TRAVₑLS
WITH MEMBERS

A CLERK IN PARLIAMENT, FROM WILSON TO BLAIR

BILL PROCTOR

Published by New Generation Publishing in 2021

First Edition

Cover: some images contain parliamentary information licensed under the Open Parliament Licence v.3.0

Paperback ISBN: 978-1-80031-023-0
Hardback ISBN: 978-1-80031-022-3
Ebook ISBN: 978-1-80031-021-6

www.newgeneration-publishing.com

New Generation Publishing

To the many colleagues, and the many politicians of all parties and of many countries, who made my thirty-six years in the service of Parliament challenging, fulfilling, frustrating and entertaining – often in equal measure – but always an enormous privilege

Contents

Foreword

This book tells the story of getting on for four decades in the service of the House of Commons and its members. It provides an account of life and work in the Commons before, during and following the Thatcher revolution. It is in a sense a political memoir, but it is not the memoir of a politician.

In the summer of 1968 I began a brief existence as "bottom boy" in one of the Commons procedural offices. Four years later I joined a small team of young men who looked after British members appointed to international assemblies of one sort or another, in Europe and beyond. As secretary of the delegation I became closely involved in the preparations for members of both Commons and Lords to join the European Assembly on our accession to the European Communities in January 1973. This included defining the policies to be pursued by the new Assembly members, not always in accordance with the wishes of Ted Heath and his government. Thereafter, even when doing entirely other jobs, the overseas – and particularly the european - work of the House service occupied much of my time and at least as much of my interest: an important aspect of parliamentary work and life of which the public – and even to some extent the academics and political pundits – were and are largely uninformed.

In 1977, after running the old Science & Technology committee for a while, I became clerk of a committee set up the previous year to consider proposals for "the more effective performance" of the House of Commons, intended mainly as the device of a government without a majority to shut up some of its more disaffected backbenchers. The committee members were articulate representatives of a wide range of views from the moderately radical to the most conservative, and the chairman was not known to have any particular opinions at all: a mix which the leadership of both the main parties were confident would result in stalemate. Despite their hopes, however, in July 1978 the Procedure Committee agreed a raft of seventy-six recommendations, for the most part unanimously. The committee's report served for the next thirty years as the blueprint for almost all subsequent procedural reforms. Its immediate outcome was the launch in 1979 of the "departmentally-related" committees, which in their mature form have become by far the most effective means of extracting information from governments and their agencies and of making them answerable to the public.

The years covered by this book span a period of profound change in the composition of the Westminster parliament. In 1968 the reference point for the generation which dominated the Commons was still the Second World War and its immediate aftermath. The benches on both sides of the House were occupied by large numbers of men (along with a handful of redoubtable women) with a reasonable claim to be regarded as heroes, either of the war itself, or of the struggle which had culminated in the victory of the party of the workers in the 1945 General Election; not a few were heroes of both struggles. By 1987, when Margaret Thatcher secured her third solid electoral victory, increasing numbers of Members on both sides of the House were drawn from the ranks of the post-War generation, beneficiaries of the welfare state and of a generous funding system which enabled we from less prosperous families to benefit from a university education and aspire to membership of the governing elite. Following Labour's return to power in 1997 the movement towards a House composed of men – but now an increasing number of women also – for whom politics was their main or only career, and their principal source of income, appeared unstoppable.

These developments, accompanied by the transformation of the Lords from a hereditary to an appointed chamber, stimulated profound, albeit gradual, change in the character of the Westminster township. In what follows I have attempted to give some flavour of a culture which is now only dimly remembered in the rather more professional – and in many but not all respects more effective - parliament of the twenty-first century.

I am enormously grateful to Ken Brown, my friend and supporter over so many years, who more or less ordered me to tell these tales and headed me back to my laptop when I appeared to be flagging; to many other friends who were generally encouraging when confronted with large chunks of manuscript, and who made many helpful suggestions, some of which I have followed; and most of all to Sue, who had to put up with it all when it happened, and continued to bear with it all over again in the retelling, always with great forbearance.

September 2021

I   In and out of Westminster

1

The College of Clerks

The Clerk's Department in the nineteen-sixties

On 1st August 1968 I started work as an Assistant Clerk in the House of Commons.

When Parliament is adjourned the Palace of Westminster is a drab and inhospitable place. It is not only that the lights are dimmed, the dust accumulates, and the corridors, other than those many which are being dug up for maintenance purposes, are silent: when Members flee to their homes, their constituencies, or to better paid occupations, the soul of the House sleeps, only to be awoken on their return.

On a miserable August morning in 1968 I made my way to Westminster from the gloom of a borrowed flat in Bayswater, carrying my letter of appointment from the Clerk of the House. I was greeted by the lone policeman at the St Stephen's Entrance, passed the end of Westminster Hall under scaffolding, and found my way through further gloom to the unlit Central Lobby. Only a few weeks earlier I had been joyfully participating in the occupation of the Registry on the country's most radical, most rural, and sunniest university campus, which had been my idyllic home for the previous five years. It was a shock from which I never fully recovered.

I was an Assistant Clerk, rather than an assistant clerk: the latter – known as office clerks, and almost all at that time male - made the tea, kept the files, still did much of the typing, and much of the rest of the work. The Clerks were Officers of the House, and not "officials". They were described by Members, with a certain degree of irony, as the "learnèd Clerks", and certainly regarded themselves as such. The Clerks shared much the same privileges as Members. They could stand behind the Chair, mingling with the people's representatives, and had their own seats in the Chamber (well, in a gallery above the Chamber, but their own seats nonetheless). They could go more or less everywhere - other than the Smoking Room (which was still a smoking room), where once upon a time, it was alleged, a confidence had been betrayed, and possibly by a Clerk. They populated the Tearoom and the Dining Room (but at clearly designated tables), and met the media (to whom they of course never revealed confidences), the librarians and disgruntled backbenchers (from whom many confidences were received) in Annie's. They could bring in guests to the Strangers' Bar and Strangers' Dining Room and take visitors round the Palace whenever they chose. As Officers of the Legislative branch they were, like Members, exempt from jury service.

Clerks could not, of course, vote. They were expected to be anonymous, and, like Iolanthe's aristocratic friends, to have no particular views at all. These Gilbertian traditions were explained to me on my arrival by Michael Ryle, then Clerk of the Nationalised Industries Committee, a radical (in Clerkly terms), a friend of Dr Bernard Crick, co-founder of the Study of Parliament Group, and slightly suspect for possible non-Clerkly sentiments. Despite his radicalism (which really meant that he thought there should be more committees), Michael's explanation of the etiquette was profoundly serious and straight-faced, he being a profoundly serious man: I was to address all Members as Sir (or, on rare occasions, as Madam); I should address all my senior colleagues by their surnames; I should have no political views; and I was therefore expected to vote Conservative. In later years we agreed to advise new arrivals that voting Liberal would be even more ok, since nothing could be less political: no doubt these days they are advised to vote Green.

My first job, during that very hot and frequently wet August, when all other Clerks were sensibly enjoying the long summer adjournment, was to read the proofs of what was claimed to be the longest ever report from a select committee, which was saying a quite a lot. Michael Ryle was of course the author; and he was no doubt delighted to have the services of an eager youth (sweating in high summer in a double-breasted blue serge suit purchased by his mother) to read everything he had written about the past and future of the Post Office together with the two enormous volumes of evidence submitted by the great and the good and the all-the-others-who-took-themselves-very-seriously. As he knew from long experience, nobody else was going to read much of it thereafter.

During the course of this brief familiarisation with the Establishment the Soviet tanks arrived, the Prague Spring came to an end, Mr Dubcek fell from power - and the House of Commons was recalled for a day to mull over the implications and to issue appropriate imprecations. Members, after much grumbling, resumed their vacations, and Michael and I carried on reading.

Parliament properly reassembled in October 1968. At last I could take up my fulltime responsibilities: which encompassed the guardianship of dip pens (quills having apparently been phased out during wartime austerities); a multitude of coloured inks (in a mahogany bank of glass inkpots); the Commons sole supply of green ribbon; and a great deal of parchment.[*] Stacked on the shelves behind my Pugin desk were the only authoritative copies of all government bills introduced into or brought to the Commons, and only I could amend them or send them on their way to their Lordships.

I became an adept of medieval French. By means of buff-coloured betting slips I would instruct the boss in a wig at the Table downstairs to

---

[*] or at least parchment quality paper

write the appropriate words: *Soit baillé aux Seigneurs*, I would write, *A ces amendmens les Communes sont assentus*, or, more threateningly, *Ceste bille est remise aux Seigneurs avecque des raisons*. In each case the amendments would be marked up in the 'House' copy in the appropriate coloured ink, and the bill tied up in green ribbon with a neatly inscribed message (in English, for the avoidance of doubt) and paraded to the Lords by one of the other men in wigs. I then awaited its return, confident that my linguistic skills would be just sufficient to master their Lordships' riposte, tied up in red ribbon. Meanwhile, I carefully transcribed all amendments made in committee or in the House, of which there were often many hundreds (in the appropriate coloured inks), sent each bill at each stage off to HMSO (who were, when not on strike, still real hot-metal printers), and checked every word, jot and tittle when they returned.

The Public Bill Office was a delightful place to work. It ran the full length of the roof of the new Commons chamber built after the wartime bombing. On the other side of the roof was the Journal Office, an almost exact replica, where they wrote the "Vote" each evening, and read the Journal proofs (which were becoming much the same thing but at that time still set by different compositors) the following day at noon, and researched arcane procedural possibilities by consulting the complete run of Commons Journals back into the mists of parliamentary time. They also possessed an antediluvian adding machine (probably an 1888 Burroughs, but maybe from my father-in-law's Kalamazoo company in Northfield, Birmingham), which was used to calculate the hours and minutes spent on different kinds of business in the House in order to compile the "sessional diary": it was probably much envied by the accountants in the Fees Office, who appeared still to be adding up Members' expenses claims on the office abacus. The JO had a view over Star Court and the roof of William Rufus' Westminster Hall (famously saved from the great fire of 1834 and again from the Luftwaffe in 1941) and suffered the morning sun. We looked over Speaker's Court and into Speaker's House and the Serjeant at Arms' palatial residence, and could monitor the arrival and departure of Ministers and Ambassadors in the courtyard below: we suffered much more acutely from the afternoon and evening sun: it was several decades before anyone thought of putting up blinds.

In between the JO and the PBO was a run of offices where the sun rarely penetrated, except in high summer through the ceiling lights; their occupants ran the risk of asphyxia for most of the year, and were near-blinded for the rest. These middle rooms housed a conference room (under whose table were camp beds for Members who wanted to jump the queue in a ballot for bills or some other competitive event organised by the Whips) and some of the real workers – the office clerks and secretaries who serviced us and the Table Office (whose main base was immediately behind the Table of the House downstairs) – and the "Fourth Clerk at the Table", soon to be rebranded as Clerk of the Overseas Office. Like many other cave-dwellers from antiquity, the latter was a man to be cultivated, since in his gift was the possibility (precious at a time of lunatic currency controls) of travel abroad. About which much of this book is concerned.

Apart from the light pollution which afflicted us in high summer, the JO and the PBO were perfectly designed for collegiate life. They were punctuated by great mahogany bookcases which housed our formal records – the Journals, the Statutes, the Proceedings of Standing Committees, the Statutes Revised, our files of precedents back to the mid-Nineteenth Century (not much of course before the great fire of 1834), our current manuscripts and proofs – which provided a small amount of privacy in each working space. In the centre of the office was a long reading desk where our manuscripts were left and hourly collected by the printer's messenger, the daily records were available for consultation, the broadsheets were delivered each day, and where the college of clerks foregathered whenever issues needed to be resolved. Our own desks were massive, and extremely uncomfortable to sit at, Pugin clearly having allocated the design of the desks and of the chairs to different people: back problems were endemic. The desks were, however, fully equipped with the latest technology of the time: the leather-bound blotters, the dip pens, the coloured inks, the racks of green portcullis stationery, the betting slips (with which I had become familiar in a former incarnation on a local newspaper), a telephone connected to a switchboard manned by understanding ladies along the corridor (and not in Bangladesh), and, each morning, a freshly filled carafe of water and a glass. In later years the pain caused by the loss of the last facility was acute: plastic bottles purchased from Charing Cross on the way into work were no substitute and only served to emphasise the loss of status which we (like most public servants other than the politically appointed) were to endure in the bad times to come.

The real joy of the Public Bill Office was its people. It was regarded as the best place in the Department of the Clerk to work, and was very definitely the best place to start work. Opposite me was a wiry young Edinburgh graduate, George Cubie, who was my mentor then and became my friend and support throughout the many crises of my life in Westminster. George looked after the Scottish Grand and Standing Committees and the office files. Beyond the first baffle was the Clerk of Private Members' Bills, Giles Ecclestone: he processed backbenchers' legislation through the House and often wrote them (he was amongst many other things the real author of Alf Morris' Chronically Sick & Disabled Persons Bill, which pioneered disability legislation in the UK and worldwide), and presided over almost as many green-ribboned bill texts as did I. A gentle man, Giles went on to work as Secretary of the Church of England's Board of Social Responsibility across the square in Church House, but died early of cancer soon after becoming a cleric in Cambridge a few years later. He and Imogen entertained me and my young wife Sue royally in their what-seemed-to-us opulent family home in Grove Park, and on my temporary departure from Westminster gave me Cornford's *Microcosmographia Academica* (being a Guide for the Young Academic Politician) as a handbook to take on my short-lived travels in the groves of academe.

In my second year in the office Giles was replaced by John Rose, who had inexplicably acquired one of the more enviable positions in the Department – that of guide and escort to the Miss World candidates who were entertained in the Palace each year, to the great delight of the inhabitants. He was particularly remembered in college mythology as the man who took a week's supply of sandwiches with him when on clerkly duties in Strasbourg, which he ate in the Orangerie gardens while others were wasting their allowances on *truite au bleu* and *Gewurtz.*

At the other end of the long table was Kenneth Bradshaw, later Clerk of the House, who eventually spent a happy retirement as administrator of the Compton Verney Opera. His then day-job was "Clerk of Supply", which meant that he supported the annual consideration of the Finance Bill, "clerked" other major government bills, and added up all the figures in the thrice-yearly Consolidated Fund Bills to make sure the Treasury had got their sums right. KAB was another who looked after my interests when looking-after was called for.

On the other side of the second baffle (filled with old Finance Acts, old editions of Erskine May, and every edition of *Dod* since its inception[*]) was the seat of the Clerk of Standing Committees. This post (which I attempted to fill with singular ineptness in later years) was then occupied by a former Captain in the Argylls, and later Political Adviser in Khuzistan and Vice-Consul in what used to be Persia. David Scott was responsible for finding chairmen and clerks for the innumerable legislative committees (then called standing committees) invariably required by each Government shortly after its arrival on a manifesto commitment to reduce legislation and red tape. He did this (as I did later) by running around the Palace of Westminster at high speed trying to track down potential chairmen in the bars and signing them on before they became sober, or by importuning their wives or secretaries over the phone.

---

[*] *Dod's Parliamentary Companion*, published every year since 1832, and after most General Elections also, was the essential *vade mecum* for anyone working in or around Westminster. In those days it was still in a format similar to a Collins Gem dictionary, and just about fitted in the pocket. Its rival, *Vacher's*, contained no biographical information but was even handier, since it appeared in paperback, and was updated quarterly. By the turn of the century *Dod* had become a galumphing hardback which would weigh down the stoutest briefcase, and by 2020 cost the taxpayer (who largely footed the bill) a cool £325 per copy. *Vacher's* (now issued from the same stable) remained reasonably portable and cost you all a mere £130 a year.

Although not bad at suborning chairmen, David Scott was in the habit of losing his wife or his car, or both, and on some days most of the calls coming through the switchboard to the PBO concerned their relocation. He seemed a familiar character: one of my favourite university tutors - Martin Dent - was a former district officer who famously "quelled the Tiv riots" in Nigeria, which had become murderous, by standing on a jeep and, with a slight stutter, inviting them to return to their homes; and who, inspired by the example of his great-great-great grandfather (Wilberforce's anti-slavery lieutenant Thomas Fowell Buxton), took the lead in establishing the Jubilee 2000 campaign to abolish Third-World debt. Martin Dent had also had a tendency to lose his car (on at least one occasion returning to Staffordshire on the train having left the car with NCP in London and, and on other occasions attempting forcibly to break into little Renaults which looked a bit like his). Like my tutor, David Scott did not always seem the most alert of colleagues, but he symbolised the fraternity of Parliament at that time, and equally inspired uncouth young men to regard themselves as at least potential gentlemen. He went on to become Clerk of Private Bills (an even more esoteric role which I found myself simultaneously performing in later years); and then had the sense to retire to his estates in Scotland and enjoy a well-earned retirement before life in London took its inevitable toll.

At the far end of the PBO was the office of the Clerk of Public Bills. This was a grand room, with circular conference table and all other appropriate accoutrements, but directly accessible from the main office. Its very distinguished occupant was Kenneth Mackenzie, a man of infinite patience. On the day of my arrival in the PBO, having heard more senior colleagues address him as "Kenneth" I did the same: KRM raised his ample eyebrows, and the use of surnames faded away throughout the service within a matter of days. He was a man who rode in St James's Park or Hyde Park in the mornings, and then dealt with the extraordinarily tedious minutiae of the legislative system with elegance and humour. He was the custodian of the Government's secrets, since all difficult draft legislation was submitted to him well in advance. These drafts were marked at least "Secret", and often "Top Secret", and KRM therefore responsibly held them in a locked drawer of his even-more-monumental-than-ours Pugin desk. But since he knew that the rest of us might have good reason to read them, or might merely be curious about the workload ahead of us, he also left the key in the middle of his desk.

KRM in his real time did more useful things. His verse translation of Virgil's *Georgics*, and his translations of Dante, remained classics in the Folio Society catalogue for many years, and there are few others who can have received the Order of Polonia Restituta not for derring-do but for translating the Polish classics into good English.

The PBO worked as a real college. If I had a problem, or GC had a problem, we would take them to the big table. But if KRM or KAB or David

9

Scott had a problem they also would do the same. [*]

And we lived a collegiate existence. Although the parliamentary recesses were still of legendary length, when the House was sitting we were there almost all the time. The notional time of Rising was 10.30 pm, but it almost never happened. It was quite usual to sit until two-thirty or three in the morning, and not infrequently until six, seven or eight. There was no "programming" of bills, and despite (or sometimes because of) occasional guillotines, voting on contentious bills or motions went on through the night if the Opposition or backbenchers so desired. Each member of the team was expected to spend two nights a week on duty until the House rose. This meant in practice that, after Monday as a straight 10-6 day, I would arrive on a Tuesday morning at around nine in order to put the papers together for a committee starting at ten-thirty. I would be in committee again at four-thirty, which might normally run 'til six or seven. The House might then continue until, say, two in the morning if we were lucky. By the time the marked-up papers had been put safely in the hands of the printer's messenger, I might leave at around three. Unlike Members, we had a taxi service, 'though by that time of the morning the cab drivers were not infrequently a trifle the worse for wear (as, to be fair, were we on occasion) and the journey back might therefore be a trifle hazardous. [†] I would be expected to be on parade again on Wednesday morning by nine-thirty, and on Thursday would repeat the performance.

In extremis, Clerks stayed on site throughout the night. Although the very senior staff had bedrooms of their own hidden in odd corners of the estate, the junior officers stayed in 'the Straw'. These were a couple of dormitories in the lower part of the Clock Tower, reputedly designed as penitentiaries for any found guilty of breaching the privileges of the House. Whereas in Elizabethan days recusants were sent to the Tower, Victorian politicians apparently planned to send unrepentant newspaper editors to their very own Clock Tower. When the latter were behaving themselves we made use of their facilities. To many of my contemporaries they may have had something of the familiarity of an inferior prep-school dorm; sleep was really possible only after a hard night in Annie's, since with irritating accuracy the entire structure turned over every fifteen minutes as Big Ben

---

[*] Office geography is all-important. The Journal Office across the corridor was an almost exact mirror-image of the PBO. But it lacked a communicating door between the head man's office and the rest: as a result the JO (which I occupied on three separate occasions in three different guises) never achieved the same degree of comfortable collegiality.

[†] A shared late night transport service for Members was actually introduced soon after the victory of the toiling masses in 1945; it was withdrawn after a number of double-decker London buses became stuck under railway bridges in the small hours of the morning, the drivers having loyally followed the directions of their elected representatives.

and his junior mates strutted their stuff.

So we lived much of our term-time lives in the office, and around the Palace, which we came to regard as home for much of the year. And so did many Members. After a late dinner (roast lamb, roast potatoes, watercress (a speciality) and half a carafe) in what was then the grand but really rather awful Dining Room (or dried-out pork-and-egg pie and pickle and tea in the very definitely awful Tearoom) it was perfectly normal at two in the morning to be discussing in authoritative tones, and probably drafting, the next raft of amendments to be put down on a government bill, or a procedural wheeze to flummox the Speaker or Deputy Speaker either later in the night or soon after Questions next afternoon - despite the disapproval of the wigs downstairs who aimed for a quiet life and did not expect insubordination (or, worse, initiative) from the sophomores upstairs.

We who laboured through the night therefore became a fraternity, who lived, worked, ate and very often drank together. Perhaps the greatest intimacy came in the late night (and sometimes all-night) sittings of standing committees on major bills, where chairmen, clerks, doorkeepers, police, Hansard writers and members sought strength from each other in trying to keep awake through the interminable backbench filibusters intended, for the best of democratic reasons, to make the Government think again. There was much ribaldry. We were a happy band. The press had long deserted us, since it was way past their increasingly early deadlines; the lights went out through most of the Palace; but we soldiered on. So strong was this solidarity that in the by then routine all-summer-night sittings of the Labour Government's Finance Bill committee in 1969 the Tory opposition whips, who masterminded the filibusters, reputedly set up a bar in the committee room next door: this could have been one cause of the treasured moments when committee members ground to a halt or even, on at least one happy occasion, simply keeled over and slept in mid-sentence. In the morning we re-awoke and repaired to bacon and eggs and mugs of tea on the Terrace – before getting back to work.

The Master of our small College was the Clerk of the House. Officially known as the Under-Clerk of the Parliaments (the Commons being the lower House in almost every respect other than the powers to legislate, to raise taxes, and to make and unmake governments), he was Accounting Officer for the House of Commons Vote and therefore our only identifiable employer. The Clerk was appointed under the sign manual, theoretically for life, although he normally had the decency to retire at an appropriate moment to make way for the next in line. For here Buggins ruled. Ideally only one new clerk would be appointed each year, and since the full complement of clerks was less than fifty, and historically most stayed for their entire career, this was the natural rate of turnover. However, if two or more young men arrived in Westminster at the same time and the same age, they were more or less obliged to devote the remaining forty-odd years of their careers trying to position themselves to take the succession: deals might be struck twenty or thirty years ahead of time to secure the proper queue for knighthoods, but when enmity ruled (which was not unknown) the struggle continued daily, with junior colleagues making intricate and desperate calculations of loyalty to the various generations of warring contenders, whose success or failure could influence their own more distant prospects.

This was a personal problem for all new arrivals, even we from the great unwashed. I, for instance, arrived on the very same day as Douglas Millar. Although I had the seniority in terms of age and marks at CSSB[1], he had the edge over me since he had acquired a Master's at Reading after his first degree at Bristol; like me, Douglas was part of the experimental "broadening of the intake", which alarmed and even scandalised virtually all the existing members of the College. Although I lost my seniority by leaving the service for a couple of years, he and I continued to eye each other nervously over the next few years, until I finally gave up the struggle and admitted defeat. But we remained good friends and, having abandoned the chase, I was eventually much saddened that he didn't quite make it to KCB.

Our evening routines were often punctuated by visits from the Clerk to discuss the next day's business, or summonses to his flat, where whisky was dispensed in tumblers at any time between dinner and breakfast. The flat was at that time located in one of those many excrescences tagged on to the building in the fifties and sixties: in this case the so-called Upper Committee Corridor North, which had attached itself to the southern end of Mr Speaker's House. It seemed quite grand to me, but was of course nothing compared to his original suite of rooms on the Principal Floor, of which only an office remained, the rest having been poached by Ministers and Leaders of the Opposition (the Serjeant at Arms held out rather longer).

The then Clerk, Sir Thomas George Barnett Cocks, was tall and of ecclesiastical demeanour and military bearing, although no known military credentials, with an indulgent smile which helped to accentuate his mild contempt for so many of his colleagues, and particularly his contemporaries. So far as the latter were concerned he could well have been the model for Archdeacon Grantly, although his enemies might have more likely associated him with Sir Ralph Brompton, the wartime "diplomatic adviser" to HOO HQ. Although he came from the same kind of background Barney Cocks appeared to have committed those indiscretions at which most of his generation still claimed to be appalled: first, he was rather brighter than most of them; second, he had not only divorced, but had actually remarried; and finally he was rumoured to be a little bit to the left of centre (this latter was the more serious). TGBC led the House of Commons service for eleven years, during which he more or less single-handedly created a real career structure for people without means who actually had to treat the job as a job

12

rather than a part-time recreation. It was he who enabled commoners like myself to become part of the cadre and, to the even greater disgust of most his colleagues (and many a raised eyebrow in the Tearoom), began the wholly successful experiment of recruiting women, some of whom turned out to be rather more able than their merely male counterparts[*]. Fellow-traveller or not (and after all in the early forties that had been a passport to advancement, not a disqualification) he was a first-rate shop steward: that, in the eyes of his contemporaries, could have been the greatest sin of all.

Barney certainly became a trifle odd as the years went by, and the frustration caused by his outrageous insistence on hanging on to the top job for so long eventually exploded into outright warfare. Old school and college rivalries, undimmed by time, re-emerged, inflamed by the contempt of those who had gone to war for those who had not. He was eventually so loathed by the Department's captains and colonels and knights-at-arms that a rival management – in the nominal command of Captain David William Shuckburgh Lidderdale[†] - was already in place and issuing orders several months before his actual departure.

When he did retire in 1973 only eight of the 100-plus colleagues invited actually turned up to bid Barney Cocks farewell (most of the remainder taking cognisance of their own prospects in the decades to come): the party, copiously supplied with the best House of Commons champagne, was hosted by the at-least-equally civilian and more-than-equally eccentric Clerk of the Journals, Dr Eric Taylor, who in his considerable spare time was otherwise occupied as a priest in the Liberal Catholic Church of Great Britain and Northern Ireland, and spent his last years as their Presiding Bishop. The party was attended only by those whose doom was already determined or well foretold. TGBC went on to write a brilliant insider's account of the working of parliament and its committees in telling the tale of the rebuilding of the Palace of Westminster and its subsequent additions and desecrations, whose subtitle (*the story of an institution unable to put its own house in order*) said much about his view of the institution he had served so loyally and for so long.[2]

As I entered my second year in the college of clerks, I began to question whether the world of procedural niceties, minute books and green ribbon, despite the elevated status which went with it, would be fully satisfying in the years to come. I had, it is true, moved up one desk in the PBO, and had abandoned the sobriquet of Bottom Boy for the grand title of Clerk of the Scottish Grand Committee, which allowed me to hear almost daily rehearsals of the direful situation in the Gorbals, or the urgent need to

---

[*] Tom Stoppard's *Dirty Linen* provides an informative gloss on the reaction of Members to the arrival of the lady clerks, as well as a not wholly inaccurate depiction of life on the Committee Corridor in those halcyon days.
[†] formerly of the Rifle Brigade; and resident of Cheyne Walk.

abolish Scotland's still-extant feudal system, so far as I was able to penetrate the patois. But as I looked along the office, and particularly as KAB continued to check the Treasury's almost inevitably accurate sums (manually of course in those pre-calculator days) I wondered whether I would want to be doing the same in twenty years' time.

I also wondered whether London was really the place for me. I had spent my childhood in a large provincial city where the best music and theatre, as well as the countryside, could be reached on foot. I had spent five further formative years in rural Staffordshire, where squirrels fed at the window of my army hut, where I could stroll in healthy air from bed to breakfast, from bed to lecture or tutorial, from bed to bed: what was I doing living in cramped quarters and commuting on dirty slam-door trains through London fog (for Sir Gerald Nabarro's Clean Air Act had not yet taken full effect)? And I wondered also whether I could ever become a congenial member of the college. I could of course take comfort that my school – which reasonably convincingly claimed to have been founded in 1140 – was a damned sight more ancient than most of theirs; and I could claim (with an equal degree of accuracy) that my university – 'though founded only in 1950 – had given me at least as good a liberal education as theirs. But I was far from sure that I wanted to enter into life-long competition with the Establishment; or, worse, to become one of theirs.

My new wife was keen to complete her degree in Manchester. My former academic muse had a job on offer there. And so we planned to move north. The college obviously did not think too badly of me because they broke all precedents and gave me leave of absence: I could if I wished return, the first clerk ever to be offered such a privilege, although all parties to the agreement thought it unlikely.

Before we left for the north the college generously offered me a first taste of Europe, of the bright lights on the horizon for those who did after all stay loyal, or who might return to the colours.

I had been overseas only twice before. At the age of thirteen, I had spent a month or so in Bordeaux: where I had fallen in love with my pen friend's little sister and learned something of the complexities of French womanhood; where I had learned to avoid the baton-waving Sergeant in the Lycée Montesquieu and to drink Dubonnet like a man in the terrace café across the road; where I had bought my first classical LP (from the Club Français du Disque) for a few francs and began the usual adolescent attachment to Beethoven (you have to start somewhere); and where, for the first time in my life, I had encountered sub-machinegun-toting soldiery at every street corner (for this was only weeks after notre Général had reassumed the mantle of French destiny), but being young and ignorant I was not in the least nervous, as I would of course be today. This trip also gave me my first hands-on experience of the British Behaving Badly Abroad: in a short run across Paris the well-groomed young boys and girls of Bristol's multitude of direct grant schools relieved an entire fleet of Thomas Cook coaches of their ashtrays and strikers, trophies which we proudly carried home and hid from our parents a month or so later.

At the age of twenty-three, and shortly before putting on my blue serge suit, I had slipped away from Finals to make my second trip to France as a fraternal participant in the great student celebration known as the *soixante-huitième* or *les événements de mai*. After a miserable trip on the ferry, arriving at the Gare du Nord in the small hours of a wet summer morning sore from SNCF's leather seats, mandatory attendance at an Alain Krivine seminar, and having thought better of hurling even a single pavé (ball games were never my forte, and I was more than a little nervous at the sight of the CRS and rumours of corpses in the Seine), I had made a rapid retreat back to the Gare du Nord, to the ferry and to rural Staffordshire, rejoicing in the benefits of a stable monarchy. After Finals I happily participated in the peaceful occupation of the University Registry as a battle-scarred veteran, leaving it cleaner than we found it, the Registrar commending us for not having touched the sherry.

My third visit to Europe, however, was as a newly-recruited representative of the British ruling elite. In the company of my new friend George Cubie I attended the fifteenth annual session in Brussels of what was then known as the North Atlantic Assembly. Previously the NATO Parliamentarians' Conference (and subsequently the NATO Parliamentary Assembly), the NAA was the unofficial parliamentary arm of NATO, unrecognised by governments but reluctantly financed by them. Having been expelled from Paris after de Gaulle's effective withdrawal from NATO the Assembly had set up a very comfortable base camp in Brussels for its staff but lived a peripatetic existence, aiming to move its annual session from capital to capital. In 1969 it had stayed put in Brussels (probably because nobody else was prepared to pay for it).

Although I had then no experience at all of international conferences I did have some experience of organising big events, the New Universities' Festival having fallen on my presidential watch at Keele in 1966. The chaos I encountered in Brussels was eyebrow-raising. My lowly job was to write a summary report of the proceedings of the Scientific and Technical Committee of the Assembly. This met for two days in a committee room at the Chamber of Deputies, where advisers stood crammed against the walls behind their delegates, where there was no ventilation, and where the interpretation system worked only sporadically on the second day, and not at all on the first. Here I learned one lesson of great value: while the committee struggled to reach agreement on optimistic resolutions on research in Arctic waters, on the need for an ocean space treaty, and on something grandly called conflict research, under the portentous guidance of Senator Georges Portmann (France) and the elegant prodding of Congressman Peter Rodino (USA), I wrote a reasonably accurate account of all that had been said in English, and a creative rendition of all the other proceedings which I had been unable to follow, drawing so far as possible on the modest scientific data store acquired through the University of Keele's Foundation Year. Nobody, to the best of my knowledge, ever challenged my largely fictional account. There were many similar fabrications to follow in later years.

On this first of very many trips to Brussels I learned other useful lessons. By the time, well after midnight, that our fictions had been dictated and transcribed and checked by the committee secretaries (who had, with the exception of the German and the Dutchman, also failed to follow the proceedings) for accuracy, there were few places still open to eat those days even in cosmopolitan Brussels. GC and I finally found somewhere comfortable and warm. We ordered, amongst other things, "local" moules marinières, and a bottle of wine. The moules revisited me for at least the next week, and I re-affirmed my lifelong vow ever to avoid seafood without fins. After we had returned the third bottle of Bordeaux Villages (which I had chosen on the basis of proven childhood experience: the father of my penfriend and his nubile sister had shipped Bordeaux wine to Bristol as the younger and effective half of Bouchard Père & Fils) as undrinkable, and finally settled for the fourth although it was almost certainly the first, second and third de- and re-canted, I vowed ever thereafter to call only for the house wine, and always in *pichets*.

So I swore that I would never have further dealings with the North Atlantic Assembly or anything like it; we shook off the dust of London; and we headed north.

2

et in academia ego

A Mancunian interlude

Manchester, despite being up north, should not have been a great challenge. Sue came from the Midlands, and so was already half-way there, and had in any case spent a year in digs in Moss Side. I came from the south-west, but had spent five years in Staffordshire, at a time when Stoke still had some industry and in its muddle of small town centres was almost a miniature of the great metropolis a few miles north. Tripe shops, pie shops and pork butchers were far from alien, although Manchester's piccalilli couldn't compete with the incomparable product of Newcastle-under-Lyme.

Finding somewhere to live was tricky. We had spent a year living on the fourth floor of a Victorian house in Strawberry Hill, in a one room flat with a drop-down bed, and like all young people felt we were being fleeced at £5 a week. Our landlord, weighed down by a thousand keys, appeared to be an organiser for the BNP or whatever it was then called, as well as an extremely prompt collector of rents. Apart from political campaigning, however, he had left us alone and happy. We explored Manchester hoping for better things – surely our still limited income would go a little further so far from the metropolis? During our search for a home we were based with friends in Macclesfield, and spent a fortnight travelling hopefully into Manchester Piccadilly. It was a damp and depressing fortnight.

After tramping many weary and wet miles through the streets of Manchester, and after innumerable viewings of dwellings with no hot water, with the summer rain cascading down the inside walls, with windows as impenetrably dirty as any Hollywood version of chez Fagin, we finally found a one bed-roomed flat at the top of a small, and relatively modern (ie post-War) block in Fallowfield. The rent consumed about forty per cent of my salary and Sue (having married) was debarred from the maintenance grants which were then the norm: the view of the state at the time was that if a female student married it was the responsibility of the husband to look after her: separate gender roles were still recognised.

Whiteoak Court had the advantage of being 30 seconds from the Oxford Road. This proved to be something of an advantage during the winters which followed, when the regular winter power cuts organised by Ted Heath's government required the journey from university to home to be undertaken in almost primeval darkness: we felt our way back from work in conditions which would have been familiar to Hardy's woodlanders, and spent the night in candle-light. Occasionally, the rodent population of the neighbourhood would put their heads round the kitchen cupboard doors to remind us that this was really their territory, not ours. Crazily, we actually tried to put up wallpaper, which peeled from the walls in the damp; but ours was a fairly comfortable camp, because we were young.

I got a job in the University's Department of Government. At that time Manchester, like most cities, had only one real university - other than UMIST, which on the whole kept to its own specialisation, or specialisms as we are now expected to call them, and didn't attempt to trespass on other people's territory. My job was the lowliest of the low, but I nonetheless felt privileged to be billed as a research associate working in a department headed by Sammy Finer.

Sammy, a flamboyant Bessarabian Jew with a line in deer-stalker hats, had been the founding professor of political institutions at the University College of North Staffordshire, which when I joined in 1963 had just been elevated into the University of Keele. All my joining papers were still on UCNS-headed paper, and it was perhaps sad that the overtly North Staffordshire connection had been obscured in the university's new title, since it was really the Staffordshire branch of the WEA which had created it. But the students had voted for the name of the local village, which without its church and Hall would really have ranked as a mere hamlet. So, for a while, I and my contemporaries were able to confuse friends and relations with the idea that we were being very adventurous in studying in north Germany – until the M6 opened up, and Keele Services became a feature in the geography of the north Midlands.

Keele was very definitely not like the kind of new institution parading as a university which has spawned all over the country since Mrs Thatcher and Sir Keith discovered that sending everyone with an IQ over a hundred into "higher" education would provide a temporary palliative to the youth unemployment statistics: a policy pursued as a permanent substitute for real jobs with increasingly manic enthusiasm by her successors. Keele was founded by a sceptical Atlee government, on a shoestring budget, housed in ex-army huts, and initially intended never to exceed eight hundred undergraduates. It was the first post-Oxbridge university institution allowed from the start to award its own first degrees, although still subject, like earlier twentieth-century foundations (Exeter, Bristol, Leicester and so on) to mentoring by London, Manchester et al.

For both staff and students Keele was a very exciting place to be. For people like Sammy Finer, elevation to the rank of professor at the early age of thirty-five (when there were only a dozen or so universities in the whole country) was a remarkable career move, particularly when you had been personally selected for the job (never mind interviews, balanced playing-fields, gender discrimination etc) by the great A D Lindsay, the Master of Balliol (whom my father as a young Quaker had assisted in providing relief for the South Wales miners after the Great Strike), who had abandoned the comforts of Oxford for the damp of the stables in the Clock House at Keele Hall (which eventually killed him), and who was determined to implement his dream of a new university for the modern man.

Sammy was in no way unique amongst the early Keele professors in being a genuinely inspirational teacher. We for whom the Foundation Year was our first experience of university life were privileged to spend two hours each morning being taught not by men who were already the leaders in their fields, but by young men who had come to an ex-military camp because they passionately believed in transmitting knowledge, and a love of learning, to an even younger generation. They presided over a remarkable educational and social experiment: a four-year undergraduate course in which natural sciences, social sciences and the arts were compulsory ingredients for all; and a rural campus, full residence for students and staff alike, and (most revolutionary of all) equal numbers of women and men (the Oxbridge ratio at the time was something like 1:11).

Although I had spent five years in rural arcadia (an Oxbridge college in 600 acres of woods and fields and the company of often very beautiful friends), I had seen enough of universities elsewhere to know that a civic institution would fall somewhat below my ideal. The Victoria University of Manchester didn't disappoint.

The Department of Government was housed in a decrepit three-storey building in Dover Street, just off the Oxford Road, with the air of a badly-converted warehouse. For my first year I sat at a utilitarian desk in a utilitarian office, occasionally vacating it when my apparently humourless room-mate met his student groups, he doing likewise for me when I tried to persuade eight groups of largely recalcitrant undergraduates to take even a passing interest in comparative government (which in those days meant the UK, the USA, France and the USSR and not much else), or to respond to what I hoped were still the inspirational lectures of the man with the deer-stalker hats. We occasionally and silently shared dreadful and already tepid coffee in flimsy cups from a dispenser in the corridor, and silently agreed that our lack of social communication skills was probably our only common métier.

That my room-mate (who went on to a distinguished academic career) appeared humourless was hardly surprising. I probably appeared much the same to him. There was nothing in the buildings or their surroundings to encourage levity, and our vain struggle to educate the unenthusiastic was sufficient to deflate the most stout-hearted. The students were awful, or at least not the most diligent.[*] It was only two years since I had ceased at long last to be an undergraduate, but the undergraduates I had known as my

---

[*] I mean, of course, awful as *my* students: they may well have found other tutors more congenial, and were of course the loveliest of people.

contemporaries were articulate, interested and acute, typed their essays, knew what they meant, and were quite attractive with it. Mine (and his) sometimes appeared borderline illiterate, uninterested, inarticulate, and waiting to be told the answers. Many had little idea of how to string a sentence together, and some at least believed that a few hundred words of indecipherable scribble on the poorest quality letter-paper (or worse) was sufficient discharge of their obligations to a system which they appeared to think had compelled them to suffer three years at England's most prestigious provincial seat of learning. This was 1970, when ostensibly only the cream were getting into universities; not 2020.

My academic superiors understood my frustrations, but were alarmed by my initial response. For the first few weeks, so-called essays were returned to sender unmarked and grades were unallocated. Eventually I was summoned by Professor Brian Chapman to explain why my students were doing so badly; and reluctantly I agreed to read the product, so long as it was at least written on only one side of reasonably clean paper, and not in palimpsest. Remarkably, their performance improved, and all went on to reasonably respectable sessional exam results, marginally better than the departmental average.

The dour atmosphere of Dover Street and its surroundings seemed to infect all, academics as well as undergraduates. The latter were mostly housed in digs, where liver and bacon and mash were evening staples, or in halls of residence often miles from the university; they, too, were forced to suffer Mr Heath's stygian nights. Their students' union, where they might have been able to develop and assert their individuality, was a disgraceful mess crammed into other equally insalubrious university premises, littered with plastic cups, and run by a few students with political ambitions. They had little incentive to shine.

Nor did most of the academics. Dover Street had its stars, but they were all somewhat dimmed. Sammy himself was dimmed. We all knew why he had left Keele for Manchester: his brother Herman was already a big wheel in Chicago: Sammy had to do one better, which in the end he did. Gladstone Professor at Oxford, yes; one of the team at Manchester, only a staging post. In this environment Sammy seemed reduced, a pale reflection of his former (and future) self: serving his time, no longer much inspiring his students or his colleagues. His greatest achievement during this interlude was to complete his first *magnum opus*, which became a staple of first-year undergraduate courses for many years to come.[3] When I arrived in Manchester he gave me a copy of the Penguin proofs to use for tutorial purposes: in practice I found it easier to rely on the duplicated lecture notes which he had flogged to us for half-a-crown a term at Keele, upon which most of the book was built.

Other academics were perhaps typical of the civic university of the time. Brian Chapman, whose *British Government Observed* made a short and unremarkable contribution to the debate which raged (if that could ever be the appropriate word) about the future of the British Parliament. Dr William Wallace, and his welcoming wife Helen: Fabians, who took the Common Market seriously, converted to Liberal-Democracy, and ended up in the Lords, trailing academic honours behind them. Only Ghiţa Ionescu – another Romanian - shone, and he perhaps because even the dourness of the Oxford Road had something over King Carol's Bucharest.

Despite the prevailing depression, Sue had achieved considerable success in an academic course called General Honours (Modern History, American Studies and Government), which was a Manchester try-on of a form of humanities tripos. This was not Keele-style co-operative jointery: all three of her academic departments were uncompromisingly insistent that the student belonged to them and them alone, and as a result General Honours undergraduates were taking what amounted to three single-honours degrees simultaneously. Sue and her year were the last to rise to the challenge, since the Victoria University finally recognised its inhumanity and the degree was abandoned thereafter. Sue did, however, have the much-appreciated privilege of being tutored in history by M R D Foot, chronicler of the SOE and a bastion of traditional academic values and standards.

Meanwhile, my own academic career was not going very far or very fast. During my first year in academia I produced a learned and intensely tedious study of the Scottish committees in Parliament. And in my second year, I laboured long and hard on a statistical analysis of private members' bills in the Commons, slide-rule ever at hand. The latter study languished in my loft for decades before being consigned to the flames. The former was eventually published, under a pseudonym,[4] in the autumn of 1972: under a pseudonym, because by then I had sent in my letter to re-join the college in Westminster. The deleterious atmosphere in Dover Street finally persuaded me that, whatever else I might become, an academic I was not to be. I had applied half-heartedly for a lectureship, which I knew I didn't merit, and was offered an indefinite extension of my Research Associateship, which I didn't want. Sue had just graduated, and it was time to move on.

II Europa Nostra

3

No 46

Preparing for Europe

Years before, when I was thinking of standing for President of my students union, Sammy Finer had advised that 'if you want to study politics seriously, you need to actually do it, although you'll end up with a two one instead of a first'.[*] He was right in both respects, and my brief experience of academic life in Manchester had reinforced the wisdom of that advice. I had the impression that some of the academics with whom I worked there were studying a subject which they little understood because they had little hands-on experience: they had some grasp of the mechanics, but little familiarity with the chemistry. I decided to follow Sammy's advice and head back towards the national political scene – albeit as a janissary. I asked Barney Cocks to redeem my return ticket: which he did with alacrity, since he needed new bodies for his new enterprises.

I moved back not to the Palace of Westminster but to a rather undistinguished and by now decrepit townhouse in the bit of the end of Whitehall known as Parliament Street. The acquisition of No 46 was the first step in the expansion of the Clerk's Department (and what is now known as the "House of Commons Service") into the immodest empire which it has since become. It was one of a terrace of Georgian houses which had declined into offices (the Parliament Street Post Office was next door) whose skeletons remain as part of 1 Parliament Street, the first major new build undertaken for the House of Commons following the post-war reconstruction of the Chamber[†]. The skeleton of No 46 was eventually transformed into a comfortable official residence for the Serjeant at Arms.

The basement of the house had been allocated to an emergency printing plant (whose existence was not intended to be widely known, particularly amongst Labour Members) which could be activated on the not infrequent occasions when the traditional printers at HMSO went into traditional strike mode (previous 'emergency' prints of the Order Paper were said to have been produced in the shed in the back garden of the man whose job was to

---

[*] My English professor, the Chaucerian John Lawlor, merely told me to go away and come back in a year's time if I was still interested in getting a degree of some kind.

[†] Apart from some dreadful bits of infilling in the main building, some of which have now, thankfully, been removed.

liaise with the official press). On the remaining floors were offices for one or two of the experimental specialist select committees launched by Richard Crossman in the late 1960's; for the new "scrutiny" committee in process of being established to monitor European legislation after Britain's impending entry into the European Economic Community; and, near the top, for what was briefly known as the European Office. In the attic above was sleeping accommodation for the lady Clerks now belatedly making their appearance: territory on which we were not of course permitted to trespass (although for some years I retained a key and could at least get a shower there).

So from July 1972 the European Office became my new, albeit shortlived, home. Before my arrival the office comprised a mid-career deputy principal clerk, John Taylor (known to all as JPS) who was rumoured to be the unofficial secretary to the Tribune Group, my exact contemporary Douglas Millar and a (thankfully extremely efficient) lady secretary, Susan Copeland. We were joined in the autumn by Robert Rogers (RJR), who appeared to have had some former military experience (and purportedly went on in later years, as Clerk of the Defence Committee, to emerge from a British minesweeper off Land's End to arrest an errant Russian trawler at the height of yet another war about fish), already sported a magnificent beard appropriate to a future Clerk of the House, and on his first day in the office disappeared for a long lunch for the final fitting of his top hat, with which he returned triumphant, to our considerable confusion.

For the first few months, Douglas and I had a mission: to write a guide for the new UK members of the European Parliament, which would ensure that they knew something about the organisation they were joining and, most important, that they would not miss a procedural trick once they were there. This continued a great tradition established in 1951, when Barney Cocks had produced a manual of procedure for the newly-established Consultative Assembly of the Council of Europe, of which many subsequent editions continue to appear, and which carried in Strasbourg the same kind of authority which Erskine May[5] claimed in Westminster.

Our book was to appear in Barney's name, but since he was by then largely ignorant of the subject he had decided to farm it out to others who were probably even more ignorant but at least had more time for creative writing. This involved trips to Luxembourg (where the European Parliament offices were for the time being based), and to Strasbourg, where it usually met, an arrangement much to the profit of SNCF and the trucking company which transported the files, whose first *patron* was said to have retired as a dollar millionaire. Since the book had to be published by the time the enlarged Parliament met in January 1973 we were working to a very tight schedule, and since we were the people who would hold our Members' hands on that momentous day we also needed to get the logistics right. So much of our time was spent sorting out hotels, buses and office accommodation, and only briefly did we actually look in on the odd meeting of the Parliament or any of its committees.

For a book produced by young men with almost no knowledge of the subject it was something of an achievement: it told MEPs what they could do (to somewhat devastating effect when first deployed in action) and what were their rights, and it contained, amongst other gems, the very first consolidated text of the 1957 Rome Treaty, incorporating subsequent treaties including the Luxembourg Treaty (the first of those relatively innocent adjustments which periodically moved the federalist cause one step further), the Treaty of Accession and the amendments resulting from Norway's praiseworthy decision to remain independent: nobody in Brussels or Strasbourg or London had thought such an obviously basic aid was necessary (particularly for the elected hoi polloi).

My first visit to Luxembourg allowed me a first immersion in the true spirit of the Community which we were about to join. JPS, abandoning for the time being the chicken farm near Sevenoaks from which he had, at unpredictable times of the day, cycled to No 46, had been appointed Director General of Research & Documentation, taking up the UK's allocation of posts at that rank (the beginning of a trend which resulted in innumerable senior posts being created in the Parliament and the Commission to satisfy each new member state, whether or not the post was needed). When I arrived on the Plateau du Kirchberg, I found a building deeply *en grève*: inside the main lobby were a vacant reception desk and two large notices listing those members of management and those union representatives entitled to enter the building during the strike for negotiation purposes: the name of John Taylor appeared on both lists. I finally found JPS in his grand new office, which was bare of all but a bare desk and an empty bookcase. He explained that under the germanic bureaucracy imposed on the Community which he had just joined he needed a pad of requisition forms to acquire any of these things: but he had no such pad and could not requisition one without the appropriate form; and he could not ask his brand new secretary, since she was, of course, *en grève*. JPS negotiated with himself and the strike was resolved ('though there were many more to come).

With John Taylor's departure from No 46 I acquired a few job titles, and an office of my own. I became, progressively, Secretary (or one of the Secretaries) to the UK Delegations to the Consultative Assembly of the Council of Europe, the Assembly of the Western European Union, and the North Atlantic Assembly, as well as to the European Parliament itself. The office I acquired directly from JPS. John had a brilliant filing system, presumably known to experts as the chronological system. This meant that he left me several pillars of paper, three or four feet high, stacked on the floor in strictly date order: "If", he said, "you can remember roughly speaking when something happened, you only need to feel down the piles to fish out the relevant pages". After playing patience on the office floor for some weeks after his departure I left it to Sue Copeland to sort it out: she very sensibly resorted to the newly-invented office shredder, and I was thereafter free to ignore or create precedents with impunity. But I utilised his filing system many times thereafter: it was a perfect means of covering your tracks and confusing the enemy (sometimes co-terminous with your successor).

As well as writing The Book, the autumn of 1972 was a period of frantic activity to otherwise prepare the new British MEPs for their new tasks. From the point of view of the Clerks this was a fraught time. The Official Opposition remained officially opposed to our Community membership, and accordingly had decided to provide no Labour members from either House for the United Kingdom's first delegation to the assembly in Strasbourg. Indeed, so sensitive were feelings on the subject that then, and for many years thereafter, the official House of Commons records referred to the "European Assembly" or "the Assembly of the European Communities", despite the fact that the said body had unilaterally adopted the title of "parliament" back in March 1962, and nobody had demurred at the time. It was a particularly unhelpful practice, since it made even more confusing the distinction between the European Parliament and the Consultative Assembly of the Council of Europe, whose premises in Strasbourg the European Parliament were for the time being poaching. * But at least we could say to Labour Members that we were "off to Strasbourg" for a meeting of the "Assembly" in the hope that they would think we meant the latter rather than the former. Or was it the other way round? I often couldn't remember which myself, since the two assemblies met in the same building, and we occupied the same offices.

For our own boss-men it was especially difficult. By centuries-old tradition the Clerk of the House and his assistants had provided services universally for Members of whatever political persuasion: but they had provided those services for all or for none. On this occasion they were really being asked to provide services for the governing party alone: there was one Liberal, Mr Russell Johnston, amongst the thirteen otherwise-Tory MEPs from the Commons. The Lords were an altogether more colourful bunch, including several Tory Peers from exceedingly ancient families, along with the Liberal Gladwyn Jebb – who with the assistance of my second cousin Brian Urquhart had effectively created the UN in 1945 – and Lord Charles O'Hagan, who claimed his seat as an independent and avowedly Marxist crossbencher, and naturally transformed himself into a loyal Tory Whip

---

* This terminological debate, of almost medieval proportions both in respect of the passions aroused and the obscurity of the substance, was rendered further irrelevant by the fact that the body had in any case been known as the "parliament" in both Dutch (*het Europees Parlement*) and German (*das Europäisches Parlamant*) since the founding treaties of 1957.

(and elected Tory MEP) in the following years. Barney Cocks took the risk, feeling that he was giving effect to a majority decision of the House of Commons, and conscious that by tradition it would be the larger Commons service who would be expected to provide the bag-carriers for the Upper House; and in doing so he gave exactly the firepower his opponents required: David Lidderdale and his successor Richard Barlas were waiting in the wings to pounce, paradoxically accusing him – long regarded as a socialist and probable fellow-traveller – of consorting with the Conservatives.

The truncated United Kingdom delegation to the European Parliament was eventually promulgated in the late autumn of 1972. At that time MEPs (like members of other international assemblies) were delegates from the national parliaments. Other parliaments had at least the veneer of an election for this purpose, but in Westminster they were appointed on a puff of smoke from No 10, since the actual election of anybody other than the Speaker had been frowned upon since the time of the Protectorate.[*]

The Commons delegation consisted largely of Tories who had previously served in the Council of Europe Assembly, and most were committed pro-Europeans. Their leader was Peter Kirk, the member for the quiet country constituency of Saffron Walden in rural (as distinct from estuarial) Essex: a constituency which over the years has spawned a number of worthy but not-exciting-enough representatives: viz Peter Kirk's famous predecessor Rab Butler, a never-to-be-occupant of No 10; viz his successor Alan Haselhurst, long-time Chairman of Ways & Means, aspirant (and a very worthy and almost certainly more reliable one) to the speakership after the ignominious departure of Michael Martin. Honourable men, but not ones to set the political world alight.

Except this once. Peter Kirk was still a young man in 1972. He had been the "baby of the House" when first elected for Gravesend in 1955, he had spent much backbench time at the Council of Europe Assembly, and had seen service as a junior Minister in the defence departments under both Alec Douglas-Home and Ted Heath, of whom he was a rare devoted supporter. Equally rarely, he actually believed in the European project.

When he was appointed leader of the delegation, we gave Peter Kirk an office (again on the penultimate floor of No 46) and asked him what he wanted to do. He replied that he merely wanted something new and newsworthy to say when he arrived in Strasbourg in his new clothes. With his earlier ministerial training, he reasonably assumed that he was relying on civil servants of the kind who had populated his private offices, backed

---

[*] There was at least a brief debate in the House on this occasion. The outrageously undemocratic nature of the appointment of UK delegations to international assemblies was finally exposed for all to see at the Council of Europe plenary session in May 1992 (see chapter 32 below).

up by a full departmental team, across the road in Whitehall. Instead he got me, with half-a-secretary's time in support.

Although Peter Kirk was unspecific about what exactly he wanted to say, we agreed for a start that it might be worth suggesting some way of enlivening the proceedings in Strasbourg and Luxembourg, where the assemblies followed the traditional continental practice of giving all power to the leaders of the political groups, and no scope for initiative to the backbencher: we should therefore stress our support for "democracy in Europe". Otherwise I was instructed to think of something which would be worthwhile, "make a difference for the future", demonstrate our commitment to the Community ideal (the dreaded term "communautaire" had not yet become part of the patois), and which might even be picked up by the papers.

I have always had difficulty delivering copy on time (this book, for instance, is almost two decades behind schedule). The plan was that a draft paper would be produced first for Peter Kirk as Leader and then, sensitively revised after appropriate party and government consultations, submitted to the rest of the delegation to read over the Christmas recess. But my brief was vague, I was preoccupied both with Barney's Book and with the logistics of getting them to Strasbourg on time, and the whole enterprise took rather longer than anticipated. After Christmas I at last produced a radical and forward-looking document, the product of a young man's enthusiasm to change a world about which he knew as near as damn-it nothing: Peter Kirk had little time to read it before, given the limitations of the then available technology, copies had to be produced for the rest of the delegation. He had had no time to consult his own political masters. The rest of the delegation read it (if they read it all) en route to Strasbourg.

4

The Book of Revelation

A new rulebook for Europe

At midnight on 31st December 1972 the UK joined the European Communities. At one minute after midnight on the morning of 1st January 1973 HMSO published The Book.[6] Although mainly intended as a *vademecum* for British parliamentarians, we hoped it would have a wider readership, not least because there seemed to be virtually nothing else available in any language. Indeed, in Strasbourg we did pick up considerable sales – particularly amongst the Benelux delegations who understandably loathed the Germans, despised the French, and despaired of the Italians; and who looked to Westminster to inject a bit of democracy and real politics into the tedious proceedings of what was still a largely advisory instrument for the approval of the diktats from Brussels. For a while The Book became a useful tool for all participants in the Parliament, even British diplomats and the Parliament's own secretariat being occasionally spotted surreptitiously checking out what "Cocks" had to say on a tricky point of procedure. This was no surprise, since "procedure" had up to 1973 been a matter of little or no importance in the assembly of the Six. The *Times* "Political Staff", evidently well-briefed by the Clerk of the House, announced on the morning of publication that his book was going to be "as indispensable a work of reference" as Erskine May: equally evidently they had not read it.

The other British newspapers eventually got round to reading bits of what they rightly regarded as little more than a technical tome, and when they did they found exactly the kind of story they needed to put our self-important new representatives in their place. Pages 142-143 contain a mere four paragraphs dealing with the matter of Members' expenses. They were helpfully included to inform our Members what they were entitled to claim when travelling on our behalf. They told the wider World that they would be paid 2,500 untaxed Belgian francs (about £25) "expenses" each day when on European Parliament business (with a day for travel at each end), and that, worse, they would be paid BEF11/km for the first 400 km travel, BEF3/km for the remainder of the journey, and, even worser, that they could choose for themselves whether to charge from home or from Westminster. Well obviously if you had a home of any kind in Orkney, Ulster or the Hebrides you would officially be travelling from there every time you set off on European duty. Compared with a Westminster MP's pre-tax weekly salary of only about £86 this didn't look too bad.

Encouraged by Opposition backbenchers (temporarily denied these lucrative opportunities), the newspapers, broadsheets at least as much as tabloids, had a minor field day, albeit a short-lived one. We had unintentionally triggered the first expenses scandal, but no heads were on that occasion to roll.

Our instinctive reaction to the media (which in those days meant the newspapers, since the BBC had not yet interpreted their charter sufficiently flexibly to get in on the act) was the traditional one of wounded outrage. This after all was still the silver age of newspaper largesse (if not quite the golden age of the thirties, the age of *Scoop*). From the age of thirteen, and before departing for the sylvan pastures of North Staffordshire, I had spent every Saturday and almost every week of the school holidays as a copy-boy and thereafter cub reporter for what was then an extremely successful local daily, the *Bristol Evening Post*, and during my many undergraduate years I continued to spend profitable long vacations working from the old shoe factory in Silver Street. Even though I only made it to the rank of Golden Wedding and Flower Show King I was soon acquainted with a system which ensured that my nominal salary represented only a modest proportion of my total take-home pay (in cash) of a Saturday evening. The journalists really did swan around, in Westminster and particularly in Europe, with apparently unlimited funds to wine and dine anyone willing to talk, and it ill behoved them to start talking morality and propriety to the relatively impoverished representatives of the people who were just trying to make ends meet.

Nonetheless the papers had a point. The European Parliament's expenses system was largely a by-product of the exchange-rate controls still in force in post-War Europe. UK citizens at that time were still limited to a ludicrously small amount of foreign currency (a total of £50 or thereabouts each year) and it was simply not possible to travel abroad for more than a few days without some kind of circumvention of the rules. The same applied to everyone else in Europe, although French members of the Parliament were distinctly advantaged by having the seat of the Parliament on their own territory. As one of my first duties as a newly-fledged delegation secretary at the other international assemblies which we serviced I had had to learn the system of brown envelopes for which I was responsible: a junior consular officer would parcel out the cash into numbered envelopes which I then handed on to delegation members the moment they arrived on foreign soil: they then spent it as they wished. But at least we – and theoretically also the British taxpayer – knew what was being paid out, knew for certain how long our delegates were staying and for what purpose, and had established some rudimentary rules of entitlement.

The European Parliament was different. Although Members were not then paid a salary by the Parliament, it was nonetheless the Parliament which met their expenses. In other words they were paid out of the

Communities' own budget, for which nobody was, or indeed is now, clearly responsible: on how many occasions has the European Court of Auditors issued an unqualified opinion on the Community accounts?

The rules which pages 142-143 exposed said that expenses might be paid "either in cash during meetings, or direct into the Member's bank account". Payments were, of course, almost invariably made in cash or into local French or Belgian accounts established for the purpose. The ritual had become well-established, and in committee meetings was so refined that the real business rarely began until the matter of expenses had been completed. Members would arrive at the meeting place, to find the appropriate *fiches* on their desks, on top of the agenda. The first unwritten item was the filling-in of the forms, which were then collected and taken to the vaults. There would then follow a happy social time, when coffee and appropriate accompaniments (which might in the case of the more senior committees include bootleg Havanas and the best local cognac) would be consumed, while colleagues caught up with the news from their respective capitals until the return of the young men or young ladies from the vaults. The envelopes would then be distributed and the meeting proper would begin – but rarely until at least some of the nominal membership had picked up their coats and any remaining cigars, and departed – the agendas only too often left behind for the incinerator.

The expenses provisions applied not only to the more-or-less monthly plenary sessions of the Parliament (mostly in Strasbourg or occasionally in Luxembourg), and its many committees (mostly in Brussels), but also to all other individual jobs to which Members managed to be appointed. Thus every time a committee secretary required the attendance of his chairman in Strasbourg, Luxembourg or Brussels, the said chairman could claim the same largely unverified travel allowance, and the same subsistence. And there were many alternatives for those to whom the political deals within the Bureau had not yet delivered the prize of a chairmanship. Most unwearisome, and potentially lucrative, were rapporteurships. Unlike the UK Parliament (where all committee reports are made in the name of the chairman) all the European assemblies followed the French practice under which a committee separately nominates a member to act as *rapporteur* for each matter under consideration. Occasionally the *rapporteur* would have a serious interest in the subject and play a real part in preparing the relevant committee report. In most cases they were merely happy to have their names attached to a report and have a few moments of limelight when they read out a previously prepared text in the plenary. In all cases they were more than happy with the resulting enlargement of their expenses entitlement.

Certain groups of delegates were notorious for pouncing on every chance which came up. Early in my association with the Parliament I witnessed an apparently routine procedure enacted at the airport in Luxembourg: I shared a cab from the Parliament offices with a committee secretary carrying a slender file, accompanied by a junior official with a briefcase. While I waited for my flight to Brussels, my EP colleagues went through security and welcomed a man off a flight from Milan. Through the glass partition I watched as the draft report was produced from the file, which was immediately signed. Then another single piece of paper was produced from the file, signed, and handed to the man with the briefcase. The briefcase was then opened, an envelope passed over, and a chit signed. All shook hands; my EP friends returned from airside; and the man from Milan returned to his seat in the aircraft from which he had descended, ready for the return flight home. The whole transaction took no more than ten minutes. As he departed the committee secretary (who just happened to be an Italian) called to me cheerily "He'll soon be back: that was only the first draft", and emerged into the wintry sunshine to pick up another cab.

By longstanding tradition Italian communists were expected to hand over a portion of their takings to the PCI back home: so Italian delegates were by far the most assiduous in seeking rapporteurships on all committees and on any subject: how else could the PCI supplement the declining subventions from Moscow? But the Italian communists were by no means the only players in the game: there were plenty of pickings – and even more if you could get a few more exciting items onto your committee's agenda, which happened to interest you or your party or your country, but probably nobody else; even better if they required (as was so often the case) investigations in the further-flung reaches of the globe.

This encounter at Luxembourg airport was a moment when youthful enthusiasm for the new Europe merged into doubts about who exactly the new Europe was really designed to serve. I told a few newspaper friends about this encounter: they did nothing: the expenses thing was already old news. Indeed, within a very short time, The Book itself was largely redundant, thanks to the revolutionary zeal of the new British members who set about re-writing the European parliamentary rule-book itself.

5

Flight to Entzheim

Getting to Europe

On Sunday 14th January 1973 the politically unbalanced United Kingdom delegation arrived at Strasbourg Entzheim for the historic first part-session of the newly enlarged European Parliament. The vacant spaces on the charter aircraft created by the absence of fifteen so-far un-nominated Labour MPs and Peers were fully taken up by new members from Ireland and Denmark (who had found getting to Europe's alternative capital an almost impossible challenge), by further British and even US pressmen to supplement the broadsheet representatives who had somehow managed to get there in advance (almost all never to return), and by the assorted sisters, cousins, aunts, wives, daughters, bag-carriers and other uncategorized companions of the United Kingdom delegation itself.

Most of the latter came well-prepared for Strasbourg's central European weather, decked in furs and mufflers and at least one astrakhan hat. Most came with relatively modest amounts of luggage, but appropriately prepared for the receptions, parties and *vins d'honneurs* which were to occupy most of their time, and that of the well-provisioned restaurateurs of the town, for the next few days. The final abandonment of formal dress for international parliamentary events, which was effectively confirmed (with the tacit assent of Buckingham Palace) in 1974, and which thereby marginally reduced the volume of luggage, had not yet come into force, although there was already no chance of any of the Scandinavians appearing in tuxedos. One of the Tory Peers (the fourth Baron St Oswald, hero of the winning side in the Spanish Civil War, and of World War II) in any case made a significant political point on his arrival at Entzheim: bearers toiled from the Trident's hold carrying seventeen items of baggage, including a portable brass-bound baronial library: this caused great delight, created some problems for the consular car service, but wholly reassured us that the age of our Empire was not quite dead. That he was not sporting a topee was due entirely to the wintry forecast; I avoided asking later whether all the baggage fitted into the St Oswalds' modest publicly-funded suite in the Place de la Gare.

I had arrived in advance, along with a conference officer (George Clayton, who presided over the logistics), and this was one of the rare occasions when I was able to demonstrate to Sue that I had actually been doing something to earn my keep abroad, and not merely pursuing unauthorised trysts with the secretaries of the *équipe anglaise*. She had already heard much about my charter flights, and there was much more to come, but at least on this occasion the BBC Nine o'clock News provided evidence of my enthusiastic welcome, in my all-weather M&S crimplene travelling suit, of "my" Members as they rushed across the tarmac, through the rain, to the simple comforts of Entzheim.

And Entzheim was at that time a very comfortable place to be. It was a provincial airport of the old style, largely timber-built, with a central island bar, little or no security (nobody much bothered whether you were going in or out), and wonderfully friendly staff. Even by this time I had got to know most of them: I was, after all, a fairly important customer who occasionally brought whole planeloads out of the sky. Most important was the airport manager, who invariably emerged just before my flight left for home (or occasionally more than once when we were fog-bound), to present me with a few bottles of the very best gewürtz or even better edelzwicker. These were sometimes consumed on the flight home, particularly if that happened to be not a return charter but the quite dreadful Air Inter service to Orly, when there was often nothing to eat or drink, and occasionally not even light to read by. On one of the latter occasions Robert Rogers and I broke into a bottle or two of edelzwicker, accompanied by a modest quantity of *saucisse d'Alsace*, whose odour filled the darkened cabin, stimulating the juices of the other passengers, and generating much Gallic fury. Remember never to travel without your Swiss army knife, which can open bottles and even more important cut through the stoutest sausage.

Access to Europe's parliamentary capital was a considerable challenge then, and apparently still remains so. It was at the far end of France, and a political embarrassment to the Germans (who had only recently had to abandon it for the second time, leaving behind largely unhappy memories – but also not a few sympathisers); and Strasbourg had at that time not yet developed sufficient commercial or tourist activities to support direct air flights from most of Europe's real capital cities. The French provided short-haul flights, and there were by then some flights from Germany, Italy and odd bits of the French *Communauté*, but all were irregular, low priority, often withdrawn on a whim and operated with unreliable aircraft without adequate avionics to cope with the airport. The latter was more or less essential since, like so many military airfields, Entzheim was built on a swamp: fog would embrace the airfield almost without notice and almost any time of the year. In the winter months it was endemic.

Being a military airport had some advantages: at least the local air traffic controllers were a bit less likely to go on strike than in the rest of France. But there were also some downsides. Arrival or departure might at any time be delayed by military exigencies – the *armée de l'air* might after all at any time be scrambled to put down a rising somewhere in the remnants of the French empire. And occasionally genuine confusion might arise about who was military and who was not.

In May 1974 I accompanied the Lord Chancellor (the charmingly fulsome Lord Elwyn-Jones) and the Deputy Speaker and Chairman of Ways & Means (the celebrated, very definitely fulsome but far from charming George Thomas) to a ceremonial meeting in Strasbourg to celebrate the twenty-fifth anniversary of the Council of Europe. We flew from RAF Northolt in an aging Hawker Siddeley aircraft of the Queen's Flight. It was all very comfortable, and extremely leisurely: the RAF cabin crew polished the silver before serving up somewhat inadequate canapés about five minutes before we began our descent to Strasbourg; and the famously teetotal George Thomas found the polite service of small measures more than a trifle frustrating. We landed more or less on time, however, which was just as well as for once the Ambassador, the Secretary-General, and half the local CRS were standing to attention, with even a red carpet unrolled by my friend the Manager. We landed, and moved slowly to our designated stand – which turned out to be deep inside a military hangar on the other side of the airfield. As the hangar doors began to roll shut I tapped a flight lieutenant on the shoulder and asked "Shouldn't we be on the other side? "Can't go against the French air force", he replied. Forty-five minutes later, after being ignominiously towed out of the hangar and towed round to the terminal we met the maire (most others having sensibly departed) and rushed off to join the delayed lunch out of town. At least for once it was the French who were wholly to blame.

Direct scheduled flights from the UK were out of the question, at a time when nobody had any money to travel on. The alternatives were legion, but all tedious and time-consuming. When Strasbourg first came to prominence in 1949 as the seat of Europe's parliamentary get-togethers the problems of travel were recognised by concentrating the main sittings of the Council of Europe Assembly into three or more weeks in the late summer or early autumn: getting there was so laborious that it was better to get through the work of the assembly and its committees in one long burst of activity, although it was profoundly unsatisfactory from a political point of view, where topicality means all. Members any distance from the Rhine travelled by whatever means were then available: from the UK this meant the boat-train from Victoria to Paris, and then a very slow train to Strasbourg.

By the time I arrived on the scene there were all sorts of other alternatives, all equally inconvenient. You could fly from London to Le Bourget, travel by coach to Orly, and then use Air Inter if there happened to be a flight; or you could go from one or other airport into Paris and take a *couchette* on the Strasbourg train. Or you could use the ferry or the boat-train as far as Paris. Or you could take the ferry to The Hague and get a train from there. You could even fly from Lydd to Le Touquet (in the Pas de Calais), and then take the slow train to Paris.

At one time or another I tried all these and other variants, and all were fairly awful: although taking the *couchette* by the old-fashioned route meant that you at least had the chance of meeting some interesting or even mildly exciting characters, such as the lady from Paris who ran the Delegates' Bar during sessions at the Maison de l'Europe (who did a fantastic line in minute steaks and genuinely sautéed potatoes), who I first encountered in the dark of the Strasbourg-bound sleeper.

Eventually my predecessors in the Commons Overseas Office had invented the Strasbourg Charter, a marque of which I became the temporary, and increasingly nervous, proprietor. The Strasbourg Charter was wonderful. It was provided by British European Airways (the old much-loved European wing of what was to become the rather-more-boring BA). Seating was club-ish class, but the service was first class or more from start to finish. The start took place not at Heathrow, but at BEA's downtown terminal on the Buckingham Palace Road (later the home of the National Audit Office): we found our way to the West London Air Terminal, checked in for the flight, and then boarded a champagne-fuelled Routemaster for the airport; having already checked in, there were no more formalities, and at Heathrow we proceeded directly to the Trident or the 111. On board the service was quite fabulous: quite apart from the drink, which began to flow again the moment we stepped on board, the food was excellent, of many courses, and served at first-class standards (and with real knives and forks). On more than one occasion we had to circle around Entzheim for some time while we finished wining and dining. And before arrival we were presented with gifts appropriate for our spouses, partners, children.

BEA, understanding where their political interests lay, always treated the Strasbourg Charter as a priority. In my time there was one potentially embarrassing Sunday afternoon when BEA's caterers had gone on strike worldwide, their entire Heathrow-based fleet was grounded, and I had had to telephone as many as I could to warn them that we might be going on the boat. But the caterers were not on strike in the Channel Islands, and so our flight to Entzheim was delayed by only a few minutes while we awaited the arrival and turn-round of the only fully catered short-haul in the BEA fleet: and they made up for the delay with the most expensive perfumes for our wives and partners. Occasionally the purser gave me a few left-over bottles of champagne on the return flight, an offer I eventually refused after my aging and well-travelled suitcase fell apart in the middle of Charing Cross station under the weight of half a ton of documents as well as the illicit hooch: I thanked my stars that it hadn't been in the then ferociously policed customs hall at Heathrow.

The charter flight for the opening session of the enlarged parliament was the only one I remember organising for the European Parliament delegation; responsibility for their travel arrangements was soon taken over first by the Conservative group, and then by the Parliament itself, and in any case I was shortly to move on to other things. But we did continue for a while with charter flights for the thrice-yearly part-sessions of the Council of Europe.

For the avoidance of doubt, and in view of the many expenses scandals which were yet to come, I ought to stress that these opulent BEA charters were no kind of hidden subsidy. This was a straightforward commercial deal. BEA provided a first-class service; we paid a premium price for it; and because it was so good (and anyway, how did you get to Strasbourg otherwise?) we expected to be able to find enough passengers to pay for it. For most of the time both BEA and the House of Commons could claim to have made at least a nominal profit out of the venture.

The thirty-six delegation members, even supplemented by their wives, sons, daughters and concubines, could not of course fill all the seats which needed to be filled. Instead, we worked on a simple rule-of-thumb: that when the figures were added up the per capita cost for each member of the UK delegation on the plane should be no more than the notional cost of flying them by scheduled airlines via Paris, or by train, or whatever. To meet this objective we worked out a tariff appropriate to the passengers. There was always, for Council of Europe sessions, a substantial tranche of UK parliamentary staff (who comprised the *équipe anglaise)* travelling at the expense of the Council of Europe itself: the latter could at least be charged the higher of either the scheduled air or first-class rail. And we could normally fill the seats in those days with others – some delegates from other countries, but mainly government officials or journalists – who needed to hitch a lift to Strasbourg in relative comfort: for them we worked out a seat price which would more than cover our actual costs. Normally we ended up with a small surplus.

The whole arrangement came unstuck during 1974. It was a year of two General Elections and, with a minority government, ferocious whipping and continuing uncertainty about who was or was not on the Delegation; it was the year when BEA was absorbed into BOAC to form BA; and it was a year when newspaper interest was understandably concentrated at home and not abroad. We struggled through the first two part-sessions of the Council of Europe Assembly (in January and May), but were finally snookered by the second General Election, which coincided with the autumn part-session of the Assembly. The Charter was booked and ready to run, but passenger numbers were falling precipitously. I consulted the House of Commons accountants (the Fees Office as they were then known to us all) about what to do. It was only at this point that they let me into a small secret: since the House of Commons as such had no corporate existence at that time (that's why we never knew the identity of our employer, for instance) it was not possible for the House of Commons to have entered into a commercial contract of this sort: whoever's signature was on the contract would have to bear the liability. The charming Deputy Accountant, Tony Lewis, was absolutely charming about it: he even bought me a drink in the Strangers' Bar to soften the blow. "You, chum, carry the can – unless you can get out of it, which I very much doubt".

The total cost of the Strasbourg Charter was something like £2,500 each way, so the return trip was getting on for my annual salary. I didn't say a word to Sue, of course, but went on bended knee to my erstwhile friends in what had been BEA, Europe's undoubtedly friendliest airline. But they were now BA. I asked them to reduce the cost: "No good, chum, this is a commercial contract" they explained, in those same familiar RAF tones. I asked them to carry over the cost to the next charter, when I was fairly confident that we could muster a full complement: "No chance, chum, each contract stands alone". In the end, having unsuccessfully trawled every one of the small companies operating out of our less glamorous provincial airports, I pulled the plug before it was too late. And delegates, the entire *équipe anglaise*, the journalists and the johnny-come-latelies from the rest of northern Europe – all had to take the ferry, use the *couchette,* pay the full price. I was only too relieved that at this moment I had to hand on to a successor.

That BEA generally used Hawker-Siddeley Tridents for the charter flights was undoubtedly sensible. In its early configuration it was about the right size of aircraft for our purposes. More importantly, the Trident was apparently the only short-haul aircraft flying which had a genuine blind-landing capability. Very useful indeed at fog-bound Entzheim, even more so, as it turned out, at Heathrow.

For my last operational charter the Trident showed its full potential. We landed at Heathrow in unexpectedly deep darkness. The captain asked me forward (in those happy days when the crew doors were open most of the way) to apologise that it would be "some time" before passengers could disembark, but they would try to keep Members and their supporters reasonably happy. Most unfortunately there appeared to have been a major electrical fault at the airport, and rumours of a bomb, and the whole ground control system was out of operation – there were no lights on the runways, and only emergency lights in the terminal. The Trident however had been able to land: indeed, it was probably the last plane to land that night. The captain asked me to keep the troops under control until it was safe to disembark. I assured him that I would, without remembering the full effects of his airline's hospitality. After half an hour or so, two elderly Labour MPs, both of them heroes of many campaigns, particularly in Spain (and one an alleged KGB agent), insisted on leaving the aircraft by the rear door for "a bit of fresh air"; we assumed they had gone out for a smoke, but they had actually decided to find their own way to the Terminal. By that time Heathrow was, we were later told, crawling with the SAS, and with tanks. "My" Members were eventually found safely back in Terminal 1, enjoying the delights of the hospitality suite in emergency lighting, and volubly asking to know why "the other buggers are so slow getting off the bloody plane". The search and rescue operation was thereupon called off, and the rest of us found our way back by torchlight to the terminal, and eventually to the bus. In the great tradition of the public service, I was asked on my return to the House whether I had deliberately put the lives of members of the House at risk: to which I was too exhausted from running round the tarmac to have the presence of mind to reply that I hadn't fully appreciated that such an opportunity had been available to me.

6

à la Maison

Our first European home

On the morning of Tuesday 16th January 1973 the new British members of the European Parliament took their seats, along with new members from Denmark and Ireland, in the chamber of the *Maison de l'Europe* in Strasbourg. The meeting was due to start at 11.00 am sharp, and actually kicked off at about 11.20 – not a bad performance in continental European terms, where the time on the clock was determined by the whim of the presiding officer rather than, as in Westminster, by Big Ben.[*]

The *Maison de l'Europe* was a ghastly building. From the outside it looked like a very large prefab; on the inside it was one of the most uncomfortable buildings man was ever condemned to work in. On a prime site at the end of the allée de la Robertsau (now inevitably re-named the Avenue de l'Europe), along which General Leclerc's Legion had been allowed by the allies to redeem French honour by driving the Germans out of occupied Alsace, and opposite Josephine Bonaparte's Orangerie (destroyed by fire in 1968, and rebuilt without oranges), it had been hurriedly assembled in the early summer of 1950 to provide a home for the Consultative Assembly of the Council of Europe, since the Great Hall of the University, used in 1949, was needed for more serious purposes. A few years later it was put to use also as the seat of the Common Assembly of the European Coal and Steel Community (the organisation which kick-started the Schumann Plan), and since 1958 had therefore also housed the European Parliament.

By 1973 the House of Europe looked and felt like a building which had long overstayed its time. While the chamber (*l'hémicycle*) fulfilled its functions tolerably well (although it was getting too small for both assemblies) the offices and surrounding facilities were simply dire. They reflected the era of post-War austerity in which the building had been erected, and merely putting up the whole complex in such a short time must

---

[*] On one occasion in the late seventies I waited, along with the drummers of the National Guard, for almost two hours outside the office of the President of the *Assemblée Nationale* in Paris while he sorted out the latest political crisis before taking the *fauteuil*: so on this occasion Herr Walter Behrendt did quite well.

have been a considerable achievement by the *Ponts et Chausées* or whichever French agency had been responsible. An English local authority faced with the same challenge as Strasbourg would probably have dusted down the drawings of some town hall planned in the thirties but aborted by the War, and delivered it (late, of course) irrespective of its suitability, but of such monumental construction that it would be around long beyond the demise of the institutions it had been built to serve. Instead the French appeared to have stitched together a number of military prefabs of various sizes, and delivered on time. It was eventually replaced in the seventies by the magnificent *Palais de l'Europe* on the site next door.

The *hémicycle* occupied the middle of the ground floor of the building, and was surrounded by a range of offices which were for the most part used only during sittings of one or other of the Assemblies. These provided space for the proceduralists (the *service de la séance*), and the interpreters, the stenographic service, the summary writers, the press and others who arrived only for the sessions. For meetings of the European Parliament these mostly came down on the train or by road from Brussels or (in those days) from Luxembourg, large pantechnicons disgorging a vast quantity of crates containing all the documents and equipment needed for the week's business, and the staff fanning out through the building to get the operation up and running.

While the centrepiece of the *Maison de l'Europe* was the hemicycle, during sessions the most important area was probably the *Bar des Délégués* alongside. Presided over by my lady friend from the night train (who as well as minute steaks and *pommes sautés* served every alcoholic beverage known to man – where else at that time could you chase your Aalborg with a bottle of Tiger?), it was the main centre both of social dialogue and of political intrigue: of which there was plenty, despite (or more likely because of) the almost total powerlessness of both assemblies: backbenchers free of their whips enjoy nothing more than a bit of intrigue, even if they're only bidding for a rapporteurship.

The Delegates' Bar was across a narrow and dark corridor from the chamber, close enough to allow members (and delegation secretaries) to keep an ear open for what was going on without having to face the tedium of participating.

Those too challenged by the previous night's celebrations were able, however, to repair to the delegation offices, which surrounded the hemicycle on the floor above. Each national delegation (irrespective of size) had two rooms – a conscious gesture towards the Churchillian belief in parliaments properly divided between government and opposition. These offices contained *haut-parleurs* providing a direct feed from the chamber (with which high technology we were all most impressed), two telephones, and Remploy-style tables and cupboards, with leather armchairs apparently inspired by SNCF's third-class carriages: if you fell asleep (which would be not altogether surprising) you were likely to slide slowly to the floor unless previously bolstered by other chairs, or saved by a considerate conference officer or secretary. The latter, who really ran the team, were in any case briefed to wake up all other occupants whenever the division bells rang.

Apart from its general dowdiness and discomfort, the *Maison* had two particular features which made a barely bearable week more or less completely unbearable. The first had been there from the start and had presumably been designed by some unreformed Vichyite official to encourage by-elections throughout the member states and accelerate the turnover of delegates. The floor of the main entrance hall was composed of slightly-sprung rubber, which when damp became as good a skating rink as Somerset House in the Christmas season. Whenever it rained in Strasbourg (which was not infrequent) delegates, staff, the media, visitors of all descriptions – each performed an elegant cachucha as they entered or departed or tried to book an official car or claim their expenses in hard currency. Breakages were frequent, so much so that one of our famously redoubtable lady Members – Dame Joan Vickers, she of the blue-rinsed hair who had seen off Michael Foot (to the delight of all parties) in the 1955 General Election – after a series of bruises and breakages, insisted on having a room at the Sofitel next door to any Maltese delegate, since he would almost certainly also be a doctor of medicine.

The second endearing feature was the European Anthem. This was chosen by the Council of Europe, after prolonged deliberations in the Assembly, at the beginning of 1972, and was – perhaps inevitably – a pasteurised version of the Ode to "Joy" from Beethoven's Ninth. It was intended to be used only on ceremonial occasions, a practice facilitated by the installation of a large box, with a play button (but not, as I recall, a stop button) which was conveniently located at the bottom of the stairs leading from the delegation offices to the delegates' bar. Given its great bulk, we speculated that the whole contraption might contain either a worn-out jukebox from the nearest US air base across the Rhine, or one of the original magnetophons liberated from Großdeutscher Rundfunk in 1944: the appalling sound quality suggested the latter. It was supposed to be operated by one of the Assembly's *huissiers* at the beginning of each session or at the arrival of heads of state or government or other notables. Because of its location, however, the play button presented an irresistible temptation to any passer-by wishing to enliven proceedings, or who simply happened to be unsteady on his feet. Although delegates eventually learned not to stand to attention every time the awful noise filled the building (and it got worse as the tape – or was it a 45 - began to wear out), a whole generation of politicians, officials, translators, waiters and messengers developed a deep-seated loathing of Bonn's most famous son.

Few of the new British members of the European Parliament were unfamiliar with the House of Europe and its idiosyncrasies. Fourteen of the twenty-one (and all but two of the House of Commons members) had already served time as members of the Council of Europe Assembly - some, such as Peter Kirk himself, for more than a decade. They knew the town, they knew the building, they re-occupied their old leather chairs in the delegation offices, and were welcomed back as old friends by Madame. Their nomination by Ted Heath's government reflected the obvious need to have people on the ground already well familiar with the European political scene, and with European parliamentary procedures. In most cases it also reflected their own personal commitment to the idea of European co-operation: which did not mean that they all necessarily subscribed to the federalist agenda; and at least two of the Tories (Sir Derek Walker-Smith and the Ulster Unionist Rafton Pounder) were well-known campaigners against joining or remaining in the European Community.

Most of the new British members had served with some distinction in the Second World War. Sir James Hill, for instance, had volunteered for the Royal Fleet Auxiliary as a teenager; John Hill had spent the war in the Royal Artillery, and then the RAF; John Peel (by now also President of the Assembly of Western European Union, still a member of the delegation to the Council of Europe Assembly, and President of the North Atlantic Assembly) had survived the Japanese prison camps; Jim Scott-Hopkins had served with the Ghurkas on the North-West Frontier and in Burma; Sir Tufton Beamish had been injured in the BEF's retreat to Dunkirk, had escaped Japanese imprisonment by rowing the whole way from Singapore to Ceylon, and then transferred to the Eighth Army; and the only woman in the delegation (this reflecting both the paucity of women MP's and, perhaps, Ted Heath's own inclinations), Baroness Elles, had spent the war in the WAAF as a codebreaker at Bletchley Park.

Although they may have looked and behaved a bit like their caricatures, these were not the Colonel Blimps or the Sir Bufton Tuftons of *Private Eye*'s imagining, but mainly intelligent and in any case uniquely experienced men and women who shared with their European counterparts an absolute determination to avoid further European and global conflicts. Although most had served as junior ministers or party spokesmen, they were not of Cabinet 'calibre' (which was on the whole to their credit) and some were perhaps disappointed that they had not moved further up the political tree: one, Sir Douglas Dodds-Parker (colonial service, colonel in the SOE, légion d'honneur, croix de guerre, parliamentary under-secretary for Foreign Affairs at the time of Suez) reflected something of this sense of frustration, and rather stole my thunder, by publishing his memoirs in 1986 under the title *Political Eunuch*: which would otherwise have served as an appropriate title for this book.

7

Scott-Hopkins Goes Forth

Taking charge in the hémicycle

On the day before the formal opening of the newly-enlarged Parliament, the Speakers and Presiding Officers of the national parliaments met in Strasbourg in celebratory mood to consider mechanisms for improving relations between their parliaments and the European Parliament, with an appropriately generous lunch.

Meanwhile, the Tory members had spent much of the day at last reading the memorandum we had prepared in London in their name and persuading the other members of the newly-created Conservative Group (namely two Danes) to support its progressive (if not radical) proposals. Given their background, it was not surprising that they all signed up to the document: but it was just as well, since it would have been technically impossible to produce a new version with the equipment then available to us in Strasbourg; and although there had been no leaks the document's mere existence had been so hyped to the media that it was politically essential that it should be delivered on time.

'Mr Kirk's' memorandum[7] did what Mr Heath had asked (to "shake up" the European Parliament), and indeed what most of the existing members at least claimed they were hoping for. Many of these had made clear that they expected the British to inject new life into an institution widely regarded as moribund, and would have been greatly disappointed if the by now celebrated document had not at least moved in that direction. Indeed, following an EP Bureau meeting in early December, the Parliament had agreed in advance to Peter Kirk's proposals for the introduction of some form of Question Time, and for spontaneous debates to follow statements and reports from the European Commission – both of which developments were already scheduled into the January agenda.

The memorandum therefore contained much that was to be expected. It acknowledged the limited nature of the European Parliament's formal powers, but insisted that they should be used to the fullest extent. Both the power to dismiss the entire Commission, and the power to reject the administrative budget of the Community institutions were blunt instruments, but they should nonetheless be exercised, the European Commission being thereby reminded of its ultimate dependence on "the continuing support of Parliament", and as a means of clarifying "the

45

political divisions which exist within the Parliament on major policy issues, and the degree of support which exists for the Commission's overall policies". The Parliament "should not feel the need to shelter behind unanimity in order to influence the Council of Ministers and the European Commission. It should make its political differences clear, for these reflect the political divisions amongst the people of Europe".

The Parliament should therefore "concentrate its attention on matters of political substance", arrange more topical and spontaneous debates, strike a better balance between the examination of the detail of legislation and of the underlying policies, give individual members (and not merely the political groups) some right of initiative on the floor, use its committees as more effective instruments for the scrutiny of administration, and increase what we would now call "transparency" by holding committee hearings in public, and by the rapid publication of full or summary reports of proceedings in all languages. All this was sensible encouragement to the European Parliament to use its "latent powers" and to give up acting merely as a "technical and advisory agency".

But against all public expectations the memorandum also included a small bombshell, which I and Peter Kirk knew that the whips on the delegation would have removed if the time and the technology were available. Despite confident predictions in the *Times* and other broadsheets (well-briefed as usual by Downing Street) that "the vexed subject of direct elections" would not be raised, the Kirk memorandum concluded that "as democratic parliamentarians we will not be happy until the European Parliament both acquires real decision-making powers and is elected by the people of Europe". And in his opening speech, followed closely by European governments as well as by the world press, this unprepossessing man, calling on the ghosts of "the dead of countless battlefields", told the European Parliament that "Initiatives are not there to be given; they are there to be seized. We can, and must seize them. … By this means this Parliament will live and the peoples will clamour to be directly represented in it."

This was not really the stuff of revolution, but it sounded a bit like it. Direct elections for the European Parliament were anticipated in Article 138 of the Treaty of Rome, but until now nobody had taken the prospect at all seriously. The "Assembly" was empowered to draw up proposals, but these had so far been ignored, largely to the relief of the governments of the big states, a group now enlarged by the admission of the UK. Until now the Community had been run by the Chancellor in Bonn and the President in the Elysée; and the assumption was that Downing Street would now be joining this comfortable arrangement. But here, from a man who was thought to be Downing Street's spokesman, came what seemed like a clarion call for elections, democracy, and responsible government in the Community.

In consideration for the considerable antiquity of most of the delegates,

Peter Kirk was not actually carried shoulder-high out of the hemicycle by the quaestors, but in every other respect he was given a hero's welcome. Mr Heath, a federalist by nature and by conviction, may have been privately amused, but publicly he was very much not. He was reminded at a press conference the next morning that only a fortnight earlier he had told a Hampton Court banquet that he hoped that "our objective of a democratic Europe is not going to be misdirected by a desire to see direct elections", but could now only lamely endorse his delegation's "very specific concrete proposals as to how the European Parliament can build up its power and influence". But the damage was already done. Everyone took Peter Kirk seriously, the United Kingdom appeared to have given the green light, and the previously remote prospect of direct elections moved to the top of the agenda. Peter Kirk got his knighthood, but relations between the parliamentary delegation and No 10 developed a healthily cautious distance thereafter. It was one of my finest hours, much though I lived to regret it thereafter.

Very sensibly, the Conservatives had followed the example of the Gaullists in establishing their own political group in the European Parliament, resisting pressure to throw in their lot with the dominant German and Italian Christian Democrats. By establishing their own group they gained the immediate advantage of dual membership of the parliament's management body, the *bureau élargi* (both a national Vice-President and the leader of the new group), direct control of the allocation of members to parliamentary committees, their own offices in Luxembourg, travel expenses for group meetings, and a small paid secretariat - to which they had already appointed Mr Dunstan Curtis, a former naval commander, DSC plus bar, and croix de guerre, former deputy secretary general of both the European Movement and the Council of Europe, successful international lawyer, and an impressively effective operator. Equally important was that it gave them freedom of manoeuvre: although they liaised closely from the start with the Christian Democrat Group (indeed they held a joint meeting of the two groups on the very first morning before proceedings began), they were able to vote any way they wished, table whatever amendments they liked and, most important, carry over the Westminster practice of allowing their members to speak for themselves in the plenary: their speeches were not going to be constrained – or, worse, drafted – by the group secretariat. As a result, anti-marketeers like Derek Walker-Smith were able to play a continuing role (constructive or otherwise) in the Parliament, even if they were not committed to its long-term future. As many of its own MP's felt at the time, if only the Labour Party could have been so grown-up! The Tories even managed to force the Liberals and the *non-inscrits* to sit on the right-hand wing of the hemicycle (where they had initially been condemned to sit), and upstaged the Gaullists by sitting in front of them near to the centre, to great Gallic alarm.

The British Tories therefore made an improbable, but immediate, impact as a progressive force in the enlarged Parliament, and swung immediately into action. Although the remains of the first week were fairly routine (after the excitements of day one) by the time they returned for the next round they were up and running, and began to get down to the detail.

At the February session in Luxembourg (which I missed, having returned to Strasbourg for yet another Council of Europe session) the Brits managed to refer back to the Commission a draft regulation on ethyl alcohol (designed before enlargement to protect French, Italian and Belgian agriculture, but highly prejudicial to the whisky industry), forced through a resolution on the monetary crisis (when is there not a monetary crisis?) specifically tailored to City of London interests, and combined with the Gaullists and the Italian communists to require the Council of Ministers to consult the Parliament prior to the ratification of trade agreements. In March, I was back with the team in Strasbourg, but only just – the British plane was almost the only one which made it through the snowstorm into Strasbourg, and Peter Kirk had had to go ahead by train. The delegation managed to head off the most trenchant criticism of the UK for refusing to participate in a joint float of Community currencies and to go it alone in the defence of sterling in the latest international monetary crisis, and led the attack on the Council of Minsters for agreeing the annual farm price review ahead of any debate in Parliament.

The honeymoon period was obviously drawing to a close: members of other national delegations were beginning to mutter that if the British wanted to take the lead in reforming the institutions of the Community they ought also (in the great spirit of consensus) be prepared to co-operate to help other member states and currencies in difficulty, even occasionally at the expense of their own national interests; and that although the British had proposed ways of expediting consideration of more "technical" legislation (to allow time for more grand policy debates and administrative scrutiny) it appeared odd that any legislative proposals which cut against British interests seemed not be regarded as "technical" after all. These criticisms were not entirely without foundation.

At the April session of the Parliament – back in Luxembourg –a real clash at last arose between the resentments of the older member states and the undoubted adeptness of the Brits in matters procedural, all in their different ways reflecting their national interests, but all of course in the name of the Community interest.

The Parliament now met in a new building on the plateau du Kirchberg, thrown up by the Luxembourg government in one of a series of vain bids over the years to upstage Strasbourg. It was the first of several such buildings to clutter the streets of Europe as the European Community continued its inexorable growth. Getting to Luxembourg was not quite so difficult as getting to Strasbourg, and our already seasoned travellers were beginning to get the hang of the system. There was a passable rail service from Brussels, which was not far away, and as the national capital of a micro-state Luxembourg boasted reasonable air services so long as you chose the right time of day, or day of the week. Hotels were definitely below standard, and their staff almost British in their surliness. The new parliamentary building was only just big enough for the enlarged European Parliament: if the Norwegians had joined as planned there wouldn't have been enough room for them and their bag carriers also to sit in the dark and claustrophobic auditorium provided, so that was yet another good reason for their very sensible decision to stay away.

On the agenda for the April 1973 session was the delayed consideration of the farm price review. The Common Agricultural Policy was of course one of the cornerstones of the original Common Market – a straightforward deal between primitive French farming and post-reconstruction German industry – and was probably the main reason for British opposition to membership of the Community. We were mostly loyal to the Commonwealth, and in any case wanted cheap New Zealand butter and lamb: they were putting up barriers to Commonwealth imports and trying to force us to pay high prices for food we didn't as yet realise we wanted: who ate pasta in 1973, other than as one of Heinz 57 varieties?

This very first debate on the CAP was a typically European moment. The Council of Ministers and the Commission proposed an across-the-board rise of 2.76%; the Germans, the French and the Italians wanted 4%; the Benelux countries accepted the Commission proposals; the British and the Danes – new members with much more efficient agricultures, and who still happened to believe in free trade – really didn't want guaranteed prices at all, but were prepared to settle for no change in the price regime for the time being – pending the real negotiations which they confidently hoped would lead to the early demise of the CAP.

So, on the evening of Thursday 5th April, the first great debate of the enlarged Parliament began, on a motion from the agriculture committee to accept the Commission's proposals. The Christian Democrats put down amendments to increase guaranteed prices further; the Conservatives put down amendments to keep them level. The debate ebbed and flowed, but it was clear to all that the old European alliance would win if we didn't do something dramatic. At which point Sir James Scott-Hopkins, the Tory whip, began to ruminate the possibilities of a roll-call vote.

In the dark and dim corners of the auditorium, Sir Barnett Cocks' Book was at last consulted. A series of spectacular manoeuvres followed. First, Robert Rogers was sent forward to the presidium to warn them of the possibility: heads wagged, and Barney Cocks' old friend Hans Nord, the Dutch Secretary-General, warned that this was not the way things were done in the Parliament: it was wholly alien to the tradition of understanding and compromise. Robert returned to us, and we discovered from the Book that the last time a roll-call vote had been called was all of five years previously, and that there appeared to be no record of a roll-call then actually taking place. Jim Scott-Hopkins then went to the presidium and warned them that the Brits were serious. On his return I (as Barney Cocks' representative) was summoned by Hans Nord and told in no uncertain terms that what we were proposing to do was "unacceptable, and against the spirit of co-operation and compromise which has characterised the European Parliament since its inception".

Finally, convinced that we had every right to call for a roll-call vote, Peter Kirk himself went to the presidium and demanded one. He was told that the request had to be made by ten members, and in writing; he returned to the back of the hall, obtained ten signatures, and returned to the presidium, "waving", as the Times reported, "a sheet of paper". On a point of order, a Belgian Socialist suggested that we appeared to be in a cinema or a theatre rather than a Parliament, with messengers arriving stage-left and stage-right, a comment entirely appropriate to the building in which we had been constrained to meet.

Meanwhile Mr Nord himself began to consult the rules of procedure and, we were glad to see, our own Book. He then invented a way out, and the usually calm but now understandably agitated Dutch President – Mr Cornelius Berkhouwer – ruled (on no authority other than his own) that a request for a roll-call vote had to be made in advance of the sitting. Peter Kirk played the gentleman he was, and merely said that for future reference his group might always want a roll-call vote. Eventually another Dutchman, Liberal Jean Vaas, revealed the unpalatable truth, that if a roll-call vote were held it would demonstrate the lack of a quorum, and the proceedings would have to be adjourned to the following day – a Friday, when everyone was expecting to be on the way home. What he didn't say – and what the media failed to pick up – was that the reason for the lack of a quorum was that the entire German delegation was absent – because on Thursday evenings they, by tradition, all went out to dinner together.

The result, after ten hours' debate, was that in the small hours of Friday morning the Parliament voted, by sitting and standing (which technically did not reveal the absence of a quorum – although it was evident to all present), to reject both an increase and a decrease in farm prices, and also to reject the operative clause of the draft resolution, which would have endorsed the decisions of the governments and the Commission. A few hours later the Parliament sheepishly asked the Commission to look at the problem again. It was a result wholly in the United Kingdom's favour: all British parties wanted the cosy arrangements of the CAP to be re-examined, and we had demonstrated to all the leaps which had to be taken before the assembly could begin to claim to be a real Parliament.

8

L'équipe anglaise

The Clerks in Strasbourg

The European Parliament was only a tenant (and a not altogether welcome tenant) in the *Maison de l'Europe* in the *alleé de la Robertsau* in Strasbourg. That building was first and foremost the home of the Council of Europe and its own consultative assembly (which in 1974 added to the general confusion by insisting on renaming itself the "Parliamentary" Assembly). It was also something like home from home to many generations of Westminster clerks as well as Members – mostly from the Commons but with always a few from the House of Lords, some of whom added a certain colour to the mix.

The Council of Europe had from the start the sense to import the expertise required to run its plenary sessions, rather than maintaining a full kit of interpreters and proceduralists on its permanent books. That they were able to do this was partly because even after travel became easier they kept the number of plenary sessions to only three a year, and partly because they followed the wise precedent of the League of Nations and the United Nations in limiting the number of official languages: in the Strasbourg case to only two, a position they have admirably managed to maintain (with a certain flexibility in the case of German and Italian, and then Russian), even now that the organisation's reach has extended from the eighteen member countries of the early 1970's to the full forty-seven states generally recognised as "European" by 2012.[*] This has always meant that the number of fulltime translators and interpreters could be kept to a minimum, and that procedural complications could be resolved largely between the francophone and the anglophone. The European Parliament, of course, chose to go down the opposite route – of allowing every member state its own language (or languages): a practice which was just about manageable in the Community of the Six, became challenging and expensive (and already faintly ludicrous) in the Community of the Nine, and became clearly lunatic in the European Union of the Twenty-Seven and rising (or perhaps falling).

For meetings of the Council of Europe Assembly staff therefore appeared from all over the organisation's still rather limited bit of Europe.

---

[*] with the exception of Belarus.

The multi-national but compulsorily francophone permanent staff came merely across the way from *bâtiment B*, a utilitarian, hideous but unpretentious office block (which on the top floor contained probably the worst staff canteen in the civilised world), which was their home *hors session*. Interpreters and translators came from whichever other European city had most recently tolerated their extravagantly expensive services. And the shorthand writers and proceduralists came (apart from the odd Dutchman, Irishman, Norwegian or Dane thrown in for the sake of political correctness) almost exclusively from the national parliaments in London and Paris. For the latter the occasional trip to Alsace was a change from work (and lavishly paid), but no great excitement: for the time being it had ceased to be abroad, but still had the distinct drawback that the local patois was so adulterated after 80 years or so on and off of German occupation as to be unintelligible to the true-born *haut fonctionnaire*: one expected pomanders to appear whenever an *Alsacien* (or for that matter a Brit) dared to pass them by in the corridor.

For the Brits, on the other hand, suffering from acute exchange control-induced travel deprivation, a trip to Strasbourg was worth fighting for (and hence the prime importance of the Fourth Clerk at the Table and head of the Overseas Office, in his lair above the Commons chamber). Established from the foundation of the Council of Europe in 1949 (when the recently-retired Clerk of the House, Sir Gilbert Campion, was appointed the first Clerk of the consultative assembly), the *équipe anglaise* provided an English-language summary report, and an English version of the presidential *dossier* required for running the sittings; they vetted Questions and draft Resolutions, compiled the lists of speakers for plenary debates, and produced the formal minutes of proceedings. The *chef de l'équipe* wrote the *dossier*, briefed the President and guided his hand in the plenary sessions, and was in overall charge of what amounted to a local version of the House of Commons Table and Journal Offices. French versions of the same documents were produced in parallel, and entirely independently, by staff from Paris and Brussels (but who, for unknown reasons, were not known universally as the *equipe française*).

The two teams kept as far apart as possible, so what was officially recorded as having happened in the plenary sessions depended to a large extent on which language was being spoken by (and therefore fed to) the president or vice-president in the chair. By the time I got involved as team leader in the 1980's there was general acceptance that the British interpretation of events was likely to prevail: despite the overwhelmingly "continental" form of the Assembly's rules of procedure, and despite the fact that the nominal head of the procedural service for the first few years was from the Belgian Senate, it was difficult and often visibly painful for the French and their Belgian co-frères (this was a rare arena where the Parisians accepted the Bruxellois as such) to accept the reality that the *anglophonie* was fast overtaking the *francophonie*.

The English *équipe* was regarded by the Strasbourg authorities as also including those who produced the verbatim report of proceedings in English: but despite the fact that they mostly came from Westminster, domestic demarcation lines and status were just as rigidly enforced. So the Hansard writers stayed elsewhere (and in rather superior accommodation), dined elsewhere, and were only contacted when procedural embarrassments required some creative embellishment of the official report: although in practice more than one romance between clerks and shorthand writers blossomed in the parc de l'Orangerie, despite discouragement from the powers-that-were.

My own first taster of the Council of Europe had been in the autumn of 1972, when I accompanied JPST on his last assignment before leaving for Luxembourg. On this occasion we comprised a two-man and one-girl team to support a Council of Europe offshoot, the Conference of European Local Authorities. Run by a man and a girl of relatively lowly status in the permanent secretariat, the local authorities conference had presumably been set up to discourage local counsellors and the equivalent from complaining that the national parliaments got all the good trips. In later years it has established itself (as such non-essential organisations tend to do) as an indispensable feature in the European landscape (now grandly known as the Congress of Local and Regional Authorities), handing out awards to progressive cities but, rather like the Newspaper of the Year awards, ensuring along the way that each country and region gets its turn, and encouraging town twinning and other worthy causes.

The Local Authorities Conference in 1972 allowed me to hone those essential skills, first learned in Brussels in 1969, in writing convincing but largely inaccurate summaries, but also gave me the chance to familiarise myself with Strasbourg, which was to become my second home for the next couple of years. On this first occasion I stayed with JPST, thankfully for the only time, in the *auberge à l'horloge astronomique*, a singularly unsavoury boarding house across the way from Strasbourg's famously hideous (and never completed: it should have had two spires but only got one) cathedral and its eponymous clock. When the drains began regurgitating through the bidets I suggested to John that perhaps it was time to find slightly more commodious billets, even if they charged more than 5 francs a night.

Thereafter, the English team became more or less permanent residents of the Hotel Gutenberg, in the *rue des serruriers*. The Gutenberg was run by Monsieur Jean Lette and his son, and claimed to be a family enterprise of great antiquity. It had a chequered and invitingly notorious history, having variously served (depending on which version you believed) as the headquarters, torture chamber, or brothel (or all three) of either the Gestapo or the SS during that war which still figured so largely in our memories or imaginations, but was definitely not to be talked about: the rather flimsy four-posters in the larger rooms suggested the latter, although the voluminous, echoing, bathrooms hinted at more uncomfortable, if equally traditional, SS past-times. The hotel remained, even then, Strasbourg's centre of buonapartist resistance to the Republic: the staircases were illuminated (to the extent that they were illuminated at all) by patriotic paintings of Napoleon's greater victories, and of England's greatest defeats; but when M Lette's confidence was eventually gained you had the ultimate privilege of reading illegal pamphlets in his private office behind reception, encouraging thoughts of rebellion, the resurrection of the Grande Armée, and the creation of a new empire, this time presumably centred on Alsace, the true beating heart of the real France.

Despite M Lette's hopes of empire and of renewed campaigns against the English and the Brandenburgers, the Gutenberg was extraordinarily welcoming to the English team. Although it had no restaurant or bar to look after them in the evenings (which was probably just as well), it served excellent café au lait, fresh jus d'orange, decent croissants and oeufs á la coq from the earliest hours of the morning in the lobby at the bottom of the stairs: so if you could manage to negotiate these in the gloom after a typical soirée de Strasbourg, you had a reasonable chance of facing the day, fortified by an excellent petit déjeuner, a brief glance at the *Dernières Nouvelles d'Alsace*, and a bracing walk along Strasbourg's innumerable bridges, rivers and canals.

The Gutenberg was also conveniently central to Strasbourg's multifarious attractions of a more uplifting character. If you turned right out of the hotel you soon found yourself at the protestant equivalent of a cathedral, the church of St Thomas, where I attended some wonderful choral and orchestral concerts over the years. If you went on you reached Strasbourg's *petite France*, famous for its Maison des Tanneurs (a *location touristique*), but full of restaurants and bars of rather greater quality and character. My favourite was the Taverne des Tanneurs, where much of an evening could be spent in the upstairs room discussing with Madame or her buxom daughter what best meal could be produced from their daily trip to the market: there was never a printed menu, and if you got a table you were there until the menu was created in co-operative manner, the food cooked in a great central stove *à la russe*, and the finished product presented unceremoniously before you, very late in the evening, but always exquisite.

If you turned left out of the Gutenberg you were immediately amongst restaurants varying from the very best to the dire. The Maison Kammerzell, a fifteenth century edifice fronting the cathedral, was probably the most prestigious: here the English team held occasional celebrations, the most memorable in late 1974, when the Council of Europe celebrated its twenty-fifth anniversary by decking the cathedral in fireworks: a magnificent meal, threatened by what appeared to be and sounded like a reliable reconstruction of Verdun. There were others of equal provenance: *au crocodile*, or *l'ancienne douane*, but most were, even then, and even on generous expenses, normally out of our range: in any case, after a hard day's inventive summarising, what was needed was somewhere a decent omelette could be ordered at short notice. So our works café was in the Place Gutenberg itself. The *aux Armes de Strasbourg* was at that time still a family-owned restaurant which would serve anybody and anything at almost any time: although (like most of the town) it packed up in the late evening, it offered for the rest of the time a wonderfully complete menu – which meant that if it wasn't on the printed menu you could simply ask for it: its omelette jambon and pommes (genuinely) sautés, or even better its rognons sautés, had no rivals. Sadly, the *aux Armes* eventually became part of a chain and its more useful attributes were lost forever. Most important to me, just round the corner in the *rue des tonneliers* was *au Pigeon*, which had been in the same family for a mere couple of centuries (surviving revolutions, invasions, re-occupations) and a restaurant for much longer. The food was bland at best, but the atmosphere unique, and it was here that I not infrequently escaped from the team, and settled for the coq au vin blanc or tarte strasbourgeoise, along with copious pichets, happy in the illusion that I was following a tradition of centuries, and that notables back to Martin Bucer, or even Gutenberg himself, might have sat on the same benches.

So central did the Hotel Gutenberg become over the years in the lives of Westminster clerks that in the 1990's, when management awaydays became de rigueur in the otherwise economising public sector, the Heads of Office of the Clerk's Department briefly entertained a proposal that the hotel, then up for sale, should be acquired as a permanent base for such outings: but like all my more imaginative proposals this was regarded as merely frivolous. That they failed to act resulted only in that the hotel, as part of a chain now going up-market, and putting up its charges, became less accommodating to the whims and idiosyncrasies of the English team, and that we were all collectively less well-off than we otherwise would have undoubtedly become as joint proprietors of such an iconic feature of Strasbourg life. For many years we had managed to keep the secret of the Gutenberg from British MPs (being deliberately evasive when asked where we were staying), but eventually – probably tipped off by the Dutch and the Danes – they discovered it (Mr Russell Johnston was, I think the first intruder), realised the savings they could make by staying there, and poached the best four-poster rooms. So it was no longer a safe haven from the politicians who otherwise blighted our lives.

The post of *chef de l'équipe* was, after the top fulltime job which guaranteed a KCB, one of the most coveted in the whole clerkly service. It had been created by Barney Cocks in the early fifties, and then held by a whole string of illuminati, including David Lidderdale, Kenneth Bradshaw and JPST. By the early 1970's the role had been taken over, and was superlatively performed, by John Francis Sweetman TD. JFS – scion of the

Royal Artillery and still active in the territorials - was hearty, a trifle portly, volubly but misleadingly humorous, who tolerated neither fools nor incompetents: we all sought his favour (and for much of the time we mostly succeeded) and were terrified of becoming one of those who had lost it.

JFS, like JPST before him, led the team with glorious confidence. When invitations were not forthcoming through official channels to the soirées which gave purpose to Strasbourg's otherwise unmotivated and largely unemployed diplomatic corps, it was John Sweetman who led the way into receptions, even dinners with *placements* already arranged, masquerading as whichever member of the British delegation he knew was safely on the way back to London. On more than one occasion he and a secretary were announced in the mairie as, for instance, Sir Frederic and Lady Bennett, only to be fulsomely introduced by M Pflimlin[*] to his other habitual guests as '*M John Sweetman et sa nouvelle épouse*'. John guided the hand of the President of the Assembly, solved the not infrequent financial and emotional problems of his team, enforced strict protocol in any unavoidable contacts with the French, attempted to ensure that relations with the Hansard writers were limited to the minimal courtesies, and took charge of his team's social programme - which largely entailed deciding which of a hundred restaurants was to be chosen for dinner, how to gate-crash the autumn session's Sunday awayday for Members, and (most important of all) where the works outing was to be held.

In terms of flamboyance, even JPST and JFS could not really compete with the scions of their lordships' House who occasionally added lustre to the Strasbourg team. This was still an age when the largely hereditary house was supported by men of the same ilk, men who regarded their tenure as clerk as a minor interruption in their far more interesting social round. Particularly celebrated was Euan Douglas Graham (Eton, Christ Church, RAF), the immensely tall grandson of the Fifth Duke of Montrose, and close friend of Alan Clark, who listed his recreations in *Who's Who* as deer stalking and mountain "bicycling", but didn't there admit to his real life-long addiction to snakes. The discovery of the latter in his desk in the Lords Private Bill Office may well, in the words of his *Daily Telegraph* obituarist, have "contributed to his failure to succeed as chief clerk of the Parliaments". It was Euan who drove me off one winter Saturday afternoon to the Rhine in his Morgan, there to induct me into the art of hurling lumps of concrete into the locks and the local hydro plants, declaiming "sals boches" as the night descended: we got hopelessly lost trying to avoid the frontier guards (sirens blaring, but machine guns mercifully silent) on the way back, and

---

[*] Pierre Pflimlin (1903-2000); mayor of Strasbourg 1959-83; for two weeks in May 1958 he served as the last democratically elected prime minister of France before the accession of Charles de Gaulle (and was therefore entitled to be addressed as 'M le Président' in perpetuity).

spent most of that foggy night in a friendly (and thankfully francophone) bar on the safe side of the Rhine.

Although the immediate attractions of service in the Strasbourg team were (a) money and therefore (b) the chance of going abroad without using your sterling allowance, there was also the opportunity to do well in Strasbourg the job we were already paid to do at home, but here the chance of shining was much greater. In the longer term, the exposure of Westminster clerks (and, indeed, of Members) to the different procedural challenges of the Council of Europe (as well as the WEU Assembly in Paris, and the peripatetic North Atlantic Assembly) proved of enormous benefit to both chambers in Westminster. By this means we began to shake off inherited prejudices in favour of the "Westminster Model", and to absorb rather different approaches to the parliamentary challenges faced by all national parliaments at that time. In particular, clerks as well as Members began to appreciate the advantages of specialised committees, and of more flexible legislative procedures, an appreciation which from the 1980's onwards bore fruit in the development of the new committee systems, and of new methods of considering primary legislation, at both ends of the Palace of Westminster.

Academics might claim their authorship of such changes, but it was really their hands-on experience of being chairmen or rapporteurs at international assemblies which altered the mind-set of so many backbenchers; and, equally or more important, several generations of Westminster clerks had begun to realise the potential of specialised committees, not only for backbenchers to make their mark, not only as a means of opening up the democratic system to effective influence from outside the Palace, but also to create a new and far more interesting career path for the clerks themselves. So Strasbourg offered a significant educational experience for MP's and clerks alike: an experience which radically transformed the British Parliament a decade or so later.

9

Secrétaire de la Délégation

Bag-carrier in chief

As delegation secretary in these early days I held only honorary membership of the English team. The team, although fulltime employees of the whoever-it-was-who-employed-people-in-the-House-of-Commons, were, when in Strasbourg, also temporary employees of the Council of Europe, and handsomely paid as such; moreover, under the treaty by which the Council of Europe was established, they had no need to declare their winnings nor were they liable to income tax back home. Their first task on arrival in the Maison de l'Europe was therefore to draw the first tranche of their pay from the caisse; thereafter they travelled around Strasbourg with the confident, occasionally over-confident, air of the newly-enriched. Sometimes their reputation went before them and they came to grief at the hands of the local criminal fraternity, despite frequent advice from the House authorities to always hide the loot under the mattress at the Gutenberg.

The Delegation Secretary had the privilege – for purposes of, say, invitations to mayoral receptions, or weekend visits to the local Clochemerle and its co-operative wine-bottling plant – of being ranked alongside Members of Parliament; but he also received the same meagre living allowance as did his political masters. He (and the conference officer and secretary who accompanied him) therefore just about broke even on a trip to Strasbourg, while the team actually made money. Hence the unseemly scramble back home to get onto the team, the strict rules of rotation which applied to the choice of team members, and the general popularity of the Clerk of the Overseas Office.

The effective running of the British delegation to the European Parliament was soon to be taken over by their political groups, and the role of delegation secretary soon faded away. Although always less well known, the delegation to the Council of Europe Assembly – eighteen full representatives and eighteen substitutes – played a far more important part in the politics of Europe than might have been supposed by the almost complete disregard paid to it by the Government back home or, for the most part, by the media. In view of Britain's role (inspired by Churchill) in the founding of the organisation, it was not surprising that the parliamentary delegation had always played above its weight, taking the chairmanships and rapporteurships of the key committees through most of the Assembly's early existence, and contributing far more actively in plenary debates than others, with the possible exception of the Germans (who had much to prove) or the Dutch (who shared our democratic instincts).

The importance attached to Council of Europe membership by the UK political parties (as distinct from Governments and their civil servants) since 1950 rather belied the myth of British isolationism or anti-Europeanism: many leading politicians in Westminster (Butler, Callaghan, Douglas-Home, Gaitskell, Gordon-Walker, Healey, Roy Jenkins and David Steel, to name a few) had at one time or another served in Strasbourg also; and in 1973, active participation in the Council of Europe became of particular importance for the Labour Party as a mark of their unqualified support for other forms of co-operation within Europe, despite their opposition to the federalist ambitions of the European Economic Community.

While the Conference Officer (in those days usually the redoubtable George Clayton) looked after travel, accommodation and expenses, the delegation secretary was supposed to do more clerkly things. These included drafting Questions to the Committee of Ministers (in the case of the Council of Europe) or to the Commission (in the case of the European Parliament), drafting amendments to draft resolutions, and even drafting speeches. In practice, even in the early 1970's, the political groups had already tried to assert their right to take over many of these functions in both assemblies, but with little result so far as British members were concerned, since they were as a breed (and most unlike the Germans, the French or the Italians) rarely amenable to anyone else telling them what to say.

There was much else for the delegation secretary to do, but it was often of the indefinable nature of clerkly support at which we were all seasoned hands. I would be pleading with the Hansard writers to launder politically awkward speeches for the record; I would be running round the building setting up meetings between anti-marketeers on our side and covertly disloyal French, Germans or Dutchmen; I would (perhaps most importantly) be clearing up the raft of embarrassments which arose each morning as Members remembered (or failed to remember in sufficient detail) the commitments and indiscretions of the previous Strasbourg night.

This latter job was of particular importance during Fred Peart's brief tenure of the leadership of the Labour group. A former teacher and captain in the Royal Artillery, and Leader of the House during the great struggles over Barbara Castle's industrial relations legislation, and with another Cabinet career still ahead of him, he seemed far too senior to be leader of a mere national party group in Strasbourg, and of course was there only because a high profile happened to be needed at that moment. Not surprisingly, Fred seemed to find the official bit of his current job somewhat tedious, but nonetheless managed to enjoy his return to Strasbourg (this time with an official car) enormously, presiding (in the great tradition of Labour group leaders) over a number of generous collations in Strasbourg's better-known inns and taverns, at several of which his dancing-on-the-table skills (as well as the choral skills of his companions) were generally commended.

On the mornings following such evenings there was just the small task of fending off the waifs and strays (Algerians, Armenians, Palestinians, Yemenis, or whatever) with political axes to grind who had received his benediction the night before (or the blessings of his team mates, or of any other British delegate who happened to have also been out for a post-reception night-cap, or two), and who then arrived at the Council of Europe to receive their promised tickets to the public gallery, questions immediately asked in the plenary, interviews with the BBC World Service, UK visas or (better still) passports. This was a real job for the delegation secretary, who was assumed to have attended all such happenings, to have entered fully into their spirit, and even, somehow (and even more surprisingly), to have full recall of what had transpired and what commitments had been entered into. While the rest of us regarded the CRS vans lined up across the road with some trepidation, such seasoned and street-wise lobbyists seemed to be able to penetrate the Council of Europe's own rather basic security with impunity, and other measures had to be taken to deflect them from their supposed benefactors: on one particularly painful occasion I cleared everyone out of the delegation offices for a few minutes while I persuaded a relatively respectable representative of the Roma community that the entire British delegation really had been recalled at short notice on a three-line whip.[*]

The delegation created other hazards for its bag-carrier-in-chief. One distinguished Tory got it into his head that the best way of disposing of his difficult, even tempestuous, daughter (who had more than a few of the characteristics of the Laird of Mugg's great-niece from Edinburgh) was to bring her to Strasbourg and pair her off with some unsuspecting parliamentary clerk who might be temporarily off-guard; and despite my commonplace background, unprepossessing appearance (in crimplene suit) and limited prospects I briefly found myself the principal target. After a few days of very public manoeuvrings I was compelled to parade several of my colleagues before the Conservative leader to vouch for the fact that I was already spoken for, and the hunt was called off, albeit with a certain bad grace.

The Conservative leader would have found all this immensely amusing:

---

[*] Fred Peart returned to his old job of Minister of Agriculture when Harold Wilson returned to Downing Street in March 1974. He was joined there, first as Parliamentary Secretary and (after the October elections) as Minister of State, by Ted Bishop (see p 71 below). This inspired combination of two drily humorous men, of apparently inexhaustible energy, constituted a formidable weapon in the renegotiation of UK membership of the European Communities: they could wittily talk every other agriculture minister under the table – and did so, not infrequently, over the next few months.

Sir John Rodgers Bt[*], the MP for Sevenoaks, was renowned not only as a pioneer of the British advertising industry, but also, and particularly within the English équipe, as an incorrigible admirer of well-bred young ladies. According to well attested sources one of my predecessors as leader of the clerks' team had around this time the rare privilege of physically assailing the leader of the delegation in defence of one of his young and pretty charges – and of doing so with impunity.

Even the Liberals posed the occasional problem. Normally there were only two British Liberals, but as one was usually Lord Gladwyn they made up in experience as well as pomposity what they lacked in arithmetic, and punched further above their weight even than the rest of the UK delegation. In order to maintain and reinforce their credentials as leaders of the European liberal movement the British Liberals held an annual party, the cost of which was partly defrayed from the small entertainment allowance allocated to the whole delegation from the Westminster budget. It was yet another of the responsibilities of the delegation secretary and the conference officer to assist at this modest event, held during my time in the Liberal leader's suite at the Sofitel. Most of those who attended appeared to be from northern climes, on the rebound from the prohibitionist tendencies of their respective governments, and matters were always at risk of getting out of hand.

One of the more notorious of such occasions occurred on my watch, when I was instructed by the Liberals' leader to accompany an over-excited Scandinavian back to his room and put him safely to bed: which somewhat offensive and distinctly un-clerkly duty I loyally carried out. Towards the end of the next morning's plenary session a bandaged and turbaned Scandinavian was released from hospital and rejoined his Liberal colleagues in the hemicycle; the story spread immediately through the assembly that another country's delegate had been beaten up by the British delegation secretary: there seemed to be an encouraging implication here that if you beat up your own delegates it might in some ways be excusable, or anyway explicable, but that others were off-limits. Some time later the politician in question owned up that so far as he could recall he had slipped in the bathroom and hit his head on the porcelain; but by then my reputation had been sullied for life, and my chances of getting onto the Liberal Party candidates' list (loyal Liberal voter though I had ever been) had been reduced to zilch.

Probably the most important regular social event of the Council of Europe part-sessions was the British Delegation Party. This was traditionally arranged to take place after the last assembly sitting of the week, usually early on the Friday afternoon. It used the bulk of the delegation's entertainment allowance, but was on the whole good PR for the

---

[*] one of the very last hereditary baronetcies, created in 1964.

UK. All delegates from all member states, together with the resident diplomatic corps, were invited, we being safe in the knowledge that almost all delegates as such would by that time have departed, and that, thankfully, the diplomats would therefore feel no obligation to attend. As the week drew on, and the regrets poured in, we extended invitations to more or less anyone who might happen to be in town by Friday afternoon: this invariably included the English team, even any of the French team who were not already leaving for Paris or the country, and all our friends and colleagues from the permanent secretariat.

There was a strictly enforced rule that the premises of the Council of Europe were not to be used for purely national functions; and so it was also a traditional duty of the delegation secretary to spend the first few days of the part-session negotiating with the Clerk of the Assembly (at that time a fiercely francophile and anglophobe UK national, Mr John Priestman) for this rule to be waived; which it invariably was, but late enough for invitations to be circulated in confidence of the traditional non-attendance of the original guest-list.

It was a further traditional duty of the delegation secretary to get in the drink. Although we recruited a few of Madame's remarkably sour waiters, and allowed her to lay on limited quantities of food (not in much demand), edelzwicker and gewurtz, we had another, and widely envied, source of sustenance for the serious party goers. Accordingly, on the last morning of the part-session I commandeered one of the official cars and made my way to the British Consulate General, in the cellar of which lay one of the largest stocks of decent champagne available anywhere in the neighbourhood. Allegedly inherited from the retreating *Wehrmacht*, it had refreshed the parliamentary delegation since the earliest days, was greatly superior to anything laid on in the *mairie*,[*] and was apparently inexhaustible. As the always tedious final session wore on my car would arrive none too discreetly (despite the injunctions of the Secretary General) at the back of the *maison de l'europe*, and would disgorge appropriate quantities of this precious wine, along with the duty-free spirits. The sight of the British delegation staff staggering through the back doors with ancient, and rapidly disintegrating, cardboard crates invariably raised an optimistic cheer from their multinational *confrères*. Later in the afternoon, with luck, we got them all back on board the charter.

---

[*] M Pflimlin's champagne at the Town Hall produced seriously ferocious headaches (worse even than the whiskey distributed in tumblers at the annual Irish delegation party), and was thought by members of the diplomatic corps to be the worst available anywhere west of Bucharest.

III Our Atlantic Allies

10

The madness of the Clerk

A double life in the Journal Office

In April Sir Barnett's patience ran out. As the good shop steward he was, he pulled the troops out. At about three o'clock on the afternoon of Thursday 19th April 1973 I was at my desk in No 46, innocently putting the final touches to our arrangements for the next sessions of both the Council of Europe Assembly and the European Parliament, when the internal phone rang. It was Maundy Thursday, and so far as I knew almost everyone else on the parliamentary estate had already departed for an albeit brief Easter recess (do not believe all those stories – including my own - about invariably long holidays). At the end of the phone was David Scott – he of the lost cars and disappearing wives, and still Clerk of Standing Committees. He was as always charming, and was merely asking to inquire if I could see myself being free to act as clerk of the standing committee on the new Education Bill, which was due to start in committee after the break. I politely replied that I had always enjoyed standing committee work, but he had perhaps forgotten that my job in the European Office required me to be out of the country quite frequently – indeed that until July I was already booked to be abroad every other week. He in turn charmingly rejoined that I needn't worry about any of that – "After all", said he, "your current office doesn't actually exist any more; I'm only phoning because it looks as though you won't have that many duties in the Journal Office". The Heads of Office had met and decided our fates.

Assailed by complaints from both sides – from the new Tory MEPs (who wanted more office accommodation and staff devoted exclusively to their needs), and from the Labour members of the other international delegations (who complained that the limited resources of the European Office were being monopolised by a partisan delegation to the European "Assembly"), the Clerk of the House decided to close the European Office altogether. With a total staff of all ranks of less than a hundred, he was expected to keep the Chamber going, run half-a-dozen or more legislative committees at any one time, man about fifteen "scrutiny" committees or sub-committees (and seven housekeeping committees), and between times support dozens of newly-independent Commonwealth parliaments. Now, apparently, he was expected to provide expensive bag-carriers for yet another European circus, and one, this time, which had the nerve to meet getting on for a dozen times a year. In the days before the establishment of parliamentary financial independence under the House of Commons Commission, the Clerk, although Accounting Officer, had little control over his own budget, which was an easy target whenever the Treasury embarked on another cost-saving or "efficiency" drive (an annual event then, as now). In effect, Barney said "sorry, gentlemen, it's time we got back to our core business" and although those of us directly involved were more than a little disconcerted by the abruptness of the change some had at least a sneaking respect for the decision.

So we Young Turks were redeployed to desks in the Palace to do real clerkly jobs. Douglas and Robert moved off to work for the Expenditure Committee, while I re-appeared in the offices above the Chamber, this time in the Journal Office, the mirror of the Public Bill Office I had left in 1970. No 46 was left with its long-suffering secretary, and a solid and reliable conference officer, George Clayton (soon to be joined by Colin Watson, who developed considerable expertise in maximising income from expenses), to book hotels and find some way of getting people to and from Strasbourg, Brussels, Paris and the far reaches of the then-known parliamentary world where European committees and the NATO parliamentarians chose to meet. Peter Kirk remained for a while in lonely occupation of the office at the top of No 46, until the Accommodation whips found him a room in the Palace more appropriate to his new status.

Although officially demobbed, Douglas and I continued to carry out our basic functions in support of the three original delegations – Douglas looked after the WEU Assembly, which met periodically in Paris, and I continued to have charge of the delegations to the Council of Europe Assembly and the North Atlantic Assembly. And various Clerks (notably John Rose, the lothario of the Miss World competition) were surreptitiously recruited to cover the meetings of the European Parliament. So far as the Clerk of the House was officially concerned the Department's services to the delegations (other than "conference" services) were terminated or at best suspended. So we were officially required to pretend that we weren't carrying them out. In practice, Barney Cocks knew very well where we were and what we were doing but preferred not to be reminded. Instead I reported via the then Clerk of the Overseas Office (my friend Kenneth Bradshaw) to the Clerk-of-the-House-in-waiting – David William Shuckburgh Lidderdale – who after the notorious Heads of Office meeting on Maundy Thursday had set up what amounted to a parallel administration, with its own command and reporting lines.

Despite the Clerk's insistence that his boys were needed for real work, I was strictly supernumerary in the Journal Office during this first brief sojourn, a fact which did not go unremarked by the full-time inhabitants. The JO was presided over by the Rev Dr Eric Taylor, who in his youth had published one of the very first popular readable accounts of parliamentary procedure, and who had also written the first rules of procedure for the North Atlantic Assembly: he was for this reason if no other at least vaguely sympathetic to my under-cover activities, despite his loathing for the new regime waiting in the wings. Now more than happily occupied by his duties to his Liberal Catholic flock, and his life-long interest in the poetry of James Thomson, he emerged but seldom from his room at the end of the office, where each day at noon the "Vote" was solemnly read and corrected. There was a somewhat uncomfortable resemblance to the incarceration of Corporal Major Ludovic at No 4 Special Training Centre ; it was a role I reprised to perfection thirty years later. Eric wisely left the day-to-day work in the hands of his two deputies, David Pring MC (ex-Royal Engineers), who lived in the Guard's Van at the other end of the office, and Jim Willcox (ex-RNVR). With their distinguished service backgrounds both had little time for the bishop at the other end of the floor; both were frustrated by the promotion of lesser men and the lack of promotion for themselves; and both looked upon my nefarious activities with suspicion at least: Jim Willcox in particular took delight in getting to any incoming calls before I did in order proudly to announce "Non, Monsieur Proctor n'est pas la; Non, il n'est pas ici; vous comprenez?", thus leaving me with the labour of trying to place yet another international call through our antediluvian switchboard.

As an aid to rapid research in the event of a late-night procedural difficulty, the Clerks since the early nineteenth century had laboriously produced not only a meticulous index to each annual volume of the Journal, but also an almost equally detailed index to each decade of Journals, which was still at that time separately researched and edited. Checking the Accounts & Papers sections of the decennial index[*] was one of the most tedious of the many tedious jobs in the Journal Office; at a later date it was down-loaded to the 'non-graduate' office clerks in the unlighted offices in the middle of the Clerk of the House floor, but since much of their time of an evening was in those days still occupied in manually checking and counting the names on public petitions (for which they received a small extra pro-rata payment), the index checking was still at that time undertaken by graduate clerks. This seemed an appropriately mind-numbing punishment for me as an interloper. Thankfully, nobody expected me to make much progress with this and other similar tasks, but it kept me ostensibly occupied during my occasional guest appearances in the Journal Office, and ensured that any evidence of my real-time work was safely buried under mounds of authentic JO proofs.

So immediately after Easter 1973 I settled down to eight months of a

---

[*] the Accounts & Papers are all the multifarious documents from government departments and agencies, and from committees of the House, which are required by statute or standing order to be formally presented and laid on the Table of the House, but which have little or nothing to do with what goes on in the Chamber.

double life. I had a desk in the Journal Office, piled high with untouched proofs and Journals; I had also an unofficial desk back in No 46, where any incriminating evidence of my continuing international affairs was stored out of view. When in the Palace I was either trying to run a standing committee on behalf of my erstwhile colleagues on the other side of the floor, or desperately running for the JO telephone before Jim Willcox could intercept some portentous call from the FCO or from Monsieur Deshormes or Monsieur Rémion in Bruxelles. And for about a third of the time I was out of the country, inveigling colleagues – sometimes actually paying them - to cover my only-too-frequent absences. All this required a considerable amount of subterfuge, not only in dealing with the then Clerk of the House, but also in persuading the members of the various Assembly delegations that all was operating as normal, and the old European Office was still in business. There was a degree of double-bluff: the Clerk of the House had to be persuaded that his aspiring successor really believed that he, Barney, was in charge and that he knew nothing about what we were all doing – although of course he did, and so did the other.

By the autumn of 1973 some small sense had been restored. By tacit agreement a relatively senior colleague, Hugh Maben Barclay (ex-Royal Artillery) had been drafted in to serve as head of a revived European "Section", and had taken over Peter Kirk's former desk in No 46. I had an assurance that after regime change on 31st December I would return to the same office (or section) and be free to devote my uninterrupted time to the affairs of the Council of Europe and the North Atlantic Assembly. Which was just as well, since the then leader of the UK delegation to the NAA, Sir John Peel, had more or less dropped us in it.

11

L'Assemblée de l'Atlantique Nord

Getting to know the NAA

Following initiation at the Brussels session in 1969, my subsequent long involvement with the North Atlantic Assembly really began when I was tipped into the role of secretary to the British delegation in time for the Assembly's eighteenth annual session in Bonn in November 1972. The NAA was a gem amongst international organisations. It was a peripatetic show, with a tiny permanent secretariat, and no formal recognition from governments. The US had an Act of Congress, but this was needed only to legitimise the payment of expenses and a sizeable chunk of the Assembly's relatively small budget. The assembly had first met in Paris in 1955, at the invitation of the Speaker of the Canadian House of Commons and the Norwegian Storting, on the initiative of Canadian and British MPs, but in the teeth of opposition from a number of NATO governments (notably the British). The cost of the first conference had to be guaranteed by a handful of backbench politicians, and most of the usual services such as translation and interpretation were provided for free by idealistic friends. The European NATO governments in the end agreed to cough up sufficient funds to pay their own Members' expenses and laughably small contributions to a regular budget, but the Assembly only just about survived for its first five years with a small rented office in London, largely on the charity of individuals and a personal guarantee from the elected Treasurer. The organisation managed to go a little up-market in 1960, by moving its offices closer to NATO headquarters at Rocquencourt, only to find NATO kicked out of France a few years later. The Assembly were then told by the Americans that they also must leave Paris if they wanted any further dollar support, followed SHAPE to Belgium, and re-grouped into small but rather splendid offices in the Place du Petit Sablon in Brussels, occupied by a new Secretary-General and an almost entirely new staff, the originals having been left behind in the retreat from Paris.

The Assembly's standing committee debated long and hard what kind of man they needed to lead what they hoped would be a revitalised organisation – a politician, a parliamentarian or a diplomat – and it must have been a rather curious or even discomfiting experience for Gladwyn

Jebb (effective creator of the UN[*], UK Ambassador to the UN and to France, then deputy leader of the Liberals in the House of Lords, and a man of enormous dignity) to find himself sitting on a plane to Paris in late 1967 beside John Taylor (my predecessor JPST, the man with the Sevenoaks chicken farm), to discover that they were both going for the same job. Neither got it. Instead the Assembly sensibly opted for an insider, a former diplomat with extensive experience in the wider international lobbies working towards both European integration and Atlantic solidarity – and a Belgian to boot, no doubt in the hope of at least keeping on good terms this time with the host government.

Philippe Deshormes had all the right credentials: a former *chef de cabinet* to Paul-Henri Spaak, and subsequently secretary-general of the *campagne européene de la jeunesse* (an off-shoot of Spaak's European Movement), he had eventually become director of studies of the Atlantic Institute, established in Paris in 1961 on the initiative of the NATO Assembly (supported by a raft of former US Presidents and Secretaries of State) and wholly funded by the Ford Foundation.[†] The latter factor was probably crucial: Philippe already knew how to run an international body, with derisory official funding, and no official recognition, but somehow ensured that it punched above its weight. With his aloof mien he was a formidable ambassador for the NATO parliamentarians – although, after a short acquaintance, you discovered that the apparently impenetrable sang-froid was a mere cover for no small degree of insecurity and a considerable tendency to panic. We brash young men from Westminster always found it a trifle hard to take him entirely seriously: maybe it was the discovery that his first major job after the War had been as Belgium's equivalent of the Chief Scout: it was difficult to reconcile the high seriousness of the Secretary-General with the image of "Des" in bush hat and khaki shorts.

Although Philippe's impressive demeanour was usually an asset to the Assembly, his sense of personal dignity, and of the gravitas of his office, occasionally backfired. Not least when, in the summer of 1973, Philippe invited the Clerk of the House of Commons to pay an official pre-retirement visit to the Petit Sablon. The laudable purpose of the invitation was to thank Barney Cocks for his help in keeping the NAA on the road and, in particular,

---

[*] with the able assistance of my cousin (well, to be honest, second cousin twice removed) Brian Urquhart.

[†] By the time Philippe Deshormes left the Atlantic Institute to join the NAA the use of the Ford Foundation as a conduit for CIA funding was becoming widely known; it was murmured in the corridors that he should have known long before; but if he did he probably wouldn't have been too troubled, since in the terms of the times they were all working on the same "side". There were after all many other organisations with a less obvious community of interest with the CIA (such as Britain's National Union of Students) whose officers had regularly to deny allegations about who was making up their budgetary shortfalls.

for providing the many Commons staff who ran the support services without which the Assembly couldn't function. An equally important aim, however, was to recruit the Clerk in aid of the next round of budget increases: the Assembly was asking for something in the region of 20%; the FCO and the State Department were refusing any increase at all. Philippe made two major errors on this occasion. First, civilised chaps don't talk about money. Second, you don't show off your grand official car, and fulltime chauffeur, when asking for money. Barney had a splendid weekend in Brussels – receptions, dinners, the opera, and, of course, the exclusive use of the Secretary-General's car and chauffeur from arrival to departure. Despite the cat-and-mouse game currently in play on the Clerk of the House floor, and the uncertain nature of my job description, it was for me to make the arrangements for this trip. After the weekend, a tall shadow fell across my desk and smilingly delivered its conclusions: "No more money under any circumstances", it said, "after all, the Clerk of the House of Commons has to make do with the Government carpool". In very short order, Philippe Deshormes found himself welcoming an FCO accountant to "advise" on the better use of our money and, most dangerously, to examine the accounts.

The finances of the NAA were to be a major preoccupation throughout my period as delegation secretary, and particularly the following year, when the Secretariat sought yet again to hike the budget by a fifth or so when most national governments were struggling to impose real-money cuts on their domestic budgets. But there were more immediate problems to resolve.

The NAA was forever searching for somewhere to meet. Although by 1973 its secretariat was comfortably settled in Brussels it was a welcome guest there only so long as it stuck to the bargain which required it to meet elsewhere as often as possible, with the host government or parliament footing the bulk of the bill. After meeting in Brussels in 1969 it had therefore begun its peregrinations, with plenary sessions held in the Hague, in Ottawa, and in Bonn, and in 1973 it was due to meet in that famous bastion of democracy just outside the fringes of Europe, Ankara (and thanks to the Colonels the Greeks were for once not there to complain). Nobody, however, had signed up for 1974. At a meeting of the Assembly's standing committee in November 1972 the leader of the UK delegation, Sir John Peel (by then the Assembly's acting President), had succumbed to flattery and agreed that the 1974 plenary could be held in London in November 1974: this despite the fact that earlier soundings with the British Government and parliamentary authorities had made absolutely clear that the best they could manage was a lecture theatre in the University of Edinburgh. In January 1973 John Peel asked the FCO to play ball and they, knowing that some international face might now be lost, eventually agreed that the Assembly could be accommodated in London and that "in principle" some financial support might be forthcoming. It was this ominous news which I had carried with me as I transferred to my desk in the Journal Office.

The truth (which Sir John Peel and his fellow delegates then and thereafter failed to grasp) was that there really was no money for this venture. Throughout its history the House of Commons had until then never played host to such international ventures (and had certainly *never* allowed strangers, let alone foreigners, to sit on its hallowed benches[*]) and they had in any case no budget of any kind to support one now. If the event was to go ahead it would be for the FCO, itself under serious budgetary pressure, to find a location well away from the Chamber, and to foot the bills. In December 1973, after extended to-ing and fro-ing between Brussels and London, they finally agreed to do so. I was designated as "UK Co-ordinator", with no additional staff support.

By this time I had gained some useful experience of the North Atlantic Assembly in the field. As a tyro I had spent an uncomfortable weekend in Brussels. As newly appointed delegation secretary I had attended the 1972 session in Bonn. There I had witnessed the Assembly at its comic best. Mr Ted Bishop, MP for Newark but a Bristolian born and bred, was the retiring chairman of the Assembly's Economic Committee.[†] A man who had built his political career on his ability to pun his way through constituency party meetings, local council meetings, and on the floor of the Commons, he had determined in advance to confound the interpreters in his last speech to the Assembly with an untranslatable display of verbal subtlety. The international union of interpreters was not, however, to be confounded. With advance intelligence about his intentions, they interpreted Ted's brilliant speech in the same spirit. He was delighted by the laughter which accompanied his speech throughout, only slowly awaking to the conceit that many in the hall were being entertained to completely different jokes.

The Bonn session also provided an opportunity to witness the extent to which our European parliamentarians were in practice in thrall to the North Americans. Hard-working and very serious-minded MPs from the Hague, from Oslo, from Bonn, even from Paris and Rome, gathered together to try to say wise things about the future of the western alliance and their response to the continuing cold war, with absolutely no media coverage. A small number of hard-working Congressmen with relevant domestic agendas (notably the prospects for their local defense contractors) also attended and did sterling service as chairmen or rapporteurs on the relevant committees.

---

[*] Members of the UK Youth Parliament have since 2009 been allowed to hold an annual one-day debate in the Chamber; one of Mr Speaker Bercow's better decisions.

[†] Although MP for Newark, Ted Bishop and his wife Winifred remained active in Bristol's politics, and when he received a life peerage in 1984 he even named himself after an area of Bristol (Bishopston) close to his place of birth. They both ranked high in my mother Anne's extensive personal demonology, and she probably wrote them almost as many slightly barmy letters, some of which Ted once read to me with wry good humour, as she did to the second Viscount Stansgate.

But for the media there was only one event of importance: the senior Senator for Massachusetts, nominally vice-chairman of its military committee, arrived in the former girls' gymnasium in Bonn, surrounded by cameras, walked purposefully to the rostrum, delivered a five-minute speech, and departed immediately for Washington (or perhaps Chappaquiddick), accompanied by cameras. Teddy Kennedy came and went, and the media circus likewise.

I had quite enjoyed my brief introduction to Bonn in 1972. We stayed in modest but modern hotels, were wined and dined as appropriate to our status, and were impressed by the efficiency of our German hosts as well as the remarkable frigidity of their secretaries. Bonn in 1972 was by no means as exciting as my visit a few years later with the Science & Technology Committee: on this later occasion we stayed in Bad Godesberg at the very hotel patronised by Neville Chamberlain and his team back in 1938. My room then was a gruesomely baronial suite, decorated by many scenes of hunting and seventeenth century massacres. The largest picture seemed out of sequence and was in any case awry. Knowing that I wouldn't be able to sleep with a picture a-kilter I tried to adjust it but it came off the wall. It was an unprepossessing portrait of the then President of the Bundesrepublik, which it was no doubt assumed all well-intentioned guests would wish to venerate. When I enquired at Reception whether they could re-hang the picture which had come off my wall I dared to venture to ask the provenance of the picture on its reverse: 'Ah, Herr Proctor', replied Reception, 'we have many elderly visitors for whom a picture of our late Führer is, shall we say, more comfortable, and after all our little township is for some you know a place of memories: we like to make all our guests as comfortable as we can - so when they come the pictures may sometimes be turned around; it is the same in some other of the rooms, you know'.

So Brussels in 1969 and Bonn in 1972 had been quite fun, an unchallenging initiation into the rites of the north Atlantic alliance and a cause for quiet mirth. The nineteenth annual session in Turkey in 1973 was to be different: here I would have to study and concentrate hard, since next time round it was going to be my own show, and I needed to find out how the operation really worked, and what was required of the host parliament.

The session was timed to coincide with the fiftieth anniversary of the proclamation of the Turkish Republic, and was divided between the great new Asian capital on the Anatolian plateau, where most of the working sessions were held, and that most ancient of surviving Christian cities at the tip of Europe on the Bosporus.

In Ankara the British delegation (like most others) was housed in a large and even by the standards of the day extremely flashy hotel (*free* mini-bars included) just across the road from the Turkish Parliament.* Although only across the road, getting across the road was far from simple. Turkey was, for the purposes of the NAA session and the celebration of the Republic, going through a brief spell of nominally democratic government. As a result, there was, most unusually, scant military presence on the streets. Unfortunately, the army had been providing the traffic police as well as carrying out their usual functions of rounding people up. Having been despatched back to barracks, the military – greatly piqued - had collectively decided that they couldn't in that case continue to provide support for the civil police. As a result there were no traffic police: even crossing the road to the assembly sessions required considerable nerve, and one or two delegates (and many spouses) were said to have remained corralled indoors for the entire weekend.

The building which housed the *Türkiye Büyük Millet Meclisi* was probably the apogee of totalitarian shrines to democracy, designed in 1938 at the height of the totalitarian caprice, restarted in 1957 and completed in less confident times in 1961. Its vast exterior was matched inside by endless marbled corridors, and we worked under ceilings higher than our own houses back home. It had some particularly endearing features. At the end of each grand corridor lurked one or two cherubic youths, whose functions were ostensibly those of the youthful messengers who assist the Canadian House of Commons and the US Congress, but who were said also to offer services in keeping with the proudly masculine character of Atatürk's secular republic. I noted also with interest around this time the facilities for screening those entering the chamber, which appeared to be applied to the politicians rather than the public – gun battles on the floor apparently being a tradition of parliamentary debate in Ankara (and, as we learned from our television screens a couple of decades later, a tradition subsequently exported to the new democracies of eastern Europe). I concluded, albeit a little sadly, that neither of these facilities would be deemed necessary in London.

So we spent a happy few days in Ankara, avoiding the debates so far as possible, smiling sweetly but not too enigmatically at the delightful boys in the corridors, dodging the traffic, familiarising ourselves with the questionable culinary delights of Anatolia, and enjoying greatly our visit to the Atatürk mausoleum, where we admired the array of whips and other instruments of delight and approved the practice of placing the wreaths of subordinates on small tripods, so that they could be re-shuffled whenever the political climate so required: so much more cost-effective than chiselling

---

* I noted for future reference that the United States delegation were sensibly booked elsewhere – although in practice few of them actually turned up, many having turned round, literally in mid-flight, following the resignation of Elliot Richardson, Nixon's latest Attorney-General, in the midst of the unfolding Watergate affair.

the plaques off the Kremlin wall.

However, my attention was really focused on Istanbul. In respect of which we had been confronted by something of an impasse. The Turkish authorities were anxious to keep the foreign parliamentarians in Turkey for the highlight of their fiftieth anniversary celebrations, but equally anxious to remove them from Ankara and from the limited number of suitable hotels, to make way for the army of heads of state and government and their supporters who were expected to roll into the new capital for the great day.

Instead, the NAA was to finish its business in Ankara and then decamp en masse, to reassemble for a great military parade and other jollifications planned for the old capital and symbol of Turkey-in-Europe. Unfortunately, and almost at the last minute, the FCO in London decreed that while it was entirely open to British MP's to enjoy a couple of nights by the Bosporus if they so wished, the costs could not be met from public funds, since their work as Assembly delegates would by then have ended. Other governments indicated that they would follow London's lead; and despite the undoubted attractions of Byzantium our MPs were certainly not prepared to pay out of their own pockets. About 24 hours before we left London we finally sorted out a compromise: the Assembly was to complete all its real work in Ankara, apart from the election of its officers for the next session; this latter ceremony was to be held in Istanbul – not, as it turned out, in somewhere appropriate like the *Hagia Sophia*, but in a suburban cinema which turned out to be the only hall not already booked for other celebratory junketings.

So it was that on 30th October 1973 Mr Knud Damgaard was installed as President of the North Atlantic Assembly, delivering an entertaining speech in Danish and inventive English which went uncomprehended by most of the company, since the Assembly couldn't afford the interpreters' fees for any longer than originally planned. He was photographed leaving the scene of his triumph under hoardings advertising the latest re-run of the Turkish version of *The Guns of Navarone* or some equally appropriate but indecipherable title.

The days in Istanbul were full of incident. There were incidents of an aeronautical character; there were incidents of a pyrotechnic character; and there were incidents pertaining to the collapse of stout parties. Very early in the morning of our departure from Ankara I took the first plane out, leaving a conference officer in charge of despatching the delegation at a more civilised hour. After my arrival in Istanbul, having ensured that the Consulate-General had organised the required fleet of limousines, I waited nervously on the air-side of the arrivals terminal, watching the latest Turkish Airlines aircraft burning itself out at the end of the runway on which I had recently landed. The delegates eventually arrived, cruising slowly over the still-smouldering wreck, and by early afternoon we were able to send them all safely to the delegation hotel.

This was the Park Hotel, once a destination for English arrivals on the

Orient Express, and now decaying gracefully, its string quartet playing softly in the tea room to the very end.[8] Having been up at about three in the morning, having an official cocktail party and dinner to face in the evening, and having ensured the safe arrival of my flock, I decided to take to my bed for what remained of the afternoon. As Secretary of the Delegation (which everywhere east of the Curzon Line meant - quite properly - the most important member of the Delegation) I had been allocated a magnificent room, on one of whose king-size beds I collapsed in near-catatonic exhaustion. A couple of hours later I was awakened by the amplified call of the müezzin next door to find myself on the floor: my timber-framed bed had collapsed irrevocably beneath me. Hastily putting on my glad rags to ensure that I was on parade to usher "my" Members into the cars, I stopped briefly at Reception to ask what they might do about this small catastrophe. "Never mind, Mister Proctor", said Reception, "you have two beds in your room, eh? You are paying for only one person, eh? What are you doing in the bad bed, eh? And how many people do you want to sleep there, eh?" The next morning, when I really did feel I had earned some respite, a carpenter and two of his apprentices arrived – at 6.30 – fully equipped with workbenches, saws, adzes and other tools familiar to the father of Christ, and proceeded to rebuild the offending bed. But to be fair, I had already been awakened again by the müezzin.

The following days in Istanbul unfolded with the kind of inevitability which we sometimes experience in bad dreams: if there is a chance of something going wrong, then it certainly will, and it may well trigger hysteria along the way. October 29th was the important day, the day of the Revolution. Recovering ourselves from nights at the Consulate, collapsing beds, and the amplified calls to the faithful, we were herded into ancient buses and transported to Istanbul's parade ground, which looked suspiciously like an unfinished stretch of dual carriageway. This was quite an important moment for many – the Turks and their armed forces, obviously, but also for some British and other west European politicians, who were still of the generation to have served in the war and some even in the Balkans. The North Atlantic Assembly was quite properly placed in a stand immediately opposite the saluting platform, and therefore able to appreciate and be impressed by the formidable fire-power of their NATO ally.

It was an inordinately hot day, made inordinately worse by the corrugated iron roof of the temporary grandstand. Opposite we dignitaries, the military brass sweated in their dress uniforms, weighed down by medals. The march past began. In our honour, American-built jets swooped dangerously low over the grandstand, and the serried ranks of army, army reserve, navy, naval reserve, air force, air force reserve, fire fighters, red crescent, boy scouts, girl scouts, university professors, schoolteachers, doctors, nurses, midwives - just about everyone who was anybody -

marched past us.

And finally came the veterans of the civil war. They were a magnificent sight, dressed in the traditional garb of true revolutionaries, bandoliers full of ammunition, grizzled, still dangerous. As they approached us, and the saluting platform, the flag of the Republic was dipped, and then raised in their honour; and all saluted. And then the flag fell off the flag-pole. Much-bemedaled senior officers rushed forward to retrieve the offending drape, and (we were told with authority after the event) were immediately put under close arrest. But the procession moved inexorably forward. And as it did, the lead jeep, succumbing to the intolerable heat, burst into flames, its ferocious occupants scattered around the parade ground. Solemn-faced, we departed.

The next and final day again broke warm and sunny. We paid our visit to the cinema and then crossed the Bosporus on ferries, fortified by deliciously sweet tea, to witness what for the United Kingdom was the most important event of the weekend: the opening of the first Bosporus Bridge, the symbolic uniting of Europe and Asia. It was a big event for us because the bridge – which bears a remarkable resemblance to the Forth Road Bridge and the first Severn Bridge[*] – was designed by Brits, and largely built by Brits, and we could therefore bask in the achievements of our British designers and engineers. As we settled down in yet another grandstand we were able to join the official representatives of the secular Republic in averting our gaze from the ritual slaughter of sheep which was proceeding apace ahead of the official ceremonies. Then the moment came, the bridge was declared open in wholly secular terms by the President of the Republic, and the people moved in to experience this wondrous meeting of two worlds. Hundreds of thousands of Turks had amassed on the hills on the southern side of the Bosporus, and hundreds of thousands then descended onto the great bridge to try it out, to see if it was real and safe.

It was probably a good thing that the municipal reception at the end of the day was well-fuelled. As we stood in line to shake hands a messenger in the form of an Embassy Second Secretary arrived to whisper in my ear that all was not entirely well. Under the weight of an estimated million pairs of peasant feet, the carriageway of the great bridge had by the end of the day faltered, and the bridge had had to be closed. The Brits and their engineers were now a bit less popular than at break of day, and some of us at least were only too glad to make our apologies and head for home. Eventually it

---

[*] for which I have always had a particular affection, notwithstanding a Bristolian's instinctive horror at the facility thus provided for the invasion of the South-West by the inhabitants of Cardiff Bay. As a cub reporter on the old *Bristol Evening Post* I had the extraordinary honour, shortly before the completion of the bridge, of interviewing the designer's father, none other than Alexander Kerensky, the last vaguely democratic prime minister of pre-Soviet Russia: an experience which greatly enhanced the immediacy of my university studies of Soviet politics.

emerged that the blame rested almost entirely with Danny Kaye (he of *Hans Christian Andersen* fame) who after the important people had departed had led the Anatolian masses across the bridge in strict dance formation, thus setting up vibrations for which the great new bridge had not been designed. All turned out well in the end, after a few months of structural repairs. A few years later Freeman, Fox & Partners and their engineering partners got the contract for the Fatih Sultan Mehmet Bridge, a few kilometres along the water, and the original bridge still stands in all its iconic splendour – although pedestrian traffic is, for obviously very good reasons, now banned.

After mooching anonymously around the bazaars the next day we took our leave of Istanbul, anxiously looking out for downed Fokkers or Boeings, and looking forward to a pleasant flight with BEA, having had enough for the time being of our friends in the near orient. Heathrow, however, was fogbound; and so in the middle of the evening I found myself with a dozen or so apoplectic British MPs hanging around at Birmingham's still primitive municipal airport in the gloom waiting for a bus to take us all back to Westminster.

It is already becoming difficult several decades on to appreciate what going to the wrong airport and sitting in a bus to take you down the foggy M1 meant at this time: no mobiles, and so no way of letting colleagues, offices, mistresses, whips and families know that you were going to be inordinately late; and at their end no internet to track the progress or otherwise of your flight. So after more than a week away, with only very occasional contact by landline, the fury of my Members was understandable – and that they took out their frustrations on the nearest dumb object (in this case the delegation secretary) was more or less inevitable.

But at the end of every fairy story there should be a knight in shining armour, and it turned out that we had brought our own. Sir Fitzroy MacLean Bt, the Member for Bute & North Ayrshire, was chairman of the Military Committee of the NAA. Amongst his very many other accomplishments[*] he was the proprietor, with his wife Veronica (daughter of the 16th Lord Lovat), of a hotel at Strachur in Argyll, and therefore always concerned for his fellow creatures' comfort. In between chairing the Military Committee

---

[*] Fitzroy (Eton and King's, Cambridge) had served in the Moscow Embassy to the end of 1939 and discovered more about the Soviet Union than the NKVD wanted him to know. He went on to become Head of Churchill's mission to the partisans in Yugoslavia, survived his dealings there with Evelyn Waugh, and ended his military career as Major-General (while also serving as MP for Lancaster) wrote biographies of both Tito and Guy Burgess, and was a junior War Office minister in the 1950's. He became a baronet in 1957 and a KT in 1994. He was probably most proud of his appointment in 1981 as the 15th Hereditary Keeper and Captain of Dunconnel Castle, although his posthumous appointment to the Order of Prince Branimir by the President of newly independent Croatia would have no doubt chortled him.

at the beginning of the week and providing me with a detailed narration at the great military parade the following weekend, Fitzroy had taken time off to follow his well-travelled trails into the Soviet Union and Yugoslavia, to meet old warriors and to delight in confusing the famously trigger-happy guards on both sides of the frontiers.

Fitzroy's trips no doubt contributed much to the friendship of nations, but from our point of view had more immediate benefits. As we shivered in our seats while the bus negotiated the fog, glumly contemplating the inevitably icy reception we would receive in the metropolis, Fitzroy produced from the innumerable pockets of his trench coat bottles of the very best local vodka and the very best local slivovitz, together with those miraculous sets of cups (in this case, silver cups) invented by the military for those in extremis. After ten minutes or so, we relaxed into dreams of the orient, and were awakened only as the driver negotiated with the police at the gates of New Palace Yard.

I at least was confident that I had a small offering to placate the household gods. So hours later when I arrived back in Kent this offering was immediately disentangled from much dirty underwear and proudly presented to my sleeping partner. In the unpressurised hold of the aircraft the hand-made and beautifully gift-wrapped Turkish delight from the banks of the Bosporus had turned into a solid block of starch and sugar. My sleeping partner had real work to do in the morning, and turned over, and slept.

12

The Alliance in London

The 1974 NAA plenary: strapped for cash

Back in London, returning for most of the time to my desk on the penultimate floor of No 46, I was determined that there should be no incidents at the twentieth annual session of the NAA of the kind which had so enlivened the nineteenth session in Ankara. However, I had returned from the holy city of Byzantium to the byzantine politics of yet another bankrupt imperial capital. So there were some small problems to be resolved.

There was, for instance, still no money. Not just not much money, or not enough money, but, at the turn of the year, no real money at all, the only funds so far committed comprising the princely sum of £320 generously offered from their official entertainment allowances by the incoming Clerk of the House and the Clerk of the Parliaments for a fraternal lunch for the visiting delegation secretaries. In all the enthusiasm in 1972 for holding the session in London no thought at all was given by the politicians to how much the enterprise would cost, and who should pay for what. So the Assembly's Standing Committee decision in November 1972 was taken in total ignorance of the financial implications. In the whole of the following year nothing more definite was extracted from the FCO beyond guarded undertakings to provide "what other host governments have provided", from HM Treasury to give "some financial assistance", and eventually from the Civil Service Department that the FCO should assume "host department" responsibilities.

It was not until January 1974 that estimates of sorts were produced by the FCO and the Assembly and submitted to the Treasury. Our original and already very modest sum of around £33,000 was reduced by March to £26,575, the Treasury having refused to agree to a "state" opening session in Westminster Hall and having reduced the per capita cost of official receptions from £3.00 to £2.50. This (equivalent to around £280,000 in 2020) remained the total within which we had to work, like it or not. I compared it ruefully with the grant of £150,000 (or about £1.6 million) only recently provided by HM Treasury to fund the Commonwealth Parliamentary Association conference in 1973. But it was difficult to deny "the radically changed economic circumstances we now face" (Mr Heath had just asked the electorate to decide "who governs Britain?") or (in my already antiquated and definitely-not-politically-correct view) that money spent on bolstering the Commonwealth was actually money better spent than most.

We had at least agreed on where the North Atlantic Assembly should meet. We managed to avoid Edinburgh (although a few years later it did meet there, but in something rather grander than a lecture theatre). The powers-that-were in the House of Commons had greeted the prospect with unqualified horror, no "stranger" who had dared to sit on the hallowed benches having previously escaped with anything less than quartering; the powers in the House of Lords, although some there were tempted to set a revolutionary precedent, in the end felt that they couldn't be seen to be offering something regarded as demeaning or even criminal by the lower House; and both County Hall and Central Hall were already booked. So we opted for the most uncomfortable of all solutions. The committee meetings were to be held in Lancaster House, the setting for many diplomatic conferences of some substance, but woefully inadequate in the services it could offer for the relatively large numbers involved; and the plenary sessions were to be held in Church House, the administrative HQ of the Church of England and its committees, which had in its time played host to bodies as august as the UN Security Council as well as to the House of Commons itself, but whose offices were by now otherwise wholly occupied and its conference services primitive.

In December 1973 I was given the grand title of "UK Co-ordinator" and told to get on and find the money and "co-ordinate" the great event. In conformity with the praiseworthy tradition of the Clerk's Department that in a crisis you just muddle through I was given no staff in addition to the services of Mrs Susan Copeland, who was already in any case doing the job. She was expected to continue to carry out all the other secretarial duties for the other staff in the re-constituted European Section (who were now almost fully occupied with the European Parliament), and I was similarly instructed to continue to act as Secretary to the delegations to the Council of Europe and the Western European Union, and to continue to attend all their meetings. It was only just before the NAA London session began, in the autumn of 1974, that my eventual successor Robert Wilson was appointed in advance and allowed to relieve me of some routine delegation duties. Those Westminster Clerks who were to carry out specific functions as part of the NAA's version of the *équipe anglaise* (such as committee secretaries and the Head of Protocol) were to be nominated especially early in case their advice might be sought, but were also specifically instructed not to take time from their desks for the purpose.

This all seemed fairly daunting, if not impossible, if it had not been for the FCO. And the FCO's assistance would have been somewhat less impressive if it had not been for Crispin Tickell, one of the most imaginative and flexible of his generation of British diplomats. With whatever indifference the rapidly shifting cast of Ministers may have regarded the event, Crispin, in a mid-career London posting, recognised the potential benefits to the UK of the NAA meeting in London and drove Western Organisations Department, and they in turn drove the FCO's Protocol and Conference Department, to ensure that the UK at least gave a good account of itself.

So I "co-ordinated"; and some very good professionals did the real work. At what my diaries suggest were at least twice-weekly meetings on the other side of Whitehall in the first half of 1974 I grandly took the chair while Brenda Chaplin and her occasionally bemused, and not infrequently amused, team from Conference & Visits Section took notes and translated my fanciful aspirations into a surprisingly coherent administrative plan. The meetings were occasionally enlivened by visits from the NAA's administrative director, Jean Rémion, and even more so by one or two state visits from Philippe Deshormes himself, when official bemusement was apt to ascend into something closer to diplomatic hysteria.

We also had occasional meetings involving the politicians, in whose name the whole operation was supposed to be organised, although this became increasingly difficult as 1974 progressed. Not only was there not much money; there was also for most of the time no British delegation. Just as we began to get the show seriously on the road, Ted Heath and his Cabinet colleagues took their disastrous decision on 7th February to ask the electorate "Who governs?", the inevitable response being delivered on 28th February. And in September Harold Wilson and his colleagues took their apparently inevitable decision to ask the electorate "Do you expect us to carry on like this?" (to which the electoral response was "yes, but not too freely") after seven months of not unsuccessful minority government, an experience by no means new in British political life (1923 and 1929 were not so long ago) but nonetheless regarded by the media and the newly-engrossed political scientists as a more or less revolutionary event. Little could any of us know what was to follow forty years later.

Two general elections in the space of ten months meant that Parliament was out of action for at least two and a half months in addition to the then still more or less mandatory three-month shooting season. For most parliamentary staff this was of course a golden year, with many opportunities either for unplanned vacations or for long-overdue decorating, and even I managed to put up a good deal of wallpaper during the year's electoral longueurs. But so far as my main preoccupation was concerned the parties' obsession with consulting the people was more than a trifle annoying.

The moment the first Election was announced the Leader of the British delegation, Sir John Peel (the original author of our woes) disappeared from the scene, his Leicester South-East constituency having been abolished, and neighbouring constituency parties having shown little enthusiasm for an MP who spent almost all his time in Europe.* Although the rules of the Assembly allowed members to continue for a few months after an election, or until their successors were appointed, their status at home was decidedly uncertain: there was in particular doubt whether any of their expenses could be paid (and in those days during election periods they were not even allowed to set foot in the House of Commons or its outbuildings). And after an election the nomination of a new delegation always took time while the parties agreed on their share and deployed their troops to the more important jobs first. As a result I spent much of the rest of the year furtively consulting ex-members and potential future members of the delegation, often by landline to their homes (we easily forget how hellish life could be before the arrival of the mobile phone) during the repeated periods of their expulsion from the Estate, to get some idea of their wishes in respect of the conference being organised on their behalf. And if the commoners weren't available I had to rely on the peers of the realm.

At the Commons end my main interlocutor from now on was Sir Geoffrey de Freitas. Sir Ghastly (as he was fondly known) was more than somewhat disappointed at having been passed over by Harold Wilson for high ministerial office, despite his immaculate track record as a former squadron leader (albeit on the engineering side), renowned athlete, high-performing QC, highly successful High Commissioner in the newly independent capitals of Accra and Nairobi, family friend of Clement Atlee, and inheritor by marriage of north American wealth (which in most of the previous century had been a certain passport to preferment - and would of course be again today): it says something positive about Harold's judgement that Sir G was not appointed, even as Solicitor-General or something equally harmless.

In his early post-war days as an MP Sir Ghastly had argued vociferously, and laudably, for the North Atlantic Alliance to be demonstrably an alliance of the democracies, and had been the key player in London in the establishment of the North Atlantic Assembly, backing it for many years with his own (or his wife's) money. He had meanwhile been a little bit compensated by Harold Wilson, and his dignity a wee bit mollified, by becoming leader of the Labour group at the Council of Europe Assembly, and thence rapidly catapulted into the presidency of that Assembly in the late 1960's.

Geoffrey de Freitas was amiable, amenable, and (not a bad point) a real friend of staff such as myself, with whom he shared many interests, not least a taste for the fine, or if necessary the less fine, wines of Alsace. He was,

---

* At the time of his departure from the House of Commons, John Peel was simultaneously a member of the European Parliament, and of the British delegations to the Assemblies of the Council of Europe and Western European Union, and had finished two years as President of the NAA.

however, and despite his many qualifications, a man without any very discernible qualities of leadership, a lack which Harold Wilson had obviously noted. He had originally had one great asset, of which I had taken great advantage during my very early encounters with the delegations. His secretary was almost the very best Member's secretary I had the pleasure of dealing with over the decades (and they were a very formidable army)[*]. A former Tiller Girl, Betty Boothroyd's great quality, from my point of view, was decisiveness: if I phoned her in desperation of a Sunday night after two or three days of abortive calls to Sir G, she would guarantee his attendance on parade the next morning. She continued to display this quality when called to higher office in 1992. But unfortunately Miss Boothroyd won a by-election in May 1973, and so had more important things to do in her own right, although she occasionally adopted her earlier role of disciplinarian in the crucial early months of 1974, and was herself helpfully added to the NAA delegation after the October election, after which she effectively acted as Sir G's PPS.

So for much of the year I was at least able to deploy Sir Geoffrey de Freitas, masquerading at various times as Leader of the Labour group, or putative Leader, or eventually (about ten days before the NAA plenary) pulling rank at last as the actual designated Leader of the UK delegation. Other actual or potential members of the delegation from the Commons end of the Palace were otherwise so preoccupied with their electoral prospects that they had little time to concentrate on the forthcoming conference, although some, such as (later Sir) Philip Goodhart and (later Sir) Jerry Wiggin offered their services (or really their wives' services) to orchestrate a social programme for delegates' wives (which through no fault of their own proved not far short of disastrous).

In this situation I was compelled to fall back on the services of the members of the delegation from their Lordships' House, whose continued participation could be assured. This was particularly important since in the midst of the fairly chaotic planning for the NAA in London, the small matter of the Assembly's budget had again to be resolved. As previously recounted, the NAA had a tendency to demand an annual increase in its budget of around 20 per cent, at a time when national budgets throughout the Alliance were being frozen or reduced. The Assembly's main paymasters were the US and the UK, based on the anachronistic "civil budget" formula devised when NATO was set up, and when the FCO had a remit to demonstrate that

---

[*] The very best, of course – an opinion which Lady Boothroyd herself would undoubtedly endorse – was Beryl Goldsmith, who served as Peter Kirk's secretary until his death in 1977. She went on to greater things (including serving as Norman Tebbit's secretary, and therefore moving rapidly from Europhile to Europhobe) but failed to achieve her own ambition (like Betty's) of becoming an MP in her own right, although she had considerable influence in the Conservative Party in the House.

the UK, although broke, could still punch above its weight, and certainly harder than mere Europeans.* In both cases the lines of authority were confused: in the USA the North Atlantic Assembly had a form of official recognition, in an Act of Congress providing for a budgetary contribution and the payment of delegates' expenses; the NAA was however not established either by treaty or by Executive agreement, and therefore not recognised as an international body by the State Department. In the UK the Assembly had no official recognition at all; the delegates were nominated by the Speaker (according to the time-honoured formulae of party balance) and the costs were covered by a "grant-in-aid" through the Foreign Office, which was exactly as it said: a grant, which could be granted or withdrawn on the whim of HM Treasury.

In 1974 the American delegation was itself in turmoil, coping with the fallout from Watergate, could not spare heavy-weight delegates to turn up for budget meetings in Brussels, and deputed their in every way impressive delegation secretary, Mr Peter Abbruzzese, to sort things out, with a brief to veto any increase at all in the Assembly's budget. At the UK end, the FCO, as the grant-aiding department, didn't recognise the North Atlantic Assembly as an official body, and was therefore not prepared to enter into any negotiations about its finances. Instead the drill was for the FCO to advise the Leader of the Delegation what level of contribution they would be prepared to make, and leave it to the Leader to vote accordingly in the Assembly's budgetary discussions. This had normally worked ok, since the nominated Leader usually had sufficient political clout to come back to London and say "Well, I didn't hold the line completely but we've settled on a reasonable compromise, so you'll have to pay up". In 1974 we unfortunately had both a major fiscal crisis in London, and no Leader of the Delegation.

Instead, Sir Ghastly suggested that I might make use of the services of the ranking Labour member of the delegation from the Lords. Lord Wynne-Jones, who was elevated to the peerage in 1964 while still serving as Professor of Chemistry and Pro-Vice Chancellor at the University of Newcastle, had a distinguished academic record as a pioneer in heavy water research in the 1930's, and as head of chemistry at the Royal Aircraft Establishment during World War II. He was undoubtedly firmly committed to the North Atlantic Assembly, serving for many years as the chairman of its scientific committee, as well being fully up to the intellectual challenge of the finances of a relatively small NGO in Brussels, but he wasn't actually interested (probably having endured more than enough budgetary manoeuvrings in his university). As our temporary representative at the

---

* The extraordinary result was that while the (bankrupt) United Kingdom paid 19.5% (and the USA 24.2%), the booming Federal Republic of Germany contributed 16.1%, and the Italians (the European tiger of the day) a mere 5.96%.

NAA's standing committee in April 1974, he was voluminously briefed by me, on behalf of the FCO, to resist all budgetary increases, and was told very firmly that the US expected us to do our duty on their behalf.

Kenrick Wynne-Jones fell asleep early in this crucial meeting, claimed when awoke to have lost his papers (of which I of course had spares), and merely nodded when the full 20 per cent increase was approved; only the French saved the day: they needed to consult the Quai d'Orsay. When the Standing Committee met again to review their irresponsible decision (irresponsible, because nobody was actually going to pay up), I was prevailed upon to take the train from Strasbourg to Brussels on a wet September evening, and not for the last time in my career to personate a real living politician in casting the UK's votes against the Assembly's budgetary proposals: I took the late-night train back for the rest of the Council of Europe's session, more than a little disgruntled at having missed the annual weekend *vin d'honneur*. It is symbolic of a wasted life that when the standing committee met again it was in the midst of the euphoria of the London session, and Sir G happily over-rode my earlier veto, and voted the whole budget increase through, able – with the threat of adverse publicity while the rest of the alliance was in town - to out-face the FCO, who eventually increased their grant-in-aid accordingly.

Their Lordships were, however, enormously helpful in other, and more immediate, matters relating to the event which we were struggling to put together in London. The main reason for the reluctance of senior politicians to take the twentieth annual session of the North Atlantic Assembly in any way seriously was the certainty that almost nobody of any importance (other than the Canadians, who, although dependable allies, weren't to be taken *too* seriously) would be coming across the Atlantic for the event. Mid-term elections were due on 4th November, and, following Nixon's resignation and Gerry Ford's elevation as the first-ever entirely unelected President, these were to be mid-term elections of more than usual importance. It was assumed in Whitehall that few or even none of the US delegation would actually be turning up; in consequence, it was also assumed that there was not much point pushing the boat out for a scattering of neutrally-inclined Scandinavians, Frenchmen of dubious loyalty to the Alliance, west Germans loyal to the Alliance at any cost, and assorted Turks and other Mediterraneans (such as the Italians) incapable of either contributing much to the conversation or (of rather more importance) contributing much to the defence of the Alliance.

Ministers had, accordingly, already vetoed a "state" opening of the Assembly in Westminster Hall, which had been our first objective – ostensibly on grounds of cost, but really because they thought it unwise (as one of them put it to me) to waste Her Majesty's credit by rolling her out for an occasion of not much importance. Instead, tortuous negotiations were set in train for a private audience with the Queen for the leaders of the various national delegations, followed by a budget-level reception given by the Foreign Secretary in the Banqueting House or some other appropriate venue. This was the game-plan by the time we reached the summer, and the draft list of attendees from across the water seemed to justify this low-key approach.

Ministers and the FCO had, however, failed to recognise the importance of the small House of Lords contingent in the United Kingdom's own delegation to the Assembly, nor of their commitment to Atlantic solidarity, nor indeed of HM The Queen's own political nous. Shortly before Parliament rose in the summer for yet another adjournment, and shortly after I had returned from a somewhat surreal Breakfast with Kissinger in Washington (during the NAA's annual committee sessions), word came from the Palace that far from merely shaking hands with the leaders of the delegations, HM The Queen would like to offer them all a party. Behind the scenes both Lord Strathcona, the Tory Whip,[9] and the young Charlie Lyell* appeared to have used their influence at court to good effect. It was, we were told, to be the first large evening reception offered by the monarch at Buckingham Palace in more than a decade: and all the delegates and their wives and their attendant diplomats were to be on parade.

The whole tempo of the conference suddenly changed. Ministers began to take the whole thing profoundly seriously; the military were instructed to put on a good show for the delegates; the British Tourist Authority was told (to no avail) to pull out all the stops; and No 10 was told that the Prime Minister (whoever he might happen to be by then) would definitely have to make the keynote opening address. Most importantly, there was a sudden rush of interest in Washington. In May we had expected an American delegation of half a dozen at most; by September we had thirty expected, together with partners and even wives.

By October I seemed to have become the centre of international attention and flattery as the scramble for tickets to the Palace got seriously underway. I also had the rare experience for a few weeks of regularly visiting the Master of the Household about the logistics. For although as a young man of the sixties I was of course expected to be a trifle blasé about royalty, and although intellectually closer to marxism-leninism than to anything currently on offer from the mainstream parties, in practice I was of course a monarchist to the core. To be able to stroll across St James Park to Buck House, wander the corridors, and chat to the staff had remarkable, albeit temporary, effects on my self-esteem, or at any rate on my self-regard, to

---

* Charles Lyell, the Third Baron, who had succeeded his father (killed in action in 1943) at the age of four, and was one of the most charming if slightly scatterbrained men I had to deal with during this period.

the not surprising disgust of most of my colleagues.* The rules of eligibility for the Palace reception were very tight; and unlike most such occasions there were no spare tickets hanging around.

All had to meet the predetermined criteria, and all had to be written out in copperplate in the FCO, on behalf of the Palace itself. There were therefore many disappointed applicants, including many disaffected colleagues. There was also a major potential glitch: when the draft of the invitation card was sent over to me it contained wording which implied that the politicians from around the alliance were expected to parade in evening dress or uniform (with medals), and their wives were expected to appear in long dresses. The latter would probably have not minded too much, or indeed might have risen to the occasion. I knew in my bones, however, that the democratic representatives of the Alliance might be prepared, at least in theory, to fight the commies, but would not be prepared under any circumstances to do so in silly costumes. On one of the rare occasions in my life when I think I actually influenced something I told the Master of the Household that "You can't do it this way; none of the Scandinavians, and almost none even of the Americans, will appear in clothes of this kind, and I'm more than a trifle uncertain about the Labour Party". When the invitations were finally issued, they required only lounge suits and (as the Palace advised me over the phone) "short dresses". Interparliamentary functions of this kind were henceforth, around the world, regarded as lounge suit affairs, and dinner jackets and even grander could at last be left at home, which greatly assisted in meeting the airlines' baggage allowances.

So, having finally sorted out the dates, a rather larger number of delegates than originally expected and their wives (and more than three times the number of variously-defined "observers" and other hangers-on) arrived in London for a conference due to assemble on Monday 11 November 1974. This latter date created its own problems because it was, in some countries at least, Armistice Day, and the French and the Belgians (secular politicians to a man) refused to attend meetings of any kind until they had paid respect to the fallen at appropriate religious ceremonies at the relevant embassies, national churches, or the many war memorials with which London is so blessedly endowed. The programme was accordingly re-jigged, with nothing other than the delegation secretaries' lunch at the House set to start until the late afternoon of 11th November, when the politically driven obsequies were well out of the way.

The whole conference went remarkably well. The committee rooms at Lancaster House were too small for the purpose, with supporting staff crammed along walls, the interpretation equipment worked only

---

* I had already bored and aggravated most of my colleagues with tales of entertaining and dancing with Princess Margaret in north Staffordshire, and twice lunching with the Queen Mother – all true, but not endearing.

sporadically (an NAA tradition), the electrical sockets were incompatible even with the rest of the UK, the catering services were inadequate, the Ladies Programme (organised by something which we were embarrassed to acknowledge as the British Tourist Authority) was disastrous. On the other hand, the Royal Military Police turned up in force in their red caps, guarded every portal, and wowed the delegates into believing that they were being taken seriously and properly protected, although the American professionals rightly regarded the security arrangements as no more than a band-aid; and the Royal Marines not only provided a magnificent lunch midweek, but also paraded their band in torrential rain on the square in Greenwich, which had not yet been abandoned to academic use.

While the Marines were doing their stuff, the entire conference (documents, nameplates, printing equipment, as well as bodies) was within a couple of hours miraculously translated from Lancaster House to Church House – despite the sacrosanct institution of the HMSO porters' lunch hour. Typically British, said the Belgians – a fair enough comment before the dawn of Thatcher.

On the afternoon of Thursday 14th November 1974, after the usual opening formalities, Harold Wilson, who had survived the recent General Election with a resounding majority of three, addressed the representatives of the NATO parliaments in the Assembly Hall of Church House. Backed by uplifting ecclesiastical homilies around the walls and benches, he pledged his country's total commitment to the alliance, but called for greater burden-sharing amongst the allies; only a few days earlier, unbeknownst to the wider world, the Chief of the Defence Staff had just returned from informing President Ford in Washington that the UK would finally be withdrawing from east of Suez by the spring of 1976.

Although for the most part fully aware of Britain's perilous financial situation, the delegates were in any case that day not so much dismayed by the country's faltering armed might as beguiled by the fairyland magic of its monarchy. Off they all trooped to Buckingham Palace, not only to bow and curtsey to HM The Queen, but also (an unexpected privilege) to wish the Prince of Wales a happy twenty-sixth birthday. The whole evening was organised with that professional genius which characterises all royal events (to standards which others often seek to emulate but never quite achieve); and it was choreographed on the ground by Robert Rogers, who as acting deputy head of protocol for the Assembly (as well as already aspiring Clerk of the House) drilled us in how to inscribe on our cuffs the list of interviewees for whom we were responsible, exactly how to time their interception, how to arrange that thereafter they were encountered as if by accident in a crowded room by the Queen or the Prince, and how to ensure that they were under no circumstances to be further introduced (having already bowed and curtsied on their way in).

But the stars of the evening were the royals themselves: the Queen and

Prince and their minders progressed through the company as in a stately saraband, succinctly briefed by the Foreign Office, memorising all the essential details of their guests and therefore always able to launch the next conversation, allowing just enough time for each interview (but no more), and also allowing time for the unplanned encounter and the untrained punter. Nobody could have come away from the evening other than entranced; and no other firm – even a royal one – could have done the job so well (as indeed I was to discover next year in Copenhagen, and only too often thereafter).

At the end of the session, on Saturday afternoon, following a memorable service of celebration in St Margaret's, Westminster, there were plaudits all round as the survivors (by now almost all staff) headed across Parliament Square for a final British Atlantic Committee "bash" in the Members' Dining Room, during the course of which Sir Ghastly advised me portentously that "there's definitely a gong in this for you, my boy". For the first and only time in our lives, Sue and I, in honour of our success, were then whisked away from Speaker's Court in a government Bentley (for which the Government Car Service eventually billed me at the end of the year) – our arrival home causing some alarm and consternation to our quietly law-abiding neighbours in south-east London suburbia.

On Monday I took up my new post as second Clerk to the Science & Technology Committee[*]. On Wednesday I was summoned to the presence of Captain Lidderdale, expecting, not entirely unreasonably in view of Sir Ghastly's confident assurances, at least some acknowledgement of two years' hard labour without remission and in trying circumstances. I was not invited to take a seat. In strained tones the Clerk of the House, also standing, managed this much: "I am advised that you, no doubt like others, should be thanked for your contribution to the apparent success of the recent conference. I am accordingly so thanking you. You would be well advised to remember that this is not the kind of work which I expect members of my Department to undertake. I hope that you will in future try to confine yourself to activities of a more clerkly nature."

---

[*] I write "clerk *to*" because this was the curious appellation we all enjoyed at the time. The boss clerk was Clerk *of* the House of Commons, but the rest of us were mere clerks *to*: this idiosyncrasy no doubt had some obscure historical rationale (probably the Clerk *of* the House sent one of his assistants *to* a committee) but was quietly faded out in the early 1980's.

13

Wayne's Circus

Around the Alliance with the Political Committee

When I left the Overseas Office for more "clerkly" duties it was generally assumed by the departmental cognoscenti that my travelling days were over.

I was not terribly keen on this idea. I had acquired a taste for travelling. I knew that it was better suited to my limited talents: I was a natural bag carrier. So when the "trips" list for 1975 was promulgated by the Clerk of the Overseas Office from his lair a few weeks later I for once kicked up. I pointed out that I knew more about international assemblies than anyone else of my relatively lowly grade; that I had more recent hands-on experience than anyone else in the service; and that having lived on mere subsistence for the last two years I thought it an injustice that I should now be deprived of the financial fruits enjoyed by others. I could have added that if a gong was to elude me I might at least be rewarded with some cash in hand (much needed, since we had just bought a first small house, and base rate was running at the staggering rate of 11.25%). After much haggling, and having antagonised almost all my colleagues, I was nominated Secretary of the Political Committee of the North Atlantic Assembly, a post I was able to hang on to for the next seven years.

The job of committee secretary at the NAA was strictly limited. The real work – taking chairmen and rapporteurs on trips, liaising with the military and the universities, arranging meetings, writing (often enviably learnèd) reports – was the responsibility of the two fulltime committee directors, in whose appointment the much-mocked Des showed surprisingly good judgement. The committee secretaries, like the rest of the temporary team, arrived a day or so before the meetings began (wherever in the western hemisphere that happened to be), glanced through the documents, noted any changes in the membership, instructed the messengers and the summary-writers in their duties, checked that the interpretation equipment was at least in principle operational (and that the interpreters had not yet gone on strike), and found the bar.

When the committee assembled, the secretary's job was to write the formal minutes and edit the summary report of what was purported to have been said (one of the few truly creative tasks in a clerk's otherwise humdrum life), to draft resolutions and amendments, and to advise the chairman how to hold the ring, applying whatever version of parliamentary procedure seemed appropriate at the time. The Assembly's own written rules were sensibly brief and permissive. Accordingly, if the chairman was procedurally weak, the secretary could impose order simply by drawing on the rules of his own parliament (in my case the House of Commons, in other cases the Bundestag, the Assemblée Nationale or the Tweede Kamer), just as he did at home. If, on the other hand, the chairman either fancied himself as a proceduralist (there are many itinerant backbench politicians of that kind) or else regarded himself as a man of power, the committee secretary had no hope of influencing events, and happily settled for the role of the man who merely wields the quill pen.

I had several chairmen during the next seven years, since such offices were held for short periods to allow for rotation between nations, and individuals came and went according to the whim of their electorates or of their political leaders (if you lost your seat, you couldn't last for more than six months or so before someone found you out; if you were offered a ministerial job and a ministerial salary, you left on the next flight home). Two made a particularly long-lasting impression.

The first was Michel Boscher. In his early fifties by this time, M Boscher was the epitome of the French parliamentarian, operating at all levels of the system and revered locally as the "father" of the new town of Évry, in the Paris suburbs (and, indeed, of the new towns movement in France as a whole, the results of which were – at best – mixed). Rotund, avuncular, moustachioed, largely bald, he seemed a far cry from the cinematographic image of the Gaullist *résitant* who was said to have been the General's hit man in the clean-up of Paris at the *Libération*. But his *anglophonie* probably gave him away: years of exile in London had given him not near but more-than perfect English; his main concern in the committee was that the French and English texts (whatever their substance) should always be exact translations unlikely to be censured either by the Académie or the editors of Fowler. The principal duty of the committee secretary was to arrive armed with large quantities of Senior Service cigarettes, obtainable only with great difficulty and at great cost at that time on his side of the Channel (when my appointment was confirmed I received a phone call from the Petit Sablon reminding me not to forget). He and I had no difficulty in interpreting and enforcing the *reglement* in easy harmony, since we were both concerned more with form than substance, and neither of us shared the high seriousness of the cold war warriors from Bonn.

My second remarkable chairman was of an altogether different stamp. The long-serving representative from California's 5th district, Congressman Phillip Burton was a US Democrat who would have found a happy home in the Tribune Group or even perhaps on the benches of the PCF or the PCI. He was a fighter for ideals, not for high office. Having fought in real wars – notably in the USAF in Korea – he loathed US entanglement in overseas adventures, famously one of only three congressmen who had the prescience to vote against the appropriations demanded by Lyndon Johnson in 1965 which led to the mire of Vietnam. At home he espoused popular causes – a gigantic statue of him stands overlooking the Golden Gate as monument to his fight for the establishment of national recreation areas and parks; and also the less popular – he was one of the first US politicians to recognise the need for research and funding in the fight against AIDS. And in 1974 he particularly endeared himself to Europeans in general by taking the lead in the final dissolution of the House Committee on Un-American Activities.[*]

While Michel Boscher presided upright, dapper and beatific over the impassioned debates of the Political Committee, Phillip Burton – tall, heavily built, carelessly dressed and hair awry – engaged in the political battle, draped over the conference table, and argued succinctly but commandingly for his beliefs, in often very colorful language. To some extent his prime belief was that Europe was a very long way from the West Coast (even further than Washington), and it was time Europe started looking after its own affairs and its own defense – a view probably and understandably shared by the majority of US delegates (and its possible consequences feared, equally understandably, by their European counterparts). Even amongst the minority of atlanticists, nostalgia for the old congressional stand of isolation from Europe's murderous infighting – reflecting very much the sentiments of their electors – remained strong.

Representative Burton by this time carried with him a reputation as something of a procedural wizard, having in 1973, and for the first time in 50 years, passed a bill out of committee without the block of the "closed rule", thus reverting to the old practice of allowing new amendments on the floor of the House of Representatives, and a resultant, no doubt unintended, explosion in lobbying. His main interest in procedure, however, was properly in how to use it to get the results he wanted, and I noticed (thankfully) nothing of that finesse in drafting and even promulgating rulings from the Chair which is the sign of the true and tedious proceduralist. When his attention was occasionally drawn to the rules of the North Atlantic Assembly his response was "Look, son, while I'm in the Chair the rules of the US House of Representatives rule – OK?" A sentiment more volubly expressed from the Chair of the plenary Assembly by Congressman Hays.

Wayne Levere Hays, the Democratic representative from Belmont County, Ohio, was one of the founders of the North Atlantic Assembly. He was, according to Phil Burton, "the meanest man in Congress. He's also the most powerful. Everyone is afraid of him".[10] He had served as President of the NAA in 1956-57 and 1969-70, and was re-elected for a two-year term in the same job in 1975. He was, most importantly in Washington terms, chairman of both the House Administration Committee and the Joint Committee on Printing.

---

[*] Phillip Burton died young of an aneurysm in 1983, greatly mourned.

Although I already knew that I was supposed to revere Congressman Hays as a great atlanticist and father of the Assembly, it was not until the London session that I fully realised in what respect he needed to be held.

In order to meet the alarmingly pacific inclinations of the European and even some British members of the alliance, we arranged a service in St Margaret's Westminster – the parish church of the House of Commons – to celebrate the twenty-fifth anniversary of the alliance, and to pray for peace and harmony - on the final day of the London session. The service was to be ecumenical and multilingual; Canon David Edwards, the then Speaker's Chaplain (and notable scholar) had taken enormous pains to involve as many as possible of the national churches in London, and we were due to pray in the many languages of the alliance, to proclaim the pater noster in whatever language suited us, and to sing the great hymns of the worldwide church. Despite the United States' reputation for Christian devotion and observance, the large majority of the US delegation to the London session (and their wives in particular) made it clear that they would not under any circumstances attend a religious event of this kind (Christian or otherwise), particularly on a Saturday afternoon, and planned to devote what was left of their week in Bond Street. Wayne's response in our support was swift and uncompromising: if you want to get back to Washington on Air Force 3 (or whichever) you attend the service and sing very loud; if you prefer to spend your own money on a Pan Am ticket, feel free. Barring funerals, it turned out to be the best-attended service in St Margaret's in centuries, and Americans of all persuasions helped to lift the roof.

Wayne's circus rolled on across the capitals of the Alliance. In Copenhagen in 1975 I had my first encounter with the brilliant invention of the *pater noster* lift, which we were assured by Danish colleagues had been deliberately installed in the Folketing in order to increase the likelihood of by-elections and ensure the regular rejuvenation of the national parliament – it seemed an extremely good parliamentary precedent. Several of us took the hydrofoil across to Malmö, waving enthusiastically to the little mermaid, hoping for duty-free akvavit, but being offered only vast quantities of duty-free chocolate. At the end of the session we were entertained by the still young Queen Margrethe: it was an occasion much enjoyed – and in particular we all appreciated being personally welcomed (she, like her relatives in London, also remembered our names, ranks and titles), and also personally served canapés and gin-and-tonics by the reigning monarch, who proved to be a damned good waitress – a rather attractively downbeat version of the Buck House reception of a year earlier.

Next year was the turn of the United States Congress itself. It was the 200th anniversary of the Declaration of Independence, and the Assembly was to meet in Colonial Williamsburg, the historic home of the Republic: it was an occasion designed for Wayne to demonstrate his patriotism and his mastery of the House. Unfortunately, by the time we were due to assemble in the fall of 1976 Congressman Hays, although yet again elected President of the North Atlantic Assembly, was no longer chairman of the House Administration Committee or of the Committee on Printing, nor even a member of Congress. In May 1976 a disgruntled mistress, a rather compelling southern blonde by the name of Elizabeth Ray, claimed in the *Washington Post* that she had for two years been provided with an empty office and a good salary as an HAC staffer with no other duties than to provide comfort services for Congressman Hays; and she provided graphic details. Most uncharacteristically, Wayne apologised on the floor and then, on 1st September, resigned from the House in order to avoid the jurisdiction of the Committee on Standards of Official Conduct.[*]

Wayne Hays' little local difficulties created major problems for the North Atlantic Assembly. When we arrived at the Convention Hall in beautiful Williamsburg, there was no printing equipment of any kind, and not even any paper; the promised unlimited supplies having been cut off, we were informed that all such would now have to come out of the congressmen's individual paper and printing allowances. It took a great deal of international arm-twisting (and, inevitably, under-the-counter subventions from Executive agencies of one kind or another) to get the show on the road just in time for the arrival of the great and the good.

Their arrival was something of a miracle in itself. So far as the staff were concerned the visit to Williamsburg had acquired a rather picaresque quality long before the lack of a printing plant had been discovered. The original plan had been for all local and international staff to arrive at Brussels airport, and then to be transferred from the civil to the military side of the airfield, whence they would be flown by the Belgian air force to Washington, and thence onward by local transport to the old capital of Virginia. The staff duly arrived in Brussels, but only late in the evening did the air force admit that their few available aircraft were unable to make the crossing against the Atlantic headwinds. Philippe Deshormes having already gone ahead on Pan Am, the small permanent staff were then faced with the problem of what to do with fifty or so British and other foreign officials with nowhere to stay and, crucially, no money (we were still in the days of currency controls and long before the days of internationally-accredited holes in the wall); and the Assembly's finance director (the otherwise always helpful M Guignet) had very sensibly gone ahead with his boss, and with most of the available cash.

As is so common on such occasions it was the underpaid and under-rated ladies of the Secretariat who turned to, faced the fury of the polyglot crowd

---

[*] Amazingly, Wayne won the 1976 congressional primary for his district (although he subsequently withdrew) and then went on to serve a term in the Ohio legislature and subsequently as chairman of the local Democratic Party in Belmont County.

in the stairwell of the Petit Sablon, found a way into the safe, and tracked down hotel accommodation. The following day, the headwinds still unfavourable, half a dozen "key" staff were put onto real planes: we made it to Williamsburg only a day late. The remainder of the team reached landfall – having travelled via the Azores – a mere hour or so after the committees they were supposed to be staffing were scheduled to meet. Colonial Williamsburg was, however, unsurpassable, brightly garlanded in a golden carpet of the leaves of the fall, and I was able to take home a genuine late eighteenth century colonial cookery book (printed in 1972) and a pewter teaspoon made on site by a young craftsman whose convincing Virginian drawl belied his recent emigration from East Ham.

A week or so later the *Aviation Militaire* managed to get us all back to Brussels, with only a few hours of enforced idleness in the cockroach-ridden lounge at Gander (while refuelling in the snow), and a briefer stop at Shannon (almost equally cold and equally infested). I was personally responsible for driving most of the other very weary passengers, scarcely sustained on army rations for the best part of a day, to near distraction by rehearsing my lines – and also some of the actions, including a tricky backwards fall into the arms of my butler, which was repeatedly tried out down the central isle of the aircraft – for the part of Lord Arthur Savile, which I was to play on the amateur stage only three days later. I was greatly assisted in inflicting this torture by George Cubie and other companions who together occupied the back row of the plane, and read me my cues.[*]

Despite his own departure, Wayne's circus moved on. In 1977 we met in the Senate in Paris. There Robert Rogers (although still only 2IC of the protocol service) confirmed his future as a man of power, running affairs from Napoleon's second-best imperial throne. The following year the ménage moved to Portugal, a longstanding member of the NATO alliance, but only recently delivered from Salazar's sclerotic dictatorship. Although the initial enthusiasms of the revolution had waned since 1974, the NAA's arrival in town signalled Portugal's admission at last into what Mikhail Gorbachev later famously described as the "European House". We were garlanded with carnations, magnificently entertained at the Gulbenkian, and, in the true tradition of revolutionary socialist solidarity, we were each allocated a beautiful young lady to look after us for the week.[†]

---

[*] *Lord Arthur Savile's Crime* is a brilliant dramatisation by Constance Cox of a somewhat tedious short story by Oscar Wilde. It is superior to all Wilde's own stage plays other than *The Importance*. The production went well, and could have run for weeks, and it was one of those occasions when I wished very much that I had stayed on the boards (a view probably shared by my parliamentary colleagues, particularly en route from Gander to Shannon).

[†] My charming escort helped me buy a sumptuous art volume of Portuguese paintings as a parting gift from the English team for Sir Geoffrey de Freitas, who

In 1979 the Assembly met again in Ottawa, where there was early snow, and only a qualified welcome from parliamentary officials as jealous of their House of Commons as so many of my colleagues in Westminster were of ours. My wife never fully forgave me for bringing back a real Indian drum for our newly-adopted son, and nor did our neighbours[*].

After many entertaining plenaries, and many rather tiresome committee meetings in Brussels, I was lucky to be able to say my farewells to the North Atlantic Assembly after a series of committee sessions on San Giorgio Maggiore in the summer of 1981. I spent four nights at the Graspo de Ua, a small, grubby but otherwise exquisite hotel by the Rialto, with a balcony overlooking a private canal, and with a private chapel attached; I went to work by boat; I spent the evenings alone by the Grand Canal with a book and spaghetti and the local vino rosso; and on the last day, in something of a trance, I followed the one-man band around town before boarding the vaporetto for the airport, and home. It is tedious to wax lyrical about Venice: we all know that it's unhealthy, falling back into the Adriatic, vastly expensive, exploitative of visitors and locals alike, and that it would be shut down altogether if any middle-ranking official from the British Health & Safety Executive were to spend a long weekend anywhere near the San Marco. It is nonetheless a magical city. If given a free choice of final earthly destination I would probably opt for Saigon or St George's – or even somewhere on the Sussex coast; but if offered somewhere to stay for eternity, given the demise of both Alexandria and Byzantium, I would have to opt for my room at the top of the Graspo de Ua.

---

was at last retiring from the Assembly, and from the House. He wept real tears, and we were all rather moved by the occasion, a reminder to still over-confident young men that most careers – apparently successful to the bystanders - whimper to an end in sadness and disappointment.

[*] In his hands, the drum did not long survive, much to our collective relief.

IV In Committee

14

The power of prayer

The Science & Technology Committee; seven samurai in the faubourg St Honoré; the Angus diaspora in California; the last of the Keystone Cops

It says something about the standard of training provided for House of Commons staff at the time (and it says even more about my own indolence) that before I took up my new duties as second clerk on the Select Committee on Science & Technology I had never once attended any other real select committee meeting, even in the gallery.[*] Although there was a brief running-in period in the procedural offices there appeared to be an assumption that committee clerks would leap fully fledged from the groves of academe, fully equipped to advise Members, negotiate with lobbyists, and confront the permanent secretaries they would invariably encounter within days of taking on their jobs. So, like most of my contemporaries and successors, I joined the committee service both innocent and ignorant.

I nonetheless arrived in 3 Dean's Yard drawing great confidence from my education. It was surely for precisely this that Lord Lindsay of Birker had created Keele's Foundation Year and provided me with an introduction to all that modern man needed to know. Although I had emerged after five years in the Staffordshire countryside with a degree in English and Politics, three years of physics had also taught me (following the footsteps of Professor Millikan) how to measure the charge of an electron; I understood the principle of the lever; and I even more or less understood the rudiments of the atomic bomb. I could pick my way through a French or Russian text, and I had Plato as well as Hegel. All this self-confidence, or arrogance, was, of course (to use a contemporary colloquialism) balls. The fact that my new boss, Jim Hastings, was an Oxford historian, or that his immediate predecessor John Sweetman was a Cambridge lawyer was, as it turned out, just as irrelevant as that my successor Dr Christopher Ward was a real chemist. Probably much more relevant was three weeks' work experience at the end of my second sixth form year with the E S & A Robinson Group

---

[*] I had served in my first year in the House as the second (Commons) clerk of the Joint Committee on Consolidation &c Bills, which vaguely followed the procedures of select committees (and whose proceedings were followed by nobody else) but was otherwise *sui generis*.

(the packaging people), several summers spent sweeping waste tobacco (an extremely valuable commodity) off the floors at the W D & H O Wills No. 1 factory in Bedminster, several Christmases clutching my lift-driver's licence (of which I am still the proud possessor) in the Temple Meads parcel sorting office, and innumerable Saturday afternoons and many school and university vacations as a very junior reporter, but often also reserve copy-boy - with frequent access to the hot metal compositors when running late copy for the "fudge"- in the old shoe factory in Silver Street which then housed the *Bristol Evening Post*: all this gave me at least a feel for what it was like actually to work on the shop floor, which is where new technology actually mattered.

Just as it was becoming clear in Westminster that a research chemist could make a damned good political leader, so it also became clear to me that what was needed to be a damned good committee clerk was not any extensive knowledge of the subjects under scrutiny, but political nous, and a flair for ambiguous drafting; expertise could be brought in and paid for at a daily rate – but the art of handling a committee was a precious mystery. The key ingredients were: the ability to convince all concerned that you were always on their side, and not on the other side, combined with the art of feeling equally, genuinely and wholeheartedly committed to both; the ability to acquire instant understanding of a complicated subject and persuade both sides that you knew more than they did; and the ability to jettison all that knowledge as soon as it became irrelevant to the next task in hand, to make way for the next committee inquiry. With all these built-in qualities good parliamentary clerks would (or perhaps that should be 'will') make first-class recruits for the Records Department of the Ministry of Truth come regime-change time.

In keeping with longstanding tradition the Science & Technology Committee was ordered by the House simply to "consider Science and Technology"; it was given no other or more specific instructions, and was therefore required to do as little or as much as it chose within its very broad brief. Its fourteen members had in practice chosen to be very busy, and kept their tiny staff even busier. I inherited five separate sub-committees, all pursuing fairly major inquiries simultaneously, and the egos of an army of specialist advisers from the universities to be soothed and flattered. And all this was done with two graduate clerks, an executive officer, and half a secretary, in those days before computers when secretaries really did have to do a great deal of work[*].

---

[*] In September 1975 I was able to swap notes with my opposite number on the Hill: the Executive Director of the House Science & Technology Committee was supported at that time by 51 graduate staff, including an astronaut who had flown to the moon and back and who also happened to be a well-qualified international lawyer.

The committee had been dominated since its first appointment in 1966, as part of Richard Crossman's tentative procedural reforms, by Arthur Palmer, a well-qualified hands-on electrical engineer (and representative of the Electrical Trades Union), who had served successively since 1945 as a Labour or Labour/Co-op Member for Wimbledon, Cleveland, and various parts of Bristol.[*] In the brief interregnum of Ted Heath's unhappy government from 1970 to 1974 the chair had been taken over by Airey Neave, the rather dour hero of Colditz Castle, who when I joined the committee was again serving as chairman of the second-ranking sub-committee, then known as the Science Sub-Committee, for which I (then the second-ranking clerk) became responsible on my arrival. Neave only lasted until February 1975 when, having masterminded Margaret Thatcher's leadership triumph, he left the committee to become her chief of staff, and unfortunately for him, shadow Northern Ireland Secretary.[†]

Airey Neave's replacement as the lead Conservative on the S&T Committee was a less flamboyant character. He was however a man of determination, who eventually achieved his lifetime's ambition by becoming the founding father of the Parliamentary Office of Science and Technology, in which I was able to assist him when, ten years or so later, I was free to interpret an ambiguous decision of the House of Commons Commission as a positive vote in favour of his scheme, and of the resulting expenditure commitments. Few backbench MP's have ever made such a decisive and permanent contribution to the work of Parliament, and none have been so little regarded or esteemed for their success.

Ian Stewart (later Sir Ian) Lloyd was a South African by birth, but fought for Britain as a spitfire pilot, and during his time at King's was elected President of the Cambridge Union. Despite having left his home country for good in 1955 in principled protest against the apartheid policy of the post-war Nationalist government, Ian Lloyd was regarded by more or less everybody on the British political spectrum (including most in his own

---

[*] Like all Bristol MPs, Arthur Palmer was subject to a barrage of highly critical and articulate letters from my mother Anne. Both he and Tony Benn suffered particularly from her entirely sensible campaign to convert redundant aircraft and armaments factories into producing prefabs, thus solving housing and unemployment crises by the same stroke of the pen. Michael Cocks, MP for Bristol South from 1970 to 1987, and Labour Chief Whip under Jim Callaghan, suffered his own particular purgatory in finding himself living across the road from my mother and therefore facing the risk of running into her without notice in the local grocers, or while innocently cutting the front grass.

[†] In the early afternoon of Friday 30th March 1979 I was putting the Votes & Proceedings to bed in the Journal Office, waiting for the messenger to take the copy to the printer, when a large explosion rocked the by-that-time normally somnolent Palace of Westminster; our departure from the building was delayed for some time following Airey Neave's assassination in the New Palace Yard car park.

party) as incorrigibly and objectionably right-wing, since he opposed the effortless option of sanctions against both South Africa and Rhodesia on practical grounds and spoke out against what he regarded as the dictatorial tendencies of the leaders of most of the former British colonies in the rest of Africa. Political correctness did not begin with the Blair Government.

My new chairman knew as little about select committee work as I did, and so from early 1975 we worked to educate each other in our new roles. The first problem we confronted was dealing with the other committee members, most of whom were regarded (or regarded themselves) as big beasts.

They included on the Labour side: Ron Brown, almost a clone of his older brother George, who argued with everyone in sight, including all committee members and staff as well as all witnesses. Ted Leadbitter, an equally pugilistic former teacher, who in his youth had fixed posters to the top of telegraph poles to ensure the successful election of Manny Shinwell (and the defeat of the despised Ramsay MacDonald*) at Easington in 1936, and was, most notoriously, Colonel George Wigg's instrument in 1979 in the unmasking of the Surveyor of the Queen's Pictures as a Soviet spy. Tam Dalyell described him in his obituary, affectionately but accurately, as "blustering, opinionated and verbose". David Ginsburg, a Sandhurst-trained intelligence officer, a highly successful (and high-earning) economist and market researcher, a fellow Balliol man who had succeeded Roy Jenkins as chairman of the Oxford Democratic Socialist Club, and who (like Ron Brown) eventually went down with most of the rest of the SDP when he switched from the Labour Party in 1981. And Frank Hooley (Sheffield Heeley), a university administrator by trade, pugnacious and (so far as I could see at that time) a somewhat humourless enthusiast for 'alternative' energy sources, who evangelized for the Severn Barrage: a man ahead of his time.

---

* Here I have to declare an interest. My mother and her sister Peggy Angus (eventually the long-term châtelaine of the über-Charleston across the Sussex Downs at Furlongs) were bosom pals of Ramsay's daughter Ishbel, who filled the role of First Lady from her father's first appointment as Prime Minister in 1924: she was then only 21, and became a media personality. My father George achieved brief notoriety by leaving a copy of the illicit 1929 Mandrake Press edition of *Lady Chatterley's Lover*, in an envelope personally addressed to the Prime Minister, on a bus on his way to tea with Ishbel at No 10. Despite frantic police efforts the package, with its incriminating wrapping, was never recovered, and there were fears thereafter that Macdonald might be blackmailed. Both my parents in later life regarded Manny Shinwell as something of a hero: so they must privately have shared the view that Macdonald, despite his sweet nature, had betrayed the movement. Since Ishbel refused to join "National Labour" in 1931, one must assume that she shared these sentiments, even while continuing to preside over her Downing Street salon.

The Tories on the committee seemed at the time an altogether more pallid crew, although most eventually achieved rather higher things. Christopher Tugendhat (City of London and Westminster) was a journalist who went on to become Vice-President of the European Commission; Neil Macfarlane (Sutton & Cheam), who made it to the giddy heights of deputy minister for the Arts and minister for sport, and for "children's play", and who after all that probably deserved his knighthood; Norman Tebbit, the member for Chingford, and former RAF and commercial airline pilot, who these days needs no further introduction, although at the time was largely unknown and a rather tamer political presence; and Ken Warren, a hands-on aeronautical engineer by profession, more fully attuned to the aggressive character of the select committee, who eventually (after the humiliation of several years as a PPS) emerged as an extremely effective chairman of the select committee on Trade & Industry. He was forever beloved of Commons clerks for his name alone (which may also of course have been the reason for his getting his constituency party's endorsement in the first place): in the division lobbies he rasped out his name and constituency in time-honoured fashion: it always produced a small frisson to hear the name "Warren Hastings" called out again in those hallowed halls in the small hours of the morning.

In the eight years since their first appointment, the committee had concentrated on matters relating to aviation, high-speed land transport, energy conservation, and nuclear power. The latter had not surprisingly become by far the most important part of their self-imposed brief, and much adrenalin had flowed in their regular punch-ups with the chairmen of GEC (Arnold Weinstock), the Central Electricity Generating Board, the South of Scotland Electricity Board or – best of all – Dr Walter Marshall of the UK Atomic Energy Authority. In providing a highly publicised forum for the opponents as well as the supporters of nuclear power the committee did much to defuse public unrest on the issue. Although Britain was by then both a military nuclear power and home of the world's first civil reactor programme, street protest was surprisingly muted; we were spared the serious riots in Paris and across the Federal Republic of Germany, and French and German politicians were duly impressed by the sophistication of our political system.

Ironically, since most of the committee were actively pro-nuclear, their continuing and often well-informed debates about rival reactor technologies, boiler capacities, reactor safety, and the chimera of the fast-breeder reactor, made a major contribution to that British institutional indecisiveness which ensures that good money is never thrown after good. Just as it was becoming clear that British gas-cooled technologies (or even better the steam-generating heavy water reactor) were potential world-beaters (and both a damned sight safer and probably cheaper in practice than the Westinghouse PWRs which thereafter held sway) the continued debates had left the way open for populist politicians – led by the second Viscount Stansgate – to hide behind the prospect of North Sea oil as a short-term solution and allow Britain's nuclear industry to collapse. The French economy, for one, has subsequently thrived on nuclear power and a much reduced dependency on fossil fuels: such are the advantages of a dirigiste state.

When I arrived in 1974 the Science & Technology Committee was beginning to turn its attention to other matters: the scope for alternative (ie non-nuclear and non-fossil) sources of energy (which led them into the absurd cul-de-sac of the Severn Barrage), and the fundamental (and age-old) problems involved in transferring British scientific prowess at university level into profit-making new technologies. The latter was the main focus of the science sub-committee, and reflected Airey Neave's aspirations, and Ian Lloyd's ultimately successful efforts, to bring 'pure' science closer to the centre of parliamentary consideration of policy options and governmental funding decisions.

It was with the science sub-committee that I first learned the arts of travelling with select committees. The most important point – which was something of a shock - was that, unlike members of international delegations, select committee members expected their clerks to know something about the subjects they were travelling to investigate. So although select committee trips were often great fun, they were also quite hard work. Lengthy negotiations were required with overseas posts about who was to be met and about the logistics of travel and lodgement (usually, in those early days, indirectly through the agency of the Foreign and Commonwealth Office, and subject to their frequently unsympathetic gloss). Briefs had to be prepared in advance to guide members in their meetings with eminent interlocutors (ie to tell them what to ask) – which not infrequently meant translating the sophisticated gobbledegook provided by the specialist academic advisers into simple concepts, and language, which laymen could be reasonably expected to understand. Notes had to be taken of all meetings, sufficiently decipherable (despite the consular gin & tonic) to be of some use in preparing subsequent reports. And the clerk was expected to minister to the personal crises of his Members, as well as handing out the expenses payments, in local currency and in brown envelopes, at every port of call.

In search of enlightenment, the science sub-committee first set out in July 1975 on a relatively modest trip to France and the Federal Republic of Germany, predicated on the simplistic notion that the two countries' post-war "miracles" could somehow be explained by the superiority of the gymnasiums in producing technologists, and the prowess of the écoles supérieures in producing technologically articulate civil servants. I suggested in vain that they might do worse than merely go to Edinburgh and

Glasgow to discover how skilled but civilised engineers and scientists could be produced and used in industry; and a minority pleaded that maybe neither the educational system which had facilitated national socialism nor that which nurtured dirigisme was necessarily a model to be followed in a country still at least nominally committed to some form of open and liberal economic as well as political system.

This initial trip provided only a few useful clues to how to bridge the notorious gap between science (at which we were rather good) and industry (at which we must have been even better once upon a time, since our ancestors managed to invent the industrial revolution); not least because the formal mechanisms, and the criteria, for funding research and innovation were remarkably similar in France and Germany (and, as we discovered later in the year, in Canada and even much of the US). There were of course the obvious shibboleths of the trades unions and poor middle management, both easy targets when attributing blame for the UK's economic woes. But the sub-committee, creatures of their time, were initially obsessed by apparent malfunctions in the relations between institutions (universities, manufacturers, research councils, government departments), and (whatever their nominal political differences) wedded to the idea that it was the responsibility of "the Government" to find the capital needed for investment in wealth-creating innovation in industry.

Only as the inquiry progressed did these overwhelmingly conservative members of Parliament begin to acknowledge that there might be something fundamentally wrong with attitudes in the revered city of London. The obsession with short-term profitability characteristic of the latter was in stark contrast with both the relatively long-term perspective of the industrial giants in the Federal Republic, and the skilful deployment of public money into targeted sectoral leaders (nationalised or not) in *la France du Plan*. This growing perception of what was probably the major underlying problem was reinforced a few months later during an exhausting ten-day visit taking in Ottawa, Toronto, Boston, Washington and San Francisco.

It was much to the credit of the Committee, and of Ian Lloyd in particular, that after almost two years of painstaking investigation – with several dozen formal evidence sessions as well as many visits around the country, as well as abroad – their final report, in October 1976, while making scores of routine proposals for tinkering with the institutions, managed to hit some nails firmly on the head. They regretted the demise of the pre-World War II industry-based apprenticeship and postgraduate training establishments at Metropolitan Vickers, Rolls Royce, and elsewhere[*]; they rightly deplored the elevation of the CATs[†] into universities which immediately began to offer courses in the arts and social sciences[11]; they effectively demolished the credibility of the much-lauded National Research and Development Corporation which, having a statutory duty to at least break even, applied the same cautious criteria to innovative developments as would any high street bank; and they found it "abundantly clear" that "the process of innovation in industry is dependent on the availability of *private* capital" – a view which may seem self-evident now, but which at the time was regarded as almost breath-takingly audacious.

In a subsequent brief inquiry into a specific machine tool under development at Cranfield (for what was described in those pre-computer days as "numerically controlled" gear grinding) the Committee similarly concluded that the Department of Industry's relevant Requirements Board, which in effect supported only low-risk ventures, could never be of more than "marginal assistance" to companies struggling to launch innovatory products with a long lead time towards profitability. It is sad to reflect fifty years on that – despite the replacement of keynesianism by monetarism as the economic orthodoxy, despite the undoubted revolutionary effects of Margaret Thatcher's personality, and despite the obvious lessons of the more recent world economic crises – short-termism remains the City's essential characteristic: any major company which fails to increase its profits year by year is marked down as a failure and ripe for takeover by the asset-strippers; and it's so much smarter to make a quick mega-buck by trading futures.

I felt reasonably satisfied (and maybe justifiably) with these first parliamentary blue books to come from my pen[‡], and I was particularly chuffed by the comments of the professional journals to the effect that at

---

[*] My older brother left school after O-levels but progressed through the apprenticeship scheme of the Bristol Aeroplane Company at Filton, and then through Imperial College, to a highly successful career in steel tube manufacturing. Imperial College of course survives and thrives; quality apprenticeship schemes of that kind were fast disappearing by the 1970's.

[†] The Colleges of Advanced Technology, formed in the 1950's out of local technical colleges, and just finding their feet as centres of excellence in engineering teaching and research. The Committee (or I at any rate) thought that their transformation reflected "the distressing British habit of attempting to bestow status and prestige on institutions and individuals by changing their names rather than by encouraging them to do well the things for which they are best suited". The bestowal of B Ed degrees in place of the professional Cert Ed qualification, and the subsequent elevation of teacher training colleges into also-ran universities was another manifestation of the same baleful trend.

[‡] The first of something like 70 in all – and in those days they did of course come from my fountain pen: the switch to keyboards in the mid-1980's seemed very painful at the time, although eventually I like most of my contemporaries found wielding a pen a somewhat uncomfortable experience.

last they had proof that members of Parliament [*sic*] could understand technological issues. A D Lindsay would have no doubt been a little bit satisfied also. Inevitably, as was usual at the time, the select committee's conclusions and recommendations were politely acknowledged by Ministers and then largely forgotten: many of them remain relevant half a century later.

The visits to Europe and North America in 1975 provided some fascinating insights into the way other countries tried to achieve the same objectives. But from my point of view they were even more a valuable training ground in my chosen trade. The first lesson was to instil a healthy distrust of the FCO abroad which I was careful not entirely to discard later in my career. I had previously developed very amicable relations with the FCO across the road in Whitehall, when dealing with the North Atlantic Assembly. But it was only when travelling that I discovered the extent to which UK diplomats "go native" when overseas, and treat their own nationals (including – or perhaps even in particular - MP's or even Ministers of the Crown) according to the lights of the host country.

We were reasonably well looked after in Bonn, staying in that down-at-heel but nevertheless historic hotel in Bad Godesberg, were well-briefed by the Ambassador, and treated with great courtesy and deference by the Science Counsellor, who seemed glad to have been provided with an additional entrée to the higher reaches of the federal government and the academic and research community. In Munich, our prestige seemed to have dropped a peg or two (and our local minders had of course dropped a rank or two), and we were housed in a passably clean *früstückspension* about half a mile from the centre of town in an area which seemed to have missed the worst of the bombing, and were advised to call for a taxi to get to the Max-Planck-Gessellschaft.[*] From there we flew on to Orly. We were welcomed by an individual who couldn't have ranked higher than a third secretary, bundled into taxis, and unceremoniously dumped at an at best two-star hotel half a kilometre from the famous Paris embassy.

As the ladies of the night ascended the stairs to entice these rich pickings from Westminster, Dr John Cunningham eventually made a connection to the FCO in London, and finally got through to the number for the Paris Embassy which we had been given in case of emergency. He explained, with his usual politeness, that for the middle-aged chairman of a House of Commons select committee (and war hero to boot) to be billeted in a brothel was frankly unacceptable. The Embassy caretaker fully agreed but

---

[*] Only a few years later select committees were being up-graded. On my next visit to Munich I stayed with the Transport Committee at the *Vier Jahreszeiten*, enjoyed a magnificent steak tartare in what purported like so many others to have been Hitler's private room, and downed a few beers in the Hofbräuhaus – which to be fair I suspect the Science & Technology Committee also managed to track down but for the usual reasons I can't now recall.

explained that the duty officer was at that moment not available, and so nothing could be done. Eventually, at around three in the morning, the Embassy duty officer was found in a Paris night club, in no condition to deal with any kind of emergency, and the Head of Chancery or someone of his ilk was awoken from his bed.

Early the following day, while we set off in limousines rather grander than the taxis of the previous evening, to the Centre National de la Research Scientifique, our possessions were moved to the very much grander hotel de Castiglione, across the road from Britain's most opulent embassy in the Faubourg St Honoré, just down the road from the Élysée. That evening the committee (having been given no serious diplomatic briefing of any kind) were at least invited to a garden party at the great embassy across the road. Fulminating at their appalling treatment, they refused a belatedly offered lift and walked from the hotel and across the embassy lawn like the seven samurai, expecting at least some kind of apology, Ian Lloyd white as much with embarrassment as with fury. When a rather obsequious second secretary asked me why the members of Parliament seemed slightly out of sorts this evening (had it been a tiring day? was it the heat? or had they perhaps been over-indulging in the exquisite local cuisine the night before?) and I had tried lightly to explain that there seemed to have been something of a *faux pas protocolière*, I was directed towards someone claiming to be rather more senior: he explained from his lofty eminence that there had of course been no mistake, the committee having been lodged in accommodation "appropriate to their status". The much-admired antennae of the foreign service had on this occasion failed to note that Dr Jack Cunningham, although a relatively new Member, happened also to be the parliamentary private secretary of the Foreign & Commonwealth Secretary, their political boss. It was with not a little satisfaction that we heard shortly after our return of a number of staff changes in the Paris Embassy: although most probably those concerned were at best recycled to other posts, and continued to misrepresent their political masters and otherwise lie abroad for their country.

In early September the Science sub-committee set off on their travels once again, this time to Canada and the USA in search of the same pot of gold: what was the key which opened up the wide vistas of Silicon Gulch? As we were still deep in the long summer recess[*], we had not had the

---

[*] In those civilised days the Commons summer adjournment ran uninterrupted (bar international crises) from late July or early August (depending on how speedily the Finance Bill could be run up to the Lords) until after the end of the party conference season. This was not only one of the perks of the job for most parliamentary staff (who the rest of the time worked inordinately long hours), but also enabled what was still then a division of the Ministry of Works to get on with the scheduled re-cabling, wallpapering and painting (let alone re-building) of the great Victorian palace without interruption.

opportunity to meet in Westminster before departure. Since Members needed to approve the itinerary for the trip, we shanghaied the upper cabin of our 747, other first class passengers being politely told that the cocktail lounge would be unavailable for an hour or so. We accordingly achieved a first: a formal parliamentary meeting officially recorded in the sub-committee minutes as having taken place "somewhere over the Atlantic". It was also never to be repeated, as BA and other airlines began to cram the upper deck with the newly-designated "club" class passengers, and as the House of Commons (under Thatcherite pressure) began to withdraw the privilege of first class travel. Most subsequent trips were Club if long enough and otherwise strictly Economy.

After the usual friendly exchanges with our Canadian cousins we travelled across the frontier to Boston, Washington and el dorado. En route from Toronto to Boston we flew with Allegheny, known to aficionados as "Agony Air", whose captain kindly gave us all a second "flip round the Falls", ostensibly for the entertainment of the distinguished party of Britishers on board, but probably because of traffic congestion. Norman Tebbit (ex-RAF, ex-BOAC) admitted as the flight came to its end to being "something of a white knuckle flyer", and when we appeared to land at Logan nose down his suspicion was confirmed that we were in the hands of an Air America pilot recycled from Saigon. Ian Lloyd, the only former active combat pilot in our own crew, remained white-faced in his pencil grey suit to the end.

While the sub-committee were being entertained by the great and the good at Harvard, I had a pre-arranged assignation with Professor Eric Robinson, formerly of the Victoria University of Manchester and then of the University of Massachusetts. He was (and remains) notorious in the academic world as the man who controlled the study of an English poet more than a century dead by purchasing the copyright in the unpublished works of John Clare from Whitaker's Almanac for a quid (literally) in 1965 and then claiming royalties (or at least acknowledgements) from all other editors, authors and publishers. Eric proved to be a reliable guide to Boston's nightlife. After enjoying the various attributes of what claimed to be the last embodiment of the Supremes (minus Diana Ross and all the other originals by this time), performing on a bar top down by the river, I was equally invigorated by the imaginative tactics of the Boston hookers all the way back to my hotel. I have no doubt that my evening was more stimulating than that of my committee members, from whom I had for once broken the rules and played hooky.

After these breath-taking experiences, and another day's hard grind round the seminar table, we flew down to Washington late on a steamy September afternoon, to be met by a couple of embassy Checkers. These were due to take us direct to our hotel for a quick turnround before a reception and dinner with the Ambassador. We arrived at our hotel in driving rain, inordinate heat and way-above-the-scale humidity. Ian Lloyd and the team were drooping, but anticipating an air-conditioned hour or so in which to recuperate before going on parade for Washington's minor glitterati. The luggage was all stored in the trunk of the second Checker, securely locked and separated for security reasons by a grille irremovable from the front of the automobile. I shepherded my wilting flock towards reception and returned to attend the routine ceremony of decanting the bags. Unfortunately, the key wouldn't work[*]. We all tried it, and we all eventually tried forcibly to remove the internal grille. After twenty minutes or so, as angry exhaustion palpitated from the hotel lobby into the storm outside, I opted for the route of last resort. I went down on my knees in the rain; the driver went down on his knees beside me; and we prayed together. And low and behold, without recourse to any keys, the lid of the trunk rose up, and we were saved.

36 hours later we were off again, heading for California. I enjoyed many remarkable flights during my career – remarkable most often for discomfort and sometimes alarming risk. Flying United Airlines on the 8.00 am departure from Dulles to Los Angeles was the most opulent. We were in a relatively small Boeing, and the sub-committee occupied the whole of the first class compartment, which was set out to replicate a comfortable hotel lounge as far as seat belts would allow. As soon as we had reached cruising height the delightful air hostesses served a light breakfast of fresh croissants, fresh coffee, and decent champagne, and subsequently the chef appeared – fully accoutred, with hat – to ask what we would like for lunch. Slightly fazed, we asked what the choice was, whereupon he invited us into the galley, from which we were able to choose our duck, rack of lamb, steak, trout or lobster fresh from the icebox. We dined over the Grand Canyon from real tables, off real linen cloths, from fine bone china, and with real silver cutlery. We then descended into the nightmare of Los Angeles International, where disputes between operators had resulted in no through ticketing, no interline baggage handling, and no inter-terminal buses or even, so far as we could discover, baggage trollies. My charges, having been so wonderfully entertained across the continent, were somewhat deflated by the time we made the shuttle to our destination up the coast, early on a sunny Friday evening.

A first visit to San Francisco provides memories which you never forget. A bit like Venice. While several committee members had of course been there before, for me it was a very special experience, for which I had carefully, and most uncharacteristically, planned (or at least my Mother had – entirely characteristically – planned for me). My main objective was to get rid of the committee for as long as possible over the weekend since I had family commitments to meet. The California state legislature kindly

---

[*] remote locking had not yet been invented, even in America.

obliged, and took the committee off to an out-of-town country club, where they could play golf, shoot wildfowl and relive their childhood dreams by dressing up as cowboys and Indians.

As soon as the committee were out of the Mark Hopkins, I phoned my cousins. Within a few minutes St George Holden, who lived across the road, arrived to show me the sights. St George (pronounced *Saint* George) arrived not in any old pickup, but in one of Lyndon Johnson's presidential limousines, which he happened to have acquired at auction a few months earlier (he appeared also to have acquired the chauffeur). In the rather cramped rear of this enormous and heavily armoured automobile we settled back to consuming the local family staple of very large tumblers of neat Scotch, and travelled over the Golden Gate and around the Bay while Moira prepared a "traditional Scotch" meal – consisting of an odd mixture of unsalted mince and giant beefalo steaks – in their wood-framed mansion on Filbert Street, just on the other side of the hill.

George was the grandson of my maternal great uncle James Angus, who had emigrated to the States in 1874, became secretary to James Fair (one of California's "silver kings") and built a fortune in real estate, the most valuable having turned out to be the lot of six large houses, with interconnecting gardens, at the top of Nob Hill, which almost uniquely survived the 1906 earthquake and in 1975 remained as the family residences. Moira was from a distant branch of the Kennedy's, but her Irish ancestry and almost aristocratic name did not prevent her being a loyal partisan of the Angus tribe: on her Bechstein was a well-turned copy of the same edition of *Songs of the North* as on the pianos in all the family's households in Britain; and the same sentimental family stories were recycled, albeit with Pacific variations.

The following day George took me on a pilgrimage as important to him as to me, since the separate branches of the Angus diaspora had fallen out over the decades, and few were on terms of civility with their second cousins once or twice-removed. We went first to visit Mary Angus, known to the whole family on the other side of the Atlantic as Mary San Francisco, who had offered to adopt all my older siblings in the worst days of the blitz, and had subsequently showered food parcels on us all until well into the 1950's: the whole chicken canned in jelly (with wonderfully crunchy bones) remains one of those cherished childhood tastes which it would be foolish to try to revisit.* Then to see his cousin Angus (known universally as Bill) who still at an advanced age presided over the family's real estate empire

---

* My next visit to San Francisco followed shortly after Mary San Francisco's death. Her adopted daughter Elspeth offered me an original and extremely rare Japanese print (with a slightly risqué theme) as a memento. This I hid in my luggage for fear of the federal statutes against the export of works of art. It took Christie's only a couple of minutes to identify the picture as an extremely good fake. But it has a place of honour in our downstairs loo.

from the same rolltop desk his grandfather had used in the previous century (and with the same Black Label whisky on offer). Finally we crossed the Bay to meet up with the sprightly remnant of the other side of the Angus family in Castro Valley. Cousin Hal was the grandson of William Angus (brother of James)[*], who had also made a fortune in silver[†]. Hal also happened to be one of the last survivors of the Barnum & Bailey Circus and the Keystone Cops. He was still chasing: well into his eighties he had recently married a knock-out of a young lady who looked about eighteen, and they welcomed me into their rambling timber-framed mansion with copious quantities of iced beer – and Black Label – and much laughter. They already had two children.

The next few days were spent visiting just about everyone who mattered in Silicon Valley, and everywhere receiving the same message: the secret was a combination of ingenuity, at which the British were still pretty adept, together with capitalism, about which the British seemed to have lost the plot. This was music to the ears of the young Tories on the committee, most of whom went on to pursue the free-enterprise agenda as senior members of Margaret Thatcher's administrations; and a message not lost on Labour members already heartily weary of the poor economic performance of their own party in office.

Most of the rest of my time with the Science & Technology Committee was spent taking voluminous evidence and visiting industrial sites around the UK, examining the interstices of gear-grinding machines, magnetically levitated rapid transit trains (in which, again, Britain could have led the world if either the City or the Government had been able to look more than a couple of years ahead at a time), prototypes of what would become the dvd recorder, and prototype nuclear reactors of one kind (gas) or another (heavy water). And we produced some interesting reports as a result.

The committee had by then developed a taste for travel further afield. A number of other committees in that pre-modern era had already managed to

---

[*] My maternal grandfather David Angus was one of their many younger brothers. David declined the opportunities offered in California, and instead, after completing his degree at Edinburgh, became an apprentice lighthouse builder in place of his friend Robert Louis Stevenson (in whose memory my mother Anne, born at the railhead in Valparaiso Chile, received Louis as one of her given names). David then built a career as a latter-day Brunel, prospecting and building railways and harbours in south-west Africa, Brazil, Argentina, Peru and Chile, with his wife, the majority of his thirteen children, their nurse and the cook usually in tow. His memories of his epic crossing of the Andes on a donkey with my eldest aunt Nancy provided another boyhood friend, Conan Doyle, with some of the detail, and much of the atmospherics, of *The Lost World*.

[†] William Angus was unable to enjoy the considerable fruits of his labours since he and his foreman inadvertently stepped into the shaft of their own mine when the lift had already descended to the bottom.

persuade the informal chairmen's Liaison Committee (which distributed the funds) to approve extravagant expenditure on trips to the middle and far east. S & T members were not to be outdone, and during 1976 appointed a sub-committee, containing all the most vociferous, whose admitted purpose was – to put it as simply as possible – long haul travel. They all wanted to visit Japan. In a special report to the House some vaguely plausible reasons were advanced: they had "noted the success" of Japanese industry in "translating the fruits of research into marketable products", and had appointed a sub-committee in order to gain "first-hand knowledge of the situation". At this point, in October 1976, they were extremely miffed that their arrangements (which the Liaison Committee had approved on the back-scratching principle) were scuppered by the whips – not of course on grounds of principle or financial probity, but simply to protect the minority government from the risk of a hijack in the division lobbies.*

I was due to go on this highly questionable trip, but its original timing coincided with the North Atlantic Assembly in Williamsburg and – much more important – my starring role as Lord Arthur Savile with the Imperial Players in Chislehurst. As a result Dr Christopher Ward took over the running of the "Japan" sub-committee, and eventually travelled with them in March 1977, by which time I was too busy in rehearsals for *Tartuffe* to be bothered about one trip or less to Tokyo. The sub-committee met everyone who was anybody in Japanese industry and even "delivered a Message from the Prime Minister", which surely will have greatly enhanced the prospects for British exports. The committee had pushed the boat out a little too far, and their misdemeanour was not forgotten. My own committee travelling days were to be severely limited for the next couple of years. Those of the S & T committee were shortly to be suspended for all of thirteen years.

---

* Most visits away from Westminster in the 1974-79 Parliaments were closely policed by both the Government and the Opposition Whips. It was usually ok to get away so long as you had an entirely reliable 'pair', but when the Whips expected a really close call they were particularly wary: ministerial posts and even peerages were on offer to government backbenchers who reneged on a pairing arrangement. Numerous delegations and committees were recalled to Westminster, sometimes in mid-flight.

15

The Conversion of Enoch

The 1978 Procedure Committee

In the summer of 1977 I returned from 3 Dean's Yard to the Journal Office, to take over the Procedure Committee from Clifford Boulton, who was moving on to higher (and higher) things, eventually becoming one of the longest serving Clerks of the House.

Procedure committees were by that time two-a-penny. In the previous twenty years they had been set up in all but three parliamentary sessions, and had made no less than forty-four separate reports to the House. Only the Government could bring these forward for consideration, since in those days the Government controlled the entire agenda. Many reports had therefore been left in limbo since they didn't meet the wishes of the Executive, irrespective of party. Although there had been some rather wider reviews such as that which led to the establishment of the Expenditure Committee in early 1971, most had addressed relatively minor points about the day-to-day work of the House, since the terms of reference of the annually-appointed committees were usually carefully circumscribed.

The committee appointed in the summer of 1976 was a different sort of animal. It was not at first intended to be a select committee at all, but a rather grander commission of inquiry including captains of industry, trades union leaders (then at the peak of their power) and a raft of specialist advisers from the universities. This original scheme, put forward by the then Leader of the House, Ted Short, was widely ridiculed in a debate in the House in February – as most Members realised, this would have been a device to "keep us quiet for a while", and to delay (with luck indefinitely) any significant changes in the work of Parliament, or of Government. When the committee was finally set up in June his successor, Michael Foot, was one of the great traditionalists to whom the idea of including "outsiders" of any kind was anathema, and giving them votes more or less treasonable.

So the new committee was established on orthodox lines – which in those days meant by the Whips. Although Ted Short had failed in his original scheme, the Whips had no intention of letting the backbenchers take control, and reverted to time-honoured practice and devised alternative ways of emasculating the process. Membership of the new procedure committee was in their gift. They therefore nominated Members of the most widely divergent views in the expectation that there would be little chance of them agreeing anything coherent which could seriously rock the institutional boat.

This resulted in a mix of enthusiastic young men of an academic bent, who could be guaranteed to argue at least until the deluge (Kenneth Baker, George Cunningham, John Garrett, David Marquand, Giles Radice); of more eccentric enthusiasts for causes (Jo Richardson, for the feminist cause, Michael English, an amateur proceduralist of the most dangerous kind,[12] and Nigel Spearing, a charming but obsessive anti-marketeer and pioneer of cycling to work);[13] and a couple of Very Safe Hands – Sir David Renton, who had just completed a monumental, highly influential and largely unread report on the Preparation of Legislation;[14] and on the Labour side Sir William Thomas Williams, an improbable mixture of Baptist minister, highly-paid Queen's Counsel, socialist internationalist, and circuit judge, a man of no particular opinions: he was therefore the natural choice of the Whips for Chairman of the committee.[15]

The coup de grace, from the Whips' point of view, was the appointment of the two representatives from the minority parties. The Liberals inevitably proposed Alan Beith, a former politics lecturer, who had managed to retain Berwick-upon-Tweed after his wafer-thin by-election win in 1973 (and held onto it for the next 42 years) and was firmly of the reformist tendency. But the other appointment was in the gift of the other small parties (the Irish, the Welsh and the Scots); and they opted for the biggest name they could deploy, and one whose reputation as a procedural purist was unchallengeable – namely, the Rt Hon J Enoch Powell, cast into outer darkness by Ted Heath for speaking what he regarded as home truths about immigration, and now Ulster Unionist Member for South Down. The Whips no doubt believed that Enoch's combination of dialectical prowess and social conservatism would provide the crucial block on any over-ambitious plans for procedural change.[16]

The Whips and party managers had made some miscalculations.

The first was that the inclusion of Sir Tom Williams, as chairman, and Sir David Renton, as lead Conservative, would temper any untoward enthusiasms amongst the younger members of the committee. Sir Tom just about held the ring while he was in the chair. But he had no opinions of his own, no inclination to promote the opinions of others, and lacked the skill to lead discussion to any kind of conclusion. He was the most passive of the multitude of chairmen I dealt with over three decades, and left no mark, other than his name, on the report which he famously made to the House in August 1978. Indeed, he was so unengaged that when the report came up for two days of set-piece debate in the House in February 1979 Tom was elsewhere, going about his duties as President of the Inter-Parliamentary Union. He provided no kind of protection against any radicals who had made it into the Procedure Committee. And, as it turned out, he was unwell during March, April and May 1978.

114

During those months the chair passed, in accordance with tradition, to the senior Member from the "other" side, Sir David Renton. David Renton had laboured for several years as chairman of a committee of inquiry tasked by Ted Heath to consider the methods applied to the drafting of legislation, and to seek greater simplicity and clarity in statute law. His report had been published in 1975. But by now Sir David was less than happy that there were few signs of progress towards the implementation of any of his committee's recommendations; he was therefore a trifle disgruntled, and open to suggestions of changes in parliamentary procedure which might achieve some of his objectives by alternative routes.

The Whips' second miscalculation was understandable. Members of select committees – although less openly partisan than on the floor of the House or in the legislative "standing" committees which replicated House procedure – were at that time nonetheless assumed to acknowledge the basic divisions between the parties, and if necessary to dance to their party's drums. The Whips could not have been expected to know that this committee would behave any differently from its predecessors.

The third miscalculation was the assumption that since most of the committee were outspoken characters, each capable of making a great deal of noise, their conflicting opinions could be guaranteed to result in stalemate.

Finally, the belief that select committee reports are fatally weakened if not unanimous was shared by all involved. The Whips' confidence that the involvement of the Rt Hon member for South Down would undermine any prospect of a unanimous report was therefore also misplaced: first because it assumed that Enoch Powell was not open to persuasion from his well-known scepticism about select committees, and second because all other members of the committee were also open to compromise.

When I took over the committee in the summer of 1977 they had already made considerable progress under Clifford Boulton's guidance. Early on they had roughed out the main areas of "procedure and practice" to be examined, and had agreed to concentrate initially on "the process of legislation"; but this could not be considered in isolation, and all issues were already in play.

Prompted by the Study of Parliament Group,[*] the committee turned their attention to the experience of the Canadian House of Commons, which a few years earlier had set up a new system of nineteen "specialist" committees. This seemed to be something like the ideal structure favoured by "the academics": largish committees shadowing each government

---

[*] The SPG had been established a few years earlier by Bernard Crick – regarded as the leader of the academic pack at the time – and Michael Ryle – the leader of the growing band of reformist clerks. The latter wrote the papers in a cloud of anonymity and the former appended their names.

department and doing all the things a parliament should do in relation to the departments' expenditure, administration and policy. It seemed logical, it was a familiar feature of many of the continental parliaments with which British politicians were in increasing contact, and it conformed largely to the model propounded in the politics departments in the expanding university sector. Largely, but not entirely: Crick and some others favoured 'subject' rather than 'departmental' committees – a theological argument which had brought many a postgraduate student to grief but which the Procedure Committee eventually managed, with some brilliance, to resolve (or at least to fudge).

Ottawa was an appropriate analogue as a leading member of the Westminster parliamentary family, and had the great advantage of not being Washington: there was such suspicion of the congressional model (of powerful, over-staffed, law-initiating committees) that most of the committee's witnesses – even those with aspirations in that direction – and the committee itself avoided any open reference to the Capitol although its dire (or welcome) example could be read as a subtext in much of what was said to or by the procedure committee during its three years of activity.

However, the sub-committee sent to Ottawa under Kenneth Baker's chairmanship soon rejected the Canadian model. This locked the Canadian committees into agendas set by the federal Government, compelled them to concentrate on government legislation and expenditure proposals, and denied them the freedom to initiate their own inquiries into administration or policy. Such freedom was the hallmark of the existing "subject" committees in London - on race relations, overseas development, the nationalised industries and science and technology – and even of the umbrella Expenditure Committee and its sub-committees (despite the fact that their orders of reference tied the down in theory to the examination of the Estimates alone). The sub-committee concluded that importing the Canadian system "would almost certainly mean the suffocation of some of our select committees by legislation, and a great diminution in the financial and more general work done by them". They refrained at this stage from mentioning their main concern – that if Westminster's select committees were to have formal responsibility for the committee stage of government bills they would end up under the control of the Whips, and lose their long-established freedom from party control and the freedom to set their own agendas.

The committee's rejection of the Ottawa model paved the way for compromise, since it de-coupled the two most contentious issues before them: the future of the investigative select committee system on the one hand, and the detailed consideration of government legislation on the other. Both reformers and traditionalists could claim some victories. The establishment of an across-the-board system of investigative committees, covering the activities of all government departments, was the holy grail of the reforming party: but the traditionalists could also claim victory, since those new committees were to have, at best, only a consultative role in the system for considering legislation. Accordingly, the detailed, line-by-line consideration of bills in what were then called "standing" committees, actively policed by the party Whips, would continue; but the relief of the traditionalists was such that they were happy to concede the possibility of the legislative committees also taking evidence, at least on an experimental basis.

The solution for the committee stage of bills was to retain the inherited structure of standing committees (which by this time were entirely ad hoc, but largely manned by Members who either knew about the subject or wanted to); to retain the analytical as well as adversarial character of the line-by-line consideration of the text; but to allow some of these committees also to take oral and written evidence for a limited period before engaging in traditional inter-party hostilities. Careful to avoid any whiff of revolutionary cordite, the Procedure Committee proposed these new "public bill committees" as an experimental option, although hoping that "before long" they would become the norm. Members of all persuasions were not unduly optimistic about the prospects for their new scheme: they either expected or privately hoped for its outright rejection by the Government, or they expected that if approved it would languish, largely unused, in the standing orders of the House like earlier tokens of reform. None therefore would have been particularly surprised that the provision for "special standing committees", as they were initially described in standing orders, was rarely invoked more than a couple of times each session for the next twenty years, nor that when they became the norm (with their original title) more than three decades later, they did so only as part of a package which permanently deprived the committees – and, more importantly, the House – of their most important power, the power of delay.

The final deal about select committees – specialist, departmental, subject, or whatever – had to wait a while. At my first meeting with the committee in September 1977, at the end of the traditionally lengthy summer recess (a tradition no longer, alas), Members were so concerned about the prospect of an imminent General Election* that they informally agreed a draft report on the handling of public bills which could be rushed through if there was no time to regroup for more than a few minutes before dissolution.

The 1977 General Election did not of course happen. So in the new session the Procedure Committee got down to the business of establishing

---

* not unreasonably, of course. Jim Callaghan's decision to hang on in the autumn of 1977 with his rapidly vanishing plurality was regarded by some as risky; his decision to hang on once again in autumn 1978 was universally regarded as suicidal – which it proved to be.

what the new select committees might look like, and clarifying what exactly they would do, or at least be free to do, having already decided that the committees would certainly not be part of the formal legislative process. Largely to assure injured parties that they had been fully consulted, we spent the autumn of 1977 taking formal evidence from the chairmen and clerks of the main run of existing select committees. This was done in private (although later published) in order to allow the proceduralists to test their tentative conclusions without provoking a raft of premature speculation in the newspapers. Inevitably, the chairmen of the Nationalised Industries Committee and the Science & Technology Committee in particular were not prepared to countenance their abolition without a fight, and the hearings provided a fascinating seminar on what the difference between the existing "subject" and the likely-to-be-proposed "departmental" committees would mean in practice: it would have been an educative experience for the political scientists to witness their theoretical arguments rehearsed in real time by people who actually did the job.[*] These hearings demonstrated that the choices the committee were making were not cut-and-dried, and that no solution would really be able to provide the kind of perfect "coverage" of government activities or policies to which most by now aspired.

The solution was the replacement of most of the existing committees by twelve new committees "each charged with the examination of all aspects of expenditure, administration and policy in a field of administration within the responsibilities of a single government department or two or more related departments", but also free to examine matters for which the relevant department had a "leading, but not exclusive" responsibility. This convoluted definition was designed to meet the objections of those who disliked the rigidity of the boundaries between government departments, which were "to some extent artificial", and were liable to change, "sometimes with alarming frequency". The new bodies were not to be "subject" committees, but nor were they simply "departmental". When they were eventually established they were described as "departmentally related", although "departmental" in common parlance. It was to be some

---

[*] I was aware of some sense of grievance in the academic community that the Procedure Committee had not only been set up without Ted Short's "outsider" members, but had also made no use of their power to appoint specialist advisers (who would of course have been the political scientists), since Members of Parliament regarded themselves as the only true experts on parliamentary procedure and practice. As a result the academics were rather less welcoming of the Committee's Report than either the House or the newspapers, and some remained highly critical of the new system for a while, only grudgingly accepting as the years went by that it was more or less what they had wanted, and that the new committees were more or less doing what they had hoped - and, of course, taking full advantage of the fact that the new committees soon had plenty of opportunities for specialist advisers of their own.

years before the inadequacy of this largely departmental model to deal with some issues which were genuinely cross-departmental was recognised. The Science & Technology Committee was finally resurrected in 1992. Paradoxically, in its latest incarnation this paradigm of the "subject" committee is now fully departmentally-related, the Government having caught up with the need for ministers with an inter-disciplinary brief.

Having reached something approaching unanimity on their two central proposals the Procedure Committee knew that they would have to do a lot of persuading of others to overcome the sometimes furious sectional opposition which arose. And they still had other reformist aspirations to address. So from December 1977 to March 1978 we embarked on the committee's second great epic. The committee met for about three hours on thirteen consecutive Monday evenings (a total of forty hours deliberation in all) – not considering a draft report, as might have been expected by this time, but instead mulling over the issues yet again, following a similar marathon in the previous winter and spring. I was authorised to begin the drafting process, but only on matters where decisions had provisionally been made, and some semblance of agreement might be expected. Other matters – including major issues such as the procedure for considering delegated legislation and European legislation, the scrutiny and control of public expenditure, and the hours of sitting of the House – were painstakingly debated, hour by hour, while I kept notes. The theory was that as issues were resolved (or at least had been exhausted) they were removed from the running agenda and added to the running minute, on the basis of which I was authorised to base my draft. In practice just about every topic re-emerged at just about every meeting, so I had no choice but to plough on and write my own report, in the hope that some of it would eventually find favour.

One central issue remained. The committee had debated at great length the many proposals from ministers, academics, and even some misguided backbenchers, which could have resulted in the routine and mandatory timetabling of legislation. Enoch, and other wiser members of the committee, realised that delay was just about the only weapon left to Parliament against the accumulated power of the Executive. Although a Government with a sound majority could normally enforce the closure of debate, or establish a guillotine, both (and especially the latter) were wildly unpopular in the House and in the country, and a government dependent on the guillotine always got a bad press. Timetabling, it was rightly feared, would allow any government, however slim its majority, to get its legislation through on time and, if it chose, without too much debate. Having made many concessions, Enoch made clear in early 1978 that if the committee were to approve timetabling, even on an experimental basis, his conversion to the new select committee system would after all be short-lived, and he would be compelled to vote against the whole package. He

119

would have undoubtedly brought others with him, unanimity would have been lost, and the prospect of achieving anything at all in the reform programme would have gone for yet another generation.

The issue of timetabling went right to the heart of the underlying debate about what, exactly, a parliament – or at any rate the British parliament – was there to do: a debate which had certainly been in full swing since the mid-nineteenth century. Walter Bagehot (as interpreted by Richard Crossman in the 1960's) had characterised the House of Commons as little more than an electoral college, in which case the resultant Government which emerged from the college had a "right" to govern and to get its legislation through, a doctrine espoused with humourless dogmatism by Ted Short when he proposed the committee in February 1976. For those in Government (including most civil servants), or those who aspire to join or return to Government, the promise of guaranteed out-dates for their legislative proposals has a natural attraction, of immediate practical importance, and their promotion of timetabling was understandable. For impartial academics the espousal of such a system was less excusable, but had nonetheless understandable causes: first, their immersion in Bagehot during their impressionable undergraduate days; and second, their professional desire (as social "scientists") to impose order on an essentially disorderly form of human behaviour.

The concern for efficiency and order is, however, in perpetual conflict with a reality of which the electorate at least seems at least half-aware: that we elect parliaments not only to legislate on our behalf but also on our behalf not to legislate. The English parliament is, historically, not primarily a legislative machine – as well may be assemblies born elsewhere out of revolution - but a mechanism to constrain the aspirations of those who wish to legislate – and spend our money - in order to control our lives and limit our freedoms. In different ages the conflict between rulers and governed has been manifest in different forms. As the academics themselves so often remind us, elections in "democratic" Britain are usually lost, not won.

The Study of Parliament Group had magisterially opined, on no particular evidence, that "Members themselves are more interested in policy than in scrutiny of administration". Echoing Bagehot and Crossman, Bernard Crick had also concluded that "Parliament's function is not primarily to legislate, but is rather to provide a recruiting and a testing ground for Cabinet timber, and then both to sustain and to criticise a particular Cabinet". Under normal circumstances, these dismissive academic conclusions were beguilingly simple and apparently obvious. It is only too easy to observe institutions as they perform from day to day and as a result to overlook their latent powers. The problem for "Members themselves" was, of course, that if you are told often enough that the institution you serve has a merely decorative role, and is in any case largely failing in its functions from day to day, you also may end up believing this nonsense, forget that you do have powers which derive directly from the electorate, and behave accordingly. This is what eventually happened in 1997. But not in 1978.*

The Procedure Committee's achievement in not supporting the routine timetabling of legislation was due largely to Enoch's principled stand during the Committee's many months of deliberation. From this flowed a reluctance on the part of the saner or even merely the more calculating reformers to put the entire project at risk. Some had been tempted to embrace the policy as a potential bribe to encourage the front benches to accept their proposals concerning legislative and investigative committees. But the key frontbencher at the crucial time came to their rescue: Michael Foot continued when Leader of the House to hold views diametrically opposed to that of his predecessors, previous Chief Whips, and the current leaders, of both main parties. In a memorandum to the committee in early 1977 Michael Foot, while for form's sake conceding the advantages to governments of general timetabling, nailed his colours firmly to the parliamentary mast. Timetabling, he wrote (one can imagine his officials drafting this through gritted teeth), "would blunt the Opposition's main weapon against the Government – delay – and curtail the activities of backbenchers, whose prolonged and even quirkish delaying tactics can sometimes serve a valuable parliamentary function."

Whatever the pressures from other quarters, most of those on the committee who had started out in favour of timetabling realised that it was for the time being no longer any kind of bargaining counter, and that recommending it would simply discredit the report in the eyes of the one man who happened to matter at the time. As a result, support waned, and when it came to a formal vote in July only four diehards were prepared publicly to support it. Indeed, the majority went further, recommending new restrictions on "allocation of time" motions in order to constrain the Government's freedom to employ the hated guillotine at short notice. The whole idea of the orderly management of the legislative programme of course lingered on, to re-emerge a couple of decades later as the flagship "reform" proposal of New Labour.

But there now arose the prospect of a unanimous report to the House. At the end of March 1978, I produced a draft of a draft report to the House. "Informal consideration" of a draft report was by no means unique (and is now the norm); but for this stage in the proceedings to occupy a further eleven meetings (about thirty-five hours in all) was somewhat extravagant.

---

* Nor, of course, in 2019, when for a few months the Whips lost control and the House indulged in a brief (but perhaps not altogether successful) experiment with *gouvernement de l'assemblée*.

Throughout March, April and May 1978 the process of consensus-building was aided by the absence of the chairman. Although nobody wished ill of Sir Tom Williams, his unengaged demeanour as passive chairman of a standing committee or chairman of the bench, with no particular views of his own, undoubtedly fitted the aspirations of the Whips to de-rail any changes beyond the cosmetic. In accordance with tradition, the chairman's functions were taken over by the ranking Conservative opposition member, Sir David Renton. For twelve happy weeks he galvanised the committee, restored their self-confidence, and banged their heads together. By the time Tom Williams returned at the beginning of June most of the real decisions had been taken, including the vital decisions about what issues would have to be put to the vote – for the public record - even if the conclusions were by then agreed.

We got down to the hard grind of voting on the final "chairman's" draft report on 12th and 17th July 1978. Despite the deals done in the twenty-four long meetings which had gone before, they still needed a further thirteen-and-a-half hours before they delivered a unanimous report to the House (most of us feared it might take even longer). The process set a number of precedents and records. So many formal amendments (373 in all) were tabled that, almost certainly for the first time, a marshalled list of amendments was printed and circulated in advance[*]. There were forty-four formal divisions. Most of these were merely a means of putting on the record the relative strength of opinion in the committee on all the key issues considered in the previous two years.

The proceedings were so complex – involving on at least one occasion amendments to amendments to amendments – that new minuting conventions (avoiding the regular reiteration of the draft texts) had to be invented, in defiance of the Clerks at the Table who so zealously guarded our traditions, since otherwise the minutes of proceedings would have occupied more space than the finished report, and publication would have been delayed into the depths of the summer recess.[†]

---

[*] The Chairman's copy was "marked up" in exactly the same way as the amendment papers for public bills in committee (indicating how amendments might be "grouped" for discussion) which provided a familiar framework for Sir Tom, but also with rubrics advising "reject" or "accept", the latter mainly because he was largely unfamiliar with the arguments which had been so extensively ventilated during his helpful absence from the scene of battle.

[†] Writing the minutes in long-hand was an exceedingly laborious process, requiring absolute accuracy but on this occasion at very high speed. At least for once the printers were able to read the text, since I had been joined at this point by the young, but already heavily bearded and balding, Robert Rogers, who worked with me overnight for several nights, and whose immaculate copperplate was a joy to the compositors and obviated the need for anything other than a desultory scan of the galley proofs.

16

Norman pulls it off

Establishment of the departmentally-related committees, and associated manoeuvres

Thanks to heroic efforts by the parliamentary printers (and copious amounts of overtime – generously paid in their case, not paid at all in ours) the report – with surprisingly few of the typographic glitches endemic in those *Grauniad* days - was delivered to the House and the world on the day the Commons rose on 3rd August 1978.[17] To my delight, HMSO reported queues at those of their shops which still existed (although sadly no longer) in the major cities of the realm; even my own Dad, to my genuine amazement, was on the No 3 bus with the commuters to get down to Bristol's Wine Street ahead of opening time: it was almost like a re-run of the Denning Report.

The timing of publication was accidental, but it couldn't have been better. As Parliament had gone into recess there was no opportunity for the immediate public clash of parties which could have locked the committee's proposals exclusively into one or other party's programme. They had to wait awhile before anything could be said on the floor of the House. And they were thus able, indeed compelled, to engage instead with public opinion: which was expressed on this occasion (in the days before twitter, or even e-mails) by the overwhelming support of the print media. One or two tabloids unsurprisingly and excitedly picked up on the tentative suggestion that "consideration should be given to the payment of a modest additional salary to the chairmen of select committees", and on the failure of Jo Richardson and Giles Radice to secure earlier sittings of the House,* but the broadsheets (as they then were) were unanimous in their support. It would, said the *Times*, "prove to be a historic document in parliamentary history"; the *FT* thought that the House of Commons would "never be quite the same again"; the *Guardian* concluded that the Commons could "begin to claw back the authority it has steadily surrendered to the Executive over the years", but warned that the report provided "an agenda for the century": it couldn't all happen in one go. And all believed that it was up to the backbenchers of all

---

* both of which proposals came to fruition a few decades later. At the formal consideration stage, the Procedure Committee had devoted more time to the last section (on 'Organisation of Sessions and Sittings') than to any other part of the draft Report, agreed innumerable amendments after lengthy discussion, voted on twenty others, and formally divided fifteen times.

parties whether the opportunity was grasped: the *Economist* correctly advised that "there is no reason to suppose that the Tory Whips will be any more enlightened [than their predecessors]. It will be up to backbench MPs on both sides to force the changes through. That'll be the day."

The latter advice was of course entirely right; and over time they did. The serious media had recognised that buried in the report was something a little bit revolutionary, but the committee's concern was that at all costs it should be presented as a package of merely evolutionary measures, building on the existing procedures of the House, and fitting comfortably into the familiar agenda of the academic and parliamentary reformers. It was designed not to alert the fainthearted. Members of the Procedure Committee (and I) were ourselves alarmed by the extent to which our public relations exercise had succeeded, and generally hoped for a period of quiet before we had to stand up and defend what we had done.

Although there was a blessedly long interval before the House returned, there was also the complication that it was generally expected never to return at all. A General Election had appeared to be a distinct possibility in the summer of 1977; in 1978 it appeared to be an absolute certainty. This made some of us a trifle pessimistic: after an Election a new Government, upon whose goodwill everything would ultimately depend, would be likely to have a working majority, and would have neither obligation nor incentive to do anything about the report of a committee in the previous parliament, and would be delighted to be free of any responsibility for the rash initiatives of its predecessors.

However, if an election were now to take place the parties did need to have something new to offer the electorate. Despite their acrimonious recent history the main parties' platforms were in practice already getting closer and closer together, particularly in respect of economic policy, where the main difference appeared to be whether to introduce monetarism by the front door, with a great fanfare à la Keith Joseph, or quietly through the back door, as already in progress under the auspices of Jim Callaghan's Chancellor of the Exchequer Denis Healey: do you say publicly that high unemployment is the discipline the country needs, or do you quietly allow it to happen for the good of the country? In many other important areas – the NHS, the European Community, incomes policy, even the control of the trades unions – both parties were so divided that their leaderships were generally required to fudge.

The Tories were the first to jump on board. Convinced by the barrage of media support for the committee's report, the then Shadow Leader of the House Francis Pym announced his personal support for the main proposals in a speech in the West Country only a few days after publication, and by the early autumn made implementation of the report a Conservative manifesto commitment. The other parties soon followed suit, although Labour's rather cautious endorsement reflected the natural reluctance of the party in government to be hamstrung by a resurgent parliament, as well as the deep-seated scepticism of the then Lord President of the Council.

In the months following yet another autumn General Election which didn't happen, the Procedure Committee made a brief attempt to concentrate on the one remaining matter of importance – financial control – over which they had lightly skated in their main report, largely regurgitating earlier reports of the Expenditure Committee and the Public Accounts Committee. But only one committee member, John Garrett, had any real enthusiasm for unravelling the complex world of financial control. A management consultant by profession, scion of Inbucon, and former adviser to the Fulton Committee on the Civil Service (which reported in 1968), Dr Garrett campaigned assiduously for the transfer of control over the national audit service from HM Treasury to the House of Commons. The National Audit Act 1983 (which eventually achieved that objective) contributed much to the progressive weakening of the Government's control over the supply of information, and hence to Parliament's ability (and in particular the ability of the new select committees) to hold the Government to account on the basis of hard facts, rather than rumour and rhetoric.

But the rest of the Procedure Committee were frankly relieved that the baton would now be passing on to others. It was not that they didn't believe in this particular cause, but simply that they were honest amongst themselves that they had little expertise in the subject, and were maybe a little exhausted by their hundreds of hours of procedural debate. Their sights remained set on the single objective of getting the main thrust of their hard-fought report at least debated and maybe parts of it even implemented. All of which would be quite sufficient an uphill struggle against the Whips, and against Michael Foot. So they talked about financial procedure, and even managed to take some evidence from the Treasury, but they weren't really interested.

Meanwhile, the matter of procedural reform was getting closer to the top of the parties' agendas, and became a regular, even tedious, feature at Lord President's and Prime Minister's Questions (which in those days happened twice a week, not once). Finally in February 1979 the Opposition offered up one of their "Supply" days to ensure a full two-day debate, which together with added government time occupied almost fourteen hours on the floor of the House.

It is no accident that those who fought hardest to resist the development of select committees were Parliament's two last great rhetoricians, Enoch Powell and Michael Foot, and no surprise that they saw eye to eye on some other matters also (not least on matters European). Sixth formers of my own generation in the early 1960's still studied Latin, but rarely any longer Greek; and they still learned a great deal of poetry by rote. But their successors in the next decades apparently studied less of either; progressively, those entering the political profession were losing touch with the powerful linguistic tools which were part of the parliamentary inheritance. And there was a technological element at work: the introduction first of radio, and soon after of television, exposed the fragility as well as the power of the rhetorical device and eventually discouraged those who sought to maintain it in the glare of the cameras. Great speeches were still widely applauded, but impassioned debate was losing its central role in the work of parliament.

So, following the conversion of Enoch in the committee, the debate in February 1979 represented the capitulation of his friend Michael Foot – not so much to the Procedure Committee's specific proposals as to the will of the House. At a quarter to Five on the second day of debate, the Lord President was still arguing against virtually all comers that it would be "a great error" if the proposed departmentally-related committees were to be established, and that in any case the whole matter should be left to the next Parliament, which would have to live with the consequences. By ten to Ten Michael Foot had agreed that there should be "immediate discussions through the usual channels as to how we should proceed", the House having spoken with an almost united voice, although personally he would fight on for what he believed. A characteristically teasing peroration expressed his confidence that "this House of Commons, in all its majesty and its greatness, may even be able to cope with the deficiencies of this latest report on procedure, along with all the other triumphs that we can record in our parliamentary history."[18]

Nobody in the House was fool enough to think that, amidst all their other survival strategies, any of this was going to be near the top of the agenda for Jim Callaghan's beleaguered Cabinet, nor believed for a moment that Michael Foot was wrong in thinking that decisions would in practice have to be left until after a General Election.[*] Consignment to the usual channels meant an uncertain future, and no safe passage. But the Leader of the House was up against a formidable challenger in the new shadow Leader, Norman St John-Stevas. He also knew – as many of his own backbenchers were not slow to remind him during the debate – that a substantial army of Labour MPs had on this issue defected to the other side. With a government majority of one (and falling) this would inevitably give even the most partisan Lord President reason to engage with the Opposition.

Michael Foot had in any case suggested that he was also "happy to have discussions through unusual channels". This was sufficient encouragement

---

[*] Michael Foot obviously didn't have much confidence in his and his party's prospects for the coming months, for he also said at the end of his speech that "it may well be that the House will want a different Leader of the House to carry into effect such proposals. It may be from the Back Benches that I shall be making any criticisms that I may further have to make". Evidently he also did not then anticipate that within a year or so he would not be on the back benches, but attempting to lead the Opposition from the front.

for the Procedure Committee to regroup, and to devise a strategy for moving matters on from debate to some sort of decision. Within a few days of the February debate the committee had reconvened, and a few days later – driven on by the enthusiasm of Kenneth Baker and Michael English in particular - had published a special report which addressed the most reasonable objection of their detractors – that seventy-six separate recommendations were frankly too much for the House to cope with in one gulp. It also addressed Michael Foot's objection to final decisions being taken in the current Parliament. The special report therefore identified two key groups of proposals (those relating to select committees, and those relating to legislative committees) and proposed a further two day debate when what amounted to declaratory motions should be debated, open to amendment, and then approved, in each case stating that it would be "desirable" that the necessary new standing orders should be made "as early as possible" in the next Parliament. When no immediate response was forthcoming from the front benches, the committee met again on 26 March 1979 for a final attack on the establishment, declaring – driven to almost revolutionary posturing by the young Alan Beith - that they would conduct no further business, and would not meet again, until a date was set for the House to vote on their recommendations.

This mild outbreak of petulance from the committee became wholly irrelevant two days later when the minority Labour Government at last fell, by a single vote[*], following the defeat (on points) of the referendum on Scottish devolution, the Scot Nats having understandably withdrawn their support from the Labour Government which had so badly let them down.

Margaret Thatcher's electoral success on 3rd May was anticipated, but the scale of her victory presented an immediate challenge to the survivors of the Procedure Committee and their reformist supporters. They had got used to working in an environment where the government's hold on the House was so tenuous that backbenchers, and particularly government backbenchers, had to be listened to. A government with a safe working majority (at this stage only 43 – not enormous, but entirely comfortable) would be a different matter. Within a few weeks new Ministers would have settled in and been exposed to the baleful advice of their permanent secretaries, and the new government Whips would already be working hard to extend the tentacles of the patronage system. There could thereafter be no guarantee that the backbench alliance would hold together. If anything was to be achieved it had to be achieved as soon as the Commons

---

[*] For the Clerks at the Table in their wigs, and for we in the Journal Office upstairs, this was a day of high drama, when every record back to the sixteenth century was re-examined to ensure that the dreadful Mr Speaker Thomas was given the right advice about how to cast his vote in the event of a tie, and wouldn't go off at a tangent. Fortunately he was deprived (by one vote) of that delicious opportunity.

reassembled.

The Queen's Speech at the State Opening of Parliament on 15th May 1979 included the routine assurance that Members would be "given an opportunity to discuss and amend their procedures". This could mean all or nothing. By this time, however, just about every surviving member of what was by then the former[*] select committee on procedure had come to see me in the Journal Office or accosted me in the corridors or the Tea Room to discuss what they should or could do next. By the time of the State Opening the terms of an Early Day Motion had been drafted, and the text signed by the main players. In accordance with time-honoured parliamentary *politesse*, the EDM merely called on the Leader of the House to ensure that the House would have "an early opportunity" to decide on the key proposals identified in the Procedure Committee's final special report. The substance of the motion was of small importance; the number who signed up to it would be critical. There accordingly followed a great deal of running around the corridors by former committee members and, to the horror of many of his colleagues, by the former clerk of the former committee; and within a few days of the State Opening the EDM had been signed by well over half the backbench members of the House – a record at the time.[19]

Names on an EDM look impressive; votes in the division lobby are rather more effective; but votes in Cabinet even more so. So however heroic and successful our efforts to sign up the House, the eventual laurels were rightly accorded to the new Chancellor of the Duchy.[20]

That Norman St John-Stevas, a former Ted Heath loyalist, had survived so long in Margaret Thatcher's opposition team was remarkable, and that he served as Leader of the House on her behalf for the first two years of her Government was little short of miraculous. Erudite, cultured, devout, Catholic, homosexual, as well as gay and irreverent, he was the complete antithesis of the philistine world in which she moved and from which she came, and he didn't even have the slight advantage of an aristocratic background and an inherited title. His main contribution in Cabinet appears, from the remarks of his contemporaries, to have been to lighten the mood, even if (or perhaps because) his ever-serious leader could never quite get the point of the joke. He was probably there because every court needs a court jester, and Quintin Hogg, reinstated as an increasingly disputatious Lord Chancellor, was well past performing that function with any kind of conviction.

The very many apocryphal stories about Norman are all almost certainly true or true-ish. A few years later, when he had been relegated to the back benches on grounds of wetness, and I got to know him a little better as an effective member of the Foreign Affairs Committee, he rather relished the

---

[*] The Committee, having been appointed under standing orders 'until the end of this Parliament', had like all others expired when the Parliament was dissolved.

tales of transporting his Cabinet papers to and from work in a Sainsbury's carrier bag, and even claimed that he really had on one occasion left them on the bus. Indeed, I was at one stage fairly convinced that at least one leak of papers from the Foreign Affairs Committee was attributable to his studied forgetfulness – although leaks from select committees (even those with theoretical access to in any case drastically laundered classified papers) for the most part merely upset the procedural purists, and certainly posed no threat to the country. I suspect that was also true of Cabinet papers, which these days seem to be leaked to all and sundry as a matter of routine, or even of policy.

The right honourable member for Chelmsford may have seemed to trip the light fantastic, but he also had a certain amount of steel. Having eloquently led the assault on Michael Foot in February, and forced his capitulation, he was unlikely to let the issue die, particularly as Margaret had provided a window of opportunity. And he, like the former Procedure Committee, knew that the window would soon close. In a fascinating chat in a hotel lounge in Rome in May 1984[*] he told me that he had had to act at once or not at all. Accordingly, implementation of the Procedure Committee's proposals – a manifesto commitment, and what could be interpreted in bright light as a Queen's Speech commitment – was on the agenda of the first regular Cabinet after the Election.

The speed at which the new Leader of the House proceeded was quite exceptional. The new Parliament only got down to business on 15th May 1979. After almost continuous negotiations between parties, whips, alarmed new Ministers and their permanent secretaries, and clerks, and innumerable draft texts, on 25th June, only six weeks later, motions to abolish the Expenditure Committee, the Nationalised Industries Committee, and the Science & Technology Committee were all agreed (after fierce argument and divisions), and the new structure of "departmentally-related" committees had replaced them. The House argued and voted (in ten separate divisions) for eleven hours, but by half-past two on the morning of Tuesday 26th June 1979 the key elements of the package were in Standing Orders and have remained there ever since.

As a result of the enormous over-subscription of members to join the

---

[*] The FAC had spent much of the previous day as guests of the charismatic Foreign Minister, Giulio Andreotti, for lunch and everything else in Mussolini's magnificent suite in what had been designed as the Fascist Party headquarters but had ended up as the post-war Foreign Ministry. That evening members of the Committee were appropriately entertained while overnight I drafted in longhand a report on the European Council meeting due to be held at Fontainebleau, since time was pressing. The following morning the committee assembled in the hotel lounge, and I read the entire draft report to them, to the bemusement of the waiters. With a few uncontentious amendments, the draft was approved and reported to the House at a regular meeting of the committee on our return.

new committees and, more significantly, the collective determination of the whips still to keep control of the whole system, the members weren't nominated (under the new rules) until exactly five months later. But by mid-December 1979 the new and "experimental" committee system could get under way.

Only a handful of the 1978 Procedure Committee's 76 recommendations were implemented in the heady summer of 1979. But, as the *Guardian* had suggested, this was an agenda for the century. When I took stock forty years later all but thirteen of the recommendations had been implemented. Most of these were either one of Michael English's lunacies[21], proposing new standing orders for the consideration of statutory instruments and European legislation, which were perfectly drafted (I was inordinately proud of them) but entirely unworkable. The only recommendations of any significance which still remained (and remain) on the drawing board concerned the power of committees to order (rather than request) the attendance of Ministers to give evidence, and the production of papers and records by them as required by a committee, and to force a debate on the floor of the House if Ministers failed to comply. The Procedure Committee, with the assistance of an authoritative memorandum drafted in the very late watches of the night, with the assistance of copious supplies of Senior Service, by the then Clerk of the House Sir Richard Barlas, had established that although the House (and its committees) could in theory order the production of papers by a Minister of the Crown (as by anybody else) they could not do so in the case of papers in the possession of the Privy Council or any Secretary of State. It was almost certainly for this reason that most "Ministers" had, over the previous decades, been rebranded as "Secretaries of State". If these constitutional conventions were overturned it might – at least at times of a minority government – have opened all government papers to possible parliamentary perusal. Not surprisingly, the proposals have been staunchly resisted; although the government later rendered itself open to much the same kind of intrusion as a result of the Freedom of Information Act 2000 – and under those wretched provisions it isn't just Parliament which has the right to intrude, but anyone else and especially members of the Fourth Estate, with disastrous consequences for government, parliament, and for that very freedom of speech which the media claim so highly to prize.

For the rest of it, a long grinding effort by the new committeemen was needed before the full scheme could come to fruition. But in the end it did.

V St Stephen's

17

Finding a home

new staff and new offices – in buildings long condemned

The Procedure Committee were probably more conscious of the resource implications of their proposals than anyone else in the House. They had deliberately limited the number of committees, and the size of the committees, to ensure that in their first embodiment they would require the services of only a handful more Members than the committees they were to replace: this was largely a tactical concession to their opponents, although they confidently asserted that "a number of additional Members" would offer their services[*]. They had also pitched the proposed staffing requirements as low as possible: they knew that in the long run the committees would be unable to "undertake the full range of tasks proposed for them without rather more permanent staff resources than those at present available", but for the time being each committee should merely have "at least one Clerk, one executive or clerical officer, and one secretary".

So limited was the size of the Clerk of the House Department at that time that even this very modest requirement would involve "a significant increase in the ratio of executive and clerical staff to clerks: arrangements to recruit the necessary additional staff should be set in hand immediately". In practice, while some non-graduate staff were recruited fairly rapidly, the only solution available, without reducing the high threshold demanded of direct graduate entrants, was to continue and expand the practice of recruiting mid-career and usually disenchanted civil servants (on a strictly one-way ticket) as committee clerks, ignorant though they might be of procedure and suspect though their true loyalties might seem to the rest of us. They were affectionately known in the trade as "re-treads", a title of which they became touchingly proud.

As all directly involved knew, the new committees were likely to require *far* more staff than the Procedure Committee had suggested if they were to do the full range of jobs proposed for them. There was the particularly vexed question of how an entirely lay staff – however well qualified in the great generalist tradition – was to cope with the mass of technical papers which began to wing their way towards them. It was one thing for an erudite

---

[*] they turned out to be more than right: almost every backbencher immediately put in bids to the Committee of Selection for membership of one or (in most cases) more of the new committees.

Wykehamist, with the assistance of academics recruited as part-time advisers, to master the core issues involved in the stand-alone inquiries which had characterised the work of the old committees. Much more difficult was for him to stay on top of, let alone get inside, the scores of issues now presented to him every week in the form of white papers, green papers, annual reports and the outpourings of the Commission in Brussels and the Parliament in Strasbourg – all of which fell within his allotted "departmental" remit.

Within a few months of the start of operations a partial solution was found when the newly-established House of Commons Commission authorised the recruitment by the committees themselves of a small number of young graduates and postgraduates as specialist "assistants". They were expected to be in the very early stages of their careers[*], and could be appointed for only three years. For us, the attraction was to have young and keen devillers without an interest group tail already behind them who could be expected to put their backs into the genuinely hard slog of reading and manhandling all the paper[†]. From the assistants' point of view it was an enviable career break, with access to much government information not easily discovered elsewhere, the development of working and social contacts with members of parliament and - perhaps more important - with decision-makers in the government system, and an almost unique entry on their cv's. Almost all the specialist assistants I recruited or encountered in those early days moved seamlessly into jobs at least a few steps above their starting lines in industry, business, the universities or the rest of the public service, including prestigious semi-independent bodies like the Bank of England (who took the prettier ones).

Most of the assistants at this early stage were economists (since committees were desperately worried about their public expenditure remit), but often economists with a specialism: thus my first committee soon had on board a young transport economist who subsequently flew high in the world of academe. The new staffing facility meant that within a fairly short time after the establishment of the committees some at least had acquired young men and occasionally women capable of demanding real answers from the departments, and also with sufficient learning to question, and caution us against, the particular foibles and hobby-horses of the specialist "advisers" – the great and the good from the professorial ranks who were queuing up to bring their influence to bear on the tyro committees.

I cannot recall who invented the specialist "assistants", but it was an

---

[*] There was a maximum age limit of, I think I recall correctly, thirty; such an ageist job description would today probably pretty smartly land the originator in the police courts, if not the ECHR in Strasbourg.
[†] Before the internet that really did mean small mountains of paper documents on every surface and over all available floor space.

inspirational move. The Procedure Committee had said that specialists should be "on tap" but not "on top". This way they were certainly on hand, but their regular rotation ensured that they were unable to take charge: the select committees were to remain under lay control, working for lay members. Three decades later, in November 2002, following reports from the Procedure Committee, the Liaison Committee and the so-called Modernisation Committee, the Commission approved the establishment of a free-standing "Scrutiny Unit" to provide targeted assistance for committees handling financial and legislative matters; a development which I (by then an aging luddite) strenuously opposed as threatening the independence of the committees but which within months had become an invaluable asset for the whole committee operation.

To work effectively all these new staff were going to need offices in which to work. The accommodation available to the committee service was then limited to the "main" Committee Office, situated at the north end of the Committee Corridor in the Palace of Westminster and occupying space once intended for yet another committee meeting room. This contained both a grand fireplace (as did the larger committee rooms along the corridor) and a carefully camouflaged escape hatch into the Speaker's House in case of fire: the occupants of the main Committee Office were not infrequently tempted to charge through the partition wall just to check that the escape arrangements were in working order. Which was not wholly irrational, since disaster of some kind occasionally loomed, as when the upper level of the room (which had been added to double the available space for staff) began to heave and strain during an office party, and had to be evacuated in short order, the most senior staff of course being the first to abandon the sinking floor.

In addition to the Committee Office proper in the Palace of Westminster, there was a limited amount of space in No 46 of blessed memory, but this was now largely occupied by the select committee on European Secondary Legislation &c (whose future and status were unaffected by the new proposals) and others involved in unclerkly activities relating to the European assemblies (as well as the emergency press in the basement). Finally, we still had one floor of No 3 Dean's Yard, where S&T, Nationalised Industries and other condemned committees were winding down their affairs, accompanied by the glorious sounds of the choristers next door.

It was not always appreciated that if the need for additional accommodation and additional staff had not been immediately addressed the 1979 committees, if they had got off the ground at all, would never have developed from their original fledgling state to the remarkably effective instruments for the torture of the Executive into which they gradually developed. Fortunately, the Procedure Committee Report was not the only fruit of the almost-hung Parliament of October 1974. Shortly after the committee reported, the House on 20th July 1978 quietly approved the House of Commons (Administration) Act, following a report chaired by Mr Arthur Bottomley[*]. This swept away the extraordinary Act of 1812, which had entrusted the governance of the House of Commons as legislature to all the Secretaries of State, chaired by the Chancellor of the Exchequer, and therefore wholly under the control of the Executive (so much for the separation of powers). The 1812 Commission was replaced in 1979 by a new House of Commons Commission, which entrusted responsibility for the main House services into the hands of a statutory body which was not only not controlled by the Executive but in which, almost uniquely for a parliamentary body, the Government had no majority.

This was much more of a revolution than the evolutionary changes which the Procedure Committee had devised, and its long-term effect was to provide the elected parliament as an institution with a degree of independence from the Executive. Just as the new Tory government got into ritual staff-cutting mode,[†] the House found itself free to expand. As a result the "balance of advantage" really did begin to shift, at least in terms of expertise and manpower, in Parliament's favour. In 1977, seven committees and seventeen sub-committees were serviced by a mere forty-five staff, of all ranks; when I last did a head count, as long ago as 2006, the House of Commons Commission, effectively free from Treasury control, was able to deploy more than two hundred to support their successors. A similar expansion took place in the Library – and, most inauspiciously, the old Fees Office (which had traditionally comprised a handful of amiable accountants and their young ladies) rapidly rebranded itself as the Finance & Administration Department and spawned its own "human resources" empire. All this of course fundamentally altered the character of the House service. In a relatively short while the small club of Wykehamists, Stoics and Alleynians, RAF accountants and (in the Serjeant's Department) brigadiers and rear-admirals - all loyally supported by second or third generation "servants" (some actually born in the Palace of Westminster), be-medalled NCO's, and ladies from the best finishing schools – was transformed into a bureaucracy, staffed by people (like me) of the middling sort: a sad fate for an ancient institution, which has never subsequently recovered its pride and confidence.

For young career clerks the invention of the new committees was a golden opportunity (never to be repeated) when management was so

---

[*] Bottomley's report followed that of Sir Edmund Compton on the administration of the House, published in January 1975, and significantly ameliorated its impact by rejecting Compton's proposal for a separate chief executive of the House services: a dispute which again came to the fore following RJR's resignation as Clerk of the House in the summer of 2014 and Mr Speaker Bercow's badly handled attempt to impose an attractive antipodean administrator in Robert's place.
[†] hence the availability of high-quality re-treads.

desperate to get the system up and running that they actually invited everyone available to bid for whatever committee might take their fancy, rather than merely pointing staff in the direction of their next desks. Inevitably, almost everyone wanted to run either the Defence Committee or the Foreign Affairs Committee if for no better reason than that they were bound to be travelling the world thereafter. Most had to be satisfied with promissory notes for the future, since the whole range of domestic affairs had also to be catered for: agriculture, education, energy, environment, industry, even home affairs and the treasury (the latter already spoken for by the senior re-tread). I was extremely lucky, since (perhaps as an unexpected reward for services rendered) I was allocated the Transport Committee, whose scope for travel could be expected to be almost as good. If I had been faced with the challenge of nursing the Social Services Committee I might well have thrown in the towel and returned to journalism (and no doubt ended up a trifle richer).

For the first few months after the summer recess in 1979 we were mostly redeployed to the pleasantly familiar but cramped quarters in No 3 Dean's Yard, alongside the RAF accountants. Having no actual committees, we worked hard at devising idealistic plans and strategies which would almost all be rejected by our eventual political masters, and beginning that cultivation of the media (and the specialist media in particular) which would in the long run help to secure the future of the committees and protect them from the widely-expected counter-attack from Whitehall once Ministers realised quite what they had foolishly signed up for. However, we were soon on the move again.

Although the House of Commons Commission had as yet no direct control over accommodation[*], which remained for the time being the responsibility of the Office of Works, it quickly became a fairly powerful lobby for better services for the House. Within months of the establishment of the new committees, space previously said to be unobtainable had been found in a wonderfully decrepit building wrapped around the old Westminster underground station. In March 1980, the Committee Office, together with other bits and pieces of what was becoming known as the House of Commons Service, decamped from Dean's Yard and No 46 to St Stephen's House. Here we had vast acres of space, almost everyone allotted his or her own room for the first time, and conference rooms available at every turn of the many stairs. It was an appallingly inconvenient building, made almost uninhabitable by the gross odour of chips and minute steaks from the cafés below, by the continuous roar of traffic from the Embankment (despite the bomb-blast curtains installed after the latest IRA atrocities) and, every minute or so, by the arrival and departure of the District or Circle line trains in the station within us, which more or less

---

[*] This happened only in 1992 (see chapter 29 below).

turned the whole building over. St Stephen's House had been used by just about every government department or agency in transit in the post-War decades, many of which had simply abandoned their detritus in cupboards and corners and stairwells when they next changed billets, and it even boasted wartime stickers in the men's loos reminding us that "loose talk kills".

For my mother Anne my move to St Stephen's House was news of great import. For it was there (conveniently close to the Institution of Civil Engineers on the other side of Parliament Square) that my grandfather had leased an office when he returned from Chile in 1910, it was there that he had worked (presumably for not very long after 28th June 1914) on his contract for a great new railway in Serbia, and it was there that he had hoped to establish David Angus & Sons (Civil Engineers) when his sons returned from the trenches.[*] When she paid a state visit soon after our move my aging mother was immediately convinced that I was working not only in the same building she claimed to remember from her childhood, but in the very same room as my grandfather: improbable, but nevertheless good vibes for a new committee about to commission a railway tunnel or two of its own.[†]

---

[*] The younger (Archie) died, at the age of seventeen, piping the charge of the London Scottish at Messines in November 1914; the older (Stewart), who had already built a railway or two in Argentina, was killed on the Somme in July 1916.
[†] Improbable, not least because my mother was only three when her family returned from South America. She nevertheless searched my office and the surrounding corridors for any papers and other memorabilia which her father might have left behind in 1916 or thereabouts.

18

A Bridge Too Far

the Transport Committee; log-rolling; tunnelling under the Channel; and a first assault on the European Commission

By the time the new committees met in December 1979 some of the enthusiasm fuelled by the Procedure Committee's report had begun to wane. Most Members were for much of the time preoccupied by the overwhelming parliamentary question of the day: how to get a parliamentary office of your own, since many were still living out of lockers on the Library Corridor, and most others were sharing desks in crowded and often subterranean rooms in the Palace. The small committee staffs, on the other hand, were tiring of four or five months playing war games, and so all launched into frenzied activity. At early meetings committee members pursued grand schemes for investigations into just about every aspect of departmental policy and administration of interest to the interests they represented, while their clerks paraded immensely ambitious scrutiny programmes, along with wonderful new procedural devices.

I was the worst culprit. Having an obvious career interest in proving that the Procedure Committee's ambitious requirements could in practice be met by the new committees, I had long pondered on elaborate schemes to achieve them. As a result, for the first eighteen months of operation my patient executive officer laboriously filleted the documents coming our way from the Select Committee on European Legislation &c to produce an ever-lengthening list of all the European transport matters which the committee ought to examine but then subsequently failed to examine. A rolling fortnightly document listed all the transport-related statutory instruments whose passage the Committee might in some way influence, together with the dates by which their consideration *must* be completed, which were never met. I had also drawn up an elaborate annual timetable for the regular interrogation of the Minister of Transport (later re-elevated into a Secretary of State[*]), his departmental estimates, reports and accounts, his annual

---

[*] After the 1979 General Election Norman Fowler was initially appointed as Minister of State (with permission to attend all Cabinet meetings) because, according to Margaret Thatcher's memoires, "we were short of one place". In

Roads Programme, his nationalised industries (such as British Rail), and his quangos (such as the Road Research Laboratory).

If implemented in full my programme would have required the committee to meet two or three times a week before they had even embarked on any of the great inquiries their party, personal or professional interests required.[*] Under the new rules the Transport Committee was not one of those allowed to establish sub-committees, which would have spread the workload. To get over this problem I at first attempted to run a system of rapporteurs (under which individual members take the lead for different inquiries, thus easing the pressure on the committee chairman) but was ticked off by my superiors for trying to introduce a continental procedural novelty without the agreement of the House. Instead (without consulting the same superiors) we simply turned the committee into two committees: one division led by chairman Tom[22], the other by the ranking Conservative. The rules prevented Tom from attending any of the second division meetings (for each meeting of which we had to re-appoint Peter Fry "in the absence of the chairman"), but since they were dealing with things like the Roads Programme or Vehicle Testing, in which he had no great interest, Tom was merely relieved.

The new Transport Committee seemed to justify the doubts of the sceptics. Most of the members were far too well qualified for the job, and for the same reasons seemed entirely the wrong people to provide the House with anything approaching objective advice on transport policy. Four of the five Labour members were former railwaymen and/or sponsored by transport unions, and the chairman a former rail union president. The two senior Tories were very closely linked with the roads and aviation sectors – Peter Fry the main parliamentary spokesman for the British Roads Federation, and David Price a former junior minister at various times for Trade, Aviation Supply, and Aerospace, and a leading British campaigner for the creation of a European Space Agency.[23] And one of the junior Tories, Den Dover, had a career in the upper reaches of the construction industry (but at least he had a respectable degree in civil engineering).

It was a committee apparently purpose-built for log-rolling. But log-rolling was perhaps understandable at this point in history, and maybe even justified. Years of economic and fiscal crisis, diktats from the IMF, belt-

January 1981 he was elevated to the Secretariat. Norman, a former *Times* journalist, and member for Nottingham South and subsequently for Sutton Coldfield, round about this time disappointed us all by marrying one of the prettiest (and brightest) House of Commons Library Clerks.
[*] And such is youth that my enthusiasm to do everything at once was not much discouraged by the fact that I was simultaneously "clerking" the new Government's inevitably contentious Employment Bill in a standing committee across the road which met for two mornings, and often two afternoons, each week for the first four months of 1980.

tightening by governments, had left their mark on the country's transport system. Investment, in both road and rail, had been cut back savagely for more than a decade. Towns and villages throughout the country were suffocating from the stench, noise and danger of heavy goods vehicles, and from the rapid rise in private car ownership. As overseas travel increased, public awareness of the antiquity of our own rail system grew with it. Trains were overcrowded and unreliable, stations were generally filthy, and diesels belched every kind of unfriendly contaminant into country and city air: unlike, of course, the friendly contaminants of the now greatly mourned steam age. And transportation in the national capital, based largely on a century-old subway, buses designed (if not built) in the thirties, and a road system not significantly upgraded since the eighteenth century, was slow, uncomfortable, inconvenient, and hated.

There was obviously going to be vigorous competition between the road and rail interests for the limited amount of infrastructure funding which might be available from the new Government – hence the Tory backbenchers' minute examination and re-examination of the Roads Programme, and the Labour backbenchers obsessive interest in the size of the grant paid to British Rail to meet its "Public Service Obligation". There was also a slow realisation that Keith Joseph and Margaret were serious (if ultimately unsuccessful) in their ambition to roll back the state, and that the days of massive public funding for capital projects might be numbered.

If many of their interests were in conflict, there was one issue where their historical grievances were shared, and on which the whole committee could unite. A fixed transport link across the English Channel offered the prospect of regeneration for the railways, speedier and cheaper access to the continental mainland for freight, and an enormous boost for the construction industry. In early 1974 the minority Labour cabinet, stressed almost beyond endurance by the worst financial crisis since the 1930's and an almost unmanageable political situation, had insisted on an inquiry to "reassess" the viability of the Channel Tunnel project authorised by Ted Heath's government as part of his "going into Europe" strategy; and when the inquiry failed to report on time they were happy in 1975 for the necessary Anglo-French treaty to lapse without ratification. The French Government felt betrayed, the railway industry felt betrayed; the road haulage industry felt betrayed; and the construction industry faced huge redundancies.

With a new government safely installed, the Channel Link was therefore a project which might have a chance of being moved forward, and an issue on which all members of the new committee had a chance of working together. But finance was a critical issue. The previous scheme was in principle to have been privately funded, but only ten per cent of the monies put up by the market would actually have been genuine risk capital, all the remainder to have been debt guaranteed by the two governments. This time, however, the new Prime Minister had given her blessing to the idea of a channel link, but had also stipulated that there should be no guarantee from the British Government for the direct costs involved – the French could, of course, do whatever suited them within their étatiste tradition, but HM Treasury were not this time taking any risks: if a scheme came up which its backers believed profitable, then HMG would provide the legislative support such a scheme required; but HMG would not act as paymasters.

And so, true to the communautaire tendencies of the majority, we first went to Europe, in search of cash. On the books since long before the UK joined the European Communities was a draft European Transport Infrastructure Fund: what better source for funding a project which would both radically improve interstate communications and at the same time bond the United Kingdom into the Community of which it remained so reluctant a member? However, the Fund seemed singularly reluctant to get off the ground. So the committee decided, while setting up its inquiry into the Channel Link, to investigate how this stalled vehicle could be put back on the road. Their inquiry was sobering for the Transport Committee, but also for the eurocrats.

We spent a tedious March afternoon in the company of the European Parliament's Transport Committee, which was devoted almost entirely to platitudinous statements of fraternal amity. The following day the committee held the customary échange des vues with the affable Irish Commissioner, Richard Burke, in the Berlaymont, that great concrete edifice which has subsequently come to symbolise for many of its peoples the tyranny (the power, anyway) of the new Europe - the Brussels Kremlin. There it was agreed that improved transport infrastructures would, indeed, be an absolutely splendid thing indeed since it would undoubtedly facilitate the ever closer union of the peoples of Europe which was also a very splendid thing indeed (which seemed to amount to the sum total of the Commissioner's policy at that time).

We spent the rest of the day with the Director-General of Directorate-General VII and his array of transport experts. The committee had previously asked me what, exactly, they were to do (since they were new to this game), and I had advised them to do, exactly, what they would do in London – that is to say what they thought, and to ask what, exactly, it's all supposed to mean once the bullshit has been cleared away.

They took the cue. The 'draft Regulation on financial support for transport Infrastructure projects' was taken to pieces, starting with the bombastic preamble, paragraph by paragraph, line by line, word by word. By the end of the afternoon it was clear to DG VII as well as to us that there was no hope of proceeding in anything like the current form, and the whole proposal was eventually quietly withdrawn, to be resurrected only much later when the treaties had been amended and the officials had cottoned on to the fact that there were parliamentarians out there who might actually look at the wording. A few lessons were learned. First, the Commission was trying to do something for which it had at the time no treaty authority – a far from unusual occurrence. Second, the process of translation – repeatedly, as amendments were offered by other Directorates, the Parliament, the Economic & Social Committee, and the lobbies – had rendered the original intentions incomprehensible. And this in a Community using a mere six official languages (except on the rare occasions when the Irish kicked up): what chance in a European Union with twenty-four official languages? Third, the analysis of this particular text on this particularly dull March afternoon underlined the enormous gulf between British and continental law-making practice: British law simply said what could or should and what could or should not be done; continental law said what it was hoped might be done in fair weather. It was another illustration of the fundamental flaw in the project to merge Britain into the new Napoleonic condominium. There was a distinct whiff of europscepticism in the air on the return flight to Heathrow.[24]

So, no money there. Not overly discouraged, the Transport Committee set about the business of examining all the papers and interrogating more or less anyone who had anything to say about a channel link. Between May and November 1980 they talked to them all – promoters of tunnel schemes, promoters of bridge schemes, promoters of submerged tubes, promoters of half bridge/half tunnel schemes; builders of any old scheme they could bid for; trades unions, supportive and sceptical; economists, accountants; local authorities in favour, local authorities opposed; shipping interests, rail interests; government ministers and officials. They took evidence in Westminster, and they spent a very hot and gruelling day taking evidence in Dover Town Hall. And although the rules would not then allow them to take formal evidence on foreign soil, they spent a couple of days in the Pas de Calais inspecting earlier French attempts at digging to Britain, and in lengthy discussions with the mayors and business leaders of Boulogne and Calais. Despite having to eat large quantities of crustaceans, much against my better judgement, I was genuinely moved by the accolade handed to my committee – indeed, to all 'my' committees – by the then still youthful communist mayor of Calais, Jean-Jacques Barthe[*]. With Tom Bradley & Co as his backdrop he appeared on local television on the evening of 24th July 1980 to say "Thank goodness for English democracy: nobody in the *Assemblée Nationale* has so far even bothered to come to the Pas de Calais to ask us what we think about a tunnel; it was left to our friends in London to have the courtesy to consult the people of France".

In addition to the financial constraints, the committee's deliberations were complicated by the Tories' awareness that Mrs Thatcher and her husband were passionate believers in a bridge, or indeed of anything else

---

[*] who, in time-honoured French tradition, eventually ruled Calais for almost thirty years.

142

which would have allowed through-running road traffic. We were therefore compelled to go through the motions of examining all such lunatic proposals with the utmost seriousness. One, from 'Linkintoeurope', envisaged bridge spans about 2 kilometres in length, with multiple and heavily armoured island piers optimistically designed to withstand collisions in the world's busiest shipping lane; another, from 'Eurobridge', reduced the number of piers and islands by proposing spans up to 3.75 kilometres long; and the third, one of several proposed by the European Channel Tunnel Group, envisaged a tube containing a single track railway with a two-lane motorway, ventilated from an artificial island mid-Channel. The longest suspension bridge span in the world at this time (the Humber Bridge) was a mere 1.4 kilometres long, and employed deck structures of proven durability. The committee bravely (in the case of its Tory members) concluded that governments would be "irresponsible" to contemplate any such schemes. It had to be some kind of old-fashioned tunnel.

The scheme abandoned by Harold Wilson in 1975 involved the construction of three interlinked tunnels – a service tunnel flanked by two single-track running tunnels of 6.85 metres diameter. This would allow the continuous through running of conventional passenger trains and single and double decker trains ferrying heavy goods vehicles and cars. To allow the use of trains of French and continental loading gauge[*], which could not be accommodated on existing BR tracks (largely because of the size of the tunnels and bridges on the southern railway), the scheme also required the construction of dedicated high-speed tracks into London (at White City), with overhead cantilevered power lines to the west European standard.

It was an ambitious but entirely sensible project, going a long way to meeting the requirements of the railways, the road haulage industry, and also of the near-majority of the population who were by now members of the RAC and the AA. It had the particular advantage that it would use proven technology and therefore the risks were lower. But it was still very expensive, and it was understandable that Wilson and Callaghan had allowed it to fizzle out at a time of budgetary meltdown.

So in 1980 we went through all the hoops again. British Rail had this time come up with a proposal so unambitious that it is difficult now to believe that any of us could have taken it seriously. They proposed merely a single track tunnel, built to continental loading gauge but not big enough to carry heavy goods vehicles. It certainly might meet the needs of the railway industry, and wouldn't upset either the ferry and port operators or the Kent communities otherwise threatened with the construction of new railway lines. The French were said to be more or less persuaded to build new rolling stock, with dual voltage locomotives, to enable the trains to transit through Southern Region's tunnels and bridges, but it was assumed

---

[*] ie the external dimensions of the rolling stock, not the track width.

that the trains would anyway have to stop for some time on arrival in Kent to allow a BR driver to take over from one from SNCF (oh what happy days!). Although prospective journey times were just about competitive with the ferries and with city-to-city airline timings, what BR were now offering was something not really much better than a subterranean alternative to a round-bottomed boat across the water.

Following very prolonged deliberation, the committee's preferred option was not much more ambitious. They also recommended a single-track tunnel, but at least of 6.85 metre diameter, which might one day accommodate road vehicle ferrying; they did not even stipulate the need for a service tunnel to cope with fires, breakdowns and other reasons for evacuation.[25] It is difficult now to understand why the Tories were prepared to go along with a scheme which merely provided a lifeline for the then apparently declining railway industry and offered only a very distant prospect of linking the road transport systems. Their compliance perhaps reflected our collective failure at this time to appreciate the potential growth of the European economies. It certainly reflected a collective loss of nerve after the trauma of IMF intervention, devaluation, and successive winters of discontent. It could also be, of course, that the Tories realised that the committee's preferred option was a nonsense, and that we'd all have to go back to the drawing board before too long.

There was a widespread fear that a tunnel with road-ferrying capacity would sink the ferries; and consequently that the UK would be dependent on a single, and vulnerable, cross-channel link, with the danger that if that failed we would have the capacity neither to invade nor to repel those who came by other routes. There were equally wide concerns that, while the ferries sank, the tunnel would be unable to generate sufficient traffic – and that therefore both modes would be at risk of failure. And undue weight may also have been given to lobbies which claimed to speak for the nation: the Transport & General Workers Union (who were just about the only organisation openly to express fears about the security implications, but who were really speaking up for their drivers' livelihoods); the overwhelmingly Tory local authorities who feared the collapse of their traditional port business or the environmental catastrophe of new motorways and new railways; and Mr Keith Wickenden, the short-lived MP for Dorking, who happened also to be chairman of Airship Industries Ltd and of European Ferries Ltd; he dreamed of a time when fleets of dirigibles would silently transport people and freight across the Channel and further afield, and in his evidence was robustly optimistic about the ferry operators' ability to cope with new traffic.

The committee's inquiry publicised fascinating information about the possible options, in a form intelligible to the layman; it provided a public platform for local communities (in France as well as Britain), environmental groups and others to air their fears and concerns; and in both these respects it served an important democratic function. That its main recommendation was almost universally ignored was, in retrospect, a considerable relief. Indeed, within a few years common sense had prevailed, and the much more ambitious scheme which had been aborted in 1975 was back up and running, within a short time supported by the Transport Committee itself. By the summer of 1987 it had been approved by the parliaments in both London and Paris; tunnelling was renewed in 1988; trains were running by 1994. And a couple of decades on the opposition of the local authorities had been overridden, and the high-speed link to London (St Pancras this time, instead of White City) was in business and pulling in the passengers. And, at last, both Eurotunnel (who own the tunnel) and Eurostar (who run the passenger trains) were showing an operating profit and paying a reasonable dividend, even if, in accordance with the inexorable laws of railway development, the original loans might never be repaid. The traffic gradually rose because it really is better to travel from central London to central Paris in under two-and-a-half hours than to struggle with your luggage out to Heathrow, and back into Paris from Roissy, however brief the nominal time in the air might be.

19

A Touch of Gout

*Riding the US subways; confronting NORAID in
Manhattan; a private consultation for the Chairman;
putting Ken Livingstone out of a job*

Very soon after the establishment of the new committees a trip around North
America had become *de rigueur*: no respectable committee could survive
the span of a Parliament without finding some plausible reason for crossing
the Atlantic, or even better the Pacific, and since early 1980 they had been
lining up before the Liaison Committee with implausible cases, almost all
of which were admitted. Those whose bids failed knew that until the next
Parliament they were relegated to the second division. Remembering only
too well the very bad marks achieved by the old S&T committee, I
successfully headed Tom Bradley and Peter Fry away from a trip to Japan
(to which they were very much inclined, and for which there might have
been some justification in this case) or Australia, and my instructions were
therefore *North America or bust.*

Despite the objections of the whips,* and despite the appallingly
oppressive weather, most transatlantic trips took place in late June or early
July, largely because it took so long for the Liaison Committee to complete
the bargaining process and to work out how much cash was still available,
and also because it took so long to wake up the Foreign Office to sort out
the logistics on the other side. So in July 1981 I made my only transatlantic
visit with the Transport Committee – twelve days of untrammelled delight.

We were on this occasion seeking to remodel London's decrepit road
and rail system by drawing on the allegedly splendid examples of urban
transport planning and investment to be found in far off parts of the globe.
As the committee's report later recorded, we had already taken evidence
from transport operators, local authorities, transport users' organisations,
road lobbies, environmental lobbies and, of course the many unions still
involved; we had visited London Bridge, Charing Cross, Waterloo and
Liverpool St stations and much of the London Underground; and we had
become the envy of train spotters worldwide by visiting a great multitude of
signal boxes, above and below the ground, ancient and hand-pulled, and at

---

* Long-haul trips, whether in July or the early autumn, had a tendency to coincide
with divisions on the Report stage of the Finance Bill and other flagship legislation.

London Bridge, state of the art and powered by primitive mainframe computers. At maintenance depots throughout the south-east we had examined ailing buses and rolling stock inside, outside and from underneath; we had learned of the terrible combined effects of chewing gum and coca-cola on station forecourts (which problem was apparently absorbing a good proportion British Rail's research budget); we had walked the route of the Rochester Way Relief Road – the first and to date still just about the only improvement to the roads south-east of the Thames and north of what eventually became the M25 ; we had visited the eventual site of Heathrow Terminal 4, and mulled over the tunnelling problems which this would involve for the Piccadilly Line. We had been assured by British Rail and London Transport that a common ticketing system for the whole metropolitan transport network was unthinkable and, since it would be beyond the capabilities of any foreseeable modern technology, would involve the employment of hundreds of clerks manually checking millions of tickets each day to establish each operator's daily revenue.[*]

So we went to the Americas well aware of London's problems, and generally depressed about the prospects of ever making any significant improvements; we were saddled with a Victorian infrastructure, no money, and transport managers more than somewhat lacking in either imagination or initiative; and had the feeling that we the commuters – and even the tourists – would just have to put up with it as a yet another of London's ineffable attractions.

My memories of the two days spent in Toronto are hazy, largely because of the enormity of what followed, although we certainly travelled around on a lot of trains and buses rather cleaner than our own, and of course held discussions of great high seriousness (this being Canada). On 14 July we flew down to what had then become known, for no obvious reason, as the Big Apple. Darkness had already fallen over La Guardia, but the temperature was still advertised as 82^0 Fahrenheit, and relative humidity around 80%. These were bad auguries.

We were shipped to the Berkeley Hotel, a grandiose but fading leather-upholstered monstrosity in Midtown Manhattan, which would have earned much praise from the Kremlin, with appalling service and primitive, noisy and vastly over-efficient air-conditioning in rooms with sealed windows (of which the Kremlin would also have much approved).

We emerged exhausted from the Berkeley (pronounced, and maybe even

---

[*] An authoritative statement on the inability of any computerised system to cope with all-London ticketing was provided by Sir Peter Parker, then chairman of British Rail, at a convivial tea party at the Charing Cross Hotel; Sir Peter also advised me in the strictest confidence that afternoon that the chewing gum problem, which was particularly evident on the station concourse below us, was one of the main obstacles to the mainline station improvements "which we would all otherwise wish to see".

spelt, Burclay) for our first day in New York. This was largely devoted to riding the subway and inspecting the Transportation Authority's engineering works. As we rose falteringly up the timber-clad incline into Queens at the maximum permitted speed of 10mph, we began to appreciate that ours was not the only ageing metro in need of support. And as we witnessed 1930's bus engines being cannibalised to keep the fleet on the road, replacement parts recreated on nineteenth-century machine tools, and nineteenth-century safety standards rather casually observed (as visitors we were warned that we were in serious danger of electrocution), we began also to appreciate that London Transport had not completely failed us, despite the impact of the blitz (which New York had not, of course, had to suffer, but in places very much looked as though it had).

In the evening, after being critically assessed by the extremely handsome Afro-American hookers in the bar (who eventually got the message that we were on parliamentary expenses), we headed for the British Consulate-General for the customary "briefing", supported by the customary unlimited (and very welcome) duty-free gin. The Consulate-General was housed on an upper floor of one of the many thousands of identikit blocs which make New York the characterless city we are all supposed to love, testimony to HM Treasury's loathing of the foreign service in general and its pleasure in humiliating those below the strictly diplomatic ranks: the consular service was the first to suffer, although in later years many a prestigious embassy building would also be sacrificed in the name of economy and as public testimony to Britain's loss of nerve.

Although we were innocently investigating the organisation and financing of public transportation, the Committee had arrived in the middle of the Maze hunger strike and at the peak of anti-British agitation in New York, largely organised by NORAID[*] and Clan na Gael, who were ostensibly raising cash for republican prisoners and their families, but in practice also for the purchase of weapons by the Provisional IRA. Bobby Sands, having won the Fermanagh & South Tyrone by-election in April, had died a few weeks later, and by the time we arrived the death toll was already standing at six (and eventually rose to ten). That Irish Republican sympathisers were by this time outraged was no surprise, particularly in view of the repeated and clearly provocative Commons statements of the Secretary of State for Northern Ireland, Humphrey Atkins, to the effect that the deaths should simply be regarded as suicides. Anti-British demonstrations had become a daily occurrence in New York as well as other North American cities. United Kingdom diplomatic, commercial and consular premises were an obvious target, and the fact that the streets around the Consulate-General were already filling up when we arrived for polite discussions was no surprise, and probably had nothing at all to do with our

[*] The Irish Northern Aid Committee.

presence, although once we had arrived in the building the word quickly spread that British politicians were in town. Within a short time of the Committee's arrival the famous NYPD had a genuine security problem on their hands.

The police detail at the front door of the building had no immediate idea what to do, other than to tell us all to stay inside. The consular staff (and the one or two grander diplomats who were there as a courtesy) were equally nonplussed and supported the view that we should all stay put until it was all over. But George Barrington Porter was having none of this fucking public school pusillanimity (a bowdlerised paraphrase of the words he used on the day).

Barry Porter was the kind of MP that every constituency should pray for. Then the member for Bebington & Ellesmere Port, and subsequently (after boundary changes) for Wirral South, he was an Oxford-educated solicitor, but a Birkenhead man by birth and in all his attributes; he spoke the language of a man from Merseyside, he was deeply loyal to his own people on the Wirral, when he espoused causes he espoused them passionately and without qualification, and since he was never offered preferment he was free to treat the Tory whips with the disdain they deserved. Robert Rhodes James (a former clerk and therefore also another habitué of Annie's) described him succinctly: "He had guts, compassion, and courage as well as conviviality – in the best Cavalier tradition".[26]

In New York Barry exhibited his passionate support for the Unionist cause, and even more his guts and courage. Ignoring the advice of the diplomats, the urging of his chairman and the instructions of the police, Barry took the elevator down to the ground, walked out into the tumult in the street, and delivered a diatribe in scouse so loud, so powerful and so dismissive that the demonstrators were confounded, and what had all the makings of a riot declined into a mere grumble, while several erstwhile protestors insisted on shaking Barry's hand and thanking him for his loyalty to the cause of the people of the Emerald Isle. At which point the committee were happy to take the opportunity to leave the scene and head back for a burger round the corner from the Berkeley, in good time before Clan na Gael realised their slight mistake and sought to regroup their forces.

In a more heroic age, Barry would have been knighted on the field of battle.

The next morning the Transport Committee and its clerk and advisers were due to set off to discuss New York's wider transportation problems with city, county and state authorities, after an early-morning helicopter ride to view the rush-hour at its worst. The commercial councillor, the science councillor, the specialist adviser, and most of the committee set off in the limousines on cue. The committee chairman, and his clerk, were otherwise occupied.

At about five-thirty in the morning there was a brief ring on my phone, and I assumed that a domestic crisis must be looming five or six hours ahead in south-east London. But it was chairman Tom on the line. In strained tones he said "I don't think I'm quite up to a helicopter trip today, Bill". He was clearly in some discomfort. When I got to his room, I found Tom prostrate, feebly trying to move his right leg to minimise what was obviously acute pain in his foot. So I ordered tea, which all well-brought-up Englishmen know is the first line of attack against pain, alerted the rest of the team that they were on their own for the time being, and called the consular service for the phone number of a doctor.

This seemed a not-unreasonable approach to the problem, but was not so regarded by our ever-helpful consular service. It was explained to me that doctors in New York were inordinately expensive, and it was a matter of policy not to make any suggestions in case the FCO was later thought responsible for the high charges. "But we're talking about the chairman of a parliamentary select committee, one of whose members even gave the IRA their comeuppance only last night, to the greater glory of our nation. You should be proud to help". "Doesn't this man have insurance? And please remember that we're not in the business of picking up the tab".

The Berkley's reception desk was marginally more helpful, and I eventually made contact with the nearest medical practice, which happened to be located a mere couple of blocks away, at what I think was the Waldorf Astoria. I mentioned that Tom was immobile, and innocently asked if they could arrange an ambulance. "Well, sure", they replied, "but it could take hours to reach you", and mentioned a dollar sum which would have consumed both our Barclaycard limits and probably the entire committee's travel allowance as well. But the hotel again came up trumps: an ancient wheelchair was discovered in the garbage area in the basement, and placed in my care. Half an hour later, having assisted Tom into some loose clothing, I emerged from the goods entrance at the back of the hotel (having been required to use the service elevator, and very definitely not the front entrance, since these would be "bad for trade"), my chairman's leg projecting horizontally onto the baking streets of Manhattan.

Negotiating New York's sidewalks and street crossings can be hair-raising enough even when not in sole command of an un-oiled wheelchair with protruding fibulas, and my troubles were far from over. Presumably for security reasons, public access to the hotel was at this time (and perhaps is still) limited to an external escalator, which ran up to the grand entrance lobby of this most distinguished of hotels. Tom was adamant that he couldn't get out and simply hang on to the rail, and the management (following voluble exchanges with and between bell captains up and down the stairs) was equally adamant that in the case of this hotel anyway we were certainly not permitted to use the service entrance. Some kind of bellboys' union rule also seemed to have been discovered which prohibited assistance with wheelchairs into hotels for non-residential guests, particularly those with extended fibulas, and even more so those piloted by heavily perspiring and bearded foreigners in M&S suits. In the end a very nice central European gentleman came to my aid, and between us we hoisted Tom up the escalator, and located the elevator to the higher floors of the Waldorf.

Even in those politically-incorrect days, a doctor's surgery emblazoned with advertisements for the medicinal benefits of cigarette smoking was an unusual sight, and for a moment I felt transported back to the happy world of Bedminster's WD & HO Wills factories, where as a young man I had learned the art of serious floor-sweeping. The physician we had chosen appeared to be largely engaged as medical adviser to one of America's largest tobacco companies (presumably Philip Morris, since the main advertisements were for their Peter Stuyvesant brand). After a brief examination he declared that Tom was suffering from gout. An undisclosed sum then changed hands. Tom was to go home as fast as possible, rest up, and take the tablets which were immediately prescribed and dispensed.

This was all very well, but there were complications. Gout is almost as certain an exit route for a politician as a front page story in the *News of the World* (or membership of the Liberal Party) and Tom's defection to the Social Democratic Party already made him highly vulnerable. Before we had even left the surgery, I had been sworn to secrecy: until he was dead and buried I was not to reveal the truth to a soul. I accordingly spent the rest of the day in continual, and I hoped consistent, obfuscation. I had to get the permission of the accountants in the House of Commons Fees Office to send my chairman immediately back across the Atlantic, against all the rules, and at great cost. I had to explain to somebody much more senior in the foreign service that the committee chairman was actually ill, and I really did need their help to get him home. I had to assure the committee that Tom was merely suffering a mild viral infection, and wished them well for the rest of the tour. And I had to explain to his wife Joy that there really would have to be a waiting wheelchair at Heathrow, but that she was "not to worry". I think I managed to obfuscate sufficiently (and Joy of course soon had the full story). And there were no stories in the press.

Later that afternoon, at last provided with an official car, Tom and I, complete with wheelchair and an affable young escort from the FCO, headed for JFK. The affable young man arranged for me to have an airside pass and – very nobly – headed back to town on public transport. And BA – by then evidently nervous about hosting an ailing Member of Parliament – were only too happy for me to keep charge of Tom until he was safely stowed in the front seat of Concorde. It is therefore to Tom Bradley that I owe my only experience of a Concorde in service: it seemed very cramped.

Tom went home, and rapidly recovered, and I never leaked the truth, despite ruthless interrogation by the accountants. I returned to the Berkeley in the company car, and collapsed from heat and exhaustion.

Next morning, again bright and bushy-tailed, we survivors set off for

Washington DC. A few smouldering shop fronts on the way from Dulles suggested that there had been a little more local rioting than officially admitted, but this did not deter my intrepid crew from enjoying a rather-more splendid embassy reception than the usual and some fascinating rides on the loss-making Washington Metro. Next day we flew to California. I had insisted that we flew on the 8.00 am flight on United, following my exceptional experience with Ian Lloyd in 1975; on this occasion even the first class accommodation was cramped, the food was plastic, and the cabin crew worthy of Lufthansa. The committee were never thereafter sure that my judgement could be trusted.

In San Francisco I had again fixed the committee up for a day or two without me, and had another happy, Black Label fuelled, party with my wealthy relatives on Nob Hill. But not before we had all (my cousin Saint George included) been off to the San Francisco Golf Club where, after a Californian champagne breakfast, Barry Porter again proved his mettle. Somewhere there should be photographs of the Hon Member for Bebington & Ellesmere Port, successfully driving his ball back onto the eighth green from halfway up the tree wherein it had lodged. Before leaving we were, as intended, beguiled by the sophistication of the Bay Area Rapid Transit system (an essentially simple, largely overground, metro) but also warned about costs: a BART executive whispered in my ear while we were waiting for yet another almost unoccupied train that the real cost of each ride was around $10, although the standard ticket price at the time was a mere $1: the system survived on repeated public bond issues, which were expected to be replicated indefinitely. As in Washington, BART had encountered the grave disadvantages of running an incomplete system, which discouraged the rides needed to finance the extension of the system to make it even vaguely profitable. Even my Tory members began to see the advantages of straightforward public ownership.

A couple of months later we set out again, this time for Europe. In Munich we admired the extremely sleek bus system; in Hamburg we trembled at the massed ranks of ticket inspectors as they invaded the suburban platforms like avenging angels dressed for a gestapo reunion party; in Paris we marvelled at the quiet of rubber traction wheels (while also noting how quickly they wore down to shreds) and the grime and litter of so many of the stations on the Métro; in Paris also, as in Hamburg, we noted that a common ticketing system had not presented the insoluble problems alleged to face London.

Back in Westminster we settled down to vast amounts more evidence, and then, after long gestation, produced a Report. By this time, in July 1982, the main issues confronting the committee had ceased to have much to do with transport policy, and a great deal more to do with party politics. Ken Livingstone had in May 1981 become Leader of the Greater London Council, and had immediately sought to implement "Fares Fair", designed significantly to reduce London Transport fares and if necessary to run the system at a loss, supported by increased local taxation. A single London borough, Bromley*, challenged the policy in the courts and eventually, in December 1981, the House of Lords killed it completely. By this time Red Ken – and, by extension, the Greater London Council as an institution – had become anathema to the lady in Downing Street, and the relevant orders of the day went out to her troops. On the Transport Committee she seemed to have found at least one willing instrument of her policy in Den Dover (Denshore to his friends), who had previously worked for Laings and Wimpeys, but had ended up before becoming MP for Chorley as Director of Housing Construction for the said GLC: he was therefore an insider who knew the full enormity of the GLC's alleged failings.

For their own largely disreputable reasons, the rest of the Transport Committee caved in to this pressure from Downing Street, and produced a Report[27] which would have stripped the GLC of all its transport functions. Since most other local government functions were already the responsibility of the individual London boroughs, the Report, if implemented, would have left the GLC with few functions of any importance. That was what was intended, and in 1986 the Council was dismembered, with all remaining responsibilities absurdly divided amongst the thirty-six boroughs and, for a brief period, a now directly-elected Inner London Education Authority. The Transport Committee bore a lot of the responsibility for this farcical outcome, although it did at least give the necessary nudge to the introduction of the London Travelcard, which eventually spared us all from carrying a multitude of cardboard tickets to work. Some of the old-fashioned and reasonably sane non-Thatcherite Tories were appalled by what was proposed; but Tom Bradley, by then on behalf of the SDP, had no love for Lambeth socialism, and the mainstream Labour Party had even less. So much for select committee reports being based entirely on their evidence. The dismemberment of 1986 was a short-term disaster for London government; but Red Ken at least had the last laugh, when he was returned triumphantly in 2000 as the first directly elected Mayor of London, independent of the parties for a time at least and therefore doubly loved of the people.

---

* my own, I regret to say.

VI Foreign Affairs

20

Ascension

to the Falklands and back

Once my insights into the future of London had been safely put to bed with the printers (and I had left Tom and my successor Jacqy Sharpe to work out a better way of getting across or under the Channel), I sorted my possessions and shipped back to the main Committee Office, and to a desk with a splendid view over the parliamentary terrace and the river. My translation to Clerk of the Foreign Affairs Committee had been much hoped-for, but was certainly not expected half-way through the Parliament.

I inherited a second clerk, whose main job was to look after the overseas aid side of the shop, sometimes through a sub-committee specifically appointed for that purpose. This charming young man was related to one of the country's leading and most accoladed economists and apparently also to one of the country's second-ranking but still notorious spies. He eventually moved on to teach Scots English in (I believe) Japan. His replacement, Crispin Poyser, became both a real friend and a helpful foil to my occasionally excessive exuberances.

I also inherited several dozen specialist advisers, whose recruitment by my predecessor but one had in a couple of years almost choked the initiative of the many talented members of the committee and in itself largely explained why a third clerk in as many years had had to be recruited to attempt to let them do their own thing. My first objective was to retire the great majority of the advisers as soon, but also as humanely, as possible. I was the right man for this particular job, since I continued to believe, with the old Procedure Committee, that advisers should be on tap, but not on top, and that if there were specialists who had something to say they should be invited to do so on the record from the witness bench, rather than surreptitiously, and off the record, over the Chairman's shoulder. I had managed at the Transport Committee with no more than two advisers (always very eminent) for each inquiry, and had pensioned them off as soon as each inquiry was over. This time I had to do a wholesale cull, which proved fairly easy: the parliamentary session, for which they were appointed, came to an end a few weeks after my arrival, and I simply failed to reappoint them. There were a few grouses, but in the end we settled for only three long-term advisers, and were very careful that any others were recruited for a specific task, and then sent on their way.

The running disagreements between clerks, and between clerks and committee members, about the use of specialist advisers had little to do with *amour propre*, but much to do with our perception of what Commons committees were about, and our tolerance of the demands made upon us. For a committee clerk there was, superficially anyway, much to be said for having other people available – and people with much greater expertise – to draft the questions, and write the committee's reports. Being the clerk of a committee was quite hard work. The clerk was expected to anticipate as far as possible the often conflicting interests and wishes of his members. He had to agree with them their programme of business. He had to obtain finance for the overseas visits his members thought desirable, and then sort out the logistics. He had to identify the best people to give evidence. He had to negotiate with those so identified, about the substance of the meetings and how they would actually get there. He had to draft the main lines of questioning as an aid to the committee, and simultaneously brief the lined-up witnesses about what they were to be asked and not infrequently also about what they should say in response. He had to stay awake during the long and usually tedious interrogations which followed. And subsequently he had to read all the often substantial volumes of written evidence, digest and fillet the transcripts of hundreds and sometimes thousands of oral questions, produce some sort of report outline, and finally produce a polished and literate draft report for the committee's perusal, drawing ostensibly only on the formal evidence the committee had received but in practice also on the often-much-more-useful off-the-record briefings from officials and un-named overseas visitors. Sometimes the clerk's draft might be approved; sometimes it would be fought line by line, but it would in any case be he (or increasingly she) who also drafted everybody else's amendments and who finally incorporated them into a finished and publishable document. And quite often there would be three, four or more substantive inquiries running in parallel, and all at different stages.

In these early days most committees had only one graduate career clerk (so on the FAC I was especially privileged), one executive officer, one shorthand typist, and the services of perhaps half a clerical officer, who was often largely employed in the physical tasks of carrying paper around the parliamentary estate, distributing the post, and running the Gestetner or even (if we were lucky) the smoke-and-heat-belching photocopier/printer of the new age.* Some committees already had the services of a fulltime specialist assistant, as had the Transport Committee, but not, curiously, the FAC. Hard information not already in the formal evidence had to be acquired from hours of devilling in the House of Commons Library; Wikipedia had not yet arrived.

---

* When, with permission and a donation to charity, I was able to bequeath one of these early behemoths to my children's primary school PTA I needed the whole of the back of our people carrier to transport it.

Given all this the temptation to call in as much additional help – expert, authoritative, distinguished, part-time – was very great indeed. But the problem was that if you went down this road you soon lost control of the enterprise: and the only objective of the enterprise was to produce a report which reflected the lay views (warts and all) of mostly intelligent laymen who happened to be members of Parliament – if "expert" conclusions were needed they could be obtained two-a-penny from the burgeoning universities and from the Executive itself. My personal aim was that the reports produced in the name of my committee should be intelligible to the committee itself; I did not want my chairman to ask me at the press conference what the hell paragraph 97 or whatever actually meant; he should have "ownership" of the text.

My most important support in my new job was our executive assistant, Kennedy John Brown. Ken was a real House of Commons man, in a way which we transient citizens of the Westminster township could never be. He was part of a dynasty. His father John worked round the corner for the Services Committee. His grandparents had actually lived in the Palace at a time when numerous corners of the building were still occupied by the people who kept the place going, a medieval tradition eventually destroyed not by the great fire of 1834 but by late-twentieth century drives for "efficiency". Ken had happy memories of playing cricket along the main Committee Corridor on Christmas morning, knew everybody who made the system work, and appeared to be on friendly speaking terms with just about every Member. He was also pretty good at making the committees work. After a spell in the Marines, chasing Eoka gunmen around Cyprus and otherwise enjoying the many delights of that blessed isle, Ken had returned to the family business. Before the new committees came on the scene he had worked with the former Expenditure Committee, with the members of whose Defence Sub-Committee he had forged long lasting ties.[*] When I arrived on the scene he knew that his new task was to whip me into shape. If I failed in meeting all his aspirations it was not for want of his trying.

The FAC had been chaired since the start by Sir Anthony Kershaw, the Tory member for Stroud, in Gloucestershire, from 1955. The vast majority of Members, as well as every member of staff, regarded it as a real privilege - a feather in their caps - to work with and for Tony Kershaw. A monocle-sporting Etonian who had spent his early childhood in Cairo, a former Harlequins rugby player, a barrister whose fluent German had helped in the interrogation of the Nazis after the war, and an advocate able to charm and intimidate his interlocutors in equal measure, he had won the Military Cross

---

[*] Ken eventually moved up through the "ranks" to become a very effective Clerk of the Committee of Public Accounts, blazing a trail for others. His OBE was probably the only "gong" for which I ever actively campaigned and one of the few which I ever actively applauded.

in tanks in Tunisia, and returned for a while after the war as lieutenant-colonel in the Royal Gloucestershire Hussars. As a politician he had been an LCC councillor in the late forties, and after joining the House had permanently blotted his copybook by serving as PPS to Ted Heath as leader of the Opposition, and by his staunch Europeanism. That Ted Heath rewarded his loyalty only by junior ministerial appointments (albeit at Defence and the FCO) was typical of the man; that he was thereafter punished and ostracised by Mrs T was equally characteristic of the Lady. There was general agreement amongst all but the most partisan that he was well-qualified for a Cabinet position, and that after his retirement from the House he should have gone straight to the Lords. I always felt a slight pang of guilt that I might have contributed to the latter failure. But Tony Kershaw's innate modesty and humanity would have forgiven me, as also for one or two outright faux-pas which occurred on my watch but in his name. All of which had to do with the events of 1982 in the South Atlantic.

I joined the FAC just after the end of the Falklands War. This had been an exciting period in all our lives, and particularly for those of us who had been nurtured on films on our black & white TV's invariably starring Kenneth More and/or Michael Redgrave, who had not lived through the realities of conventional war (even if we had been terrorised for a while by fear of its nuclear alternative), and who therefore found it hard to shake off the image of the chivalrous Brit going forth to bring the barbarian hordes to heel. Even if we were not totally convinced about "our" war aims, most of us were genuinely gripped by the radio and tv coverage of "our" boys down in the South Atlantic, and whatever our feelings about the Thatcher regime we were more or less unanimous in wanting the great Fleet to arrive safely and then win a signal victory. Post-mortems - political, military and diplomatic – were of course inevitable; and it was therefore also inevitable that to the Falklands the Foreign Affairs Committee would eventually have to go.

There were, however, some demarcation disputes to be ironed out. The Defence Committee, who shared offices with us under the command of that same Douglas Millar who had joined the service on exactly the same day as me back in 1968, claimed proprietary rights to all the military and defence aspects of the famous conflict, and did not want the mere diplomats across the room philosophising and confusing the issues. After protracted negotiations we devised a formula which allowed them to concentrate on defence issues, while we were to be concerned solely with the *future* diplomatic, constitutional and economic prospects of the island; and under some pressure from the Government we agreed in theory not to re-examine the events leading up to the Argentine invasion. This reasonable arrangement lasted for a while, but did not survive the resurfacing of the *Belgrano* eighteen months later, after which we found ourselves obliged to poach on our committee colleagues' territory, and to retrace the diplomatic steps in the minutest detail.

The indomitable Ken set about the logistics of sending both committees to the South Atlantic. No mean feat, since there was as yet no formal end to hostilities, no civil transportation was in operation other than a slow cargo vessel out of Bristol or Liverpool, and both committees insisted on taking formal evidence if for no other reason than to demonstrate to the Argies that Stanley was again and would remain British sovereign territory. If civil air transport had been available, the cost of shipping eighteen Members, four permanent staff, four advisers and the intrepid Mike Phoenix (a shorthand writer who agreed to break union rules and do the whole job single-handed) would have completely blown the Liaison Committee's budget for the year. Thanks to the RAF, we were able to travel in style at peppercorn rates.

In late January 1983 the FAC left a very icy Brize Norton on board a VC10 of RAF Transport Command, a comfortable workhorse which had provided the airbridge for personnel to Ascension during and after the war, and was said to be Mrs T's favoured mode of transport. We stopped briefly in blazing sunshine at Dakar-Yoff International Airport[*], where Tony Kershaw was commissioned to convey HM Government's formal thanks for Senegal's critical logistical and diplomatic support to President Abdou Diouf, an elegant graduate of the Sorbonne, who had dropped by at the airport especially for the purpose.

If it was warm in Dakar, already half a world away from the snow of southern England, Ascension was blissful: the volcanic clinker burned through our shoes and our regulation suits, the dry heat ameliorated by a gentle Atlantic breeze. There we had a couple of nights at the Reknown Transit Centre, a 24-berth portacabin in Concertina City, the great military encampment which had blossomed beside the airfield. Wideawake (and Ascension as a whole) was technically British sovereign territory, but under the wartime 'Cruisers for Bases' deal (confirmed by the 1956 Bahamas Agreement) the airfield had become a US base, although by then operated on contract by Pan-Am. On our free day members wandered in various configurations, and hitched lifts from the RAF in various directions, some playing golf on the ash course halfway up the Green Mountain (as temporary members of the Volcano Club), some venturing to meet the small herd which provided fresh milk, some going down to make suitable obeisance to the empire's dead in the church in St Mary's, some swimming in the shark-infested seas off English Bay, some even trying to get into the duty-free. Some like myself sat outside the cabin, re-read the official

---

[*] Now renamed Léopold Sédar Senghor Airport after Senegal's first President, and said to be regarded by professional pilots as one of the World's worst. It was replaced as the main Senegal hub by a new airport, whose construction by the Saudi Bin Laden group began in 2007, was intended to take 2½ years to complete, and finally opened for business in December 2017.

briefing, and soaked in the ultraviolet.

Ascension was an island of no small importance. It contained the main BBC External Services relay station, a Cable & Wireless station, a major tracking facility for NASA, and a joint UK/US signals intercept facility. However, little actually happened there day by day. The airfield commander told us that he usually had one provisioning flight a week, and rarely anything else. He was a man of great charm and evidently also a man of steel, since he had not been traumatised by the events of 2nd and 3rd April. He had been vaguely gazing through the window, he said, when he got a call from the US warning him to expect the imminent arrival of a few planes from the UK. While he was alerting his small team of ground staff, the sky appeared to fill with aircraft and "they just kept coming and coming". Within a few hours, albeit for a brief period, Wideawake had become the busiest airfield in the world.

On the afternoon of Tuesday 1st February 1983 the FAC met formally in the UK Residency on Ascension Island (another first) to fine-tune the plans for their Falklands visit*. Woken at four o'clock the following morning, and provisioned by a sumptuous bacon and egg breakfast in the RAF field kitchen, surrounded by aircraft readying for the day's work, the air full of the delicious scent of aviation fuel, the committee then embarked for a day of solitude and quiet on board the Hercules to RAF Stanley, accompanied by assorted military equipment, reconditioned aero engines, food supplies and consumer goods.† This was a memorable flight. Massaged by the vibration of the aircraft, and prevented by the noise from communicating with even one's closest neighbour, the Hercules offered the most perfect holiday for politicians: unable to hear oneself speak, unable to read for long in the inadequate light, and dehydrating faster than the RAF's unlimited supplies of fruit juice could compensate, the passenger could, for one day in his life, be entirely his own man, living with his own thoughts and incapable for once of making a speech or raising a point of order. With the exception, that is, of the hon Member for Newham South, my old sparring partner from the Procedure Committee. Nigel Spearing put the European Community, Anglo-Argentine relations, and the rest of the world to rights continuously for eight hours or more; as his immediate neighbour along the side of the Hercules I occasionally nodded in agreement; but I never heard a word.

In between times (and I don't think Nigel really noticed my occasional absences) I wandered the cavernous aircraft, chatted to the crew, and had the privilege of standing in the cockpit to watch (and to photograph) the impressive operation of inflight probe-and-drogue refuelling, the turbo-prop

---

* The Defence Committee a couple of weeks later scored another "first" when they took formal evidence there from the military.
† On the return journey we were also accompanied by a coffin.

Hercules diving seawards to keep walking pace with its turbo-jet Victor tanker at near-stalling speed. The tanker had itself been refuelled en route, and would be again on its return to Ascension. For a mere civilian, this demonstration of the combined power of human ingenuity, dexterity, and courage in the clear air over the Atlantic was a humbling experience. If any of the operations had failed, we would have had to divert to Uruguay, the one Latin American country which had been prepared throughout the imbroglio to provide a safe haven for UK aircraft – such was their dislike of their neighbours south of the Rio de la Plata (as well as their reasonable but unadvertised suspicion that if the Malvinas owed allegiance anywhere in Latin America it was more properly to Montevideo than to Buenos Aires).

We landed in the early evening, having sent a specific instruction to the Civil Commissioner Rex Hunt that, however pleased the islanders might be to see us (or most of us, at any rate), there should be no welcoming ceremony or ceremonials, since the whole party would be exhausted as well as light headed, and we knew from experience what the consequences might be. Rex[*] met us in his trademark London cab at the airport, with no great fanfare, and invited us to a "few private drinks" at Government House immediately after we had arrived in town. On the patched road into Stanley we noticed that more than one of the Pucarás, downed by our side or abandoned by the enemy, bore the legend "Fuck Foulkes", a light-hearted greeting which we took in the proper spirit. George Foulkes[28] had taken the risk of issuing a statement before we left that a negotiated settlement with Argentina might in the long run be necessary, even desirable; the islanders' reaction to such views was at least informative.

We checked into the Upland Goose, a ghastly replica English seaside resort hotel by a waterfront more reminiscent of Seasalter or Brightlingsea or Skegness or many another bleak East Coast township, than of the south American cone (an image of course slightly belied by the crippled warships in the harbour). Close to Jubilee Villas, and surrounded by a full-blown Anglican Cathedral (but one without a Dean and Chapter) and churches of other denominations (as at home, not particularly well patronised), the hotel seemed to deny the fact that we were eight thousand miles away, and to make a mockery of claims that the Falkland Islands were anything other than truly British. On the day before our departure, indeed, Sir Anthony Kershaw joined Des King, the distinctly oleaginous proprietor, in hoisting the Best Western flag over his front door. Since then I and my family have done our best to avoid any hotel sporting the Best Western plaque, a

---

[*] Dennis Canavan uncharacteristically described the by now Sir Rex as "a pompous little man, a very minor diplomat who would have remained in obscurity if the Argentinians had not had the stupidity to invade the Falklands"; an unnecessary comment from a very decent man (and first-class MP) who might himself not have particularly relished the invasion of his own home by a company of enemy commandos (Dennis Canavan, *Let the People Decide* (Edinburgh, 2010), p 149).

determination cemented by an extremely brief visit a few years later to Brighton's Old Ship[*]. Des, as we were soon to be enlightened, was distinctly persona non grata with many of the Campers, charged with raising his prices to islanders during the occupation, as well as hobnobbing with the invaders. George Foulkes, on inspecting the inevitable portrait of HM The Queen in the hotel lounge, commented appositely "I bet there's one of Galtieri on the back", recalling happy memories of a similar phenomenon experienced in Bad Godesberg a few years back.

Almost immediately we were off to the Civil Commissioner's. With the anticipated consequences. The "few private drinks" turned out to be as near as dammit a full-blown reception, with all the military brass and the notables of town and Camp on parade, and all champing at the bit to tell us their understandable woes. All our party were crumpled, tired, dehydrated and deoxygenated. Almost all were sharing small and tatty rooms with not necessarily the most congenial partners. All were at one or another advanced stage of grumpiness. Tempers were frayed and only too ready to flare. That the outcome was merely a mild verbal altercation between the still bearded Dennis Canavan and the local Catholic priest, and did not lead to a general mêlée, was a tribute to the common sense and restraint of those present (with most of whom this notorious happening didn't even register). However, even in the South Atlantic politicians couldn't escape the tabloids. We had not been informed (as we should have been) that one of the guests at Government House was the local stringer for the *Daily Telegraph* (then, as now, the leading tabloid). Within a couple of days Dennis' conversation with the padre and a moustachioed brigadier had hit the front pages back home; and a week later, when we returned to Brize Norton, the press conference was dominated by typically responsible newspaper inquiries about the alleged "punch up" at Government House, with not the slightest interest shown in the substance of the committee's epic visit to the Camp.

We returned to the Upland Goose. Mutton dressed as lamb for dinner, as expected. To give Mr and Mrs King their due, they were dab hands with mutton, and despite the unavoidable uniformity of the main ingredient their kitchen produced interesting and varied menus throughout our stay. It was not exactly their personal fault that supplies of alternatives had dried up for the time being: the breakdown of air and sea communications with the Latin American mainland was partly responsible; the quite extraordinary monoculture of the Falklands was even more responsible.

The rest of the party sensibly retired early. In response to a covert and whispered invitation from an unintroduced fellow-guest at the earlier party, I foolishly ventured out onto Ross Road, and round the corner to the nearest (probably the only) spit-and-sawdust pub south of Land's End, where I was promised revelations. Over copious pints of Watneys Keg (much the worse

---

[*] which is invariably spelt incorrectly but more appropriately by my children.

for wear – the brew, I mean, but before long the customer also), which I was understandably expected to pay for in hard currency, the revelations consisted of: a couple of soldiers in mufti, slagging off their officers; a man from a West Falkland settlement (who gave evidence to the committee the following day), repeating unprovable but plausible accusations against the proprietor of the Upland Goose, which had already been retailed at Rex Hunt's soirée; and a heavy-browed individual who rather tediously repeated the mantra "I hate the English" over several pints and all the way to closing time.

The one secret which was not revealed to me at the Duck & Drake, or whatever it was then called, was that an unofficial curfew was in place. When I returned to the Upland Goose, at around midnight, the front door was locked, the lights were out, and there was no response to my repeated rings on the bell.[*]

Young and intrepid, I surveyed the prospects at the back of the hotel. My room was on the first floor, immediately above the meat store (into which several mutton carcasses were thrown each day, as into the other properties along the alley, presumably as a substitute for the milk which would have been delivered by Express Dairies back home). I calculated that if I stood on top of the meat store I could, with the cooperation of my roommate, drag myself or be dragged through the window. I therefore threw gravel, called out, sang a little Gilbert & Sullivan and a Wesley anthem or two. But to no avail: my roommate, our very illustrious specialist adviser on Latin-American politics, Dr Walter Little of the University of Liverpool, slept on. After pondering for some time whether I could cope sleeping alongside the dead sheep in the sub-zero temperatures of a Falklands summer night, I sought help from the military police post up the road. After fulminating against that's-what-you'd-expect-from-bloody-politicians-coming-down-here-for-no-bloody-good-reason they kindly wound up what looked like a WWI field telephone, and after an agonising wait (during which the MPs had very generously offered me their floor) they got through to Mr King. It was Mrs King, furious but nonetheless conscious of who would be carefully scrutinising the bills, who opened the door, apologising in simpering tones for their "rural ways".

We awoke the next morning to a hearty breakfast of mutton bacon and eggs. After a brief deliberative meeting in the Upland Goose lounge, the committee set up shop for the next two days in the upstairs meeting room of Stanley Town Hall. The atmosphere was a strange one. On the one hand,

---

[*] Dennis Canavan recalls the bar being peremptorily closed on the evening of our return from our trips to the Camp, and only re-opened when Des was threatened with prosecution for aiding and abetting the enemy (*loc cit*, p 151). My less dramatic but more practical solution to the committee's difficulties had been to purchase a number of bottles and wine boxes from the company store for emergency use, which helped out during press conferences and the like.

the formal rules of the House of Commons were rigidly enforced: every time a cigarette lighter appeared Ken or I leapt up to remind the owner that smoking was not permitted during public sittings of a parliamentary committee. On the other hand, the evidence was frequently drowned by the roar of Phantom jets or Army Air Corps helicopters outside the windows, and there was little we could do to stop the enthusiastic applause of the small audience in support of their fellow islanders. And the committee achieved yet another "first". All the public proceedings were recorded and relayed, in hourly instalments over the coming evenings, by the Falkland Islands Broadcasting Station.* These relays were listened to by almost every adult in the islands, thus achieving something approaching a 100% audience. Several islanders subsequently told us that the broadcasts provided temporary compensation for the recent withdrawal of *The Archers* from the FIBS schedules, with the added draw that the main actors were their near neighbours.

We then set out to meet the neighbours and their listeners on their home turf, commandeering whatever transport was available. Between us we visited more than half the settlements in the Camp, listening to their wartime experiences, and learning of their understandable fears and aspirations for themselves and their children. Three groups spent the weekend in AAC helicopters, visiting farms and settlements in East Falkland and the eastward side of West Falkland. My own group, provided with the only surviving serviceable Beaver float plane, stopped at the main settlement on West Falkland (Port Howard), and then headed for the most distant occupied islands – Pebble (where the Argies had an airstrip), Keppel, staying the night en route at Hill Cove on the main west island and travelling cross-country by Land Rover to Roy Cove, where the Beaver picked us up again and onward to Carcass, the most north-westerly of all (which Falklanders might have to visit if they wanted to see any substantial stand of real trees, with the resident night herons resting high in their branches). Frank Hooley, who seemed to have cheered up a bit since our Science & Technology days, was particularly fascinated by the itinerant New Zealand sheep-shearers plying their trade at enormous speed, and the avuncular Jim Lester and I much appreciated the Johnnie Walker which seemed to be in unlimited supply in the settlement farmhouses, and at whatever time of day.

These were extraordinary places. Only a little over 800 people, in forty or so tiny communities – some no more than a single farming family, perhaps with a couple of living-in hands, but always with thousands of sheep, communities separated not only by many miles but often also by stretches of the South Atlantic, entrancingly blue in February but threatening and storm-ridden for most of the year. Hardly any of them

---

* When the station was privatised in 2005 it sadly changed its name from FIBS to FIRS (Falkland Islands Radio Service).

possessed an ocean-worthy boat. Although their houses seemed well-provisioned, they were supplied almost exclusively by the Falkland Islands Company ship, occasional forays by government-owned Islander and Beaver aircraft, and, on the main islands, by aging Land Rovers driven along the small stretches of serviceable roads near Stanley, or otherwise on country tracks or straight across the sparse turf. Their young children were taught at home, with the help of peripatetic teachers of dubious provenance; and at secondary age were perforce shipped to board in Stanley: which at least gave the scattered population of the Camp a common youthful bond. Apart from a few cows and hens, and some vegetables grown for domestic use, there was no significant horticulture. Nobody fished, in an ocean which George Crabbe would have described as "boiling with fish". So the staple diet was mutton, not lamb but seven-year-old sheep whose wool-yield had declined. Most of the Camp settlements were inhabited by kelpers, some owners of their own land but mostly hereditary tenants of the Falkland Islands Company and other overseas landowners, and a few by people who had come from elsewhere with the positive intention of escaping the world. But almost all eventually retired to Stanley, where at least a medical service was available, which of course added to the English resort atmosphere of the town.

On the VC10 on the way home from Ascension to Brize Norton I talked for a while with the Anglican Bishop responsible for the South Atlantic. He said that he was "shocked" by what he described as the "pagan" atmosphere of the islands. Perhaps he meant "secular", perhaps he meant "materialistic". My own impression was of people not particularly interested in any economic (let alone political) initiative which might lift them out of their simple monoculture, and content to continue in the ways of their fathers, even if it meant eating nothing but mutton, and living with the odour of mutton, in perpetuity. The Falklands economy has considerably revived since this time of course – thanks to commercial fishing and oil – but more recent visitors have confirmed that little has changed in the Camp.

For obvious reasons the FAC's report to Parliament did not use the word "pagan", nor for reasons of delicacy did it refer directly to the anthropologists' studies which suggested that an unusually high level of inbreeding may have contributed to the character of society in the Camp. But such concerns certainly infected the committee's evaluation of the Falklands' future, in which they had little confidence. In this they were over-pessimistic, since the economy has considerably revived in the last thirty years, thanks to commercial fishing, oil, and a substantial British garrison. But more recent visitors have confirmed that little has changed in the Camp.

The committee's final report was to be long-delayed. After further oral evidence in London, Walter Little and I got down to the serious job of producing a draft report, while the committee attended to other matters, meeting four or five times a week to consider overseas aid matters, to examine departmental budgets, to meet ambassadors, foreign ministers, heads of state or government, and the occasional revolutionary. In the middle of April 1983 numbered copies of a draft report on *A policy for the Falkland Islands* were at last circulated to members of the committee only. On 18th April much of its key content appeared on the front page of the *Times*. On 20th April this leak was referred to Mr Speaker Thomas as a matter of parliamentary privilege, and no action followed. On 27th April the committee began to go through the draft report, paragraph by paragraph. On Monday 9th May Margaret Thatcher went to the Palace to seek a Dissolution. The following day the FAC met all morning, all afternoon and evening, and into the small hours of the morning of Wednesday 11th May. At which point they were compelled to draw stumps. A brief special report to the House explained that they had "found it impossible, in the time remaining" to complete consideration of the Chairman's draft Report. By this point they (and we) had met formally for a bit over twenty-two hours; they had considered several hundred amendments (almost all of which I had had to draft), and they had formally divided on ninety-six of them.

The reason for all these shenanigans was not that the report was badly drafted, but that, with Tony Kershaw's blessing – indeed, on his strict instructions – we had based the draft report on the evidence, as the House had for centuries required its committees to do. The leak to *The Times* was a calculated – and successful – bid to derail the report, in order to avoid embarrassing the Thatcher Government. For once the more controversial conclusions were in the public domain it was open season for the Tory whips to put every kind of pressure on their committee members to employ all the traditional delaying tactics. Probably the passage to which the Government most objected was in paragraph 2.15 of our draft, which concluded that: "the weight of evidence argues in favour of the view that Argentina's title to the Falkland Islands (or, at least, to East Falkland) was, at the time of the British occupation in 1833, of greater substance than is or has been credited by official United Kingdom Government sources". This reasonable conclusion was based on a vast quantity of historic diplomatic material, going all the way back to fifteenth-century papal bulls and to eighteenth-century Anglo-Spanish treaties, but also on the fact that British officials themselves had periodically, albeit privately, questioned the robustness of British sovereignty claims during much of the previous century.

However, any admission from anything resembling an "official" source that the UK's sovereignty claim might be anything less than 150% proof was clearly anathema to the Government and a challenge to Mrs T's amour propre. The whips accordingly went about their work: every innocuous amendment from the Labour side of the committee was fought to a division, and a stream of amendments suddenly appeared on the order paper from Robert Banks, the Tory Member for Harrogate, and from the more experienced Eldon Griffiths who, it was generally believed, was the source of the leak to the press.[29] For hours the committee slogged it out in attempts to insert references to the "paramountcy" of the Falklanders' "wishes" in one paragraph, only to be faced with counter-attempts in the next paragraph to remove references to paramountcy and wishes, and replace them with merely "the need to take account" of their "interests". And it carried on until we hit the buffers of a General Election.

The whips were triumphant, of course, since they had avoided the publication of our controversial script during the election campaign. They actually thought that they had avoided its publication altogether, forgetting that the draft, together with all the amendments and tedious voting, would eventually appear in print in the formal minutes of the committee, which duly occurred a few weeks later.[30] But a final report on the future of the Falklands – which reached much the same conclusions, and was again closely fought but this time not to the death – had to wait until the autumn of the following year, with a new committee and some changes of personnel.[31] The dogged and continuing determination of Tony Kershaw to tell the truth was thought by many to have cost him the seat in the Lords which he so richly merited when he retired from the Commons a few years later. Eldon Griffiths, on the other hand, got his knighthood.

In the interval between a draft Report that never reached the press and the publication of its successor eighteen months later, the ghosts of the *General Belgrano* and its drowned men were floating, slowly but inexorably, from the deep blue south Atlantic towards the Ministry of Defence in Whitehall, and ultimately to the Committee Corridor.

Meanwhile, when the select committees were at last re-constituted, more than six months after the 1983 General Election, the new Foreign Affairs Committee had another invasion to investigate, this time in the balmier waters of the Caribbean.

21

A Walk in the Paradise Garden

the FAC in Grenada; the Clerk risks life and limb for his Members; but his novel will never be completed

On 12th October 1983 the Central Committee of the New Jewel Movement of the Caribbean island of Grenada backed the decision of the "security forces" to place the Prime Minister of the People's Revolutionary Government under house arrest. On 14th October Maurice Bishop – a barrister of Gray's Inn - was expelled from the New Jewel Movement, and his deputy, childhood friend, and rival Bernard Coard – a graduate of Brandeis with a doctorate from Sussex - assumed the premiership, albeit briefly. On Wednesday 19th October, having been freed from house arrest by a crowd of about 3,000 of his own supporters, the former prime minister set up new headquarters in Fort Rupert (now known as Fort George), but a few hours later was captured and summarily shot (with several other ministers, as well as his long time partner Jacqueline Creft, and about forty others) by units of the People's Revolutionary Army[*]. The following day the Army chief, General Hudson Austin, announced the formation of a Revolutionary Military Council, and imposed a 24 hour curfew.

On the afternoon of Monday 24th October the British Foreign Secretary, Sir Geoffrey Howe, denied suggestions in the House of Commons of an imminent invasion of Grenada by the USA. Early the following morning a combined force of troops from the United States, Jamaica and Barbados invaded Grenada, ostensibly at the request of the Governor-General, Sir Paul Scoon. By Friday 28th October all US military objectives had been secured, with the loss of 89 dead (45 Grenadians, including 24 civilians, 19 Americans and 25 Cubans) and about 500 wounded. On 31st October the Governor-General announced his intention to appoint an interim "Advisory Council", pending elections, to fill the vacuum created by the collapse of the People's Revolutionary Government and the summary execution of its prime minister.

The United Kingdom Government were more than a little irritated by what had happened. The day after the invasion Geoffrey Howe was back in the Commons, stating that "the extent of the consultation with us was

---

[*] Three months later locals were still solemnly pointing out the bloodstains on the road from the Fort to the town.

regrettably less than we would have wished". Earlier the same day Margaret Thatcher, still not knowing that the invasion was underway, had advised Ronald Reagan to think again before it was too late; she was, she said, "deeply disturbed" about the potential international repercussions and domestic political consequences when she was about to seek parliamentary approval for the siting of American cruise missiles in Britain. A few days later she took the unprecedented step of publicly castigating Reagan, her closest ideological ally: on the BBC World Service (then as now the most-listened-to radio station on the planet) she roundly declared that western democracies should not use force to "walk into other people's countries"; and a few weeks later Geoffrey Howe told the FAC that "once one embarks down the road of beginning to pronounce judgement on the legitimacy or illegitimacy of governments or regimes in Commonwealth or other countries, there is no end to it". This was perhaps the Thatcher government's finest hour. If later US Presidents as well as UK Prime Ministers had heeded their advice we wouldn't have had the second and disastrous Iraq war, we wouldn't have had Afghanistan, we probably wouldn't have had Libya or Syria, and the world might have been an altogether safer place.

At the time of the American invasion of Grenada there was no Foreign Affairs Committee, as the whips, encouraged by the Cabinet, which had been badly-enough bruised during the previous Parliament, continued to drag their feet in the appointment of any of the departmental committees. It was a full six months from the General Election when, on Friday 9th December 1983, members were at last nominated to the FAC and others. Six days later the committee, still chaired by Sir Anthony Kershaw, thanks to overwhelming backbench pressure and despite his notorious "wetness" on the question of Falklands sovereignty, decided to carry out a short inquiry into the situation in Grenada. Funds were extracted at miraculous speed from the Liaison Committee, and a few days before Christmas the outline of a visit was agreed. On 15th January 1984 six members of the committee took off for Barbados. But without Sir Anthony, who was left at home, injured, according to whichever account you were inclined to believe, either by an accident at the Berkeley or Beaufort Hunt or by falling through an open drain in Green Park (I rather preferred the latter explanation). I attended as the sole bag-carrier.

Grenada was not new ground for the FAC. One of its members, Bowen Wells, was a renowned expert on the country's economic needs, having served for more than a decade as a senior executive of the Commonwealth Development Corporation, and having lived in the Caribbean for much of this time.[32] To my delight, this saved us the bother and cost of employing a specialist adviser. Two years previously the old committee had paid an extended visit to the area, and had devoted a lot of space in their report on the Caribbean and Central America[33] to Britain's diplomatic and economic relationship with Grenada.

By the time of that first visit Grenada was already three years into its brief flirtation with a Windward Islands version of Marxist-Leninism. The New Jewel Movement had inevitably aroused deep suspicions in the United States, where it was automatically viewed as a Soviet and Cuban surrogate, and as economic aid and business with the US and the European Community began to dry up, this had turned into a self-fulfilling prophecy. The PRG was inevitably drifting further into the arms of the established revolutionaries in Havana, who, along with Moscow, were only too happy to offer substantial development aid and also the prospect of some protection in an emergency. The centrepiece of the Cuban deal was the construction of a much-needed new airport, capable of handling long-haul jets. The Grenadians needed this if their tourist industry was ever to take off, and it had in fact been planned in colonial days, initially underwritten by the British Government, and much of the electronics supplied by British companies (notably Plessey Airports Ltd). But the US administration fulminated that it could also provide Cuba with a staging post for transatlantic traffic, military as well as civilian, to Africa and Eastern Europe, as well as for imagined operations in central America.

In their earlier report the FAC had shared the widespread international disquiet about the suspension of much of the island's constitution (including not insignificant features such as elections and habeas corpus) and the PRG's dependence on support from Havana, Moscow and Pyongyang. On the other hand the committee showed considerable sympathy for the original motives for the insurrection which in 1979 had removed the then prime minister, Sir Eric Gairy, whose nominally "Westminster model" regime they had described as "corrupt, repressive and sustained only by rigged elections", and which had "grossly mismanaged" the economy; and they commented favourably on the "considerable degree of success achieved by the economic and social policies of the PRG, and of the extent to which they have improved the lot of the ordinary people of Grenada", and hence the popularity of the regime; and they noted with approval that there was still "a strong private sector". They also showed some understanding of the PRG's security concerns, which were far from unrealistic in view of the track-record of the CIA and other US agencies in various countries of central and southern America since the 1950's, and in particular following a US naval exercise, under the transparent name of "Amber and the Amberines", which had been conducted in the northern Caribbean but was widely regarded as a rehearsal for operations against the real-life Grenada (with or without the Grenadines), and as an open threat to the People's Revolutionary Government.[*]

---

[*] Quite apart from their proximity to and familiarity with the politics of central America, both Bishop (at the LSE) and Coard (at the University of Sussex) would

After the murder of Maurice Bishop on 19th October 1983, and the establishment of martial law, other irritants in the mix became of particular concern to the United States authorities. In particular, the presence in Grenada of several scores of Soviet citizens, for the most part genuinely engaged in improving the island's educational and medical services, but including a suspiciously large contingent of forty or more 'diplomats' and 'advisers' in the Soviet embassy; of several hundred Cuban citizens, for the most part occupied in the construction of Point Salines airport, but widely suspected (rightly as it proved) of having small arms and paramilitary uniforms stashed away in their dormitories; and, perhaps most controversially, of a thousand or so US citizens, mostly students at the St George's University Medical School, a privately-financed American off-shore establishment, whose main campus happened to be sited within yards of the eastern turning circle of the Point Salines runway.

The US was still reeling from the Iran hostages crisis, which had brought down one President at the end of 1980. Ronald Reagan had no particular yen to follow Jimmy Carter's example. Already on his watch suicide bombers in the Lebanon had despatched 63 people (including seventeen Americans) at the US Embassy in April 1983; and only two days before the invasion 241 American Marines (and 58 French paratroopers) were murdered in their barracks. So just as Maurice Bishop had justifiable concerns about the risk of US intervention against his revolutionary government, so the United States administration had justifiable fears about the possibility of a further round of hostage-taking: the armed Cuban construction workers were based only a few hundred yards away from the medical students' dormitories. On 19th October, after news was received of Maurice Bishop's murder, the USS Independence and its accompanying escorts and troop-carriers, previously headed for Beirut, diverted towards the south-eastern Caribbean.

The committee's task, in January 1984, was three-fold: to assess what were now the aid needs of the island following the sudden withdrawal of Soviet and Cuban support; to discover what really happened in Grenada in the week following Maurice Bishop's murder; and to find some way of countering and correcting the allegedly widespread belief that the United Kingdom had somehow "failed" the Caribbean by not participating in Operation Urgent Fury.

In the unavoidable absence of the chairman (to use the time-honoured phrase) the team which arrived in Barbados on Monday 16th January was led by one of the committee's new boys. The Rt Hon Peter Thomas QC was that very rare phenomenon – a genuine native Welsh-speaking Tory. An

---

have been very well schooled in contemporary academic exposés of US Cold War shenanigans (eg Theodore Draper, *Abuse of Power,* Penguin, 1967; eg David Horowitz, *From Yalta to Vietnam*, Penguin, 1971).

RAF bomber pilot who had been shot down in 1941 and had spent the last years of the war in a variety of German Stalags, he had served as a junior Foreign Office minister under Sir Alec Douglas-Home, as the first Welsh-speaking chairman of the Conservative Party, and then as Secretary of State for Wales throughout Ted Heath's administration; and in his spare time was also a Welsh circuit judge, a Crown Court Recorder, and an arbitrator at the International Chamber of Commerce in Paris. He was a tall, imposing, hook-nosed and gentle man, judicious and kind.[34]

Despite his considerable experience elsewhere, Peter Thomas was not yet wholly trained up for the rough-and-tumble of select committee life. He had never before served on any investigative select committees, and the new FAC had held not a single formal evidence session before leaving Heathrow. Meetings with the charismatic young Barbadian prime minister, Tom Adams, and the Leader of the Opposition Earl Barrow were fairly restrained (each putting an eloquent but fairly formal case for and against the invasion), and there was nothing unexpected in the private briefings with the UK High Commissioner and other UK diplomats, where a certain amount of letting down of hair over gin and tonic (or in this case more likely Doorly's rum) was normal.

However, Peter Thomas admitted considerable confusion when we went on to meet the US Ambassador, Mr Milan D Bish. Within moments of our arrival Dennis Canavan and Nigel Spearing were firing from both barrels, for the most part aided and abetted by Bowen Wells and Jim Lester, who realised that unquestioning support and admiration for the Reagan administration was on this occasion definitely not required by Downing Street, and that they were therefore off the leash. Peter Thomas looked on aghast. I had provided the usual half a side of "straight" questions for him, but he told me after this magnificent encounter that he had never been into a meeting with the representatives of a foreign government without a full and detailed brief, and without clear instructions from the FCO of the line to take on each point. On this occasion, however, the UK High Commissioner sat silent, bemused and amused, at the back of the room, taking copious notes but saying naught: this was, after all, a parliamentary show.

Our leader's predicament intensified as Ambassador Bish got into his own stride. He also was no part of the politically correct establishment. What the State Department describe as a "non-career appointee", he had been a supporter and fundraiser for Reagan in the state of Nebraska, where he had made a modest fortune in real-estate, industrial machinery and cattle, and after serving as part of Reagan's presidential transition team had been rewarded with the post in Barbados, which also covered most of the small islands of the southern Caribbean (with the significant exception of Grenada, a diplomatic pariah, to which only the United Kingdom amongst Western nations had full accreditation).

Our main concern in talking to the US Ambassador was to get a clearer idea of the chronology of events leading up to the arrival of the marines and special forces, but also to establish why the UK Government seemed not to have been fully informed. Why were communications from the State Department to the Foreign Office so misleading? Was it merely a result of the ineptitude of our own diplomats in London? Or of our diplomats in the Caribbean? Ambassador Bish's responses were wonderfully robust and wonderfully informative. He had no reason to wilt under hostile questioning, since he actually wanted to tell us something approximating more closely to the truth than any trained professional would have been capable. He gave us much more detail of his own to-ings and fro-ings in mid-October than had previously been revealed, but then generously volunteered the key to an understanding of the whole episode. He looked round the room at the assembled career diplomats and said, in more or less exactly these words: "I am my President's man. If I know something needs to be done, I talk to my President. Hell, the one thing we did *not* require was the involvement of all these boys from State, with their theories and their buts and their ifs and their wait-and-see-what-the-Brits-are-going-to-do. I went straight to my President, and he and I agreed what had to be done; and number one on the list of the things that had to be done was that as far as possible *nothing* should be said to the boys at State: you could never be sure who they'd tell next."

None of this of course excused the Foreign Office and its ministers for not heeding the intelligence from their own men on the ground, who had signalled quite enough information before the invasion about the arrival of US advance units in Bridgetown. But it certainly did explain why Whitehall continued to receive a flow of reassurances from Washington until the invasion forces were already on their way in to Grenada. Their interlocutors at the State Department were probably conveying what they honestly thought the situation to be - because some parts at least of the State Department were deliberately excluded from the loop.[*] When the committee later reported to Parliament they could not of course quote Ambassador Milan D Bish. Instead they merely concluded, in appropriately diplomatic language, that "it was not the intention of the United States Government that the United Kingdom Government should be involved, and that the timing, nature and extent of the information provided to the United Kingdom Government by the United States were consistent with that position". We wondered amongst ourselves what the hell GCHQ and other grand

---

[*] This exclusion probably applied only to the career diplomats, and not to senior political appointees: the then Secretary of State, George Shultz, subsequently claimed that he was effectively in the driving seat, urging Reagan to immediate action in case Casper Weinberger and the Pentagon were to "drag out our preparations until it was too late". Quoted in Geoffrey Howe, *Conflict of Loyalty*, London (1994), pp 334-7.

organisations with MI numbers were actually doing as these exciting events unfolded.

Our conclusions were accepted by the media as fact. I for one was nevertheless slightly uncertain whether we had got it right until thirty years later when, in November 2014, the White House released the transcripts of Ronald Reagan's phone conversations with Margaret Thatcher a few days after Operation Urgent Fury. "If I were there, Margaret, I'd throw my hat in the door before I came in", he said in good Frontier tradition. He'd had to keep Britain and others in the dark for fear of a mole, but "it was no feeling on our part of lack of confidence at your end. It's at our end". This was all pretty ingenuous, since the real reason for not involving the UK was that the blessed Margaret would almost certainly have opposed the whole enterprise. But at least, all those years later, it confirmed that our story was essentially correct. The end of the hotline conversation was classic Hollywood. Mrs T was on her way to the Commons to justify cruise missiles. Reagan left her with a from-the-hip quote from one of his many B-westerns: "All right. Go get 'em. Eat 'em alive". Future transatlantic relations might have been a good deal rockier if Ronald Reagan's thespian skills had deserted him at this critical moment.

The following day, fleeing the by then rum-soaked mosquitoes of Barbados, we made a day-trip to Port of Spain.[*] Here the US, and nominal Caribbean, invasion of Grenada was still openly resented by the Prime Minister, George Chambers, and most of the local political community. The longstanding differences between the members of CARICOM (which included all the former British Caribbean colonies) and of the Organisation of Eastern Caribbean States (OECS), which comprised merely the small islands surrounding Barbados, had been bitterly exposed by the events in Grenada. With Barbados taking an active lead, the OECS states had encouraged and supported the US invasion; the remaining CARICOM states, led by Trinidad & Tobago (which had close economic and family relations with Grenada), had espoused merely sanctions, with hopes of a negotiated and diplomatic solution. As we learned on the weekend before the invasion, CARICOM, meeting in Port of Spain, had collectively supported a non-interventionist approach to the Grenada situation, although its OECS members, along with Barbados, had already formally invited the US to intervene, and Reagan had already signed the necessary orders. Although in Bridgetown the United Kingdom was being accused of "failing its friends" by not participating in the invasion, in Port of Spain the main question was "why didn't the UK intervene to stop US aggression against a friendly Commonwealth state?".

---

[*] Bowen Wells sagely advised us that you should always drink the rum from somebody else's island since the local mosquitoes always preferred their own domestic brand: good advice which some of us had foolishly ignored.

We finally flew into Pearls, the old airport in the north of the island, on the evening of Tuesday 17th January 1984. The twenty-mile-odd journey on the rough road down to the capital, St George's, was like travelling through something akin to the paradise islands of childhood imagination. The air was full of the scent of nutmeg and mace, and children played beneath the enormous banana trees which formed the centrepiece of many of the island smallholdings. As we got nearer to St George's we witnessed US Marines being taught cricket by the local boys (rather than teaching the local boys the alien game of baseball) – testimony to an unusually enlightened commander – and causing great hilarity amongst the locals.

After a close inspection of the blood-stained road down from the Fort (which was evidently *de rigueur*), we checked in to the St James Hotel, a decaying and quintessentially Commonwealth establishment, with good local food, an excellent bar (when caught open) and otherwise somewhat primitive facilities. On my first morning I watched from my bed transfixed as an army of red ants traversed my room in strict order, inspected everything in my suitcase, and then departed under the door. They were a well-disciplined army, left no mess, and I hope had picked up a good deal of protein on the march. I then took a hot shower. Even by the standards of, say, Rangoon or Hanoi, the shower mechanism was remarkably ingenious: a rubber hose was slung from the single tap in the sink, and was hooked over the top of a screen; the cold water then played slowly over a glowing electric element, which could be switched on and off by a pull switch, located alongside the water jet; with luck, warm water emerged, and the hotel resident – if still alive – could gently wash. This was not some local Heath Robinson creation; there were labels proclaiming that it was a power shower designed and made in Cuba, and the hotel staff seemed well pleased with this important technological development provided by the comrades up north.

During the next four days we managed to pack in no less than twenty-four separate meetings with interlocutors ranging from trade unionists to churchmen, election officials, tradesmen, farm managers, food exporters, the chairman and members of the temporary Advisory Council. I took a lot of notes. We visited Point Salines to get first-hand accounts of the invasion and the fighting from Plessey, we visited smallholdings, and after sometimes fraught negotiations with the Chairman of the Advisory Council, Nicholas Braithwaite, the police and the Americans, the Governor-General allowed Peter Thomas and Nigel Spearing to visit some of the forty-odd detainees – former members and servants of the Revolutionary Government and its short-lived aftermath – in Richmond Hill Prison. They were held without charge (although capital charges of murder and conspiracy were likely to be, and eventually were, preferred against many of them) and without trial (under "Peoples' Laws" of doubtful provenance decreed by the PRG itself), and there was widespread concern amongst cognoscenti in the

UK, which was only partially allayed by the reassurances our members were able to provide about at least the physical conditions in the jail.

A particularly illuminating encounter was lunch at Morne Fendué, high in the Grenadian hills, where the châtelaine was able to pass on to us more useful intelligence on the inward workings of the revolutionary regime and its young people (and their current whereabouts) than was ever available from our official interlocutors and all their documentation.

Officially, of course, our most important meetings were with the Governor-General, Sir Paul Scoon. A former UK and Canadian educated secondary school teacher, he had risen rapidly in the small Grenada civil service from Chief Education Officer to Cabinet Secretary, and at the early age of thirty-eight was appointed Deputy Director of the Commonwealth Foundation in London. He returned as Governor General in September 1978, and had held the ring during the New Jewel Movement interregnum. It is testimony to the good sense of Her Majesty and her advisers in the Commonwealth that they generally make a point of picking people with greater diplomatic skills than those required in the standard job description for what is usually a largely ceremonial post, just in case of an emergency.

Central to the allegation of the Barbadian prime minister that Britain had "failed its friends" was the claim that the UK Government had been invited to participate in a multinational force both by his own government and others in the OECS, and directly by the Governor-General of Grenada. Our investigations so far had established that three days before the invasion Tom Adams had indeed expressed his personal wish for Britain, Canada, France and Venezuela to be involved (or even to lead the expedition), and had indicated that formal requests would be issued the following day. In fact, however, no such formal requests were ever issued to any non-Caribbean country other than the United States (and theirs had already been issued before any of the others were even informed). The Foreign Office knew of the exchanges, and also knew that the OECS and CARICOM countries were meeting in Port of Spain ostensibly to discuss what to do. But since the Foreign Office was being deliberately misled by Washington to believe that there was no immediate urgency, and since it was the weekend, no action was taken other than to divert the only British warship in the area as a precautionary measure in case of the need to evacuate British nationals.

When we met Sir Paul Scoon we needed to discover whether he really had asked for Britain's help, but had then been ignored. We already knew that, despite being under house arrest by the People's Revolutionary Army, he had managed a covert exchange with the British Deputy High Commissioner, David Montgomery, in the tranquil gardens of Government House on Saturday 23rd October, shortly before the High Commissioner's own meeting with Tom Adams in Bridgetown. When we reported to the House we were barred from revealing any detail of our own conversations with either David Montgomery or with Sir Paul, although all was carefully recorded in my small notebooks. But we were able to state categorically, and with some confidence, that he had not actually asked Britain to help. In fact the Governor-General claimed that he had not specifically asked for any other country to intervene militarily since he had hoped that the situation might be stabilised by more peaceful means, although he thought he might have suggested that military intervention could "in the end" turn out to be the "only solution". The Barbadian Prime Minister Tom Adams, having been briefed on David Montgomery's visit by Giles Bullard, the latter's immediate boss, later the same day paraphrased Scoon's message by telling Reagan's special emissary Francis MacNeil that the Governor-General regarded force as "the only solution". Sir Paul's other revelation in the paradise garden was equally significant. He said categorically that he had not instigated the letter seeking American and Caribbean military intervention; although it was dated 24th October 1983 (ie the day before the invasion) he had not seen even a draft before he had been rescued a few days later and was safely aboard a US warship.

Subsequent memoirs and recollections have added detail, but not any real substance, to the picture which the committee was able to draw from its own conversations so soon after the events. Paul Scoon, in his autobiography, elaborated his account of the famous letter, adding that there were in fact four separate letters to President Reagan, and to the Prime Ministers of Barbados, Jamaica, and Dominica (the formidable Eugenia Charles); that they had been signed in a house near Point Salines after his evacuation and subsequent return to Grenada; and also that he had "temporized" when the Deputy High Commissioner had asked him, in their conspiratorial meeting in the garden of Government House, if he would put a request for military assistance in writing.[35] It was subsequently ascertained by the distinguished Caribbean socialist historian Richard Hart that the letters which he eventually did sign were actually delivered to Sir Paul by a minister in the Jamaican government (Tony Abrahams), who only reached Grenada after the invasion, and who still found Sir Paul Scoon "reluctant" to sign them.[36]

What emerged was a very human picture of a man under duress, trying hard to do his duty, seriously alarmed by the situation, but extremely reluctant to authorise what would amount to a foreign invasion of his own country.[*] The whole episode illustrates how the nuances of conversations can so easily be misinterpreted when all the participants involved are under pressure of time, are constrained by the need for secrecy, and have predetermined agendas to follow. On balance, after reviewing the literature, my own belief is that Paul Scoon had concluded that some form of military intervention was inevitable, but had no wish to be seen in any way to have

---

[*] "military intervention into one's territory was not the sort of thing I would normally advocate" (Scoon, p 145)

been its instigator – not least because if military intervention had failed (and even US invasions are not always successful) he would be faced with the wrath of General Hudson Austin and the Revolutionary Military Council which for the time being continued to be the de facto government of which the Governor-General was in legal theory still the titular head.

It was also the committee's conclusion that the British Government was rather better informed than it claimed about what was afoot (and there is evidence to confirm our impression that the High Commissioner had provided very full information to the FCO in London) but that it chose (for what were probably very good reasons) to turn a blind eye to the reality of the situation which was unfolding in the Caribbean, and to rely instead on reassurances from Washington which some at least in London must have realised were straying from that reality. It was certainly claimed by Paul Scoon and others that Giles Bullard, the High Commissioner, actually urged on London that "Britain should give its support or, at the very least, should refrain from doing anything that might weaken or jeopardize" the enterprise. This was not quite the impression we received directly from Bullard.

On our last afternoon in Grenada, while Peter Thomas and Nigel Spearing were visiting the detainees, we had a few hours to spare. Bowen Wells and Jim Lester apparently went off to look for business opportunities, while Dennis Canavan and Mick Welsh[37] probably went off in search of revolutionaries. After a brief visit to Curtis Strachan, the Clerk of the Parliament who (in its abeyance) was then serving as Secretary to the Advisory Council*, I found myself in a small go-down in the road on the other (ie the not-blood-stained) side of the St James Hotel. There I acquired, in addition to some excellent local beer, an illicit copy of *Morning Star*, an LP rather optimistically celebrating "5 years of revolution: 1979-1984", performed and recorded in Grenada the previous year, shortly before the revolution had reached its buonapartist stage, by the local music hero Peter Radix, side A featuring a lugubrious rendition of "African Man, Raise your Hand".[38] This revolutionary material had been banned by the occupation authorities, and had to be smuggled out of the country under all the many documents with which I was encumbered, and its pessimistic strains nearly drove my family to murder for a few weeks after my return home.

I also took the opportunity to make use of the Travel Wash which accompanied me round the world to restore the socks and other items which in the heat had needed changing several times daily, all of which I hung carefully to dry over the louvers which served the place of windows. In the evening we had a celebratory dinner in the hotel restaurant, fine-tuning (indeed, plotting) arrangements for the journey home, as a tropical storm

---

* Sir Curtis Strachan was a big wheel in the fraternity of Commonwealth clerks, and later served two terms as Speaker of the Grenada House of Representatives from 1995 to 2003.

lashed the walls and blew the candles out. In the morning I was up early with the sun, and gazed sadly over the rooftops of St George's, much regretting my imminent departure, and identifying the various items of my undergarments now scattered over the rooftops of the town. At least they were reasonably clean.

Unbeknownst to the interim administration (or at least officially unbeknownst) members of the committee had managed during their stay to locate the whereabouts of several former members of the People's Revolutionary Government who were still on the run from the newly installed peace-keeping force. So much for US intelligence. Before our flight to Barbados, therefore, the committee took to the hills, ostensibly to spend a last few hours with the charming hostess whose hospitality at lunch they had so much appreciated two days earlier, while I went back up the mace-infused road to Pearls, with all the luggage. This I checked in, and explained that the Members of Parliament were briefly delayed, but would be arriving shortly. I waited, and the airport staff waited. Our plane arrived, disgorged its small passenger load, and our baggage was taken on board. Time passed. The scheduled departure time came and went. The pilot eventually told me that he had to leave, and started his engines. He couldn't get even further behind his schedule than usual: his job would be at risk. But I couldn't leave seven members of the British Parliament stranded in the Caribbean without a change of clothes: my job would be even more at risk. I resorted to desperate measures. In an uncharacteristic act of bravado I stood in my suit, official-issue briefcase (emblazoned with the royal crest) in hand, immediately in front of the starboard propeller, and stared determinedly at the driver. He periodically revved up the engines, and I ruefully shook my head in reply. After twenty minutes or so of stand-off the committee's 4X4's roared onto the tarmac. They failed to run me over, and all clambered triumphantly aboard without a word of solicitude or apology to either the pilot, who had risked his job, or to me, who had risked my life.

Within days of our return to Westminster the main Committee Office was piled high with thousands of pages of captured documents from the People's Revolutionary Government and the Central Committee of the New Jewel Movement, helpfully copied on to us by US intelligence services to bolster our disdain for those their invasion had so successfully overthrown. Along with my copious notes, these were enormously helpful in enabling me to produce a substantial report in what for me (or, frankly, anybody else) was record time. Within a month the 30,000-word draft report had been circulated to the committee, the key amendments had also been drafted, and on 29 February 1984 the FAC got down to the business of considering Mr Peter Thomas' draft report.

This was a fraught time on the domestic front. In the midst of the drafting process, on 16th February, Sue and I, with two small children, moved house. As we moved in the central heating boiler, which had evidently not been much used, split apart, and the ground floor was flooded while the removal men carried on regardless. Two days later Sue's parents moved into the "granny annex" next door. On Saturday 3rd March I made a substantial contribution to the prevailing gloom by breaking my left humerus clean in two. This I achieved by tripping over the newly-installed, much-applauded, but very badly-illuminated disability ramp at the back door of our church and flying at high speed into a side wall, while accompanying our oldest and much-intellectually-challenged adopted son to a rehearsal of a great new musical on the theme of David and Goliath. In nightmare moments the strains of "He's broader than a barrel, taller than a tree, Twice around the gasworks is once round he" still come back to haunt me. That my wife ever forgave me is one of those unfathomable mysteries of the human spirit and of female endurance. So, having lost a chairman for a while, the committee had now lost its clerk – two cases of misadventure.

While I sat at home in voluble pain, surrounded by people I much loved, grinning-and-bearing while carpets needed ripping up, floors needed cleaning, and curtains needed hanging, and while attempting in those pre-internet days to give helpful advice to the office over the phone, the committee spent the next two weeks locked in conflict. In five very lengthy meetings they managed no less than ninety-six formal votes, ending with divisions on the question whether "this be the second report of the committee to the House" and even on the question "that the Chairman do make the report to the House". This was not the result of bad drafting, and was certainly not the result of bad clerking since Crispin Poyser did a widely-praised job in handling a text about which he initially knew little. Nor was it the result of bad feeling between members of the committee since they were a rather happy crew. It did reflect, however, both a real sense of post-colonial responsibility for Grenada (and therefore the need to get it right), and the determination of the Labour members, and Dennis Canavan in particular, that the Foreign Affairs Committee should follow party policy and formally and publicly condemn the invasion of Grenada. But Dennis was wrong on this one (unusually – he was right about most things): to have condemned the USA would have also meant condemning Barbados, and would have helped to perpetuate precisely the kind of ill-feeling with and between our Caribbean friends that it was in everyone's interest to dispel.

The report was published on Thursday 5th April 1984. The next day the papers had a field day. "Britain was 'lethargic' over Grenada", said the *Telegraph*, "MPs attack Howe's Grenada 'inaction'", said the *Guardian*, "Howe gets a roasting on Grenada", said the *Sun*, "Britain 'dithered' as US invaded" over "Grenada gaffe", added the *Daily Mail*. And the *Times*, recalling its glory days, thundered "While Britain Slept". Only the *FT* came up with a characteristically balanced assessment – particularly well balanced, in my view, since it highlighted what I regarded as the conclusions of the Report most relevant for the future: there had been much international hand-wringing in the aftermath of the invasion of St George's about the vulnerability of small (or, as they were coming to be known in the trade, "micro") states; but much less about "the susceptibility of apparently stable international alliances and communities to the disruptive effects of events on their margins". "As the world has so often learned in the past, and at such great cost", I had opined in leader-writing mode, "wars break out, and alliances fall apart, not so often as the result of deliberate decisions by the major powers, but as a result of the inability of the great power system, and the alliances which support it, to cope with the problems of small countries in faraway parts of the globe".[39]

Geoffrey Howe, a good-humoured sort of a politician, took it all pretty well. Not least because long before our report lighted up the tabloids it was clear that the UK had actually emerged from the whole episode with its reputation largely intact, and, in parts of the world, enhanced. It was certainly true that a small number of Caribbean states remained aggrieved that Britain had not immediately rallied to their call to arms; but a more or less equal number of Caribbean states had been adamantly opposed from the start to armed intervention in Grenada, and were therefore grateful that Whitehall had kept free of involvement. A month or so after the invasion, the Commonwealth Heads of Government had met in Goa, and the American intervention had been widely condemned. The British Government, with clean hands, could therefore assist in the process of healing wounds, and for a short time even assume the mantle of champion of the small states.

So the United Kingdom emerged from the whole episode more a winner than a loser. It couldn't in practice have contributed in any useful way to the aspirations of Barbados and others for an immediate invasion, since its forces were far away and sadly diminished. But Margaret and Geoffrey were able to play the role of good cops, to the plaudits of most of the Commonwealth, and immediately after the event to provide the kind of aid which the Grenadians actually needed – new power-generating sets and, almost as important, a training school for their own good cops.

There were other winners. The United States had demonstrated beyond any doubt its non-tolerance of anything to the left of the liberal democrats, and had re-enforced its hegemony in the Caribbean. If you wanted immediate action, there was no point looking to the old colonial owners because they were too tired and too far away, but the US of A would be there; and if you merely wanted to get on with your own local thermidor without outside interference, the US of A would also still be there, and would be watching, with at least a carrier force or two ready for action against you a few hundred nautical miles up the roads. Most of the Commonwealth Caribbean states could also for one reason or another congratulate themselves as winners: Britain's non-intervention had from one perspective demonstrated the old country's demise as a world force, but from another had demonstrated Britain's wisdom and restraint and respect for the principles of democracy and self-determination, and of Commonwealth solidarity. And so far as the Grenadians were concerned, after the trauma of invasion and the horror of the blood-letting in their beautiful streets, they at least, and at last, attracted the volume of western (and particularly British) aid needed to lift their economy in general, and even to complete the new airport and refurbish the roads to allow the banana crop to reach the coast unbruised.

Of the main Grenadian actors, Bernard Coard, his wife Phylis and the rest of the "Granada 17", tried by American-backed kangaroo courts, were definitely losers, although thanks to enormous international pressure they didn't actually lose their heads. It is testimony to the indomitability of the human spirit that when finally released from Richmond Prison a full twenty-six years after his incarceration, Coard humorously confirmed that he "never wanted to have anything to do with politics for the rest of my life", but offered to become an economics correspondent for the *Trinidad Express* instead.[40] Sir Paul Scoon was of course the hero of the hour, and eventually retired with laurels in 1992 as the elder statesman and saviour of his country. Even the idealistic Maurice Bishop had a small posthumous success: in 2009 Point Salines was renamed the "Maurice Bishop International Airport".

The Foreign Affairs Committee were definite winners. Their report was almost universally accepted as an authoritative record of what had happened, so far as what had actually happened could at that time be revealed (which was limited). Indeed, apart from the plaudits of the media and the acceptance of our analysis by the UK government, we had the peculiar honour of a second print-run required for the more-than-a-little-surprising reason that the US Navy Department had bought up the entire remaining stock (of several hundred copies) of the original print; we were never quite sure why (were they trying to suppress it?), but it was encouraging to know that somebody out there might be reading us (and even if they were simply incinerating their copies at least it meant we had been noticed). The FAC's reputation for decent detective work was definitely enhanced in the eyes of the media and – most importantly - in the eyes of the diplomatic community, upon whose goodwill and cooperation its future progress depended.*

Proud though I was of this whole enterprise, I nevertheless ended up as one of the losers, or at least one of the disappointed. The first half of the report read as not a bad novelette, albeit one with the feel of a *Reader's*

---

* In a telegram to overseas posts on the day before publication, the FCO said they had found the FAC report (of which they had advance copies in the usual way) "generally accurate and perspicacious", and in a letter to the UK Ambassador in Brazil three weeks later the head of the West Indian & Atlantic Department described it as "quite a balanced and sensible effort". This was high praise indeed.

Digest condensed book (which we had all read so avidly in holiday boarding houses in our youth). My ambition had always been to turn my much more comprehensive notes into a real novel. There was very definite Graham Greene, Hemingway (or at least John Buchan) potential, and I fancied following in my father's footsteps, even if the results were, like his, more Captain W E Johns or Agatha Christie.[41]

Much of my long summer recess in 1984 was devoted to producing, at the request of the interim administration, a new constitution for Grenada, which might have made the "Westminster" model actually workable in that small community. These efforts proved ultimately fruitless because protocol required that the finished product should be delivered in person by a very-much-more-senior member of the clerkly establishment, who in this case turned out to be the much revered Michael Ryle – one to propound a bit of fine-tuning here and there, but not one equipped by nature to propose a small revolution. My extremely persuasive text therefore went into the archives, and in September (when, in those rather more civilised days, Parliament was still in deep recess) I decided to spend a few days at home mapping the outline of my first novel (working title: *A Walk in the Paradise Garden*).

My set of half-a-dozen small notebooks, of some potential historical importance, had been very carefully archived and stored in the Foreign Affairs Committee safe. This was one of those enormous government-issue safes with a complicated combination and a wheel which had to be turned in multiple directions at high speed and with absolute accuracy. It had taken me many months to remember the code, let alone remember the required number of revolutions, but I was beginning to get the hang of it two years on - mainly because against the rules, no doubt like everyone else, I had eventually written it all down on my desk blotter. I had in any case no reason to worry since Kennedy Brown had everything under his experienced control.

The FAC safe was used for a variety of purposes. That we had one at all was a form of flattery, since HMG had no intention of letting us get our hands on anything seriously "classified" (at least, not until the Argentinian navy hoved into view once again and we were able to do a little arm-twisting), but we certainly stacked up copies of government evidence which had not yet been side-lined, and papers submitted to us by anybody which claimed to be at least "Confidential". Vacant space in the safe was used for other purposes. On this occasion, in the summer recess of 1984, it became a convenient depository for the beverages which had not been consumed at the end-of-term party, in case they were needed for a beginning-of-term party in October. The safe faced the windows overlooking the Terrace, and in the months of the summer recess, when few people were moving about, and few doors opened, the main Committee Office became a trifle warm, and the safe became an oven. The cartons of long life orange were stored on one shelf of the safe. When they exploded, my prized notebooks were on the shelf below: my novel was not to be.

After all these years, some intriguing questions remain, and plausible conspiracy theories have flourished. The US administration had for long been concerned about Grenada, which they viewed as the other end of a Leninist axis from the north to the south of the Caribbean. What would they have done if Maurice Bishop had not been murdered? Would they have allowed his regime to continue? Did Bishop's murder come at a peculiarly convenient moment, when Grenada was not yet sufficiently militarised to be a threat, and when its new airport was not yet open to traffic, Cuban or otherwise? If Bishop's murder had not provided a respectable reason for intervention, would the CIA have had to find or even invent one?

22

The Phoenix rises

The Belgrano *inquiry; reading the Rules of Engagement; two contrary Reports, all based on the same evidence*

By mid-March 1984 we had signed off our elegant analysis of the invasion of Grenada and, as a spin-off, we had launched a new inquiry (never to be completed) into "the economic and political security of micro-states". It was to be a busy year: we were going through the routines of examining the accounts and expenditure plans of the Foreign & Commonwealth Office, the Overseas Development Administration and agencies such as the BBC Overseas Service; and we (or mainly I) were in the process of re-writing the previously aborted report on the Falklands (killed by hand of Sir Eldon Griffiths), in the vain hope of producing something which would propitiate the anger of the goddess in Downing Street. In the latter venture we failed miserably since, try as we would, our eventual report to the House was even more sceptical about Britain's "sovereignty" in the Malvinas than its predecessor*: but at least there wasn't another General Election on the immediate horizon. And in early April we were taking evidence from Geoffrey Howe on the forthcoming Fontainebleau meeting of Heads of Government, which was (as they so often are) billed as a "last chance" to avert a major political and financial crisis in Europe.[42]

While Ken and I were hurriedly organising a trip to Bonn, Paris and Rome to discuss these latter weighty issues with ministers and fellow members of the international fraternity of foreign affairs committees, on Wednesday 17th April a fracas in St James's Square between pro and anti Gaddafi enthusiasts led to the fatal shooting of WPC Yvonne Fletcher from an upstairs window of the 'Libyan People's Bureau', then largely occupied by a motley collection of Libyan students, no doubt nominally accredited to one of London's many polytechnics (soon to be elevated to university status). This in turn led to the launch of yet another FAC inquiry, this time into the "abuse of diplomatic privileges and immunities", which involved

---

* The Committee alarmingly concluded that "The historical and legal evidence demonstrates such areas of uncertainty that we are unable to reach a categorical conclusion on the legal validity of the claims of either country" (Fifth Report from the Foreign Affairs Committee, Session 1983-84 (HC 268-I), para 22.

the disembowelment of the Vienna Convention on Diplomatic Relations and related consular agreements and an examination of FCO and Home Office practices and procedures in upholding and policing their operation.[43]

Meanwhile, in view of mounting speculation in the left-wing and international media about who had started the shooting war in the South Atlantic, the Committee had agreed in February to enlarge the compass of its second-time-round questioning of Falklands witnesses to probe the reasons for the failure of the final round of peace negotiations conducted by the President of Peru (Belaúnde Terry) and so assiduously by the US Secretary of State (General Alexander Haig), whose shuttle diplomacy had foundered over the weekend of 1st-2nd May 1982. All this meant that by Easter the main committee had at least five non-routine inquiries already running. Half the committee's members were also occupied in looking after our overseas aid and development brief, skilfully steered by Crispin, and contemplating trips afield to undernourished parts of Africa and/or Asia. The rest of the year was therefore already spoken for; we really didn't need anything else. We were, even more than usually, looking forward to the long recess.

Too bad. At around 3.45 on the afternoon of Wednesday 18th July, Sir Thomas Dalyell of the Binns, the eleventh of that ilk, made his habitually furtive progress along the main Committee Corridor and berthed alongside me in the small, quiet and pure Pugin conference room then still attached to the FAC and the Defence Committee. Having spent the entire morning taking evidence yet again from the Foreign Secretary, I was at that moment desperately trying to make some sense of the Vienna Convention out of reach of the office telephones.[*]

Tam Dalyell[44] was an old sparring partner (as he was for most clerks) and I sort-of dutifully welcomed him but prayed that it would not be for too long. In his memoirs Tam says that he had received from an anonymous source a "postcard", which he then passed on to Sir Anthony Kershaw, "an honourable gentleman and friendly to me". In fact he passed on far more than a postcard, and he passed them on to me. Tam provided me with a bootleg copy of an internal Ministry of Defence Minute (which became known as the "Legge Memorandum") which confirmed the extent to which 'spin' was already prevalent in the MoD (but said little else); together with copies of internal MoD papers (including a draft reply to Tam's own persistent questioning in the House) which appeared to reveal hitherto unpublished information about the course of the cruiser *General Belgrano*

---

[*] When things got really desperate, and it was simply impossible to think, I was still able to return to any of the vacant conference rooms in the now semi-derelict St Stephen's House, and would let only Ken know where I could be contacted in a real emergency.

during the fateful weekend of Saturday 1st and Sunday 2nd May 1982.

Tam recounts that earlier in the day he had been advised by my old protector Kenneth Bradshaw (by then Clerk Assistant, and soon to become Clerk of the House) to make sure that whichever way he raised the issues he did so as part of "proceedings of Parliament", and would therefore be wholly protected by parliamentary privilege. The most obvious route was to raise the matter on the floor of the House while waving, and specifically referring to, the documents in his hand. Tam, however, decided to pursue his own more subtle route, which was to try to engage the Foreign Affairs Committee, which was already diving into the troubled waters of the South Atlantic. He handed the papers over to me, and I promised to get into immediate contact with Tony Kershaw.

Sir Anthony's reaction was only mildly apoplectic: he didn't much like leaks of any kind, and even less did he like leakers. His initial instruction was to send all the papers direct to the Ministry of Defence, let them sort it out, and prosecute the buggers – and certainly not to bring them anywhere near the committee; after all the mere fact that something had been given to the committee clerk surely did not and could not mean that it was necessarily formal evidence and therefore automatically "privileged"?* After a little reflection, and after more discussions with the 'Wigs' downstairs, we eventually thought it better to consult the full committee, since some at least of the Labour members would be likely already to know all about Tam's visit, and would demand an explanation.

There was no denying that the unsavoury documents were germane to the committee's inquiries, since in June the Tory majority on the committee had, with undisguised distaste, already agreed to go along with the Labour minority's demands that we should report separately to the House on "the events of 1-2 May 1982". So Tam's documents were examined at the committee's next regular meeting, the Secretary of State for Defence was summoned to give evidence – and, as a potential witness, he was provided with "the documents submitted to the Committee by a member of the House on 18th July", upon which he would be invited to comment. Tam concluded

---

* Which was and remains a moot point. There has always been some uncertainty about the status of unsolicited documents submitted to committees: if all were admitted as formal evidence, then it would be open to any Tam, Dick or Harry, to bung into the hands of the committee staff any piece of paper, however inaccurate, scurrilous or mendacious, and of however little relevance to the committee's work, and thereafter claim "privilege". In this case, the status of the documents was particularly compromised because they were quite obviously bootleg photocopies, and were certainly not being submitted by their authors. Tam's version was that Tony Kershaw "did what I should have guessed any officer who went through 1940-45 with the 16th/5th Lancers would do": evidently the Greys didn't think much of the Lancers (even those with an MC). Tam Dalyell, *The Importance of being Awkward* (Edinburgh, Berlinn, 2011), pp 214-15.

that Tony Kershaw was the villain in the piece, who landed Mr Ponting in court. I have to own up to the fact that it was I who took the lead, well-advised but maybe unadvisedly, and I remain only too happy to take the rap.

The House of Commons went into the long summer recess on Wednesday 1st August; it had been another long haul, but by no means the very worst: on a mere 86 evenings that year had the House sat after midnight, and on only twenty did it sit after two in the morning. The following session was marginally worse, but it was the peak, and thanks to subsequent "reforms" of dubious efficacy, the old life of the Commons went into steep decline thereafter. In 2013-14 the Commons sat only once after midnight, and never again took breakfast as the summer dawn rose over the Terrace.

While some of my colleagues were following the traditional summer past-times of their Victorian and Edwardian predecessors (including much travel overseas as well as to the grouse moors[*]), the long recess of 1984 was for me an exceptionally busy time. I was in the office more often than out of it while rewriting the constitution of Grenada (to no ultimate purpose). And in mid-August came the not wholly unexpected announcement that an Assistant Secretary in the Ministry of Defence was to be prosecuted under the dreaded, all-encompassing, section 2 of the Official Secrets Act. Almost immediately after this, the documents submitted to me by Mr Dalyell appeared in part in the *Observer*, and a few days later in more or less complete form in the *New Statesman*. What might have been contained as a not-unusual tiff between a parliamentary committee and its corresponding government department had broken out into a major *cause célèbre*, which was to preoccupy us and the media for much of the next year or so.

And what, in essence, was the dispute about? The central facts were that around noon London time on Sunday 2nd May 1982 the War Cabinet in London[45] had authorised changes in the Fleet's Rules of Engagement to permit submarine attacks on all Argentine surface ships outside the 200-mile Total Exclusion Zone around the Falklands, extending earlier ROE which had permitted attacks only on the Argentine carrier the *Veinticinco de Mayo*[†]; and that at 7.57pm BST (or 3.57pm in the South Atlantic) a British nuclear-powered submarine, *HMS Conqueror*, launched three mark 8 torpedoes, two of which struck the Argentine cruiser *General Belgrano*, which an hour later rolled over and sank. The accompanying frigates were slow to react, and at least 323 Argentinian sailors were drowned[‡]. Theirs

---

[*] It may be remembered that the annual Appropriation Act (which gave legislative force to the Government's expenditure for the year) needed to be approved by early August in order to ensure that the long summer adjournment could begin before the Glorious Twelfth.
[†] Built by Cammell Laird, and launched in Barrow in 1943 as *HMS Venerable*.
[‡] The final unhappy death-toll (a number died after rescue) is generally put at 368, out of a complement of 1,138.

was the first blood shed in the war to recover the Falklands (although a handful of Argentines had already died, and several Brits had been wounded, during the invasion).

The *Belgrano* had had an eventful, unusually long, and on the whole very successful, life. It was built by the New York Shipbuilding Corporation in New Jersey between 1935 and 1938 as one of seven Brooklyn-class light cruisers, with a displacement not exceeding 10,000 tons, and guns not exceeding 155mm calibre, designed to carry the maximum possible power and speed while respecting the provisions of the London Naval Treaty of 1931. Amazingly all seven of this first batch of light cruiser survived the Second World War, although several suffered severe damage. Our own ship was launched in March 1938 as the *USS Phoenix*. As such she was one of the few capital ships to survive Pearl Harbour[*], and then spent much of the remainder of the war as a platform for attacks on Japanese shipping and land-based forces, while successfully seeing off aerial and eventually kamikaze attack. There appears to be no published tally of the number of lives taken by the *Phoenix* itself in the course of the Pacific War, but since its direct hits included the Japanese dreadnought *Yamashiro*, only ten of whose crew of 1,636 survived its sinking in October 1944, the total must have been substantial.

Doubts about the motives of the British Cabinet in authorising the attack on the *Belgrano* had begun to circulate soon after the end of hostilities, and in December 1982 Tam Dalyell used the floor of the House of Commons to accuse the Prime Minister of "calculatingly and deliberately" ordering the sinking in order to "switch the whole war from second into fifth gear". His specific charge against Mrs Thatcher was that "along with her Defence Secretary and the Chairman of the Conservative Party, but in the absence of the Foreign Secretary and perhaps the Home Secretary, she coldly and deliberately gave the orders to sink the *Belgrano*, in the knowledge that an honourable peace was on offer and in the expectation – all too justified – that the *Conqueror's* torpedoes would torpedo the peace negotiations". He portentously reminded the House that his charge against the Prime Minister "could hardly be more grave".[46] There was the exciting whiff of impeachment in the air.

The 'charge' depended on three groups of questions. First, the course of the doomed ship when attacked: was the *Belgrano* sailing towards the British fleet as part of a planned attack, or was she steaming towards home because her political masters believed that a peace deal had been secured? Second, was a peace deal – that is to say, an "honourable peace" acceptable to both sides - actually imminent at the time of the Conqueror's attack, and did the British Cabinet know this was the case? And third, did the British

---

[*] There are iconic pictures of the *Phoenix* proceeding unscathed among the wrecks of the rest of the US Pacific Fleet in the days after 7 December 1941.

War Cabinet – and Margaret Thatcher personally – therefore deliberately order the cruiser to be sunk because they preferred glory on the field of battle to an ignominious peace?

During the following year a succession of parliamentary questions and what the committee described as "occasional discoveries in the press" revealed more facts and, much more exciting, many more rumours about the events of the first weekend of May 1982, and also demonstrated that the official British Government versions of those events contained omissions and contradictions. All of which inevitably aroused suspicions amongst the more conspiratorially inclined. The latter were further inflamed by the Conservatives' convincing General Election victory in June 1983, with many on the left alleging or presuming that Margaret Thatcher had won the Election as a result of her victorious Falklands conflict – ignoring the fact that the Conservatives' overall vote had actually fallen, but that the Labour, Liberal and Social Democratic parties had so effectively divided the opposition vote that they had brilliantly finessed Margaret's return to Downing Street by their own inability to work together. The Falklands campaign had no doubt helped, since before General Galtieri's imprudent invasion Mrs Thatcher's chances of winning the next General Election were at best evens. But the ineptitude of the divided opposition parties undoubtedly helped her home in 1983.

Egged on by well-orchestrated Argentinian spin, which played in particular on the spectre of a "nuclear" submarine in the South Atlantic, an effective and increasingly noisy campaign had developed in the media. Leaks of not altogether accurate Argentine naval intelligence, magnified by memoirs and revelations from Argentinian generals and admirals with their own agendas, and political insights from tame Argentine academics enjoying the hospitality of Britain's ancient universities (some of whom unfortunately found their way from time to time to our quiet haven at the end of the Committee Corridor), encouraged the fatuous idea that the Argentine people and their government – which had launched the invasion of the Falklands as a classic diversion from their failed domestic policies – were in some way the victims of perfidious Anglo-Saxon gunboat colonialism, rather than themselves being the perpetrators of unprovoked aggression against an innocent and peaceful population of shepherds.

When such a campaign is launched, there are always going to be Lenin's useful idiots around, who will prefer to believe the grossest calumnies of their country's adversaries to the tediously honest truths (or even half-truths) of their own country's government. Paradoxically, this largely reflects their unrealistic confidence in the efficiency of their own governments, and an unwillingness to believe that the US or UK intelligence services could actually have failed to read the other side's signals. Our own side must be invincible, and therefore if dreadful things happened our own side must have been responsible.[*]

In the case of the *Belgrano*, the useful idiots included not only the usual suspects, but also journalists of some repute, including the veteran PA correspondent Arthur Gavshon, highly regarded amongst Tory as well as Labour politicians.[†] *The Sinking of the Belgrano*,[47] co-authored with Desmond Rice, a South African writer of fiction who had also spent several years working for Royal Dutch Shell in Argentina, created not only a small stir amongst the leftward-leaning chattering classes north of the Thames, but also some genuine concern even amongst loyalist Tories. Based largely on Mr Rice's interviews with military and political leaders in Buenos Aires, and then knocked into shape by Mr Gavshon, the book's spectacular conclusions were that "Mrs Thatcher's war cabinet decided in principle on the use of force the day Argentina occupied the Falklands, and that only unconditional surrender by the Junta could have prevented a killing war. The phase of phantom negotiations through April served only to fill the 'diplomatic vacuum' until the Task Force could be brought to bear"; and that since "British leaders were never seriously interested in negotiating, there would be little to choose between the hawks of London and those of Buenos Aires".

In the autumn and winter of 1984 two separate investigations into "the events surrounding the weekend of 1-2 May 1982" now ran in parallel: the trial of Clive Ponting at the Old Bailey, and the painstaking attempts of the Foreign Affairs Committee to discover what substance there might be in the claims of Messrs Gavshon, Rice and Dalyell.

As the weeks progressed, some of the absurdities of Britain's parliamentary and constitutional conventions were exposed to public scrutiny. The Ministry of Defence and the FCO continued to dodge their shadowing committees' questions and requests for specific documents, repeatedly fobbing us off with incomplete "summaries", falling back on the need to protect the "national interest", and when all else failed invoking the historic right of a Secretary of State to refuse to surrender documents in the possession of the Crown to either House of Parliament. As the Procedure Committee had noted back in 1978, if they had simply been called "Ministers" rather than "Secretaries of State" it would have been very much more difficult for them to resist an order for papers issued by a select committee, however lowly.

---

[*] Mr Michael Meacher's membership of "Political Leaders for 9/11 Truth" was a more recent example of this cast of mind.

[†] Arthur Gavshon (1916-1995) was a Jewish Lithuanian South African, and, like Desmond Rice, a veteran of Monte Cassino. His first major scoop had been the discovery of the identity of the *Exodus* and its Jewish cargo en route to Palestine in 1947, and later he had been one of the first to try to unravel the mystery surrounding the death of UN Secretary General Dag Hammarskjöld in Northern Rhodesia in September 1961.

Eventually, the jury at the Central Criminal Court were, on the orders of a mere salaried judge, provided with most of the documents for which we in Parliament had been repeatedly asking. Such was the much-deserved high reputation of the main Crown witness at the Ponting trial that the dedicated conspiracy theorists could come to no other conclusion but that he, the Secretary of State's private secretary, had deliberately "spilt the beans".* In truth, of course, Richard Mottram was more likely merely obeying the orders of the criminal court and honouring his oath to tell the truth.

But the fact was that twelve good men and true were made privy in the jury room to allegedly still highly sensitive British and Argentine intelligence traffic, to detailed maps and charts of the movement of ships, and to the rules of engagement which governed the actions of our soldiers, aircraft and ships in the south Atlantic. They too had sworn an oath but there was no guarantee that they would honour it forever.

We, on the other hand, were only partially privy to what was happening in the court. For a few days I was able to find a willing colleague to sit in on the trial, but our numbers were few and the trial likely to be prolonged. In the end we had a helping hand from the media: Channel 4 Television had employed a team of stenographers to produce an unofficial transcript of the court proceedings in the case of Regina *v* Ponting, and they slipped us a copy at the end of each day.

This was a humiliating situation for a committee of the House of Commons with all its famous powers to "send for persons, papers and records", and thankfully the FAC was not going to go down without a fight. If it had, the resignation of both the chairman and the clerk would have been inevitable. By this time, however, Tory committee members were for the most part as irate as the Opposition at the Government's contemptuous treatment of the House. Constant barraging of Ministers on the Floor, and constant media briefing, were eventually brought to bear against the MoD and the FCO, and probably for the first time a parliamentary committee won the media battle and HM Government had to give in.

Not of course completely: there had to be a diplomatic solution. The compromise was that the Foreign Affairs Committee (and later the Defence Committee) could see the documents – now described in the press as "the Crown Jewels" – but on similar terms to the Old Bailey jury: we could spend as much time as we liked to digest them; we could take notes, but as we were not allowed to take the notes away they could be of use only to the army of intelligence officers who my left-wing friends imagined would be pouring over them to discover any particularly penetrating insights; we could make use of anything we had gleaned as background information to

---

* "I will never know whether he did it on purpose because he was appalled by the deception of parliament or to try to help his beleaguered colleague or simply by mistake" (Tam Dalyell, *The Importance of Being Awkward*, p216)

illuminate our conclusions; but the documents themselves were not formal evidence, and could neither be directly quoted nor directly referred to in any report to the House of Commons. Our eventual report was therefore littered with a variety of circumlocutions.

As a result of this agreement, on the afternoon of Wednesday 6th March 1985 Tony Kershaw and most of his colleagues walked along the Embankment to the Horse Guards Avenue entrance of the appalling Vincent Harris building, which manages to be a blot on both Whitehall and the Victoria Embankment, originally occupied by the Board of Trade but, after the amalgamation of the three separate service ministries in 1964, home to the combined Ministry of Defence. They went up the escalator and were met by the Secretary of State's private secretary, as was appropriate, and ushered into a (presumably lead-lined) reading room. They were each given a quite substantial file, and a notebook, and Mr Mottram was there in attendance to deal with any questions of fact or interpretation, and was equipped with larger maps and other graphics in case of doubt. He was his courteous self, and after a couple of hours our team were relieved of their files and their notes, thanked Mr Mottram profusely, and – suitably awed by the efficiency and charm of the MoD and its servants – departed, desperately trying to remember what it was that they had learned from this historic encounter.

Six days later a slightly smaller team, this time comprised mainly of Labour members of the committee, set out on the same route, and Mr Mottram reprised his already very polished performance. I had the great advantage that, MoD having agreed to the participation of only one member of the committee's staff, I was able to attend on both occasions, and was therefore the only one able to review the famous documents a second time, and with an interval for reflection.

After the departure of the teams from the MoD, the frenetic scene on the Embankment Gardens should have been recorded on celluloid for posterity. Distinguished and ageing members of parliament rushed from the building to sit on the grass, to compare memories of what they recalled or what they thought they recalled from the afternoon's experience. Heads were bent together, and extensive notes were now taken.

It was obvious from an early stage that a unanimous report from the Foreign Affairs Committee to the House was a very improbable outcome. While Tony Kershaw and I set about doing our best to piece together a reasonably accurate document which would reflect the evidence (including the "informal" evidence to which we had been privy), Labour members were already hard at work producing their own account. It is revealing from their published memoirs that they had embarked on this long before they had come anywhere near the Crown Jewels, or seen the chairman's draft report. Dennis Canavan says that Labour members decided to write their own minority report because "the chairman's draft report was such a cover-up", although they didn't actually have first sight of that draft until April 1985. It is also revealing that from the start they were involving people with no standing in the committee at all, against all the House rules. According to Dennis, the Labour group met as early as the Christmas recess at the end of 1984, supported, inevitably, by Sir Tam, and also by Dr Paul Rogers from the Bradford Institute of Peace Studies, who had previously submitted evidence to the committee, and was by definition regarded as an expert.[48] We had all got quite a lot more paper to get through before we could begin to produce a report based on "the evidence", but they no doubt thought it right to get ahead of the game, irrespective of any further evidence.

The conspirators met in a small flat in St John's Wood occupied by Ian Mikardo and his disabled wife Mary. Mik, as he insisted on being known even by his enemies and detractors, had been MP for Reading from 1945, and subsequently, from 1964, for Poplar, Bethnal Green or Bow (as constituency names and boundaries changed). He was on the National Executive Committee of the Labour Party through most of the fifties, sixties and seventies, had been active in the Socialist International, and was chairman of the old select committee on nationalised industries from 1966 to 1970. A child of Jewish immigrants from the pogroms in Poland and Ukraine, he was a successful businessman, trading largely with eastern Europe. His nomination as a member of the FAC in 1983 galvanised his side of the committee to adopt a more partisan stance, but also to do their homework more carefully.

Once they had, in April, had a first sight of the draft which I had prepared for the chairman, the Labour members carved up that text between them, redrafted it, and then submitted it to revision by the others "and our two advisers". Dennis says that "we had no assistance from the committee clerks and we had to do all the research and drafting ourselves". My recollection is a little different, since my diaries suggest that another of my old friends, Nigel Spearing, who acted as the Opposition *rapporteur*, seems to have been more in than out of our office throughout much of April, May and the beginning of June. Nevertheless, I have to admit that although I did a certain amount of tidying up, between them they did a very workmanlike job, drawing on a number of published sources which I had neglected to consult (but should have consulted) as well as very carefully trawling the committee's own evidence for helpful nuggets.[*]

In the late afternoon of Wednesday 12th June 1985 the full committee met to consider the chairman's draft report and Mr Nigel Spearing's alternative. Foolishly, I was expecting a fairly long drawn out affair, perhaps involving several meetings, during which glitches in my own draft would

---

[*] Their "Chronology of the Falklands Conflict", drawing together in tabular form the known key events in London, Brussels, Washington, New York, Buenos Aires and at sea in the South Atlantic is masterly.

have a chance of being ironed out; I had a small raft of my own amendments which I was expecting to float at appropriate moments during the proceedings: my political antennae were not properly tuned in. Instead, the FAC got down to work with brisk efficiency. The 220 paragraphs of Nigel's draft report were disposed of in about five minutes, and my own mere 199 paragraphs in not more than ten; and most members of the committee then hastened off to talk to the media. I was left with an agreed Report to the House which I knew had some lacunae as well as errata, but there was nothing much I could do about it from then on.

The most glaring error was one of my own making, which I prayed would have been resolved by the simple resort of excluding the offending paragraphs altogether. In paragraph 1.6 the committee more or less directly accused Sir Thomas Dalyell of the Binns of leaking the Ponting documents to the press, and in paragraph 1.7 more or less accused Tam of breaching the privileges of the House of Commons. Just before publication of the Report, the minority report, and all its associated papers, I had to ask the committee to go through the humiliating process of allowing the mortally offended hon Member for Linlithgow publicly to disavow this slur on his character. Although Tam found this hard to accept, both Tony Kershaw and I had been assured more than once by usually reliable press contacts (who no doubt had their own agendas) that what we had alleged was the truth. But this did not excuse me from failing in my clerkly duty to ensure that an accused Member should have had the opportunity to explain before any such accusation was made. I have lain awake at nights worrying about this ever since.

It may well be that both chairman and clerk were suffering from a certain degree of overload. We had been at the UN in New York in mid-May. On 19th and 20th June we were in The Hague. On 26th and 27th June we were in Paris. We were drafting a fearsome attack on the Government over its plans to leave UNESCO.[49] We were flitting from embassy to embassy in London, and holding informal meetings with all the great and good who knew anything about the Russians. And from 8th to 17th July we were the first select committee ever to visit Moscow. When we got back, on Wednesday 24th July, the *Belgrano* Report was at last published, together with the minority report and all the associated paperwork.[50]

Ironically, after all the huffing and puffing, the majority report and the minority report were not dissimilar in either their analysis or their conclusions. What the conservative majority criticised as the Government's "excessive caution" the minority preferred to elevate into a full-blown "cover-up". No doubt carefully guided by Ian Mikardo's political sensitivity and innate caution, the Labour version steered well clear of endorsing Tam's outright attack on Margaret Thatcher, merely raising a lot of further questions which they thought needed to be addressed, and therefore calling for yet another inquiry. The committee majority also raised a lot of questions, and were very critical of Ministers' provision of information to Parliament. They did, however, conclude that "the attack on the *Belgrano* was authorised for legitimate military reasons, and not out of political design", a conclusion which has been subsequently underwritten by the memoirs of soldiers, sailors and politicians both in London and in Buenos Aires.

What all those memoirs have also confirmed is that the chance of an "honourable peace" was just as unlikely on 2nd May 1982 as it was at any other time between the Argentine occupation of the Falklands on Friday 2nd April and their liberation by British forces on Monday 14 June. There was never a possibility that the Argentine Generals and Admirals would unilaterally withdraw their newly-installed garrisons from the Malvinas, in accordance with the optimistic terms of UN Resolution 502; and that being the case, there was never a possibility that a British Government, of whatever stamp, could order the Task Force to return home, or even tread water. To that extent Tam Dalyell's belief that Mrs Thatcher intended all along to go to war, that the intervening negotiations were mere shadow boxing, and Messrs Gavshon & Rice's conclusion that the War Cabinet "decided in principle on the use of force the day Argentina occupied the Falklands", were plausible; but these were, and remain, statements of the obvious, and as allegations of skulduggery are preposterous. Neither government had any alternative.

Dennis Canavan reminds us that "One of the main functions of a select committee inquiry is to discover the truth, irrespective of any embarrassment it may cause to the government of the day", and asserts that "our minority report on the *Belgrano* was a genuine attempt to do that, based on the evidence available to us". The majority Report was also prepared and delivered in the same tradition and the same spirit.

Of all the many secrets which were revealed, hidden, even covered up, during the eighteen months leading up to the publication of the Foreign Affairs Committee's report(s) in July 1985, one was better kept on the Westminster side of the road than most of the others. On all sides of the House it was recognised that Richard Mottram was the key player – not in the war itself, but in the subsequent presentation or (according to taste) obfuscation of the facts of the war, and the elaboration of the official version of the history of the spring of 1982. It was he who had sat alongside the new Secretary of State for Defence, Michael Heseltine, when he gave evidence in the Grand Committee Room in Westminster Hall – and live on the radio – on 7 November 1984, and who silently fed the Secretary of State the right answers; it was he who starred for days on end in the witness box in the trial of Mr Ponting at the Old Bailey, supporting and protecting his political bosses and his Department; and it was he who looked after the FAC and the Defence Committee with such courtesy and charm when they were invited in to examine the Crown Jewels.

Although I had ensured that both Tony Kershaw and Ian Mikardo were in the loop, the remaining committee members were not at the time privy to the fact that Richard[*] and I had shared a stair (and subsequently an army hut) at our slightly unorthodox university back in the sixties, and that we were actually related by marriage – kith, but not kin. The younger socialist conspirators were only informed of these facts a couple of years later – on the beach of a vacant hotel, I recall, in Northern Cyprus. There were immediate murmurings from the back of the hall to the effect that "well, that explains much" and "oh, oh, oh - well, this should be looked into further", but even the Nigel Spearings of this world were beginning to grow tired of the *Phoenix* and the *Belgrano*, and looking for conspiracies of more recent provenance or potential.

The "public interest" defence of Mr Clive Ponting was upheld by the Old Bailey jury, against the advice of the judge, and he went free, to pursue a not entirely undistinguished academic career somewhere in Wales. HM Government, feeling much wounded, retaliated in 1989 by persuading Parliament to remove the possibility of a "public interest" defence from the old Official Secrets Act. But this was a pyrrhic victory. Under the Freedom of Information Act 2000 almost all their secrets became vulnerable to exposure; and today the intelligence services are supervised by a parliamentary committee, and its chiefs periodically appear on the BBC.

After re-reading the evidence at length, and reading quite a lot of the new information which has come to the surface since our report was made to the House of Commons, I am still 99% certain that Tony Kershaw and I were right to conclude that the *Belgrano* went down under the Atlantic for entirely valid and defendable military reasons. There is always at least 1% uncertainty – and it is possible (indeed probable) that we were not given access by the MoD to every piece of relevant intelligence. I suspect now that, if our conclusions were wrong, only my brother-in-law could put me right; but I am also certain that he won't.

---

[*] Sir Richard Mottram, GCB; Permanent Secretary, Office of Public Service & Science 1992; Ministry of Defence 1995; Department of Transport, the Environment & the Regions 1998; Department of Work & Pensions 2002; Intelligence, Security & Resilience 2005-07.

23

The truth about the Russian dancers

Gorbachev in London; Ian Mikardo in Lenin's bed; the KGB fail (probably) to suborn our members; the USSR jams its own transmitters

It was probably thanks to Colonel Oleg Gordievsky CMG that we embarked on our next major journey – although we didn't know it at the time.

The visit by Mikhail Gorbachev to London in December 1984 was one of the major milestones on the road towards the defusing of the Cold War, and eventually towards the break-up of the Soviet empire.

When Gorbachev became Soviet leader a few months after his visit we were all immensely impressed by the prescience of the FCO in identifying the right man and enticing him to London at the right time. It was only many years later that we learned the full extent of Gordievsky's influence: in identifying Gorbachev as the favoured candidate of the KGB to become General Secretary, and in providing the accurate briefing for both sides which laid the ground for his successful meetings with the Prime Minister. After their meetings at Chequers Margaret Thatcher famously told the world that "we can do business together". Oleg Gordievsky made a major contribution to that outcome.

Gorbachev came to London not as the guest of the Prime Minister (since he was not a head of government), not as a guest of the Foreign and Commonwealth Secretary (since he was not even a minister in the Soviet government), but as the guest of Sir Anthony Kershaw. Mikhail Sergeyevich Gorbachev was at that time for official purposes merely a member of the Politburo and one of the many secretaries of the central committee of the CPSU, with particular responsibility for agriculture, but he also happened to be Chairman of the Foreign Affairs Commission of the Council of the Union of the Supreme Soviet. He was by then front-runner to succeed General Secretary Konstantin Chernenko, who eventually survived his predecessor (a former KGB chairman) Yuri Andropov by a mere thirteen months. Andropov had recommended Gorbachev as his successor, but had then been ignored, and as the world waited for Chernenko to join the heroes in the Kremlin Wall, the young Mikhail Sergeyevich was increasingly regarded as (and, at least while overseas, played the part of) heir apparent.

Although the whole operation was initiated by No 10, and masterminded by the FCO, protocol would not permit a formal invitation from HM Government. Soviet protocol was equally adamant; indeed Andrei Gromyko, who was into his twenty-eighth year as Minister for Foreign Affairs, categorically refused to allow anyone from his ministry to accompany Gorbachev on his trip.[51] As Gorbachev himself recalled, "The Ministry of Foreign Affairs clearly did not attach much significance to our mission", and Andrei Gromyko (already aware that his job was at last on the line) asked rhetorically after the event, "a parliamentary delegation! What significance does it have?"[52] So Tony Kershaw stepped in: Gorbachev was simply invited by the Chairman of the UK Foreign Affairs Committee to lead a delegation of his own Foreign Affairs Commission for discussions on matters of mutual interest. From our point of view, this meant a great deal of work but also a great opportunity. Although many informal groups of British politicians, along with other particularly leftward-leaning worthies, had visited Moscow from soon after the Revolution,* of formal inter-parliamentary relations there had been little – for understandable, and mutually understood, reasons. If the Supreme Soviet committee accepted an invitation from us, then they would be in honour bound to offer a return visit. Although already overburdened in an already overburdened year, we therefore had much to play for.

In real time in London of course everyone knew that Gorbachev, the Soviet leader-in-waiting, was coming to meet Margaret. In real time in Moscow everyone knew that Tony Kershaw's committee could not speak for the British Government and was still only feeling its way towards any serious role in the diplomatic game. We therefore took a leaf out of the rule book of our continental friends (which showed how much we had all learned from our lengthy immersion in Strasbourg) and invented a new entity – which never had a formal name but for the purposes of this saga could reasonably be called the Foreign Affairs Committee *élargi*. We accordingly invited opposition party spokesmen, minor party leaders, the chairmen of other leading select committees, and appropriate opposite numbers from the Lords, to form up on the UK side of the parliamentary table, but of course under the guiding hand of our own Chairman. There eventually took place an historically significant but insubstantial exchange of views, without any media presence.

The organisation of the meeting was fraught with complications. The expressed need for the Soviet delegation to be accompanied by their own

---

* My aunt Peggy Angus (the "Red Angus") had participated in one of these in the early thirties, and had been appropriately (and in her case, permanently) seduced, despite her arrest and interrogation in the Lubyanka on a charge of attempting to make a drawing of the Kremlin "without a permit". Such is the magic of our unwritten constitution that she was probably not the only paid-up-to-the-end member of the CPGB to have been in receipt of a grace and favour pension from the Crown in her old age.

security detail we left as far as possible to the Serjeant at Arms and his clandestine contacts. I was much more concerned about what was actually going to happen and be said at the meeting itself. And so was the Soviet Ambassador, Viktor Ivanovich Popov. For the latter in particular, the real intentions and wishes of the man who was near certain to become the boss at any time (Chernenko himself had already become a permanent resident of Moscow's famous Central Clinic) were unclear, and he needed to avoid any solecism which (for all he knew at that time) might land him and his colleagues in a re-opened gulag. And in the home team most of the "added" members were determined to play a lead role, whilst our core members had no wish to be upstaged.

We had agreed that there should be some kind of agenda, by which we merely meant a running order of topics which might be brought up during the meeting. On the soviet side, it meant a list of very precise questions which our members would be 'permitted' to put to Gorbachev and his colleagues across the table – and a list which had to be agreed well in advance, to allow staff of the Supreme Soviet and the International Relations Department of the Central Committee (but not, officially at least, of the Foreign Ministry) to produce suitably impenetrable or retaliatory answers which were to be delivered by the relevant members of their team. What was vital, from their point of view, was that nobody should be tripped up by unscheduled questions about religion, human rights, Poland, Afghanistan etc, and that an entirely orthodox Politburo line should be paraded on every conceivable subject, lest the next General Secretary might detect any treasonable or insubordinate sentiments in his team.

We played ball, and produced a list of appropriately anodyne questions, which we confirmed with our now regular visitors from the South Kensington embassy and distributed dutifully to our own committee and their add-ons, in the confident hope that on the day they would treat the agreed agenda with whatever seriousness it deserved. Remarkably, when the meeting eventually took place in the Grand Committee Room off Westminster Hall, on the morning of Tuesday 18 December 1984, the home team played ball, and apart from a few lapses from the left or the right actually followed the general brief we had given them. I was also required to spread the message on "Privy Councillor" terms that everybody was to behave for the good of the nation and in the interests of long-term détente. The meeting was, as a result, long and tedious. But the Soviet Embassy staff appeared satisfied, and we felt that we hadn't anyway ruined our chances of a visit to Moscow.

Much to our alarm, the meeting ended with an exchange of gifts. This was a practice which we all abhorred, and we had honestly left it out of our planning for the meeting. However, my alert colleagues noticed at the start of the proceedings that one of Mikhail Sergeyevich's aides was hovering in the wings clutching a somewhat hideous (but no doubt priceless) chunk of etched and coloured metal. Ken immediately descended to the bowels of the Palace of Westminster and extracted from the Manager of the Refreshment Department an exquisite bone coffee set (appropriately gilded with the parliamentary portcullis) and returned to deposit it alongside Tony Kershaw just in time for the regulation obsequies. He had in reserve a bottle of our classiest House of Commons whisky, in case the chairman preferred the cheaper option.*

During a post-mortem drinks party in the Jubilee Room next door, under the formal auspices of the British Group of the Inter-Parliamentary Union, it soon became clear that at least one of the participants was very far from satisfied. While I was as usual keeping to a corner with at least half an eye on the nearest Refreshment Department young lady with a tray, and chatting amiably with a comfortably low-ranking embassy leg-man about those usual matters of professional and generally prurient interest to the KGB, a rather grander embassy personage intervened, urgently requiring the 'Secretary' of the Foreign Affairs Committee to spare time for a few words with 'Chairman' Gorbachev. I explained that we had no individual with that particular title, but, yes, I thought I was probably the man who performed the sort of functions which he had in mind.†

The soon-to-be-great man had already spotted me. He greeted me with a warm handshake and broad smile (sadly not the bear hug which the newsreels had led me to expect), but then said, in English, "Not good, Mr Secretary". Thereafter interpreted by one of the KGB team, Mikhail Sergeyevich explained that he had always understood Britain to be the home of free speech; here, in this famous Westminster Hall, this very morning, we had all taken part in a stage-managed event, where nobody on either side had been able to speak openly about what they felt about the very important issues which divided or which might unite our two countries; it was a scandal; this was not the way towards the friendship and greater understanding between our two great countries to which he was sure that I, as the Committee Secretary, aspired as much as he did. I explained very briefly that we had performed exactly as his embassy in South Kensington had required, but that we would of course look into the possibility of

---

* Despite all the more recent nonsense about expenses, it is not generally realised that our select committees are (or at any rate were) expected to pay out of their own pockets for any gifts they might make to overseas visitors, or when on foreign trips. Tony Kershaw paid the full price for that set of crockery, and our relative parsimony when we travelled abroad (with large stocks of House of Commons pens and pencils and ashtrays) was entirely due to the fact that when we got home we billed each participant (including ourselves) for their share of the cost.
† I should admit that I am of course not quoting exactly, but I am also not misrepresenting the tone. Exchanges such as these with pre-death-of-Chernenko Russian officialdom struck me as a strange mix of byzantine formality, oriental inscrutability, and a kind of forced international chumminess.

organising a more informal and relaxed event, if that is what he really wanted. "Yes, Yes", he said, reverting to English, "that exactly". My friend Valieri told me later that on his return to 13 Kensington Gardens he had given the senior Embassy team "what you English call a rocket", which, if true, was an encouraging start to our relationship.

Once our Soviet friends had departed to spend some conspiratorial time with their co-religionists in the trades unions and our very own Workers' Party, Tony Kershaw admitted that the soon-to-be Soviet leader had raised the same objections with him. Deploying his monocle with no doubt devastating effect, Sir Anthony had explained to comrade Gorbachev that – as in the Soviet Union – the chairman was very much under the control of the secretary of the committee, who took all the important decisions, and that he was therefore powerless to gainsay anything already decided by Mr Proctor. With this he had handed Chairman Gorbachev over to Secretary Proctor. What I had also not known when accosted by Gorbachev was that he had just emerged from a series of bruising encounters at the other end of the Jubilee Room with a trio of senior MP's, two of them leading Jewish human rights activists with their ethnic origins in Soviet-occupied central Europe, Greville Janner and Ivan Lawrence[53], together with the most eloquent (and charming) of the gay intellectuals in the House, Norman St John-Stevas (of whom we have already heard much), all barristers and all determined to nail him on the subject of Soviet Jewry. He had dismissed them angrily, but unconvincingly, and perhaps needed someone else to kick.

The FAC were originally invited to visit the USSR the following April. However, Konstantin Chernenko's ashes made their final journey to Red Square (and had the distinction of being the very last to be immured there) in March. Gorbachev's resulting elevation to the top job, a mere three hours after Chernenko's death, necessitated a pause – much to my personal relief, since we were by then deep in the troubled waters of the south Atlantic.

The first six months of 1985 were therefore periodically interrupted by visits to the gloom of the embassy and residence in Kensington Palace Gardens, or return visits from my main Soviet contact – a young and charming embassy Counsellor, Valieri Krasnov. The office area shared between the Defence Committee and the Foreign Affairs Committee had what purported to be a highly sophisticated electronic screen around it, and for that reason the committees were – at least until 2015 – able to head off attempts by the accommodation whips or the burgeoning army of administrators to kick us out of our prime site in the Palace. But for fear of the casually planted bug, and since it was assumed that all visitors from the embassy had some obligations towards their security services, all my meetings with Valieri and his colleagues had to be held on the open Terrace, Federation bitter in hand, whatever the weather.

Even after the installation of the new General Secretary, the Soviet embassy, with comrade Popov still nominally in charge, were desperate to play safe, and for several months resisted our shopping list of the people and institutions we wished not only to visit but to talk to. In particular, our requests to hold round-the-table discussions with the Procurator-General, the Council for Religious Affairs and – much worse – with representatives of the main religious communities in Moscow, provoked a horrified response, which was maintained until sometime in June, when we threatened to cancel the visit and tell the world exactly why.

On Monday 8th July 1985 (having at last put the *Belgrano* to rest) all eleven members of the FAC set off for Moscow in the relative comfort of BA, with two clerks (Crispin Poyser and myself) in attendance together with Richard Pollock, a lecturer in modern languages at the University of Bradford, as our inspiration and guide. I had by that time spent quite enough time in Strasbourg to be able to recognise an interpreter of real skill, in his case with the added bonus of considerable knowledge of the crumbling Soviet world. I was not alone in this estimation, since about half way through our first lengthy conference with the committee's opposite numbers, the Russian chairman asked Richard if he would mind interpreting in both directions, since their own man couldn't cope with the variety of accents and colloquialisms deployed by the British team. Let no-one complain (even if we very often do) about interpreters' fees. They provide our ears and our tongues. For ten days in Moscow eleven very self-important people, and their almost-as-self-important amanuenses, relied almost exclusively on Richard Pollock for an authoritative version of what was being said and what was being done. Some of us had a smattering of spoken Russian (Ivan Lawrence and Mik probably a bit more than this), and some of us had a little Cyrillic, but without our own remarkable interpreter we would have been at the mercy of our hosts.

We were met at Sheremetyevo by Leonid Mitrofanovich Zamyatin, Head of the International Information Department of the Central Committee and head of TASS, whose ubiquity in the photographic coverage of Gorbachev's visit to London spoke much of his influence at that critical time of change.[*] After minimal formalities (by the Eastern bloc standards of the time) we were transported in Soviet luxury in Zil buses, along Zil lanes, along the main highway into Moscow, and were checked in (again with minimal formalities) at the National Hotel, across the road from the Kremlin.

The National, which opened in January 1903, had more or less managed through the century to retain its status as one of the great hotels on the international circuit. Before the Great War it had played host to artists and others of the beau monde who could face visiting the already grim Russian

---

[*] His importance at this time was confirmed by his appointment to succeed Popov in the London Embassy the following year; but his independent spirit was also demonstrated by his subsequent refusal publicly to condemn the August putsch against Gorbachev in 1991.

fortress city; immediately after the Revolution it had briefly served as home to the Bolshevik government after their hasty departure from Petrograd; for a while it had been grandly restyled as the "First House of the Soviets". In 1932 it had re-opened after a major face-lift with every room and suite furnished with plunder from Tsarskoye Selo and other royal and aristocratic palaces, to become the regular abode for visiting firemen from the West.[54] As was proper, Ian Mikardo was lodged in Room 107, the room which Lenin and Nadezhda Krupskaya had occupied for all of a week in 1919; I should add for the sake of those interested in historic expenses scandals that Mik immediately volunteered the additional premium for his occupation of this great Bolshevik shrine.

The service was brilliant. Breakfast was perfect. The borscht and chicken kiev at lunch could not have been surpassed (although there was little else on offer). And that we were required to eat always in our own private dining room (well-equipped with sprinklers), with our own surprisingly anglophone staff, was, of course, entirely for our comfort, and a signal mark of respect. All our rooms were immaculate. We had cabinets full of exquisite cut glass, silver service, and Russian (or even more priceless Stoke-on-Trent) porcelain. Fruit, genuinely potable water, Crimean wine, and Stolichnaya were provided on arrival and subsequently on demand.

Justified by a fairly recent fire in a nearby Intourist hotel*, which had attracted world-wide media attention, we were also provided with what we were assured were the most up-to-date fire precautions, only very recently installed. It was, on closer inspection, the only hotel of the hundreds in which I stayed during my travelling career with sprinklers in the wholly tiled washing facilities – and, moreover, sprinklers with cables attached and no sign of any water pipes to fuel them if they were actually needed. Later in the week, as we got to know them better, our minders were very relaxed about the modern accoutrements of our rooms, and eventually I had the privilege of visiting the KGB listening room on the hotel's first floor, and shared a goodly quantity of company vodka with the over-stressed operators who were required to listen in through the sprinklers whenever our rooms were occupied, and otherwise to maintain the massive bank of east German tape machines which recorded every minute of our stay – and presumably any interesting motions in the bathrooms.

Once we had cottoned on to the user-friendly security system Tony Kershaw organised raucous committee parties in his suite; while most of us made the noise, any necessary team decisions were taken *sotto voce*. As a result of one such meeting several members were able to slip the security cordon and meet up with dissidents on the run - in Gorky Park (where else?).

---

* My wife had a few years previously stayed with a school party at the same neighbouring Intourist establishment, so she was faintly and understandably incredulous when I described the facilities made available to us at the National.

They of course knew that it was most unlikely that their movements were in fact unobserved: indeed it would have been remarkable if at least some of the dissidents had not been turned, and even more remarkable if our members had not been followed by half the non-uniformed officers in Moscow, particularly when seen furtively leaving the hotel in the company of one of our embassy men with collars drawn up, and on foot rather than in a cab. Even more obviously leaky was the great resulting coup, when one group of our members "spirited" a leading "refusenik" into one end of the National Hotel in the misplaced confidence that the attention of all the minders would be focussed on Tony Kershaw's hastily organised press conference at the other end of the hotel. But it provided many of our colleagues with a few hours of great fun. Indeed, not much fun at all to visit the heart of the Soviet Empire without engaging in a small amount of conspiracy, however effectively infiltrated.

The KGB and its allies kept up their efficient operations throughout our stay, and with generally very good humour. Our chief minder was a flaxen-haired Aryan who I thought was called Boris (or maybe my memory was confused by his resemblance to a Prime Minister of that ilk), but whom others, with better note-taking skills, called Sasha.[55] Sasha made very determined attempts to befriend us all, and particularly the younger men in the party, and appeared sometimes distraught when they made a point of moving to other parts of the bus, appealing to me for an explanation. He was extremely cultured, and of course arranged for the party to visit the dreaded ballet. Knowing that I was The Secretary, he took me aside lovingly to explain that of course he and his friends realised that more than a week away from home could be a frustrating time for men in their prime. The visit to the Bolshoi, suggested Sasha (or Boris), might be an opportunity for some - let us say - friendships, to develop, which would be a matter we could all keep between ourselves: there were very many beautiful and/or handsome young members of the corps de ballet.

I managed not even to attend the Bolshoi evening, not because I wasn't keen on the ballet or the ballet dancers (which, as it happens, at that time at any rate, I wasn't) but because I decided at the last minute that this would be an ideal opportunity to make a phone call home. Despite the relatively smooth telecommunications said to have been available to participants at the 1980 Olympics, the telephone system in Moscow had reverted to its earlier field-telephone standards by the time we visited in 1985. I of course fully understood the need to monitor whatever The English Secretary was transmitting back to the UK, but I was not particularly sympathetic with the operators who kept me waiting for two hours (and another half bottle of Stolichnaya) before eventually putting me through to my ever-patient wife for a call which faded and died after 150 seconds exactly. Half-way through the "we are sorry, we are trying to reach London, England" performance I pointed out to the operator that half the KGB was already installed in my hotel, listening to everything I did or said, and so she didn't really need to fix anything extra at her end. This evoked no more than an "I'm sorry – please, Sir, tell me again who is it you wish to speak to in London, England?" of the routine sort, so I went downstairs to remonstrate with our resident team, only to find that, on the assumption that we had *all* gone to ballet, the operation had been scaled down, only the non-anglophone engineer was there to hold the fort, and the rest of the detail had sensibly gone round to the nearest pub.

I gathered, on the evidence of their collective return to the National (I counted them out, and I counted them all back again), that all had behaved honourably, and it was evident that all (and especially Norman St John Stevas) had become deeply depressed by the galumphing young men and over-muscled female legs they had to witness at close quarters in the best, the noisiest and the most odoriferous seats in the stalls.* This evidence was, of course, a trifle superficial (since we were all aware of the expensive ladies of the night permitted in our honour to circumnavigate the National Hotel), but quite sufficient for my official purposes, and in any case I was reassured when young Sasha seemed somewhat disenchanted next morning when we set off for our weekend in the country. So no scandalous revelations, and no bonus for Boris.

Despite the occasional jollifications they worked us rather hard. Once the Soviet Embassy in London, and our own in Moscow, had concluded that we were serious about the number of people and organisations we wanted to see, and also that the prevailing political atmosphere in both capitals would permit it, they set about with sadistic energy to do what we asked. No diplomats, of whatever nationality, have much love for politicians, particularly of the backbench variety, and therefore sometimes respond to their demands with manic dedication. We ended up putting in sixteen hour days for ten days on the run.

On our first evening we attended the obligatory briefing from the chargé d'affaires (the UK was in process of changing ambassadors) in the lead-lined bunker-within-a-bunker in the famous old Embassy by the Moskva River, where we were told little that we couldn't have gleaned from the better quality weeklies (not surprisingly, since we all learned later that the bunker had almost certainly been bugged along with the rest of the Embassy), and got the routine reminder to mind our diplomatic P's and Q's.

---

* I had a similar experience a few years later in Minsk at a concert staged specially by the State Philharmonic in honour of a team sent out from Strasbourg to vet the Belarus credentials for membership of the Council of Europe. In an almost empty auditorium we sat close up to the stage while an over-weight and perspiring Russian pianist belted out Tchaikovsky and Rachmaninov in order to demonstrate the country's high cultural credentials. We gave them the thumbs down (although not entirely for this reason), and at the time of writing Belarus remains the one genuinely European state not to have found lodgings in the 'European House'.

The whole of the following day was devoted to an initial across-the-table discussion with the Foreign Affairs Commissions of both Houses of the Supreme Soviet, a discussion almost as wooden as those in London eight months earlier. It was again the Soviet side who suggested a further meeting in the last days of our visit, and on this occasion a much franker exchange took place, particularly on the UK's human rights record in Northern Ireland, on Star Wars, and on Afghanistan. On the latter subject the Russians were particularly, and very deliberately, forthcoming: after we had spent a good deal of time swapping notes about our respective countries' unhappy experiences on the roads to and from Kabul, and after Soviet military experts had very justifiably castigated the Americans for funding and supplying the Taliban, our hosts admitted that their manpower and resources were overstretched, that the war was wildly unpopular, and that – "like you British" – they would shortly have to retreat.

We were of course flattered by this openness. But, as we later learned, only a few weeks earlier Gorbachev had initiated negotiations to begin the withdrawal of Soviet troops, and no doubt wanted sympathetic contacts in the West to know this. Second, the man delivering this message was our titular host, Boris Ponomarev, one of the four members of the Politburo's original committee on Afghanistan (along with Gromyko, Andropov and General Ustinov), which had orchestrated the 1979 invasion, and so his words now carried weight. And third, as he told us with great amusement when we said farewell in his office on our last afternoon in Moscow, he had just got the sack from his main job, no doubt as a result of his association with the invasion and his proximity to the now-side-lined Gromyko: and so was perhaps a trifle more relaxed than customary about what he said and to whom. For a candidate member of the Politburo to announce his own dismissal to a bunch of visiting Westerners was probably a unique event: regime change of a serious nature was clearly in the air.[*]

The rest of our time in Moscow was spent in an endless round of visits and inspections (with a couple of passable traditional banquets thrown in for good measure). We were appalled by the rat-infested premises of the British Council, and not much more impressed by the prefabs in which the cowed clerics of the Moscow Patriarchate were compelled to serve the regime, or what could only be called the timorous servility of the lone rabbi we encountered at the one surviving central synagogue. We were encouraged by the optimism of officials at the trade, culture, sport and

---

[*] In those days Old Bolsheviks rarely disappeared completely, unless sent to run a power station in the Urals. Boris Nikolaevich (1905-1995) appears to have been finally removed from his post as head of the Central Committee's International Department only in 1986, and continued to "occupy a desk" in the Secretariat until the 1991 coup (with which he appears to have sympathised) which led ultimately to Gorbachev's downfall, the final collapse of the USSR, the rise of Boris Yeltsin, and the miraculous evaporation of the CPSU.

education ministries about the prospects for improved contacts with their opposite numbers in the UK. We were alarmed by the evident ignorance, naiveté and inefficiency of the planners at Gosplan and Comecon. And we were overwhelmed by the enormous congregations at the one Orthodox cathedral still running and at the central Baptist Church, and their enthusiasm, but inevitably wondered whether rent-a-crowd had been recruited for the occasion (and specially trained in rousing evangelical numbers).

Almost a whole gruelling day was spent in the court-room of the State Procurator-General, where many of the show trials had been staged in the Soviet Union's more robust days. It was a day well spent. Dominated by massive portraits of Vladimir Ilych, the discussions became a straight fight between our own QC's and the senior Russian lawyers, which ended with Ivan Lawrence – a son of Russian/Romanian Jews, and one of Britain's leading criminal defence barristers – causing some consternation by actually accepting an invitation from the Procurator-General to spend part of the summer inside the Russian service, in order to see how fair and independent it really was.[56]

At the weekend, Sasha (or Boris, as the case may be) acted as our principal companion on a rural ride north-east of the capital. We had asked to meet at least some local authority representatives, and ended up as guests of the Vladimir Regional Soviet. These meetings between British MP's with their constituency hats on and local Russian politicians fighting red tape and spending cuts were most refreshing, with the two teams becoming soul mates as they exchanged horror stories about the iniquities and incompetence of central government. We were all awarded honorary citizenship of Vladimir, and, after a strictly mud-on-boots and no politics visit to a collective, went off the next day for a troika ride around Russia's best-maintained tourist attraction in Suzdal, full of picturesque churches carefully restored after being unceremoniously wrecked in the heady days of Boris Ponomarev's youth.

The KGB's conscientious attention to our well-being and our whereabouts was probably just routine. But it may be that there was a certain heightened tension generated from the very top of the security system as they sought to close the net around the British spy in their midst. There was certainly a degree of tension amongst those members of our own Embassy staff who were in process of putting Operation Pimlico into effect. On the morning we left Moscow, Colonel Gordievsky took a circuitous route to Moscow's Leningrad Station, and under a false name bought a fourth-class ticket for the overnight train to the northern capital. Two days later he was 'exfiltrated' to Finland.[57]

In the autumn, back in London, we went through the inevitable process of taking more oral evidence from the great and the good, and got down to drafting a report to the House. For once I was helped by a first-rate as well as distinguished team of advisers, led by the former Ambassador in Moscow, Sir Curtis Keeble[*], and supported by an Oxford Reader in Economics, Michael Kaser, whose assiduity in penetrating the statistical disinformation regularly issued in Moscow enormously helped us explore the truly perilous state of the Soviet economy by this time. That both had already privately concluded that the certain collapse of the Soviet regime was merely a matter of time was a useful antidote to the positive vibes which had swayed a number of committee members by the time of their return from Moscow.

The committee's report was finally agreed in March 1986 after three long and closely argued meetings, with many amendments made, although the committee rarely divided. In its final form the report contained a long list of strictures against the United Kingdom Government as well as against the Soviet Government, and many recommendations of ways to improve the bilateral relationship – politically, diplomatically, in trade, education and cultural affairs, and even in the very vexed area of human rights. What was undoubtedly important was, first, that the report deliberately did not bear on the wider problem of relations between the so-called superpowers, and therefore admitted room for a genuine bilateral relationship between Russia and Britain, nominally independent of the United States; and second that it specifically acknowledged the widespread and "genuine revulsion against the possibility and prospects of war", reflecting "the different historical experience of the two superpowers, and particularly the Soviet memory of their twenty million dead in World War II".

My belief is that we all came back from Moscow convinced that the Soviet leaders would continue to wave as many swords and spears as they thought necessary to keep their end up in the worldwide media and surrogate battle with Washington, but that there was no intention of any kind to do anything which might accidentally initiate a real war. They had learned much from Khrushchev's irresponsible adventures in the northern Caribbean and had no wish to start a war or to provoke their better-armed superpower opposites to do so either. I believe that this was a correct reading of the embattled politicians in the Kremlin, already attempting to extricate themselves from their horrific and costly entanglement in the affairs of Kabul.

The report pulled few punches in its criticism of day-to-day Soviet policies and practice, and had no truck with the crumbling marxist-leninist "ideology" on which they were with increasing fragility dependent. But the report's sympathetic, although not uncritical, treatment of the real interests of the Soviet, and specifically the Russian, people was obviously

---

[*] 1922-2008. A non-public school and non-Oxbridge member of the senior Foreign Service. His charming daughter, Sally Keeble, was Labour MP for Northampton from 1997 to 2010.

appreciated in Moscow. It was clear that the committee had not been recruited to the ranks of Lenin's idiots, but it was equally clear that the Foreign Affairs Committee at least did not consist of cold war warriors and that they treated their Soviet interlocutors as fellow politicians, with the usual failings but also with the interests and security of their own constituents and communities as ultimately central to their deliberations and decisions - as such concerns were also at least supposed to be central motivations for the politicians of the nominal liberal democracies of the West.

The committee's report was eventually published in mid-April 1986,[58] with a generally supportive response from the home media. It was also immediately translated into Russian and distributed amongst the apparatchiki. It was evidently well received there also since, most unusually, a few months later the new Soviet Ambassador requested an invitation to appear in public to give on-the-record evidence to the Foreign Affairs Committee – to give, in effect, his government's official response. The new Ambassador was no less than our old friend Leonid Zamyatin, the man behind Gorbachev's shoulder in London, and our senior meeter and greeter in Moscow. Now he appeared in Committee Room 16 on the main Committee Corridor, flanked by a suitably florid colonel-general, to give what amounted to Moscow's outright approval, but also – according to policy – to denounce the fact that the Foreign Affairs Committee hadn't said anything about disarmament and arms-reduction talks. In an astute PR move Leonid Metrofanovich had also brought along his young granddaughter to witness the proceedings, to the delight of Tony Kershaw and others. Most of the session was inevitably formulaic, particularly when the Ambassador was speaking through an interpreter, for the benefit of the less Anglophone colleagues alongside and behind him, and when he needed to put something on the Kremlin record; when he spoke directly to the committee, he spoke with much greater flamboyance and confidence.

Once the mutual plaudits were out of the way, and once Ian Mikardo, with his impeccable Muscovite street cred, had seen off General Chervov's lugubrious regrets that we hadn't said anything about the current nuclear disarmament talks, it was all fairly plain sailing towards an uncharacteristically decent meal in what was in those days known as the Harcourt Room* on the Terrace, with the no-doubt fellow-travelling staff of the Refreshment Department even locating some very fine vodka of what claimed to be pre-1917 vintage in which the innumerable toasts could be drunk.

Before we left the Committee Corridor, however, there was one small

---

* Named after a much earlier Minister of Works, but subsequently (and rather tediously) renamed the Churchill Room once its ownership was formally transferred from the Lords to the Commons.

area of disagreement to be resolved. In their evidence to the committee in October 1985 the BBC had provided us with detailed information about the extent of soviet jamming of the BBC's Russian-language service, and of both the vernacular and English-language services of Voice of America and other US-financed broadcasters. They estimated that the whole operation cost somewhere between half a billion and a billion pounds sterling (at 1985 prices!), and involved the use of more transmitters than the western services employed for the broadcasts themselves. In Moscow the Russians flatly denied that they any longer jammed anything, having failed to detect that most of the committee had been kitted out by the BBC with what were then state-of-the-art short-wave receivers and were each evening experiencing the near-impossibility of listening even to the World Service, which the BBC itself did not think was deliberately targeted: the air was simply full of unwanted noise.

When Ambassador Zamyatin came to visit us in Committee Room 16, however, there was a significant change of tone. First, he admitted openly, apparently for the first time, that in fact they did systematically jam more or less everything except the BBC World Service (which evidently they didn't jam because they needed a reliable source of world news), because they objected to foreign broadcasts about internal soviet politics – after all, joked Leonid, "we are quite well enough informed to know what is going on in Moscow without being told from London". And then, when asked if it would therefore also be reasonable for the UK to jam Moscow Radio's own English-language service, he exclaimed, to the applause of his cohorts, "But you do, you do jam, and you jam very hard in the north of the country … you do it in a very simple way this jamming. You attune your own radio stations so close to the wavelength of Moscow broadcasting that it is difficult to listen to Moscow. I, for example, cannot listen to Moscow here."[59] A small amount of detective work, with the help of the BBC, established that what actually happened was that the soviets were investing far more money than they could afford in jamming the BBC Russian service on such a broad band that they simultaneously jammed their own services: information which we passed on to our friends in Kensington Palace Gardens.

On 22nd January 1987 Eduard Sheverdnadze's eloquent spokesman Gennadi Gerasimov announced to the world's press that the Soviet Union had now ceased jamming any of the BBC's services, but this decision would not apply to other stations "some of which broadcast biased information that can sometimes be considered interference in other countries' internal affairs". In later years – those brief years of Moscow's own "spring" – the expensive broadcasting suites and transmitters employed for so long for jamming purposes served a useful new function in providing facilities for at least temporarily independent local radio and TV stations throughout most of the European end of the USSR.

The Foreign Affairs Committee were already deeply embroiled in other matters, and within a year or so I was moved on to serve my country in other ways. Box 500, however, maintained their interest. Periodically over the next few years, at odd times of day or night, I received calls to check whether I had been offered any services by my friend Valieri Krasnov: has he suggested a weekend in the country? has he suggested a holiday on a barge? has he suggested a holiday in Yalta? I pointed out at regular intervals that since 7 July 1986 I had had no contact whatsoever with Valieri and his embassy friends, other than to check through the translation of his superiors' evidence to the FAC. Eventually, presumably when Valieri had been recalled to Moscow, the calls dried up (but only after an actual face-to-face meeting with the men with turned-up collars in March 1989). Ten years later, however, I spent a couple of weeks as part of a seminar team (along with much wiser colleagues from Bonn and Washington) at the National People's Congress in Beijing, and even had the temerity to visit my host's apartment and to go shopping with his charming wife and son, taking in a meal at the world's largest MacDonald's on the way. Within weeks of my return Box 500 were back on the case. It is certainly reassuring to know that our security services keep so close to the action, and follow up every significant lead: perhaps they were concerned that at the time I was still sporting a beard, and therefore might have a large bomb with a wick on the end in my regulation crested briefcase.

24

Hãng Không Viêt Nam

The FAC in south-east Asia; strap-hanging to Hanoi; Vietnamese praise for the BBC; an unplanned visit to Cambodia; up against the wall in Rangoon; an unspeakable dinner with Lee Kuan Yew

For three weeks in April 1986 most of the Foreign Affairs Committee decamped to South-East Asia. How we managed to achieve this is a mystery. We had only just agreed our report on relations with the Soviet Union, were in the middle of an inquiry into the situation in South Africa, had just got the green light from the FCO for our very long-delayed inquiry into the situation in Cyprus, and on the other side of the desk Crispin was delving deeper into the overseas aid programme and its vast but no doubt still inadequate outlays. We were seeing visiting firemen from all over the world almost every morning and afternoon of the week – tying up our own members so much that they eventually passed resolutions in committee to curtail the number of such "informal" meetings: resolutions of which I obviously took little notice, since by the summer of that year we were still running at an average of six meetings a week, with occasional peaks of seven, or even eight. But we had somehow managed to persuade the Liaison Committee to release funds for what was then, and is probably still, the most expensive overseas trip by any select committee, anywhere, despite increasing outrage from other committees whose travel budgets might have to be slashed in consequence.

The original plan had been reasonably modest – to examine the UK's relations with the member nations of ASEAN (the Association of South East Asian Nations), a bloc then consisting of Indonesia, Malaysia, the Philippines, Singapore and Thailand, created with strong US and UK prompting in 1967 as an anti-communist buffer. After some evidence in London, it became obvious that we had to look at ASEAN in context, and that we ought therefore to try to visit some of the key countries to which the bloc was at least theoretically opposed. China was too great a challenge, since the UK's relations with the Republic were at a point of maximum strain in the run-up to negotiations for Britain's withdrawal from Hong Kong, and the FCO were categorical in not wanting the Foreign Affairs Committee to muddy the waters. Vietnam, however, ten years on from the end of the war, was already putting out feelers to West European countries, as it sought some means of extricating its economy from the effects of several decades of war and of the continuing US-led trade embargo; and it was clear that the UK Government, along with its European Community partners, would not actively discourage some attempt at rapprochement at the parliamentary level, which could always be disowned by the diplomats if all went horribly wrong.

We had assumed that we would have to leave out the Philippines, for reasons of cost as well as logistics. But the overthrow of President Ferdinand Marcos and his shoe-hoarding spouse Imelda, and their replacement by the more-or-less democratically-elected and undisputedly photogenic Corazon Aquino at the end of February meant that there was real diplomatic mileage to be gained by showing the Union Flag in Manila at the earliest opportunity. So at the last minute a small group was put together – led by Sir Anthony and shepherded by Crispin Poyser – to head off before the rest of us for modest trade promotion and deep conversation with *Time* magazine's Woman of the Year, and with Cardinal Sin.

A couple of days later the rest of us set out directly for Hồ Chí Minh City, stopping off in Delhi for a few hours for refuelling.[*] Arriving at Saigon airport was an exciting experience. Eleven years after the end of the war, the sides of the main runway remained littered with the corpses of USAF and Air America aircraft which had been left behind or previously shot up before America's ignominious retreat. They might have been some kind of patriotic memorial to the Vietnamese people's triumphant defeat of the Great Satan, but they also had a more practical purpose, as a repository of spare fuselages, wings, undercarriages, engines, electronics and other essential parts for Vietnam's national airline.

It was an early indication of the desperate economic plight of the Socialist Republic of Vietnam even a decade after the end of their very own great patriotic war. At the Paris Peace Conference in 1972 Henry Kissinger (then US National Security Advisor) had promised 'substantial' economic aid. But little aid of any kind had been forthcoming, ostensibly because North Vietnam had successfully occupied the south of the country, very soon after the Americans' departure by helicopter from the nearest available flat roofs in Saigon, and subsequently because of Vietnam's 1978 invasion of Kampuchea[†] in an attempt to oust Pol Pot's Khmer Rouge. More important, of course, was the refusal of either house of Congress to contemplate aid to a country which had shed so much American blood. The result was that there was virtually no direct trade between Vietnam and the

---

[*] Sadly, in all my travelling days, this was the only occasion when my feet touched the soil (or at least the tarmac) of India, a country which, thanks I suppose to E M Forster, had almost as much resonance in my imaginative life as Russia.

[†] which from now on I will continue to call Cambodia, as we and almost everybody else did at the time.

non-"communist" world, since there was an almost total US-imposed trade embargo, there were no overt diplomatic relations of any kind with the USA, and there was no prospect of any improvement until the government in Hanoi could account for the fate of every single MIA (US personnel missing in action during the war).

The official figures we were offered (and which were confirmed on our return home) suggested a country in free fall to disaster, and it is difficult to imagine any country other than one inured to several decades of civil war which could have had the bottle to survive, and eventually thrive. In 1983 per capita GDP was recorded as $240, and by 1985 average per capita income was thought to have slumped to about $150. In 1984 Vietnam had total foreign currency reserves of only $16.6 million, against total estimated external debts of almost $4 billion; and by the time we arrived in Ho Chi Minh City the reserves had slumped further to around $10 million, while the debts continued to soar. This was all compounded by the refusal of the US-dominated International Monetary Fund to provide any support, by the refusal of the USA to release the substantial funds of the former South Vietnamese government, locked comfortably in New York banks, and the reluctance of the UK and most other European Community and western-aligned countries to offer anything other than the shortest-term credit. Meanwhile the politburo in Hanoi was, as usual in the country's history, at loggerheads with their ostensible soul mates in Beijing, and the Soviet Union, which provided Vietnam's only reliable trade-and-aid support, was in terminal decline. Only the Japanese (whose gleaming new Toyotas were just about the only serviceable non-military vehicles on the roads) and the French (who retained some post-colonial affection for Indo-China – and in any case rarely took much notice of Anglo-Saxon trade embargoes) had the sense to book front seats for the bonanza which was certain to follow Vietnam's eventual escape from international purdah.

As well as being one of the very poorest countries in the world (although one with enormous natural resources – and resourcefulness), Vietnam in 1986 was still haemorrhaging the talents needed to rebuild its shattered economy. It certainly still had armies in arms, and armies of young people at least theoretically committed to the advance of marxism-leninism, and a middle-aged population adept at tunnelling, setting booby-traps, and make-do-and-mend. But it faced massive shortages of the skills needed to build a modern economy. First, several generations had been deprived of an education in trades other than those related to war. Second, for understandable reasons of state, or allegedly for their own safety (a prominent Vietnamese parliamentarian told us that the camps were "protecting mass-murderers from popular revenge") tens of thousands of former South Vietnamese had been incarcerated in "re-education" camps, and something like two million had been through a more or sometimes less benign "screening" process. As a result, at least a million of the latter had taken to fragile boats to cross the South China Sea for new lives in Hong Kong, Singapore, Australia or the United States. By the time we arrived much of the emigration was organised through the UNHCR, but the Committee echoed a widely held lament that the "Orderly Departure Programme" was probably facilitating an exodus of "precisely those people who could contribute to the country's future development": as in more recent migrations in Europe and the Middle East, it is those with initiative and with skills to sell who are most likely to take ship.

Saigon had a distinctly down-at-heel air, but nonetheless retained at least some of that slightly raffish character which makes so many former French colonial cities such a delight to visit – despite, in Saigon, the many disfiguring reminders of a decade of occupation by other rather less cultured (but equally vicious, and equally inefficient) invaders from across the Pacific. There were still some direct colonial echoes: almost everybody, for instance, seemed to be riding Peugeots – albeit splendid replicas handcrafted in what seemed like thousands of bicycle workshops along the old colonial boulevards; and, with money, it was still possible to acquire a passable baguette or even a croissant. And even if (or perhaps because) much of the old middle class had departed, there was an invigorating sense of movement on the streets and on the faces on the streets: these beautiful people looked down but by no means beat.

Our hosts of course wanted to show us where real progress was being made. We spent most of a day at Vung Tau, south of Hồ Chí Minh City, where offshore oil and gas facilities were being slowly developed, and new petroleum engineers trained (with not-very-well camouflaged assistance from a number of western oil companies which were sensibly looking to the future). We had lengthy discussions with the Director of IMEXCO, a trading corporation already granted a considerable degree of independence from the ministries in Hanoi and staffed by some of the more dynamic survivors of South Vietnam's short-lived exposure to the capitalist system. But our hosts also had no interest in disguising their country's penury. The ex-colonial government guesthouse in which we stayed was in dire need of more than a lick of paint, and our provisions were, by the standards of fraternal parliamentary exchanges, basic. Ivan Lawrence describes our accommodation as "rat-infested";[60] Ken Brown recalls the attack of Hồ Chí Minh's Revenge which afflicted several of the party including himself, and the enormous generosity of the Saigon hospital staff who shared a single stethoscope but who nonetheless scoured the town to find the rare drugs needed to bring their distinguished visitors back to full health.

When we were encouraged to visit what is now the thriving Phuong Nam emporium in downtown Saigon, several of the craftsmen and ladies actually wept when they learned that some of us had nothing smaller than a ten dollar bill to pay for the exquisite lacquer boxes and vases which then carried a mere 50 cent price tag: overseas dollar-carrying customers (as distinct from rouble-carrying apparatchiks) were so rare that our visit apparently fulfilled their monthly profit norms in less than an hour. And we were glad to have followed unofficial FCO advice, and had all arrived with copious quantities of genuine State Express Triple Fives – a more useful currency than the locally-produced fake copies with which someone – possibly even the Government – seemed to be attempting to undermine the black economy, despite its usual pivotal role in maintaining the dynamism of a country under siege.

After four days in the relatively balmy south we set out for Hanoi, accompanied as always by our charming and fluent young interpreter from the foreign ministry.* Sadly we were unable to take the train, which was our first preference, all surface travel by westerners being then forbidden for fear of our witnessing the continuing devastation of the hinterland, but also apparently for fear of our learning from the locals what "re-education" might mean in practice. But maybe the fact that the thousand mile journey in those days took at least thirty-four hours to complete was another deterrent: certainly neither HM Ambassador nor the legmen from the Foreign Ministry could have been expected to endure conversations with Nigel Spearing or Bowen Wells for quite that long.

However, we were much compensated by the privilege of taking a scheduled flight on the national flag-carrier. Hãng Không Việt Nam was an airline which lived up to its name. It was the only flight in my experience where standing passengers were actually provided with the luxury of strap handles (which looked as though they had been liberated from the old Northern Line) to avoid excessive discomfort as we sailed over the central highlands; and where the main safety worry was whether it would be the resident cockroaches, or the passengers' live cockerels, which would manage to chew through one of the more vital electric cables which ran alongside and under our seats before we reached the ground in some semblance of order.

The descent into Hanoi provided us with an insight into (a) the population's wonderful ingenuity and (b) some reasons for the Americans' failure to subdue them. In a great ring around the city suburbs was an array of ponds, linked in places by narrow canals, which, we were told, had immensely improved the suburban water supply and eased the problems of irrigation since the end of the war. These were the craters made by the thousands of high explosives dropped short of target by USAF pilots who had the sense not to risk Hanoi's AA defences during LBJ's famous campaign to "bomb the north into submission".

When we reached Hanoi we were getting closer to the monsoon season,

---

* The next time we think we saw him was in British newspaper photographs a couple of years later, touting a pistol as he and his colleagues attempted to head off anti-government demonstrators outside the Vietnamese embassy in London.

and the atmosphere was damp and thundersome. We stayed in another government guest house, this time provided with copious quantities of local bottled beer, and bottled water which was guaranteed pure and algae-free but nevertheless a luminous green. The beer seemed at first sight a better bet for teeth-cleaning purposes, although in all probability the bottled water would have removed everything including the enamel and allowed us to appear new-born on television back home. As the days wore on we were increasingly bitten, and increasingly nervous about the incurable asiatic diseases which seemed likely to infect us in the capital of the North. We had been inoculated against Japanese encephalitis, and warned to keep clear of water courses, but as the rain began to sluice over Hanoi our chances of survival seemed slim.

But Hanoi had its own delights. The British Embassy was one. A former Chinese brothel, it had been acquired by our first Consul-General at a time when the Union Flag was sported around Hanoi on the handlebars of his bicycle and no more respectable buildings were available to foreigners from the West. An octagonal building with a central staircase and a perpetually leaking roof, it appeared to have no rooms large enough for meetings of more than half a dozen people (which presumably was more than adequate for the purposes for which it was originally designed). It was currently occupied by a charmingly vexed member of Her Majesty's Diplomatic Service and his flamboyant wife, who perhaps went some way to explaining the remark of one of their most eminent predecessors that "it is a wise policy which limits our tour here to a year: it might be difficult to report objectively for longer".[61]

We also got to experience the Hanoi-Ho Chi Minh train, although still not allowed to ride on it. On our last evening, we dined at what was billed as the best Vietnamese restaurant in town, which happened to be sited just south of the main Hà Nôi railway station. The restaurant, like many other buildings on the line, was within touching distance of the single-track metre-gauge diesel-powered Reunification Express as it began its stately 1725km journey to Saigon, flags flying, horns blaring, washing fluttering overhead, mothers hauling their children to safety, waiters and diners hanging on to the crockery, and all cowering from the monstrous noise.

On our first full day in Hanoi the committee and minders embarked in a small fleet of Land Cruisers to inspect the Hòa Bình Hydro Electric Project, on the Black River south-west of the capital. This massive construction project had begun in 1979 with Soviet money and Soviet engineering, and after many delays was not completed until 1994 (but still with Russian money and Russian expertise). The dam – until recently Vietnam's largest - is almost a kilometre long, and its eight generating sets originally produced getting on for 30 per cent of the country's power, and even now more than 15 percent. When we were there the main dam was still some way towards completion, and we could look down on the thousands of acres about to be flooded from over 400 feet above – not the most relaxing experience for someone who can suffer mild vertigo when merely walking along the side of the Grand Union Canal, and acute vertigo at the top of a church tower. While it looked and felt like that famous scene in *Dr Zhivago*, this was no film set; it had already claimed many lives, and by the time it was up and running the death toll stood at 168 (eleven of them Russians). But the Vietnamese were understandably proud that what turned out to be the key to their eventual economic recovery was already well under way. It was a brilliant use of their natural resources, Vietnam now claiming to be one of the few countries in the world dependent on neither imported energy nor carbon fuels.

Our remaining days in Hanoi were spent in the usual round of meetings with ministers and their officials, and with the heads of UN agencies and of the other European Community missions in Vietnam. The latter in particular didn't attempt to disguise their frustration with the constraints imposed on the country by the trade embargo, and urged us to "tell the world" of Vietnam's potential. It was, said one extremely angry ambassador, like Leviathan in chains. This was obviously a message which Vietnamese officials saw no need to challenge. They clearly wished to impress on us their appreciation of the UK's influence in the world, but also their regret that we continued to be tied so closely to the USA. Many spoke excellent English, all said to have been learned from the BBC. At a meeting at the foreign trade ministry on the morning of Tuesday 15th April 1986 we questioned this claim (although we were much impressed by the quality of their English English), in view of the draconian penalties in the criminal code for listening to foreign radio stations. At which point one of the vice-ministers switched on his desk-top radio to allow us to listen in directly to the World Service account of Ronald Reagan's decision to bomb strategic targets in Libya that morning (of which we had heard nothing from HM Ambassador), and of Mrs T's complicity in providing RAF Lakenheath and RAF Upper Heyford as departure points – at which all in the room bowed their heads in shame or disbelief, as appropriate.

Hanoi in those days and at that time of the year was one of those places which you were inclined to leave with relief, rather than in sorrow. The weather was appalling and the people – in contrast with their fellow countrymen in the south – looked somewhat downcast and understandably weary. However, before we left we were invited to pay our respects to chairman Pham Van Dong. We were of course fully aware of the reverence paid to Ho Chi Minh, having previously circumnavigated his mausoleum as protocol required.* We were not wholly prepared, however, for the panoply

---

* We were much entertained by the notice outside which proclaimed that "the mausoleum is closed occasionally in order to restore and preserve the body"; this

of oriental pomp which attended a meeting with the current Chairman of the Council of Ministers of the Socialist Republic which was Ho's legacy. We were seated around the periphery of the receiving room of the former French Governor-General, and served tea and cakes by what must have been the most beautiful teenage girls in Indo-China; they were meekly kneeling on their knees, a practice I have since adopted when offering mugs of Twinings to my friends and family – to the understandable embarrassment of the latter. Chairman Pham, America's nemesis, who on the whole seemed a nice sort of guy, was "wheeled out in his carpet slippers", as Ivan Lawrence recalls, looking "as though he had been dragged through a room full of cobwebs for the engagement".[62] He sat with Tony Kershaw at the head of the room overlooked by a massive bust of Ho. Many pleasantries were exchanged. We were a little uncertain when we took our leave whether kowtowing was *de rigueur*, or whether mere genuflection would suffice. Although the kings were deposed in 1945 it was clear that ancient traditions had not lost their vigour.

There was similar flummery when we reached the openly monarchist stronghold of Bangkok, although more of this seemed to be in honour of the representatives of the Cambodian resistance groups than of the assorted generals and squadron leaders, who when off-duty carried out their main business of running occasionally democratic Siam from relatively humble – and certainly more practical – twentieth century office blocks. Sadly, our group wasn't quite grand enough to merit an audience with Bhumibol Adulyadej (aka HM King Rama IX), which would no doubt have been a spectacular affair.

Our party was for the time being reduced in size, Crispin having flown straight on to Jakarta with Peter Thomas, Ivan Lawrence and Nigel Spearing to cover Indonesia and then Malaysia, while Ken Brown and I stayed to provide protection for our chairman's party in their dangerous encounters with Thai motorists, the Rangoon police, and the Cambodian belligerents. The latter was something of an accident, but it had its ironies.

Cambodia had been invaded by the Vietnamese at the end of 1978 ostensibly in order to oust the genocidal (for once the word is apposite) regime of Pol Pot, whose Khmer Rouge thugs they had foolishly helped to install only a few years earlier in the misplaced confidence that they were bona members of the marxist-leninist club or at least malleable and relatively human fellow travellers. Hanoi was in the end successful in removing Pol Pot from control of the government in Phnom Pen (after the massacre of many hundreds of thousands), for which achievement they should have been heartily congratulated not only by the country's innocent

---

reminded me of our visit to Moscow the previous year, when humorous suggestions were made by our KGB minders that I might serve as the next in the long line of Lenin lookalikes to occupy the Red Square Mausoleum.

citizenry but also by the rest of the civilised world. But since the domino theory still constrained the strategic thinking of the western "powers" the Vietnamese were instead reviled and ostracised. The Vietnamese were seen by the Americans simply as the agents of Moscow, and the whole issue was complicated by the fact that Pol Pot was supported and armed by the Chinese, Vietnam's short-lived marxist-leninist sponsor but traditional enemy, against whom they were then deploying something like 600,000 troops on their northern borders. By the time we were examining the entrails there were three separate armed groups (all theoretically allied in the "Coalition Government of Democratic Kampuchea") fighting to overthrow the Vietnam-sponsored government when not fighting each other. The most powerful (the Khmer Rouge minus Pol Pot) was financed and armed by the Chinese, the others were financed and armed largely by the USA and other Western states, and all were supplied through Thailand.

This continuing conflict was now by a long shot the main cause of the friction and violence in which the whole region was embroiled, and was at least one cause of Vietnam's continuing isolation: it was therefore obvious that we would have liked to visit the country, and to meet all four main local disputants, as well as to discuss the situation with the neighbouring countries so deeply affected.

However, diplomats from just about every country in south-east Asia, as well as the UK, had collectively and successfully pulled out the stops to prevent us visiting Cambodia – ostensibly (perhaps honestly) in the interests of our safety, but also to maintain their respective diplomatic positions. The Vietnamese threatened to veto our visit if there was any question of us entering Cambodia from the Thai border; the Thais threatened the reverse; neither side would even contemplate our brilliant, if naïve, compromise – that we visit Heng Samrin in Phnom Pen in the company of the Vietnamese, and that we visit the other groups from Thailand, from which most of their political leaders operated.

Cambodia was inevitably the main topic of our talks with Thai leaders, since they were having to cope not only with massive arms trafficking through their territory, and with massive drugs trafficking from Burma to help finance the rebel armies, but also with many hundreds of thousands of displaced persons and refugees from the war. So as well as visiting the gilded temples and palaces of Bangkok the committee also interviewed Son Sann, the Prime Minister of the coalition in exile, and Prince Norodom Ranariddh, son of the once and future Cambodian king, Norodom Sihanouk[*]. But not the now allegedly more respectable Khmer Rouge

---

[*] Sihanouk was King of Cambodia 1941-55 and 1993-2004; intermittently he also managed to serve as Prime Minister in 1945, 1950, 1952-3, 1954, 1955-6, 1957, 1958-60, 1961-6; non-royal Head of State 1960-70; and President 1975-76. He was also an internationally acclaimed film producer, director and actor.

leader, Khieu Samphan: all contact with him and his party was strictly verboten both by the Thais and by the FCO, even though the Khmer Rouge was still the biggest player in that crowded field. We had of course met them all before in the dim corridors of Westminster, but it was a delight to see some at least in their magnificent – albeit borrowed – palaces closer to their home territory.

At their pleading we went on to look at the camps on the border. What this long day in the heat and dust revealed was that although nominally run by the UN the camps for "evacuees" were, if not actual training facilities, "convenient rest and recreation bases for the armed resistance groups", their impressively efficient internal administration being almost completely under the control of the relevant private armies.[63] There were many genuine victims of the war, the maimed, the hopeless, the insane - but there was also a noticeable lack of young men of military age amongst their resident populations. That the Thai government was at that time seriously considering closing down the largest holding centre, at Khao-I-Dang, and sending them all back across the border, was understandable.

Getting across the border turned out to be a good deal easier than advertised. We had travelled to the camps in a small fleet of helicopters provided by the Royal Thai Army, armed with regulation issue boxes of savoury rice, and at the end of the day were supposedly heading back to Bangkok, thirsty and hungry, when our pilots discovered that they were lost. Although we had been provided with a navigator in the lead helicopter, he seemed not to have advanced much beyond the basic orienteering badge in the National Scouting Organisation of Thailand, and had spent most of the day pouring over his maps in some confusion about which way to go next, and even about which way up to hold them. He and his aeronautical colleagues could have made enjoyable guest appearances in *The Navy Lark*; after signalling "full ahead", "no, back a bit", "left hand down a bit", "No, right hand down a bit" with increasing frequency he admitted that he had no idea where he was. At that point I rather regretted that both my former travelling companions, Norman Tebbit and Ian Lloyd, had been unavailable for this trip.

So, thanks to the Thai Army, we achieved our ambition to visit Cambodia after all. Almost out of fuel, our little fleet glided down to the nearest air base. Amazingly, although it happened to be well inside the borders of Cambodia, nobody seemed too troubled. We never discovered (and we were pretty certain that our pilots had also not discovered) whether we had become for a while the guests of the Heng Samrin government, or of the Khmer Rouge, or of the Armée Nationale Sihanoukiste, or even of the Khmer People's National Liberation Front. Whichever way, we were treated as influential friends and with much courtesy, we liberated most of their fuel stocks, and all their Coca Cola stocks, consulted an up-to-date chart, and winged our way safely back to the capital. Politicians, diplomats and airmen all agreed that it was probably better not to say too much to anyone about our brief excursion across the border.

Of the first twenty-four hours of our stay in Bangkok I have only vague recollections, since I tried unsuccessfully to emerge on the morning after our arrival with one of those overwhelming colds which so easily afflicts anyone transferring from the edge of the monsoon to an air-conditioned aircraft (for this flight we had disloyally deserted Hãng Không Viêt Nam), out onto the tarmac for an extended welcoming ceremony in the upper thirties, and then straight back into a pre-chilled hotel room. It was a genuine twenty-four hour cold, during which I was comatose, leaving Ken Brown to run the show. I was weak and vulnerable. Ken appeared in the middle of the afternoon to inquire after my health (which was nice of him) and with a brilliant plan for cheering me up (not really needed, since a really good cold enjoyed in bed and in peace and quiet is an experience to savour): downstairs, said my seasoned travelling companion, was an absolutely brilliant Chinese tailor, who could run up a new tropical suit for me in less than a day and at half the price of Marks & Spencer. Only half-conscious I descended to the sous sol and was duly measured.

A few days later I hastily changed into my new gear, said to be entirely appropriate for the climate, and, fully restored to health apart from the suppurating mosquito bites acquired in the camps, shepherded my flock and its baggage on board a spotless Burma Airways Boeing for an extremely cool and comfortable flight. We emerged from this stretch of fine wines and perfect air conditioning into the airport at Rangoon in temperatures in the mid-forties. Although we were bang in the middle of the brief hot (ie very hot) season, when reasonably casual dress was normally acceptable, the Burmese military had decreed in our honour that the formal dress code was to apply throughout our stay. This was fine if you had some air circulating around your longyi; if you were sporting an over-tight worsted suit, with legs too short and arms too long, it was something close to purgatory. A few fading black-and-white pictures survive of our happy band laying wreaths at the Tankkyan Commonwealth Cemetery, immediately after our arrival, after travelling twenty or so miles in the ancient Australian Holdens (un-air-conditioned, and with window winders jammed) which comprised the official carpool: the inch or so of perspiration on the sleeves of our jackets can be just about discerned. The Chinese suit, which went to the nearest charity shop as soon as I got home, absorbed the small expenses surplus with which I had hoped to be able to justify my prolonged absence from domestic duties.

In Rangoon we stayed in yet another government guest house of colonial vintage, with colonial era plumbing and insect population coming as standard. My own room was a vast white-tiled enclosure which could have served convincingly as the set for a morgue in *Midsomer Murders*; it included a central drain for the evacuation of noxious liquids (just at the end of the king size bed), several showers placed apparently at random, and more than one hole in the floor to serve as loo. There were also several pre-sunk holes in the tiled walls which might or might not have been of the right gauge to receive manacle bolts. Looking back I realise that I was probably a temporary resident in an establishment which had other rather more important uses in term time. It was surely not entirely normal for a man who claimed to be the deputy chief of the Rangoon police to cook breakfast for his government's guests (to be fair, he served up some passable bacon and eggs) or to sleep on a pallet in the corridor?

After ritual meetings with ministers and ranking members of the People's Assembly (the Pyithu Hluttaw), we were given a brilliant briefing on the situation in Burma at Belmont, the compound which then accommodated both the Chancery and the embassy residences. This magnificent estate – the former home of the colonial Governor - was an asset of which the Property Services Agency was desperately trying to divest itself, as part of the worldwide drive to downsize and to place our diplomats in accommodation more appropriate to their much reduced status. However, even HM Treasury baulked at the only terms on which the Burmese were then prepared to do a deal: that they would pay whatever the nominal value was estimated to have been when the last Governor left in 1948. At some point one side or the other must have given way, since apparently the compound eventually became the Belmond Governor's Residence Hotel. For the time being, however, Belmont remained a British fastness in the more desirable purlieus of Rangoon, and events such as the Queen's Birthday party, at which we were honoured guests on this occasion, were high points in the otherwise rather unexciting Burmese social calendar.

Our diplomatic host in Rangoon was Nicholas Fenn[64], one of the leading FCO experts on the sub-continent. Unlike his counterpart in Bangkok, who had initially treated us with perhaps understandable and not very well disguised contempt (but who had by the end of our stay learned to appreciate our unorthodox brand of diplomacy), Nicholas Fenn gave us a copybook briefing on the situation in Burma, and gave us all his time. He personally accompanied us wherever we went (whether laying wreaths, or climbing the Shwedagon Pagoda, or inspecting the snake pits from which the Burma Pharmaceutical Company were developing wonderful new serums), rather than - as was the diplomatic norm - entrusting us to the care of a Second Secretary. His familiarity with both the language and the people provided us with a relaxed entrée into the otherwise rigid buddhist propriety of the ruling military caste. He was understandably revered by his staff and much admired by his Burmese interlocutors.

After a very relaxed evening in Belmont, we were summoned to the Holdens to return to our slightly unorthodox hostelry at precisely the time stipulated in the schedule agreed with our hosts. We departed on time, but without Mr Bowen Wells. Bowen, a former senior executive of the

Commonwealth Development Corporation, wanted to continue talking in a speculative sort of way about the possibilities for British future investment in Burma. The CDC had no operations at all at that time in Burma, despite its status as a former colony (and in striking contrast to the very substantial CDC investments in Thailand, which had never even been a colony), and it had proved in many other parts of the world an effective substitute for direct UK Government "aid", where political constraints had applied.

Our breakfast chef, the man who claimed to be the deputy chief of police, was not entirely happy with this departure from the agreed plan. As I was trying to work out where to hang my clothes (and particularly my new and soon-to-be-discarded Chinese suit) in my white-tiled boudoir, fighting off the desire in that tremendous heat simply to lie down and forget them all, the said officer walked into the room in his longyi and presented me with the phone. "You must telephone him now, and tell him to come straight back here at once. His behaviour is unacceptable. You must tell him, and you must do this now, this moment." I explained – a trifle ingenuously - that it was not part of my job to "tell" members of Parliament what they could or could not do; and in any case I didn't have a number to call him. At this point he snatched the phone from me, dialled the Ambassador's number, and then pushed me (by this time trouserless) against the tiled wall: "You tell him now, you understand. There is a car waiting for him".

I managed to talk briefly to Nicholas Fenn (who realised that I was under a certain amount of duress), and then to Bowen, who was greatly enjoying the FCO's extended hospitality. Bowen, understandably phased by my strangled tones, merely said that he had been promised embassy transport back to the guest house, was grateful for the offer of a Holden, but would be able to manage very well by himself, thank you very much. Since even the deputy chief of the Rangoon police apparently recognised at that point that an international incident was best avoided, he eventually left my room, merely muttering that we would "have further discussion in the morning". Bowen eventually returned to us in the company Jaguar, but remained a marked man: at one point in our stay in the white-tiled hostelry, after an apparently perfectly legitimate amble around town, he was presented to Ken Brown between two longyi-sporting guards, their leader asking "is this one of yours?" and Ken, noble and brave to the end, assured them that he'd "never seen the man in my life". Shades of Good Friday morning.

Apart from the longyi-wrapped police, and the sometimes morose generals-masquerading-as-politicians, the Burmese we met seemed utterly charming. They were, however, living under what amounted to a military theocracy, with what seemed to be a blind indifference to their own people's welfare. Vietnam, after decades of war and with a worldwide embargo more or less effectively in force, had some plausible excuses for being amongst the poorer nations of the world at that time. Despite continuing squabbles with its ethnic minorities (which conflict consumed around 35% of central government expenditure), the Burmese government really had none, yet official per capita GDP was $180, while Vietnam could at least muster $240. Substantial UN-financed efforts had managed, for instance, to increase rice productivity in this country which had not so long before been the world's largest rice producer, but the result was not an increase in output but an overall reduction in the area of land under cultivation, to something like a mere 30% of all cultivable land. Apparently happy to maintain a basic, no growth, economy, Ministers told us that they were not too worried, the people had "more than enough to eat", and that "the Burmese people are content": an early manifestation of aggressive Buddhism in action.

We were probably not the first visitors who left Rangoon feeling that overseas aid was probably an irrelevance in this kind of situation, and that in any case the country's obvious penury might be alleviated if someone took the sensible decision to sell off the 5,448 diamonds, 2,317 rubies, and the several tons of gold weighing down the great Pagoda – rather than leaving the business to the independent spirits who were said to pan the streams below the Pagoda for gold and silver dust after heavy rains (of which there were many), but who of course pocketed the proceeds. Instead, in 2009 the cash-strapped government opened a more or less full size but hollow replica to make them all feel at home in their new capital of Naypyidaw – although with slightly less valuable coverings.

After our separate journeys, the two committee teams regrouped in Singapore, we now accompanied by the beautiful Burmese Harp presented to the chairman on behalf of the members of the Pyithu Hluttaw: Ken (who had sussed out the real price of these things in downtown Rangoon) managed to persuade British customs that the solid teak case was probably worth more than the harp, and it was eventually allowed back into the country without charge. I was delighted when Sue and I attended Tony and Barbara Kershaw's golden wedding anniversary a few years later to find it in pride of place in their Knightsbridge home.

The contrast between Burma, struggling under an off-the-edge-of-the-planet regime, incompetent in all matters not appertaining to crop-spraying their minorities and enforcing house-arrests, and the immaculate island city-state off the Malay Peninsula, could not have been starker. Singapore had a per capita GDP of $6,660 (compared with Burma's $180), and was fast becoming a world (not merely a regional) financial centre. Moreover, wealth was widely (if not exactly evenly) distributed, owner-occupancy was becoming the norm, and the system of government actually worked; that at the time all but two seats in the unicameral parliament were held by the governing People's Action Party almost certainly reflected a general popular acceptance of the regime, and that the PAP's popular vote was gradually falling was generally regarded merely as a sign of electoral "boredom".

There was not much point in talking about overseas aid in a country in very many respects better off than our own. In the short time we were there we were talking about banking regulation, the protection of commercial and intellectual assets, defence agreements, and the best strategic approach to the challenges of China, Vietnam and the Cambodian imbroglio. Despite the predominance of the Chinese in the racial mix of the population, English was firmly entrenched as the official language and – at the specific request of the government – the BBC World Service was available 24 hours round the clock on local FM frequencies.

In our brief stay we did all the things visiting Brits were expected to do. We attended in the very early morning mist the sounding of the last post and reveille at the Kranji Cemetery, commemorating over 24,000 Commonwealth dead. We drank gin slings in the appallingly overcrowded bar of the Raffles Hotel, and could all think of better hostelries in Eastbourne or Bournemouth or even Blackpool. Mick Welsh[65] went searching the city for assets to add to the property portfolio of the National Union of Mineworkers. And Ivan Lawrence disappeared for a while into the market to buy up an assignment of fake Rolex's as thank-you's for his constituency workers.

Before we left south-east Asia we had several hours with Lee Kuan Yew, Companion of Honour, Knight Grand Cross of the Order of St Michael and St George, Prime Minister of Singapore, and effective creator of this particularly successful Asian tiger. A barrister with a Cambridge double first, and a sense of humour to go with it, Lee teased the committee – and particularly our more plebeian members – and ran rings around their protests about the alleged limitations on free speech and other human rights "abuses" in his new Venice in the Malay Straits. He served us a perfect Mandarin lunch, so fiery and unpalatable that I can recall its every abomination to this day, and we departed from Changi confident that at least part of the region we had visited had a prosperous future.

25

Little Hope on the Cape

The FAC speak to just about every South African in London, but is not allowed to visit South Africa; and nor is the Clerk

The committee's three week absence in Asia meant a great deal of catching up to do on our return. We had two priorities, which became three immediately we touched base. We needed to say something to the House about the Philippines, since the situation there was new and unfolding, and the committee members who had been hastily organised to visit the lovely President Aquino were the first British politicians to have talked at any length to the representatives of the new regime. And we were halfway through the process of trying to knock some sense into (or make some sense of) the British Government's determination to remain isolated from the international community's collective desire to threaten and if necessary force President Botha into conceding majority rule in South Africa.

The first task I was glad to leave to Crispin, since he had led the team to Manila, and knew the subject much better than I ever could. From his pen an extremely polished report was produced by the end of the summer term[66], which did much to consolidate his reputation, at a very young age, as a first-class draftsman. South Africa was mainly my shout, but even as we were hurrying through more formal evidence, and even more off-the-record briefings, on South Africa, on Cyprus (our next port of call), and from our new friends in South East Asia, the European Communities yet again demanded our full attention.

At the end of February 1986 the member States had signed the so-called Single European Act, which was really an inter-governmental treaty dressed up by another name. The three Communities were now to be called "the Community" – itself a significant move, but not yet the full Union to which some (and for PR purposes at least, most) of the member governments now aspired, or were said to aspire, however unenthusiastic or uninterested their electorates. The ministerial reaffirmation of faith in the onward march towards a bureaucratic and unaccountable Rhenish empire ("to transform relations" between the member States "into a European Union") was included in the Preamble. It was, of course, only a more explicit confirmation of the pledge "to lay the foundation of an ever closer union", which prefaced the original Rome Treaty of 1957, a determination whose significance was almost universally discounted over the decades by British politicians desperately anxious to reap the trading benefits of Community membership.

Any long term significance for the UK of the latest push towards a federal Europe was brushed aside in an extraordinarily complacent FCO assurance to the FAC that a preamble to a treaty was "an integral part of it but neither confers rights nor creates duties", which blithely disregarded the fact that in the Napoleonic tradition the interpretation of an individual clause in a legal document was always dependent on whatever interpretation might be given by a court to the preamble. Anyone who had sat through even a few days of proceedings in either of the Strasbourg assemblies (let alone their parallel inter-governmental councils) should have been wholly conversant with this more-than-a-little crucial point. It is extraordinary that it was only in late 2015, more than forty years after the United Kingdom joined the organisation, that a senior British minister, under pressure arising from his own Government's foolish commitment to a further referendum on membership, bravely spelt out the fact that the British people actually did not want to be part of "an ever-closer union".[67] This was hardly news: they never had been.

But in 1986 it was apparently not in the interests of the FCO and its ministers to face up to the reality of what they were allowing the Prime Minister to sign. The Single European Act might reasonably be described as a faustian deal, driven on one side by the professional federalists across the water, and on the other by Mrs T's no-doubt praiseworthy commitment to an entirely open and unrestricted market in financial and other services, which was always at the top of her agenda. In return for this, the Government conceded the extension of weighted majority voting in place of unanimity in the (now formalised) European Council, the enhancement of the legislative powers of the European Parliament (now formally so named in all languages) and the potential subordination of the FCO's role to the paramountcy of "enhanced European Political Co-operation". HMG certainly achieved its objective of gaining open access for the City to the financial services industries in which it undoubtedly excelled. In return it opened the way for the wholesale purchase of Britain's utilities by agencies of the French Government (for instance), and the subordination of much social and employment policy, as well as the minutiae of day-to-day trading transactions, to majority voting in multinational institutions in which the British Government and Parliament could no longer exercise any effective veto.

The Single European treaty involved some amendment of UK law, which was of course hotly contested at each stage, and on our return from Singapore we set out to provide some reasonably non-partisan advice before the committee stage of the European Communities (Amendment) Bill. Re-reading our report more than three decades on I remain honestly amazed by its sanity and its clairvoyance, and even more by the fact that at a time of bitter intra-party and inter-party strife over Europe the committee in a couple of sittings, and with only four divisions on relatively minor points, were able amicably to agree an otherwise unanimous report.[68] It did not, of course, dissuade the House from endorsing a treaty which eventually did more than any other to undermine the sovereignty of the British Parliament – and more than any other laid the trail which led to Brexit.

Just as they were getting out of their depth in the European imbroglio, so the South African situation was becoming increasingly tricky for the Conservative Government, and demanded equally urgent attention. HMG had rather brilliantly painted itself into a corner. Its stated policy was "to promote early and peaceful transition to a genuinely non-racial democracy", but whenever it set out its stall it seemed to feel honour-bound to add words such as "and to further the United Kingdom's considerable interests in South Africa". To the rest of the world this was an obvious give-away, since the UK was South Africa's principal source of foreign investment, and it seemed effectively to compromise HMG's proclaimed aim of achieving all this by peaceful negotiation and persuasion.

At a meeting of Community leaders in Luxembourg in September 1985 the British Government had had to fight hard against a majority demand for a more-or-less total shut-down on relations of all kinds with the apartheid regime. The following month, in Nassau, they only just managed to avoid the immediate disintegration of the Commonwealth by agreeing to the appointment of a group of "Eminent Persons" (led by the former Australian Prime Minister, Malcolm Fraser, and the former - and future - Nigerian President, General Olusegun Obasanjo) to encourage "the evolution of the necessary process of political dialogue". In November the British Government, most unusually, had to exercise its veto in the UN Security Council on the related subject of the continued South African occupation of Namibia, and used it again in May and June 1986.[*]

The Eminent Persons Group reported in June 1986, flatly concluding that "at present there is no genuine intention on the part of the South African Government to dismantle apartheid". They made no attempt to disguise their frustration with President P W Botha's refusal to co-operate with their own mission. The attacks on ANC forces outside South Africa's borders, in Harare, Gabarone and Lusaka, on the eve of the EPG's meetings with the Cabinet in Pretoria, could only reinforce this conclusion: and the Eminent Persons were instructed by the Commonwealth Secretary-General to return to London forthwith. The EPG's inevitably negative report effectively derailed the UK Government's policy of non-confrontational negotiation and conciliation, but they were not of the mettle to admit immediate defeat.

---

[*] In total, the British veto was deployed at the Security Council on the subject of South Africa and/or Namibia on six separate occasions between 1985 and 1988.

By the summer of 1986 the Foreign Affairs Committee had taken formal evidence on thirteen separate occasions from the FCO, from those involved in trade with South Africa, from the leaders of opposition parties and of the nominally independent "homelands". We had talked twice to Mr Tambo and Mr Mbeki from the African National Congress; we had talked to the Progressive Federal Party; we had talked to Chief Buthelezi, leader of Inkatha and president of KwaZulu; we had talked to the leaders of the so-called Lebowa "homeland"; we had of course talked to the democratically-inclined South African Ambassador, Denis Worrall. And since the autumn of 1985 we had also held no less than twenty-three private meetings with these and the many other groups who preferred not to appear in public, often because they feared the consequences of doing so. The Foreign Affairs Committee ended up at least as well briefed about South Africa as almost any other group in London – or, indeed, elsewhere – with the honourable exception, perhaps, of Mrs Thatcher, whose direct (and sometimes acrimonious) correspondence with President Botha sought to keep some kind of door open to the regime in Pretoria, despite the overwhelming pressure on her to join the hunt.

On 24th July the Foreign Affairs Committee produced another surprisingly unanimous report to the House, which stressed the obvious – that unless President Botha was prepared to take the risk of opening up the prospect of real progress towards the involvement of the majority black population in the government of the whole of their own country (instead of attempting to corral the majority population into subservient bantustans on the poorest land), even the United Kingdom government would be compelled to adopt the "negative" approach which was being urged on them from all quarters of the Commonwealth, in the European Community, and in the UN General Assembly.[69] On the same day, the Commonwealth Games opened in Edinburgh in the absence of thirty-two of the Commonwealth's fifty-nine nations: almost all the African, Caribbean and Asian members had withdrawn their athletes in protest at Downing Street's foot-dragging.

By this time there seemed to be not many options left for Mrs Thatcher and Sir Geoffrey Howe who, as we now know, had widely if not wildly different approaches to matters relating to southern Africa, as to other matters of foreign policy. The Foreign Secretary, as President-in-Office of the Community Foreign Affairs Council, had been deputed in The Hague at the end of June to go off to Pretoria during the summer break to see what could be done to break the impasse. On his return, with empty hands, there was the small matter of an emergency conference of the key Commonwealth Heads of Government (to review the work of the EPG) to be confronted on home ground, in London, in early August. Amazingly, given their growing personal antipathy, Margaret and Geoffrey combined to face down the rest of the Commonwealth and stuck to their refusal to support the total isolation of South Africa, the resulting communiqué openly enumerating the differences between them and the rest of the Commonwealth. Nonetheless, "at a time of heightened stress within our association" (which was about as far as even the most masterly diplomatic drafting could go), the communiqué re-affirmed collective support for this admirable, even if sometimes dysfunctional, family of nations. Margaret and Geoffrey continued to outstare the rest of the Commonwealth and the UN for the next couple of years, while simultaneously outstaring each other across Downing Street.

Although almost universally condemned for their stance at the time, there is a deal of truth in the assessment of her press secretary, Bernard Ingham, that Margaret on this occasion produced "a display of political courage and resolution": it avoided more bloodshed, averted the collapse of the South African economy and Britain's substantial economic interests there, and ensured that the UK would become one of the staunchest friends of the new democratic Republic and of Nelson Mandela: this latter achievement was not entirely paradoxical – the highly intelligent leaders of the ANC recognised the publicity value of token boycotts,[*] but they also had no desire to take over an economy in a state of total collapse: which was the burden of the private messages they were leaving wherever it mattered in London. The private interests of Margaret's husband and family were at the time less well advertised, but it would not be improbable to speculate that they had at least some bearing on the Downing Street line at the time – which of course (but unfairly) seemed to the rest of the world something like out-and-out racism.

Margaret and Geoffrey had between them at least avoided the kind of farce which had characterised Harold Wilson's blockade of Southern Rhodesia in the mid-1960's, which had sullied his reputation thereafter, and from the remains of which disaster she and her outstanding Foreign Secretary Peter Carrington had managed to secure Britain's reasonably honourable exit from colonial Africa in the Lancaster House Agreement of December 1979. In the end it was left to the common sense and common decency of Botha's initially unprepossessing successor, F W de Klerk, to

---

[*] I can claim to be one of the earliest boycotters. In 1964 the students of Keele University vowed never to touch food or buy any other product from South Africa until apartheid was no more – a vow I at least did my damnedest to uphold until 1990. Keele students and staff (almost to a man and a woman) also made out standing orders the following year to finance the Keele Scholarship for black South African students, for which we continued to pay our pound or so for something like the next forty years. The first recipient was the very brave Sam Nolutshungu, who gained a first in economics, history and politics, was a brilliant Debates Union President, and after an illustrious academic career at Manchester and Rochester was appointed Vice-Chancellor of Witwatersrand University in 1996, only to die of cancer before being able to take up the post.

extricate South Africa from its own political impasse, without a full-scale civil war, while at the same time extricating the United Kingdom from isolation in the Commonwealth without compromising its position as a major trading and financial partner of the post-apartheid Republic. As Margaret Thatcher had always hoped, South Africa had in the end found its own Gorbachev.

I had found the many months of formal and informal discussions with the men in grey suits from the South African business world, from the Nationalist Boers in even greyer suits and even greyer faces, and from the be-robed leaders of the homelands, and the more-or-less Marxist revolutionaries, an invigorating experience. I was at last dealing with issues in which, as the adoptive father of three "black" children, I felt closely engaged. As the committee's report said, the choices to be made by western governments did not require, as so many would have wished, "straightforward responses to straightforward moral questions". However repugnant the apartheid regime, there were many millions of real individuals of all races out there in what were by now relatively ancient communities around the Cape whose whole way of life was threatened with disruption, if not extinction. The moral issues were as complex as those in the American Civil War – and in much the same way the outcomes might have a very direct impact on Britain's economy, and on its reputation in the world: not least, as the committee said, "the danger of the disintegration of the Commonwealth" (that wholly benign legacy of empire) was "not to be dismissed lightly".

Our report on South Africa was widely welcomed. Oliver Tambo, variously Secretary General and acting President of the ANC (who was then living in exile in my mother's childhood haunt of Muswell Hill), wrote personally to thank me for what he regarded as a balanced and "civilised" assessment of the South African impasse, and many others from the different communities echoed his views.

A few days after the publication of the report, which was hurried through the printer at break-neck speed to get ahead of the Commonwealth meeting, I was offered a bursary by the South Africa Foundation to spend a month or so in the Republic, travelling wherever I wished, and talking to whomsoever I chose, with the aim of producing a more personal commentary on life in the Republic and on the prospects for a settlement. Most important, I was free to take my family with me. When I reminded Mr Abrahamse, the Foundation's London director, that my family was of a mixed-race character (my two sons are of anglo-caribbean origin, and my daughter of asian extract) no objections were raised – it would of course have made excellent publicity. We would stay in the best hotels - already allegedly free of apartheid - and (although there would undoubtedly have been some problems on the ground) the whole family's safety would be guaranteed. It fell to my friend and mentor Kenneth Bradshaw, by that time Clerk of the

House, to issue the expected veto: domestic political disputes on the subject of South Africa were so fraught that any such engagement might cause embarrassment. I did not believe that any member of the Foreign Affairs Committee - and few members of the House - would have objected, but KAB was of course doing his duty.

Like me, the Foreign Affairs Committee as a whole would have liked to visit South Africa (and some had of course done so as individuals), but the same political exigencies then applied to the committee *qua* committee, and they only made it in 1990 (long after my own departure), when Nelson Mandela had been released, and real negotiations were already in train for the establishment of a new multiracial Republic.

26

Letters from Ulan Bator

We talk endlessly about going to Cyprus; FAC/FCO relations slowly mature, thanks to Our Man in Mongolia

The FAC had also wished since their very first meeting in December 1979 to visit Cyprus. Not merely another post-colonial problem, Cyprus remained a legal responsibility of the United Kingdom, which was one of the three "Guarantor" powers under the constitution and independence settlement agreed in July 1960, and which also happened to own and occupy around 3 per cent of the island in the Sovereign Base Areas, somewhat anomalous survivors of the colonial era. Akrotiri and Dhekalia were not entirely different in purpose (even if they were different in legal character) from the Simonstown base in the Cape, which the UK had been reluctantly compelled to abandon, under the pressure of "world" opinion, in 1975 – a loss much regretted during the Falklands War in 1982, when the base was closed to the British Navy but could then have been of critical advantage. And Cyprus shared with South Africa the very close ties existing between hundreds of thousands of families in the UK and in the former colonies – in the case of South Africa, the enormous English and Scottish diaspora (of which my maternal grandmother's family appeared to form a substantial part), and in the case of Cyprus the Greek and (to make life more complicated) the Turkish Cypriots who had already made London the largest Cypriot city in the world.

Following the Athens-inspired coup against President Makarios in July 1974, and the subsequent occupation of the north by the Turkish army, the island – already separately governed by a Greek-speaking President and a Turk Vice-President - had been finally divided, and was policed by what was then a largely British peacekeeping force. The south of the island continued, and continues to this day, as the internationally recognised Republic of Cyprus, and now full-blown member of the European Union. The north, which after 16th August 1974 comprised about 36% per cent of the territory (that percentage being one of the main stumbling blocks in negotiations aimed at a federal solution), described itself as the "Turkish Federated State of Cyprus" from February 1975, and in November 1983 declared full independence as the Turkish Republic of Northern Cyprus, recognised as such by Turkey alone.

Visits overseas by the Foreign Affairs Committee inevitably required the co-operation, if not the active approval, of the Foreign & Commonwealth Office, for obvious logistical as well as diplomatic reasons. The committee's earlier decision to go to Cyprus in 1980 was turned down flat by the FCO, ostensibly on the grounds that a public inquiry "might compromise the possibility of progress in the communal talks then in train" – an argument which could of course have been deployed at any time during the next forty years, since inter-communal talks have been more or less continuous, and have always failed in their main objective; but in those early days there were still flickers of naïve optimism that a solution could be found.

The real reasons for the FCO's reluctance to co-operate with the committee in 1980 were not hard to discover. There had already been a stand-alone inquiry into the events of 1974 which had caused the previous Government and the FCO acute and continuing embarrassment. With their tiny majority fast vanishing the Wilson government had in early August 1975 succumbed to demands for a sessional select committee; even worse, they had suicidally agreed to limit the committee to only six (three Labour and three Tory) thus ensuring that there was not even a nominal government majority.[*] The committee, chaired by the veteran socialist Arthur Bottomley, had visited Cyprus a month later and, such was the havoc they were already causing the government's reputation, when reappointed in the next session they were allowed only ten weeks to complete their work, were not allowed any further travel, and only very reluctantly conceded the right even to take any further evidence. Their eventual report reflected the exasperation and anger of the Members who had been so cavalierly treated by a struggling near-minority government. Indeed, when a couple of years later the Procedure Committee was considering the establishment of a new select committee system the fate of the Cyprus Committee was frequently cited as an overwhelming argument in favour of a permanent structure which might limit the Executive's day-to-day influence: an optimistic aim since, as the FAC (and all the other fresh-minted departmentally-related committees) discovered, in the early days of the new committees neither ministers nor whips were yet keen to relinquish control.

The 1976 Cyprus Committee's report had long been out of print by the time we in turn reported to the House just before the start of the 1987 General Election campaign (and HMSO had apparently been specifically instructed not to reprint it), but the FAC regarded it as so important that we gave directions for the whole text, including the minutes of proceedings, to be appended to our own report. The 1976 report had been approved after a

---

[*] As in any select committee, the chairman could only vote in the case of a tie: one Labour chairman meant two Labour members and three Tory members. The latter could therefore always win: although in this case the views of the two sides of the House were never that far apart.

hard-fought battle, with twenty formal divisions, almost all initiated by the one member who had not participated in the committee's visit to Cyprus, but nonetheless should have known a great deal about it: Sir George Sinclair had in a former life served in the colonial service as, amongst other things, deputy Governor of Cyprus during the EOKA campaign in the late 1950's, which had cost the lives of over a hundred and fifty British military and police, as well as many more Cypriots of both communities. He seems to have been a realist, but tended nonetheless to accept the credibility of the British Government's animadversions. Whatever the reasons for his appointment to the committee in its last heroic weeks, he certainly fought hard to temper the anger of his colleagues. But even he accepted the main, headline-forming, conclusion of the committee: that at the time of the Greek *coup* and the subsequent Turkish invasion in 1974 "Britain had a legal right to intervene, she had a moral obligation to intervene, she had the military capacity to intervene". The 1976 committee added that the then Foreign Secretary simply refused to explain our non-intervention. After his retirement Jim Callaghan – by then ex-Prime Minister as well as ex-Foreign Secretary – acknowledged that one of the main reasons was that Henry Kissinger had simply told them not to; and since Britain was no longer a super-power we couldn't afford "another Suez".

By 1986 the Foreign Affairs Committee had gone some way towards winning its diplomatic spurs, following the mutual bruising which the committee and HM Government had inflicted on each other (and to some extent on Pierre Trudeau) during their protracted exchanges during 1981 (before my time) about how the House of Commons should respond to the Canadian government's request for the final "patriation" of the Canadian constitution. The FAC had been understandably accused in some quarters at that time of meddling not only in inter-governmental relations but in the internal affairs of an independent state[70], and had certainly not strengthened its standing in the FCO as a body fit to be let loose in any other state whose internal affairs also touched on the UK's rights, interests or responsibilities. This was of course, a constitutional doctrine invoked only as occasion required.

As the 1983 Parliament progressed, relations improved. The FCO seemed to think that the committee had mainly said the right things about Grenada (Geoffrey Howe taking the flak like a gent, while the diplomats largely purred with amusement), about the failing USSR (supporting the Gorbachev/Thatcher initiatives, and even to some extent helping to kick-start the process), and often about the European Community. And its honest doubts about Britain's claims to sovereignty in the South Atlantic, which had so enraged Ministers, struck more than a sympathetic chord with officials. The Committee had also by then, in its overseas visits and in hundreds of off-the-record meetings in London, demonstrated that Members of Parliament could be trusted, or sometimes even recruited, to ask the awkward questions which professional diplomats were forbidden to ask - and that even those of radical temperament (whether on the left or on the right) could generally be trusted to support the flag.

The committee and its staff had also done something to help to extricate the Foreign & Commonwealth Office from their isolation in Parliament, which had been so dramatically exposed in the run-up to the Argentine invasion of the Falklands. Essentially, the FCO had at that time very few reliable friends in the Commons, while the islanders had assiduously cultivated the more voluble backbenchers. Sir Bernard Braine and a handful of colleagues had run rings round the FCO in the early 1980's and noisily (and tediously) blocked the kind of negotiated – probably 'shared sovereignty' – solution which logic, commonsense, and perhaps even justice, would have prescribed. Lord Carrington's resignation as Foreign & Commonwealth Secretary at the time of the invasion reflected his own honourable view that the FCO had botched the Falklands so badly that they - and he - had at least some responsibility for the resulting war. He was one of the very last ministers to have resigned because he accepted responsibility for his officials' failures, rather than because he was being chased by the tabloids or the *Telegraph* for some sordid indiscretion in his office, or in the pool at Cliveden.*

In the early summer of 1982, soon after I was posted to the Foreign Affairs Committee, I was paraded at the FCO for a ritual meeting with my new department's permanent secretary, in this case Sir Antony Acland, who had had the misfortune of succeeding to the top job in the FCO just before the start of the Falklands conflict, and had been at the receiving end of Margaret's most unrestrained vituperations against the diplomatic profession.† I was accompanied by the FCO's parliamentary liaison officer, Allan Butler. The post of liaison officer had not been regarded historically as of much importance in the FCO, largely because the FCO promoted little legislation which required support, and had little expenditure to offer in the constituencies – which the big spending departments sought to employ to secure a reliable base of backbench friends and adherents in a mild form of

---

* It was, perhaps, a belated tribute to his erstwhile boss, Sir Thomas Dugdale, who in 1954 had resigned as Minister of Agriculture & Fisheries over the Crichel Down affair, taking responsibility for the failures of his civil servants: a case cited in every textbook and thousands of undergraduate essays as the last occasion when the doctrine of individual ministerial responsibility had been taken seriously. Lord Carrington had attempted to resign with Dugdale but had been refused. In 1982 he provided the very last exception which disproved what has now become the new rule: that you simply blame the civil servants and carry on.
† Famously, at a meeting at Chequers on 17 May 1982, after much hand-bagging, he had challenged the overwrought Prime Minister directly: "If you want to get another Permanent Under-Secretary, for heaven's sake do so". After a long pause, Margaret got the point: "All right, no more Foreign Office bashing".

log-rolling. Allan Butler was therefore not drawn from the phalanx of the graduate high flyers. Sir Antony, however, was only too aware that his department had not performed exactly brilliantly in Parliament during the last few years, and that the outcome of the Falklands war might well have been a triumph for the politicians and the military but was an episode from which the Foreign & Commonwealth Office had to find some way of recovering: for your minister to take the rap for the poor performance of your department was failure on the grand scale.

We agreed that it might help a lot if senior diplomats began actually talking to politicians other than members of the Cabinet.* During the next few months an underused FCO budget was discovered, and the following year we embarked on a programme of "Foreign Office days in Parliament", which continued at least until my own departure from the FAC. The Jubilee Room off Westminster Hall became an occasional venue for discreet luncheons at which a wide variety of MP's were wined and dined and persuaded that diplomats could be human; and diplomats on leave were offered the delight of attending meetings not only of the Foreign Affairs and Defence Committees but also of the whole range of committees which might descend on them in their next postings. The whole exercise, which included the elevation of the parliamentary liaison officer to become head of the Parliamentary Relations Unit, was approved in December at the Foreign Secretary's country residence at Chevening, in recognition of the need "as much to inform and persuade Foreign Office officials about the importance of Parliament as the other way round".[71] This deliberately unadvertised arrangement did much to improve relations between diplomats and backbenchers, and also did much to improve the latter's reception when they arrived eagerly in Caracas or Canberra or Delhi or Durban to investigate the state of the social services or hospitals or standards in the grade schools or the maintenance of the local railways. Accommodation in the local brothel became a less frequent hazard of overseas committee trips.

Despite his origins in the consular service, Allan Butler was eventually rewarded with an ambassadorship of his own. For the next couple of years our lives overlooking the Thames were greatly enlivened by the arrival of the latest handwritten letter from Ulan Bator. Allan recounted in detail, and in lyrical prose, the logistics of arranging the delivery of a whole container of good manure and topsoil, in order to recharge the Residence garden, it being the recognised role of the British Ambassador's wife (in this case the

---

* That they did not regularly do so is not a fanciful or exaggerated assertion: when Sir Nicholas (Nico) Henderson (one of the UK's greatest, or at any rate most flamboyant, diplomats, who had served as ambassador to Warsaw, Bonn, Paris and Washington) gave evidence to the FAC on the subject of the Falklands in April 1984, he commented that it was the first occasion on which he had ever been invited to address a Commons committee, and indeed that he could not recall the last time he had even entered the building.

very charming Pauline) to provide the only available supply of fresh vegetables for Mongolia's small diplomatic community. He recalled the three-month interval between the arrival of the left hand winter glove he had ordered from Moscow and its right hand partner. He told us of Pauline's long railway expedition into China to get her teeth fixed. And he claimed (probably inaccurately, because there were probably others in other quietly charming capitals around the world) to be the only ambassador in the business to spend each weekday morning sharing a bottle of Black Label with the President of the Republic, while passing on the World Service news repackaged as capitalist state secrets. I was sorry not to have seen his valedictory, which would have made good reading.[*] Allan ended his FCO career as Deputy Permanent Representative to the Council of Europe in Strasbourg where, in my long experience there, Johnnie Walker was not a merely antemeridian phenomenon.

---

[*] It was sadly not included in the BBC's splendid compilation of our ambassadors' last words (Matthew Parris & Andrew Bryson, *Parting Shots*, Viking, London 2010).

27

Crossing the Line

*Nicosia at last; we seek peace and reconciliation, and
instead win brickbats; but at least the Chairman
remembers his flippers*

So, with official acquiescence and ministerial blessings, the Foreign Affairs
Committee set off at last, at the end of November 1986, for a fortnight in
the wintry Mediterranean sun. The committee were at least as mindful as
the diplomats of the danger of our inquiry becoming "a platform for the
exchange of mutual accusations and allegations", not only between the
divided Cypriot communities, but also between the governments and
politicians of Greece and Turkey, and between their respective backers in
our own parliament. Because of this we deliberately restricted the hearing
of formal and public evidence, and, even more than was often the case for
the FAC, our analysis and conclusions would therefore have to depend
heavily on off-the-record discussions held off-limits. We had already had
dozens of private meetings in London over the previous year, which for the
most part – and most surprisingly - had not leaked either to the media or –
more importantly – to the "other" side; and we had been flooded with rival
memoranda offering totally conflicting versions of the island's pre- and
post-independence history, of its ethnic composition, and of the crimes
actually perpetrated or alleged to have been perpetrated in the cause of
Enosis or its Turkish equivalent (which when read together implied
permanent partition).

We were as usual reliant on the efficiency and integrity of our diplomatic
service to ensure that we saw the right people not only in Aphrodite's island
but also in the foreign capitals which beckoned like rival Sirens. Themselves
often frustrated to distraction by the intractability of the positions adopted
north and south of the Line, many of the diplomats were also eager to see
whether even a small amount of progress towards a settlement could be
achieved, and they co-operated magnificently to further the success of this
latest committee venture into peace-keeping. We were not unaware that in
the twelve years since the geographical division of Cyprus many astute and
experienced minds had bent themselves to the task of reunification, not least
my distant cousin Brian Urquhart,[72] and we had no high expectations of
making even a small contribution to a breakthrough in the inter-communal
impasse, symbolised by the bifurcated city of Nicosia/Lefkoşa.

Our first port of call was Athens, and there we were confronted with the full force of the propaganda battle which had been raging more or less continuously since the recognition of Greek independence from the Porte in 1830. We had already become inured to what threatened to become tons of paper arriving in our office on the banks of the Thames.*

In the Hotel Grande Bretagne of considerable notoriety, with balconies overlooking the Hellenic Parliament (housed in the old and no longer needed royal palace), our rooms were decked with flowers and fruit and unlimited quantities of the best ouzo and retsina. But as we entered we almost fell over the stacks of documents from the government, the parliament, and from a multitude of Cypriot friendship groups which occupied almost every other spare surface: not the kind of activity which would have been tolerated during the hotel's earlier manifestations as headquarters of the Nazi occupiers and their British successors, respectively before and after 1945.

Here the lower echelons of the diplomatic service came to our immediate aid. With intelligence from a well-placed mole in the hotel's housekeeping service (the kind of practical intelligence without which no decent embassy can operate with reasonable efficiency), word came fast that British MPs were decanting large volumes of paper into the waste bins, now already overflowing: an international incident was brewing. Ken and I discreetly visited each member of our team, and relieved them of the offending papers, which were sent back to London in a jumbo-size diplomatic bag for the most part consigned to the flames.

Our interlocutors in Athens – ministers, parliamentarians, party leaders and the charismatic prime minister (and former Harvard Professor) Andreas Papandreou[73] – were all desperate to assure us that they had no further interest in Enosis, that the coup against Archbishop Makarios in 1974, Nikos Sampson's eight-day presidency, and the disastrous consequences for all the Cypriot people, was nothing to do with them: it had all been the fault of the Colonels, and we should be grateful that the military had been so swiftly swept from power, and a model democracy restored in the home of democracy. The fact that Greece was at that moment engaged in mock battles and playing dare with its NATO ally Turkey was, they claimed, nothing at all to do with Cyprus, but all to do with Istanbul's nefarious territorial ambitions elsewhere (and nobody please mention Aegean oil).

When we reached Cyprus itself our hosts on both sides of the Green Line were if anything culpably polite in forgiving us for Britain's sins of omission and commission, of which there had been far too many both before

---

* It was probably fortunate that the FAC's offices had not in my time yet moved to the upper deck of the Committee Office (where it was subsequently located for a few decades), since the notorious (and proven) instability of the floor might have produced total catastrophe when the Cypriot papers arrived in full flood.

and after the botched independence settlement of 1960, which had left the great majority of peaceful Cypriots at the mercy of their native extremists and of the latter's sponsors in Athens and Ankara.

Having acted as "administrator" from 1878 on behalf of the Sultan, and having unilaterally annexed the island when Turkey joined the Central Powers in 1914, the British Government the following year offered Cyprus to King Constantine as an inducement to join the Franco-British cause. Constantine I stayed out of the war largely for family reasons (he was the Kaiser's brother-in-law), and Greece therefore didn't get Cyprus on a plate even though in June 1917, under Venizelos, it eventually and sensibly joined the winning side. The British offer of Cyprus was nonetheless interpreted, by the Cypriots in particular, as an expression of sympathy for the longstanding goal of Enosis and as a confirmation of Britain's traditional Byronic philhellenism.

Both mainland and Cypriot Greeks were therefore increasingly angered and non-plussed by Britain's subsequent opposition to Enosis, exemplified during the 1930's by colonial legislation banning the public display of Greek (or Turkish) flags and the formation of any overtly nationalist organisations. The teaching of Greek (or Turkish) history was curtailed, and the British colonial authorities attempted to control the internal administration of the autocephalous Orthodox church, which they accurately regarded as a hotbed of Greek nationalism. This resulted in a fourteen-year vacancy in the office of Archbishop (who in Ottoman times had served as the recognised spokesman of the Greek Cypriot community) and an ineradicable and not entirely unjustified sense of grievance and outrage. The Ottoman approach to their subject peoples was perhaps more nuanced.

The Turkish Cypriots had at least equal grounds for complaint against Britain. During the bitter years of the thirties and forties, the majority population's leaders' demands for "self-determination" (which meant union with Greece) escalated. The inevitable response of the Turkish population was to support, however reluctantly, the division of the island, a response which became understandably more urgent when in 1955 Colonel Grivas (hero of the anti-fascist and anti-communist Greek resistance, backed by the Greek military and by the young Archbishop Makarios III, and egged on by the mainland Greek media) began to terrorise the Turkish community, and the British occupiers, in what came to be known as the "Emergency".

The Emergency provoked an understandably urgent desire on the part of the British to get out of Cyprus, although the UK definitely didn't want to be deprived of the island's principal asset as a military staging post. Eventually they devised what seemed to at least some Turkish Cypriots a workable if not perfect solution: a wonderfully garbled "bi-communal" independence Constitution for the 97% of the island which the UK was prepared to forgo, which in theory guaranteed the rights of both the majority and the minority communities. It broke, however, the cardinal rule of federalism, of which it was a bastard cousin, which is that it doesn't really work if there are only two components: you only have to look at Belgium to understand the problem. Sir Kenneth Wheare, the author of so many post-colonial constitutions,[74] must have been appalled when the British government, desperate to leave someone else (or anyone else) to pick up the pieces, foisted this unworkable formula on a population deserving of rather better treatment.

Most important for the Turkish Cypriots in the 1960 settlement was the Treaty of Guarantee, which engaged the United Kingdom (alongside Greece and Turkey) as guarantors in perpetuity of the Constitution, of the rights of the two communities, and of the treaty prohibition on "any activity likely to promote, directly or indirectly, either union with any other state or partition of the island". However bad the Constitution, the minority believed they could be reassured by Britain's continuing involvement. At each stage in the progressive breakdown of the constitutional arrangements Britain, with "the physical means", was in a position to intervene. However, in the words of the British minister responsible for negotiating the 1960 settlement, Britain had "three times – 1963, 1967 and 1974 – evaded that responsibility".[75]

By 1963 the overly-complex Constitution, which prevented either the majority or the minority from controlling the situation (or doing much else), was already breaking down, EOKA was back in murderous action, and the Archbishop was signalling an inclination to make a run for Enosis in flat disregard of the treaties. Britain, as the only relatively neutral "guarantor" power, failed directly to intervene, but left it to the UN Security Council to create a peace-keeping force to keep the two sides apart, albeit one largely manned by the British Army.

Thereafter the two communities began to run themselves, the theocratic President in charge of the majority population, Vice-President Küçük running what amounted to a separate Turkish administration. In December 1967 the separation had been formalised with the establishment of a "transitional administration" on the Greek side, necessitated by the withdrawal of the entire Turkish component of the Cyprus House of Representatives, and of most Turkish Cypriot civil servants. Separation on communal, if not yet entirely geographic, lines was now fully under way. Britain again failed to intervene. Finally, in July 1974, the Cyprus National Guard, officered and inspired from Athens, had ousted Makarios III (who was by then less enamoured of a union with Greece, having got rather to like running his own show) and had installed an EOKA thug as President, with the aim of immediate enosis. Britain again refused to intervene either to forestall or to support an inevitable Turkish response, thousands of British troops sitting idly by in their enclaves. And within a month the island was physically partitioned.

Notwithstanding its abject failures after independence, British suzerainty had given Cypriots of both confessions a good deal to be thankful for. Apart from roads and drains, a relatively efficient civil service, the beginnings of a decent education system, and a reasonably impartial judiciary, all Cypriots had, under the British imperial umbrella, been spared the appalling population exchanges and state-sponsored ethnic violence which had engulfed much of the Balkans, the Aegean and Anatolia during and after the Great War. As a result Cyprus had retained the kind of population mix of which most of the other Aegean islands and the Adriatic had been forcibly deprived; and had as a result become an anomalous and continuing irritant in Greco-Turkish relations otherwise "eased" elsewhere by the results of the ethnic cleansing legalised by the 1923 Lausanne Treaty. If the much-abused term "protectorate" ever meant anything more than "colony", it was in Cyprus in the first few decades of the last century. But colonial peoples cannot be expected to be grateful. In the words of a once celebrated British historian, "No race, however weak, prefers a stranger in the chair of state".[76] That is, we might add with the benefit of hindsight, until they have seen what their compatriots can do.

When talking to individual Cypriots in London it was sometimes difficult to think of them as Greeks or Turks, particularly as we were now all becoming accustomed to excellent Cypriot food in Cypriot restaurants of undeclared ethnic origin. Many community leaders had been brought up and educated together, and senior politicians and civil servants had often been on amicable terms in British universities or when training at the Bar in London. One of our small tasks when crossing and re-crossing the Green Line which divides the island was to carry familial greetings (and in one case birthday presents) from one family to another. Indeed it was His Beatitude Chrisostomos I (Makarios' successor) who encouraged us to think about the similarity of the island's populations, rather than their differences, even hinting (with possible accuracy) that their ethnic origins might not be as different as both communities claimed. We were at the time watching from his study as soldiers of the Turkish Cypriot Security Force changed guard on a goon tower on the northern side of the Line, rifles apparently permanently aimed at the Archbishop.

It was of course in the interests of the Greek Cypriot leadership to encourage the legend of a happy, united, people forcibly divided by the invading Turks. But by 1977 Makarios, somewhat deflated by his treatment at the hands of Nikos Sampson and his friends, had come belatedly to accept the idea of a bi-communal Cyprus. And so by 1986 the majority was learning to eschew ideas of union with Greece; the very idea of Enosis was, according to the foreign minister, "entirely behind us". Having by then been in charge of an internationally recognised independent country for a quarter of a century they were, as the committee's report put it, "unlikely to have any great hankering to become mere provincial legislators and officials in a province of the Republic of Greece".

By 1986 the prospects of a happy reunion of the two communities were therefore already dim. True, the London-educated leaders of that time had been and might again be on civil, even friendly, terms; but the people on the streets were already people on quite different trajectories and were perforce now accustomed to their identities as Turkish or Greek Cypriots, rather than Cypriots. As the committee noted, the centrifugal forces were already very much stronger than the centripetal; for the younger generation the sense of a common Cypriot heritage and a common Cypriot identity was already fast fading.

We arrived on Tuesday 2nd December 1986 in an idyllic Mediterranean island divided already not only by military force but also by the growing inclinations of its population. There were only two telephone connections between south and north; there were no postal services; between the two communities lay a wasteland of weeds and rampant undergrowth and decaying buildings; and the militias of the two communities diligently protected their separate bastions, often face to face across what had once been a busy street, or at a greater distance across untilled fields, overgrown vines and a newly modernised international airport occupied only by peacekeepers and the local wildlife, while Canadian jeeps and British Landrovers kept up their quiet but continuous vigil, east to west, west to east. At least no more lives were being lost. And the two communities continued to provide each other with some of the essentials of life, like water and electricity, each constantly grumbling about the cost and denying their interdependence.

Our six days in Cyprus were in most respects a delight, despite minor, well-orchestrated but good-humoured street demonstrations, and despite our growing awareness that the impasse was one we would not be able to breach. We talked to opinion leaders (of whom there were many) on the southern side of the Line, and several times navigated the overgrown track into Lefkoşa, by way of the Ledra Palace Hotel checkpoint (which at that time was the only official crossing point between the two sides); an experience which could be compared with that of Lucy as she tumbled out of the wardrobe into the perpetual winter of Narnia. Nicosia was already a thriving, prosperous, noisy and distinctly European centre of tourism and espionage; Lefkoşa was set in a time warp, an almost silent colonial outpost (for automobiles were a rarity) sleeping under the Mediterranean sun, the advertisements for Castrol and Shell, Marmite, Robin Starch and Surf, pealing slowly but stately from the stucco. There we were encouraged to find that although Mr Rauf Denktash[77] was obviously fully in control of the Turkish Republic of Northern Cyprus there was, contrary to Greek Cypriot propaganda, sufficient freedom for opposition parties to operate, and that by no means all the elected members of the Legislative Assembly of this small community were happy with the adulteration of the indigenous population by waves of immigrants from Anatolia, or with the official view that Cyprus must be permanently divided.

Just as many Greeks were desperate to return to their family homes in the north, so quite a few Turkish Cypriots dreamed of returning to their own villages in the south. I was not alone in our party in feeling some real sympathy and admiration for these people, whom the rest of the world treated as a pariah when they thought of them at all. In an uncharacteristically and no doubt improper political gesture a small flag of the TRNC flew thereafter on my desk in Westminster until my retirement. Unlike some known to me, however, I honourably declined the offer of a five bed-roomed villa with pool and a couple of acres for a mere £30,000; a decision I have from time to time regretted.

Proceedings on both sides of the Line were enlivened by the ebullient mood of many of the party. While Ken Brown recalled his days chasing EOKA in the Troodos mountains and introduced committee members to the delights of brandy sours, Mick Welsh scoured the island, south and north, for prime properties in which to invest the funds of the National Union of Mineworkers (and found a few both north and south). Ivan Lawrence, who had apparently already fallen deeply for the colonial north, and ended up as a big wheel in the parliamentary Friends of Northern Cyprus, tinkled (or in his words "thumped") the ivories in a straw hat in Nicosia nightclubs and in the cavernous northern hotel opened up specially for our arrival. And I still treasure photographs of Sir Anthony Kershaw, just before his seventy-first birthday, marching into the Mediterranean from the same hotel in early December armed with the flippers and snorkel which Barbara had solicitously remembered to pack in case of need.

After a relaxed lunch with Mr Denktash and other Turkish Cypriot community leaders at Boğaz we returned to the south of the island, said fond farewells to the Archbishop, and headed off for Turkey. As the mythical crow lies, the journey from Nicosia to Ankara on the Anatolian plateau is a mere 329 miles. Thanks to the closure of Nicosia airport (mothballed inside the buffer zone, as it still is) and the purdah imposed on the north, we in fact travelled from Larnaca to Athens, from Athens to Istanbul, and from Istanbul to Ankara, a journey occupying most of a day, and along which a very exhausted crow would have clocked up something like 1200 miles instead. It was a great pleasure to be back at the *Türkiye Büyük Millet Meclisi*, and to hear again the ritual protestations of affection for Britain, confirmation of the entirely philanthropic motives of the 30,000-odd occupation force and the at least 20,000 new Turkish settlers in the island, amid assurances of the strength and longevity of Turkey's philhellenism. Some of which was plausible.

We returned safely to London direct from Ankara, and therefore hadn't again to face the inherent risks of immolation on the runway in Istanbul. Our report to the House was one of our finest. I have recently re-read it impressed by the accuracy of the information it retails, by the sympathy and even-handedness it showed for the concerns and interests of all four of the parties concerned (Greek Cypriots and Greece, Turkish Cypriots and Turkey), by its open acknowledgement of our own governments' serial failures, and by the elegance of its draftsmanship. It is almost always a shock to revisit the works of your youth. The report was, as usual, produced very late in the day, more evidence having to be taken, and tens of thousands of pages of submissions having to be absorbed. We were simultaneously completing our deliberations on South Africa, hosting visits from the Supreme Soviet (in its last gasping days), from the Federal Republic of Germany, from the Netherlands, from Bophuthatswana, from Zimbabwe, from Nicaragua, from Malaysia, from the Spanish Cortes – amongst others.

In the end, we were up against the uncertain deadline of yet another General Election, and rushed the report through two footslogging meetings in early May in time for the Dissolution of Parliament on 18 May. But publication had to wait until after the House returned, with not a few of our members (including Tony Kershaw, Peter Thomas and Ian Mikardo) already departed, and its reception by the national media, already absorbed by post-Election politicking, was muted.

However, we knew we had done well. We had spread the blame evenly. The Report was therefore denounced by all parties, including our own Government. Its central message – that time was running out, and that "Delay in reaching a bi-communal settlement can only favour the forces tending towards permanent partition" – was true then, and is obviously even more true a few decades later. At least then there were many members of both communities who actively wished for the reunification of Cyprus; today their numbers are rapidly falling, and several generations have grown up in a divided island, and lack any real motive for re-establishing a unified island, with the still attendant risk of renewed bloodshed.

Inter-communal talks continue, and UN initiatives come and go, but one day the international community, and the European Union in particular, are going to have face reality and welcome the Turkish Republic of Northern Cyprus, by whatever title it then goes, into the fold. Two entirely separate states in Cyprus would not be a disaster. As a separate member of the EU the north would, after all, be only a trifle smaller than Malta or Luxembourg. And it would certainly not be the only island permanently divided, or even the smallest.[*] Rather than indefinitely mulling over sanitised memories of what Cyprus was before 1974, Greek, Turkish and Cypriot leaders might do

---

[*] The Caribbean island of St Martin has a total area of 34 square miles (a quarter that of the Isle of Wight) and a total population of only 80,000 – and the north sends a representative to the Assemblée Nationale in Paris, while the south is a part of the Kingdom of the Netherlands: this may or may not be a useful analogue. Perhaps Ireland is a better one.

better to follow the example of the Czech and Slovak Republics, and agree to an amicable divorce and become good friends thereafter.

Shortly after the 1987 General Election, which saw Margaret Thatcher returned with a comfortable majority, Neil Kinnock's Labour Party vainly struggling to establish itself as a plausible party of government, and the famous "SDP-Liberal Alliance" vastly increasing its collective vote but failing miserably to fill the Opposition benches, and after the publication of our Cyprus report,[78] the FAC survivors met for the last time in the garden of Ivan and Gloria Lawrence's house in what appeared to be a rather grand traffic island in Ealing. Most of us were demob happy; those who had stood down from Parliament were already looking healthier, heartier and a good deal younger; and Ken and I were abandoning Crispin (probably much to his relief) for new jobs just around the corner on the Committee Corridor North. The Foreign Affairs Committee, under its new Chairman David Howell, was going on to an illustrious future. But the pioneering days, when the committee had established itself as an authoritative player in the foreign policy establishment, had now, with Tony Kershaw's retirement, come to a close.

VII The Long Goodbye

28

Keeper of Wigs & Gowns

The Services Committee discover some gaps in Palace security; and more tunnelling gets underway

I spent the next seventeen years in a variety of jobs with grand management-sounding titles, marginally better pay, but often rather too far from the coal face.

Some of my colleagues believed me to be on the well-trod road to the top of the service. This perception was understandable, since the post of Secretary of the House of Commons Commission, to which I next moved, was fast becoming the proving ground for the top job: all my predecessors as Commission Secretary[*] eventually became Clerk of the House, as did several of my successors.[†] The main reason why the job of Commission Secretary, although only a decade old, had acquired such status was that it provided for the first time a role not totally dissimilar from that of Private Secretary to a Permanent Secretary across the road in Whitehall, together with some of the attributes also of a Principal Private Secretary to a Minister. In management terms the Commission Secretary frequently acted as gofer to the Clerk's developing (although not yet formally acknowledged) role of Chief Executive in the gradually coalescing House of Commons Service; he banged other departmental heads together, intimated what was or would not be acceptable, and controlled the agenda of many management meetings. He frequently acted for the Clerk in advising the Speaker on the less important management and staffing issues, and even learned part of the trade from across the road when providing briefing for Parliamentary Questions both for the Commission (and the Services Committee) and for a real Minister in the form of the Leader of the House. In all these roles the Commission Secretary got to learn much more about the operations of other parts of the House of Commons service than could clerks in any other desk, and was also an almost daily visitor to the Government Whips offices and to the Cabinet Office in Whitehall, from which the machinery of Parliament as well as the Executive was in those days for the most part controlled.

---

[*] Sir Donald Limon, Sir William McKay, Sir Roger Sands.
[†] Dr (later Sir) Malcolm Jack, Sir Robert Rogers (later Lord Lisvane), Sir David Natzler.

As Secretary of the Commission, and Clerk of the Services Committee, I was corralled with a tiny staff in a very small office around the corner from the north end of the main Committee Corridor. I also acquired some small responsibility for the Table of the House, since in a small cupboard in my small office resided the spare wigs and gowns used by those mid-career clerks who put in occasional appearances at the Table during the then still long watches of the night, or to fill a post-prandial gap in the Table team in the early afternoons. Unlike the fully paid-up members of the team, who were kitted out in full regalia, we were entitled to only a small allowance for the purchase of dress shirts, wing collars, and white bow-ties of our own. Otherwise we of the supporting cast wore our normal workaday suits and drew on the store in my cupboard for any old gown and any old bob wig which more or less fitted: these were hand-me-downs from previous clerks at the Table who had left their kit lying around the office. Several were ancient, and visibly moth-eaten. My successor was a more responsible sort of fellow than I, and had them all dry-cleaned.

Neither the Services Committee nor the Commission was of any great antiquity. The Select Committee on House of Commons (Services) had been set up in 1965 to "advise Mr Speaker on the control of accommodation and services", following his assumption of responsibility for the north end of the building* from the hereditary office of Lord Great Chamberlain (who in the current reign was generally the Marquess of Cholmondeley), a change which may be regarded as one of Harold Wilson's few genuinely revolutionary achievements.

The Services Committee was largely manned from the whips offices or by otherwise compliant backbenchers. Although its remit was nominally advisory, it had inherited from previous committees, or members had created for themselves, a range of quasi-executive decision-making powers.

The Accommodation & Works Sub-Committee effectively told the Serjeant-at-Arms what to do about almost everything other than the more subtle and refined aspects of security, which were handled by the usual shadowy bodies in the wings. The Library Sub-Committee was more or less in thrall to the Librarian – Dr David Menhennet – and unquestioningly backed his every demand for more staff to complete the development of a research service to rival the Library of Congress, in which ambition he went some way to succeeding, at a tiny proportion of the cost. The Computer Sub-Committee, chaired by Ken Warren, an unusually well-informed computer specialist at a time when such beasts were something of a rarity in the political world, floundered around in a desperate attempt to produce an

---

* The demarcation between the Speaker's end and the Lords end was merely a line on the town map, something akin to the Sykes-Picot Line, but with a tendency to occasional movement in response to the shifting strengths of the personalities at either end of the building.

integrated IT service for the whole Palace when no effective management structure was in place to run it. The Catering Sub-Committee, chaired by Cheltenham's "leading hotelier" Charles Irving, co-operated with the Refreshment Department's equally debonair (albeit Scottish) general manager in maintaining a wildly uneconomic level of service, offering magnificently pretentious banqueting services to outside commercial interests while effectively preventing ordinary backbenchers from finding a table to give even a cup of tea to their constituency party executives, and keeping the quality of the food served to the normal run of Members and staff to something approaching the British Restaurant standards of the late War. Many Commons Officers were as a result reduced to eating, disloyally, at the Lords end of the building, which offered the only chance of getting a decent salad anywhere in Westminster.

Thankfully, the real work of the Services Committee was done by Ken Brown and others who staffed the sub-committees. My attention was only regularly engaged every few weeks when sub-committee reports and other proposals came up for endorsement by the main committee, which I clerked and whoever happened to be Leader of the House chaired. For the most part the sub-committees' reports, having been previously fixed by the usual channels, were merely endorsed by the main committee. I only got involved when differences arose between a sub-committee and its client department, or between a department and its client sub-committee.

I only got deeply involved twice. On the first occasion, shortly into my custodianship, the Accommodation & Works Sub-Committee embarked on an inquiry into *Access to the Precincts of the House*.[79] This was triggered by young Mr Jeremy Corbyn's employment of a temporary research assistant, who had served several periods of incarceration, albeit on remand. Even though he had eventually been cleared (indeed cleared himself) of IRA-related charges eyebrows were perhaps understandably raised by the security people at the time, and a photo-identity pass had been withheld.[*] The inquiry revealed the quite monstrous holes still to be found in the screen which was supposed to protect Members and staff alike, despite the greater urgency which we had been promised after the murder of Airey Neave in the Underground Carpark in 1979, and other near-misses.

The Serjeantry flailed around trying to produce the most basic statistics, such as accurate figures of the numbers of passes (of which there were 72 different categories) currently issued to advisers, secretaries, research assistants, civil servants and the media. They came up with vague assurances that the BBC, for instance, "probably had something in the region of 200 pass-holders at any one time", but they didn't have an up-to-

---

[*] The man in question ended up as a successful novelist and highly-regarded chess columnist for the *Guardian*.

date record of even their names. More preposterously, the Serjeants (citing the "security services") claimed to believe that all their doorkeepers, and any police who happened to be on duty at any particular time, could be relied on to recognise every one of the ten thousand or more people claiming a right of admission, and that there might therefore be serious dangers in replacing men by mere machines. Only with the assistance of David Hunt, the icily smiling Government Deputy Chief Whip, were we able, after protracted negotiations, to persuade Sir Victor Le Fanu (the then Serjeant at Arms) that the committee's report might include even a mild reference to the possibility of introducing electronic pass screening in the main building (it was already planned to be introduced in new premises but only to save manning costs), or even of creating more secure zones in the areas "behind the Chair", occupied by the Prime Minister, the Home Secretary, the Leader of the House, the Leader of the Opposition and other potential terrorist targets (in those days of course we were mainly thinking only of men with semtex from the Emerald Isle). Although it was a considerable inconvenience, I was glad to discover on post-retirement visits to Westminster that the Palace and the now many outbuildings had become almost impenetrable, even by old hands.

My second incursion into the routine work of the Services sub-committees resulted from my earlier role as clerk of the Transport Committee. The committee were much vexed by news from London Underground that they were planning to re-route the Jubilee Line (at that time a very short run down to Charing Cross) through Westminster, under the Thames, and all the way to Stratford in east London. While there was no lack of enthusiasm for better communications through Westminster, there were real concerns about the effects of tunnelling under or close to the great Palace, which was already somewhat unsteady on its marshy base. Surely, they said, there must be an alternative.

Since I had spent a couple of happy years in St Stephen's House pouring over undersea maps with Britain's foremost tunneller – Alan Muir Wood[80] – I turned to him for a possible solution. Between us we examined many subterranean maps and cobbled together a wonderful alternative route for the new Tube line, taking it westwards through the Pimlico area, across the river to Vauxhall and the along the south bank to Waterloo. It was by no means an implausible option, since the Pimlico/Chelsea area was badly served by local transport links, but it happened to involve even greater engineering challenges than London Transport's preferred scheme. In the end the Services Committee had to accept repeated assurances from LT that the Palace of Westminster itself would be by-passed, and had to put up with the closure of Parliament Square behind tastefully painted awnings for several years. Parliament ended up with Portcullis House and, even better, London acquired the stunning new interchange station at Westminster, which together comprise one of the finest turn-of-the-century buildings anywhere in the world. Sir Alan suffered nothing from his involvement in our maverick scheme, and went on to be a big wheel in the engineering of the Jubilee Line, and many other fine stations, along the original line of route.*

---

* Resistance to the new Jubilee Line route (of which Parliament became a major beneficiary) was but one example of the innate conservatism of Members as a breed. I also spent an enormous amount of time resisting plans to upgrade the then semi-derelict Westminster pier on the grounds that anything larger and grander might spoil the view from Speaker's House: I am glad to see that my early successes have now been overturned, and a rather more respectable landing stage has at last been provided for the increasing number of cruise boats and even regular river buses which have brought new life to the Thames.

29

In Commission

The House of Commons Commission: the Westminster divan; Ibbs empowers the House; Geoffrey Howe kicks over the traces

The other side of the job was running the House of Commons Commission. This was an even more recent creation, one of the several beneficial by-products of Jim Callaghan's effectively hung parliament of the late seventies (another, of course, was the new select committee system). There had actually been House of Commons Commissioners since 1812 but, as Barbara Castle had pointed out in May 1960[81] they rarely if ever met: indeed, they had not met once in the seven years before she first raised the matter in the House.

The new Commission, set up under the House of Commons (Administration) Act 1978, was an unusual body. Its ancient and moribund predecessor had consisted almost entirely of Ministers of the Crown; the new Commission, unique amongst parliamentary bodies, didn't even have a government majority, consisting merely of the officially neutral Speaker in the chair, the Conservative Leader of the House plus one government backbencher, their opposite numbers from the Labour benches, and a sole Liberal Democrat (who was invariably Alan Beith[82]), representing the minority parties.

The new Commission seemed to be a complete break with the past, a more or less overnight leap from the gorblimey to the sublime. The Commission's initial role was as employer and paymaster of the six departments of the House, with a permanent staff of around a thousand: so at least we now had an identifiable employer. It was also responsible for the costs of various miscellaneous services for Members: posts, telephones, embryonic computers, and more media-stimulating activities such as overseas travel by select committees, on which facility I had already made more than my fair share of demands. Its budget became unique in being the only public service estimate not to be presented to Parliament by the Treasury: in recognition of Parliament's theoretical independence symbolised by the 1978 Act, the estimate for House of Commons (Administration) (at that time Class XXA, Vote 1) was submitted by the Speaker, after approval by the Commission.

This all sounded pretty revolutionary, and I and my senior colleagues

257

happily and confidently lectured our Commonwealth co-workers at seminars around the world on the new-found "independence" of the British Parliament – and, as a result, our new model was widely copied. But there were some not insignificant flaws in the new arrangements, and at least some of the variants around the Commonwealth addressed these more effectively.

First, the Commission had not then acquired responsibility for many of the services which were of real importance to Members. Most obviously, they didn't have charge of the largest budget of all, for Members' salaries, allowances and pensions. These were all periodically agreed by the House itself, thus enabling the Government, of whatever party, to cosy up to the electorate by pressuring their backbenchers to vote against salary increases which were by any objective criteria wholly justified and already too long delayed, and enabling the official Opposition, of whatever party, to up the ante by proposing reductions. By this means the two front benches (most of whom usually had comfortable incomes from other sources) were able simultaneously to claim the moral high ground and to keep the backbenchers in place, total sycophancy being of course eventually rewarded by a junior ministerial post with marginally higher take-home pay. The downside to this, and the ever-ticking bomb, was that to compensate for ridiculously low nominal wages the House regularly voted what appeared to be minor increases in secretarial, research, housing and travel etc allowances, with little front bench interference because all were confident that neither the newspapers nor their constituents would ever fathom the implications. Not, at least, until the *Daily Telegraph*, thanks to an uncharacteristically disloyal leak, was able to catch up with them in 2009.

A second area of expenditure not yet covered by the Commission was one which Members largely took for granted. The printing and publishing of the tens of thousands of documents generated each year by the two Houses, together with the provision of office equipment and many tons of stationery, was simply provided on demand by Her Majesty's Stationery Office on what were known as "allied service" terms. There was no budget ceiling, and therefore no particular incentive for the House departments (or indeed HMSO itself) to economise or to operate more efficiently. I remember one happy occasion in 1975 when we requisitioned for a thousand packets of Tippex (a vital tool in the days of typewriters) to go into the stationery store in the Committee Office outpost in 3 Dean's Yard. HMSO actually delivered a thousand *boxes* of Tippex, which provided us with 100,000 packets. When we asked what we were to do with the unexpected surplus, we were told that there was no system for returning supplies to HMSO, and that we would simply have to work through them. Long before the secretaries had made much progress through the Tippex mountain the fragile sheets had dried out – and in any case we had already switched to computers and word processors. So far as Members were concerned their only real grouses concerned the quantity of portcullis franked stationery and envelopes they were entitled to use, matters now determined by the A & A sub-committee on their behalf.

But the main gap was any kind of responsibility for the parliamentary buildings and in particular for the accommodation provided – or more often not provided – for Members and their staffs, minute in numbers as were the latter in comparison with their counterparts across the Atlantic or even across the Channel (the newly directly elected members of the European Parliament, for instance, were doing very much better). The maintenance, refurbishing and furnishing of the parliamentary buildings – and most importantly the commissioning of new buildings – was delivered by the Parliamentary Works Office, an off-shoot of the Department of the Environment, direct successor to the Office of Works established by King Richard II in 1378, but now under a budget cash-limited by the Treasury: in consequence, building projects large and small, however much demanded by Members and however urgent, might be and often were deferred from year to year.

Despite these limitations, quite impressive progress had been made during recent decades towards the establishment of a more commodious – or even efficient - working environment. When I first worked in Westminster the "parliamentary estate" consisted almost entirely of the Palace of Westminster (blighted by portakabin-type structures around the inner courtyards[83]) and a few small houses around the Abbey. Even during my brief absence in Manchester in the early 1970's new space had begun to emerge, including the Norman Shaw buildings (which the Metropolitan Police had abandoned in 1967[*]) and No. 46 Parliament Street, the Clerks' first outpost. In 1968 it was the norm for Members to live out of lockers (albeit gloriously brass-handled lockers), and to dictate their letters to agency secretaries on the benches along the Committee Corridor. By the time I took on clerkly responsibilities for these matters in 1987 only one Member claimed not to have at least a desk of his own, and around a third actually had their own offices, although some – Enoch most famously – preferred the Library, where elegant prose could still be composed in elegant copperplate on leather blotters at Pugin's elegant tables and their excruciatingly inelegant chairs.

By 1987 the first significant new outbuilding was under construction. Retaining the mock-Georgian facades of the terraced houses running from the Cenotaph to Parliament Square (and absorbing No. 46 of blessed memory) the new 1 Parliament Street provided modern offices for at least some Members, new catering facilities and reasonably comfortable

---

[*] although film and television companies periodically returned for atmospheric shots of detective chief superintendents in conference with their sleuths, with the Thames Embankment just visible through rarely-cleaned windows.

furniture not designed by Pugin's apprentices; and at the north end of the same run the Library was about to inherit a splendidly refurbished 1 Derby Gate (the former home of numerous government committees and commissions of inquiry which had met there in sepulchral gloom), allowing its research service to go some way at last towards helping Members to compete with the Executive's still almost complete information monopoly.

Long before these buildings – known as Phase I – had actually opened for business, plans were already advancing towards Phase II: the transformation of the rest of the semi-derelict "Bridge Street site", surrounding Westminster Underground station and including the even more decrepit St Stephen's House (where my grandfather had worked a century ago, and where the rapidly expanding committee service was currently camping) and the former Members' club on the corner of Bridge Street, which housed modern radio and television studios but whose central staircase carried warnings of impending collapse.

Phase II eventually emerged in 2000 as Portcullis House, designed by the same architect who had overseen the creation of 1 Parliament Street. With a planned life of at least two hundred years, to match the Palace of Westminster over the road, and created in tandem with (and supported by) one of London Underground's finest new stations, it was bound to have turned out a trifle expensive, and therefore provided some entertainment for the media. But it incorporated every kind of technical advance, and was approved by Members specifically because it would provide a model for other major new buildings. Its cost over-run was small compared with the Victorian Palace of Westminster itself, and infinitesimal compared with the Scottish Parliament.* Ken Brown and I had one major regret: at a private dinner at the top of 1 Parliament Street to celebrate the completion of Phase I we persuaded Michael Hopkins[84] to sketch out on the back of the menu card the design he planned to submit in the competition for Phase II: it was more or less exactly as Portcullis House emerged, and might now be worth a few bob: but neither of us have been able to find it.

As all these developments indicated, the House had already found ways of asserting its demands. This was partly because, as each new generation of Members arrived, an incoming Government of whatever colour could not entirely ignore the demands of at least its own backbenchers. It was partly

---

* The outturn cost of Portcullis House was around £234 million, an 18% increase in real terms on the budget approved in 1992, and it was completed more or less on time. The replacement for the burned-out medieval palace was expected in 1837 to take six years to build and to cost the then already enormous sum of £724,986; by the time it was more or less completed thirty-three years later the actual outlay was thought to have been something over £2 million (or the equivalent of around £2¼ billion today). The building at Holyrood was originally estimated at "£10-40 million" in 1997, and £109 million when the designs were approved; the out-turn cost was £414 million, and the building was completed three years late.

because the Services Committee was in a position to articulate those demands. And partly because the new House of Commons Commission, despite its then limited functions, had already raised expectations and provided a new focus for the discontents of Members.

The whole system for managing what was tantamount to a small town, with a growing population, and burgeoning needs, was woefully inadequate. Demands for services were articulated by means of plaintive early day motions which would never be debated, through the party organisations, or through the Services Committee and its various divisions. The latter made formal recommendations either to the Speaker or, in the case of major changes, in reports to the House. They were not required or empowered to report to the House of Commons Commission, which in the case of many of the non-accommodation services was already the actual paymaster. When the House of Commons (Administration) Act was passed hastily through the two Houses in July 1978, the assumption appeared to have been that the Speaker would in turn bring the proposals which reached him, either from the Services Committee or as a result of Resolutions in the House, to the Commission for financial approval and then implementation.

This sort of worked, although in practice far more demands were being passed directly up the line from the separate House departments. These were largely for staff increases – which could be blamed in each case by the Librarian or the Serjeant at Arms or the Editor of Hansard or the General Manager of the Refreshment Department on the demands emanating from their client sub-committees, or Members generally, for improved services – and were buttressed by reports from the Staff Inspector, an extremely likeable young man, undoubtedly rigorous in his analysis, who usually sympathised with the case for more and more highly-graded staff. Since he reported directly to the Commission, and indeed was employed as its creature and not by any of the individual departments, the Staff Inspector's imprimatur was almost invariably sufficient.

There was, in other words, no supporting sub-structure – either to assess or prioritise the financial demands from the departments (and their corresponding committees) or to co-ordinate the implementation of the Commission's decisions. On their way up to the Commission there was a nominal filter for new manpower bids, which consisted of the heads of the six House departments sitting in the grandly-titled Board of Management under the chairmanship of the Clerk of the House. This was intended to further the concept of a unified House of Commons service, but there was still little movement of staff between departments, and the Board dealt almost always with the staffing concerns of each separate department. And since it proceeded on the basis of gentlemanly agreement it almost always endorsed each department's manpower bids: it was by its nature governed by the principle of mutual back-scratching. Once bids had been approved it became inevitable that the extra staff would be recruited and extra equipment acquired. The small Fees Office, located in quiet seclusion in Dean's Yard, had, as its title acknowledged, no higher pretensions. Still largely managed by former service paymasters, it produced annual Estimates of expenditure, based on the separate departmental inputs, for the Commission to endorse. Once approved, the money was then spent with meticulous attention to accounting detail, but with little or no concern for "value for money", let alone "efficiency", terms somewhat alien in the royal palace, and for which the accountants had not in any case been trained or employed, but which were slowly becoming priorities in the Treasury offices across the road in Great George Street.

Some of the medieval trappings of the control of the Palace of Westminster and its services had been removed in 1965, when the Lord Great Chamberlain surrendered his control of the building, but it took almost thirty years for more rational decision-making and implementing mechanisms to follow. For the initial effect of the establishment of the House of Commons Commission in 1979 was if anything to make the system even more opaque. The office of the Secretary of the Commission bore some resemblance at that time to an oriental divan: anyone who wanted a decision from the Speaker or the Commission – or whatever body might be deemed capable of taking a decision of any kind – came to see me, often looking furtively over their shoulders or begging an interview in a distant corridor, or on the Terrace, or even in the home of Spike Milligan at the Grafton Arms,* in the hope that I might be able to put in a good word in whatever was the right quarter. Some were disgruntled senior staff, who thought I might do something to get them the promotion they deserved, or even to rescind the dismissal-on-grounds-of-incompetence of which they had been notified, sometimes not without reason; others were heads of departments, pleading the obvious and overwhelming need for the expansion of their services. They came to me partly no doubt because I was reputed to be a friendly sort of fellow, but mainly because they had also ascertained that it was I alone who drew up the Commission's agenda, wrote the Speaker's brief, and interpreted the results.

The Commission rarely did anything so unseemly as vote, and Mr Speaker Weatherill[85] rarely felt it necessary to sum up the conclusions of any discussion with any words other than something on the lines of "Good, I think that's clear", or "You've got all that, Bill?". The subsequent process of interpretation and dissemination was confidently left to the Secretary, who sat at a separate table several yards away from the Commissioners

---

* Grafton's, in Strutton Ground, a little way down Victoria Street, was said to be where the best of the *Goon Show* scripts were crafted. Strutton Ground itself sported the best barber in town and a splendid street market: my favourite fake Giorgio Fellini shirt, purchased for a mere quid, is still showing few signs of wear after forty years of regular summer use.

themselves in the Speaker's Library and was already suffering a degree of hearing loss: in the summer months, with the windows open, the traffic on Westminster Bridge and the merry-making on the Terrace combined effectively to drown anything but the laughter around the table.

The official version of the Commission's deliberations was contained in my minutes, transcribed from usually indecipherable manuscript notes, which were never examined in detail by anyone else, nor ever challenged over the course of my five years in the job, even though on several occasions I had interpreted what I thought I had heard of the discussions in a spirit of creativity rather than tedious accuracy. Decisions were promulgated largely in the form of letters which I despatched in my own name, but on the Commission's authority, to those directly affected. On the one hand, causes which I personally espoused – such as the Parliamentary Office of Science & Technology – were given a surprisingly clear run through the Commission: in that particular case the initial financing of POST, as an entirely new service, being authorised before the House had even been asked to approve the policy. On the other hand, what seemed to me to be excessive demands were clawed back: at one point, without consulting anyone else in advance, I simply advised Dr Menhennet, the charming but thankfully realistic Cornishman who was head of the Library at the time of its transition into a parliamentary research service, that I didn't think the Commission would be "able" to accede to the latest of his bids for staff (which were increasing at an exponential rate) and cut it by half: nobody complained, and indeed none of the Commissioners, nor even Clifford Boulton (the then Clerk of the House and Accounting Officer), noticed that the staff numbers minuted as having been authorised by them were way below the numbers in the paper which they had approved without demur. Although it didn't take long for the librarians to retake the ground and make further advances.

The system which had developed by 1987 was of enormous benefit to the House, in the sense that support services which had been starved of cash for decades, even centuries, were enabled to catch up despite the fairly ruthless economies which were being enforced across the road in Whitehall. But it was inevitable that a Government committed to "efficiency and effectiveness" would eventually turn its sights on the muddle across Parliament Square. It was perhaps only with the arrival of John Wakeham as Leader of the House after the 1987 General Election that attention became more sharply focussed on the dysfunctionality of the management arrangements in Parliament. A first sign of a more active approach came when the new Leader began to ask pointed questions in the Commission about the affairs of the Refreshment Department, the only actual trading organisation within the Commission's remit and therefore a natural focus for scrutiny by the monetarists.

The anomalous position of the Refreshment Department had been a matter of concern for well over a century. Founded in 1773 as a private enterprise chop house by the deputy Commons housekeeper John Bellamy (who also happened to be a wine merchant), it was transformed in 1863 into something resembling a gentlemen's club under a manager appointed by the Kitchen Committee, who reserved to themselves the compilation of the wine list and held a weekly wine tasting to this end: competition for membership of this particular select committee was accordingly fierce. The service expanded enormously thereafter, with a tank being provided "for the preservation of turtle", and vats installed in the basement of the new Palace for both whisky and whiskey (with capacities of 1,000 gallons and 300 gallons respectively). By the turn of the twentieth century the operation comprised around two dozen eating and drinking outlets and by the end of the second World War Members and staff alike had become largely dependent on its services.

Under this "club" arrangement (even though premises, heating, lighting and printing were all provided for free) the Kitchen Committee and its Manager were by then riding on a sea of debt. This was said to have been partly ameliorated, during Cap'n Bob's short period of command, by simply selling off most of the best of the cellar at what may have been "advantageous" prices to the only bidder, who happened to be himself.[*] From the early 1950's onwards the committee had called, with increasing desperation, for its operations to be treated as "a service of the House, and not a business concern" and thirty years later (a short time by Westminster standards) this was what happened. There had been a brave attempt in 1975 to find some way of outsourcing the service; but a committee of inquiry chaired by Ian Mikardo (to which I had given eloquent evidence on behalf of the trade unions in the then gloomy conference rooms at 1 Derby Gate) discovered that none of the private catering services approached would consider providing the service without an even larger subsidy. The problem was fundamental: providing a comprehensive service for only seven or so months of the year, and at unpredictable times of day and night, was not and could never become a commercial proposition.

So an early decision of the House of Commons Commission in 1979 was to designate the refreshment service as a full department of the House. Accordingly, from April 1980 all permanent staff costs were transferred to the Commission "Vote", accrued debts were written off (ie paid off by the rest of us), and the reappointed General Manager was from then on "expected to make an overall profit". Which he did, and spectacularly well.

---

[*] Robert Maxwell MC (aka Ján Luvik Hyman Benyamin Hoch) had a brief but energetic stint as chairman of the Catering Committee during his short career as Labour MP for Buckingham from 1964 to 1970; the Bouncing Czech's notorious sale of the House of Commons cellar was perhaps an early warning of his predilection for selling off the family silver, which later was said to have included the pensions of his Mirror Group employees.

Since one side of the balance of his trading account comprised little more than the cost of food, it might have been regarded as a trifle incompetent if he hadn't. In his first year of operation under the new dispensation he turned in an operating surplus of over a quarter of a million pounds. By 1988 the annual surplus had risen to over £460,000, and there was over £1.5 million at the bank. Four years later, despite efforts to reduce the annual surplus by holding down prices, the accumulated reserve had reached over £2.7 million, thanks in part to the wonderfully high interest rates on offer in those happy days.[*]

What had been a scandal of burgeoning debt had thus developed into a tale of scandalous profits. This was not what was supposed to have happened. The intention behind the transformation of the Refreshment Department was that it should at least appear to be making a modest trading profit, but that any such profit should be ploughed back to support the capital cost of refurbishing its premises and equipment. Such, however, had become the manipulative influence of the chairman of the Catering Sub-Committee that this obvious public relations manoeuvre simply failed. Although minor contributions were indeed made towards capital improvements they were actually declining year by year although the building and refurbishment programme was increasing. But Sir Charles Irving[86] repeatedly persuaded the Commission that, in the interests of prudence, "nothing further should be done", and the justified alarm of the Comptroller & Auditor General was simply met by bland, if not very confident, assurances from the Commission that "steps would be taken".

Meanwhile, backbench Members were becoming openly restive. There were widespread complaints about the quality of the food, anger that there was a lead time of many months for Members even to book a small private dining room to give tea to their constituents, and abundant (and as it turned out justified) rumours that favourable tariffs were being privately offered to corporate "sponsors" of grander banqueting events, to front benchers or even to other of the chairman's friends.

After a few months of unfruitful exchanges with Sir Charles and his Manager the Commission asked me to investigate, but such was the sensitivity of the whole issue that I was to try to avoid intimating that I was actually acting on their behalf (I blamed it all on the over-zealous Clerk of the House), and was then to brief the Leader of the House privately. He in turn would privately advise other commissioners about what steps might be practicable to deal with the rumours and regularise the financial position. Following sometimes fraught interviews with junior managers, chefs, waiters, clerks, committee members, government agencies, and the auditors,

---

[*] As a late starter in the mortgage business, I was a victim rather than a beneficiary of 17% rates: nowadays of course the selfish side of my nature would rather welcome them.

I eventually presented my conclusions, produced (under instructions) on my appallingly noisy, and primitive, electric typewriter to avoid the text getting anywhere near a secretary, to John Wakeham in the spring of 1989. Although my forensic powers were insufficient to uncover incontrovertible proofs, I had nevertheless gathered enough second and third hand allegations to make it clear that some cleaning of the stables was called for.

In July of the same year, John Wakeham moved on to be Secretary of State for Energy, and Geoffrey Howe arrived from the Foreign Office, smarting at his obvious demotion, despite the empty title of Deputy Prime Minister (once accorded to Willie Whitelaw) with which he had been encumbered as some kind of a sop by the Lady in No 10, or perhaps as a Bernard Ingham joke.

Sir Geoffrey's reaction to my paper was decisive, although the results could not be made public for another eighteen months or so. I carried out some further amateur detective work, and he then authorised me to put my then boss Clifford Boulton in the picture, while he briefed Jack Weatherill, about some of the personal and political sensitivities which would be involved if the Refreshment Department's affairs were to unravel too publicly. In February of the following year the Commission agreed in principle that the management structure of the Refreshment Department should be "re-examined", and management consultants were duly hired, although their appointment was not made public until May 1990, and then in the context of a wider review of the "provision of services to Members".

The Ibbs process, as the wider inquiry came to be known, was the first professional assessment of the management of the House of Commons since the establishment of the Commission. It is named after Sir Robin Ibbs, a former engineer and ICI director, who had served for two years as head of the Central Policy Review Staff, and continued until 1988 as Mrs T's "efficiency adviser".[87] But the process should really to be named after Geoffrey Howe himself: after discovering the muddle into which the catering (and other) services had descended he took the initiative, enthusiastically supported by both Jack Cunningham (the Shadow Leader), and Alan Beith, who had concluded from his long experience of fielding Questions on behalf of the Commission that "responsibilities are so widely diffused that it is often impossible to know who is answerable for what".

Robin Ibbs was helped in the exercise by one of the Leader's private secretaries, a senior member of the National Audit Office staff, a deputy assistant Serjeant, and Donald Limon (next in line for the clerkship of the House) who very effectively ran the whole operation. They were only appointed in late May, and in a six-week period interviewed over eighty individuals, received great quantities of paper, and managed to commission and digest a MORI survey, to which well over half the current Members responded. It took only four months for the Ibbs report[88] to be delivered to the Commission, and a couple of months more for the House to give its blessing. Geoffrey Howe regarded the commissioning of the report "as the most important achievement of my year as Leader of the House".[89]

A first result of the Ibbs process was the departure of Sir Charles Irving, whose replacement as chairman of the catering sub-committee was quietly engineered by the whips when we gave the word. The management consultants then helpfully suggested that a new job specification should be drawn up for General Manager's post, in view of the wider responsibilities it might carry post-Ibbs. A new recruitment exercise was undertaken, and a new "director of catering services" appointed. Sir Charles was knighted, and the incumbent manager offered a redundancy package: and both may well have been relieved that reward of any kind was on offer.

For the House of Commons as a whole the Ibbs process went some way to addressing what were occasionally and not unreasonably described as the "byzantine" arrangements still in place. Despite Treasury caution, logic dictated that all House of Commons expenditure should now be brought under the control of the Commission; some nominal downgrading of the Members' committees which had hitherto called most of the shots; and the introduction of a "comprehensive financial management system". Within a few months of the report, steps were already well advanced to re-brand the old Fees Office as a Department of Finance & Administration, and to transfer the whole of the accommodation budget to the Commission; and other major services such as printing were in future to be purchased with cash rather than provided as "allied service" freebees. All this would now be under the more-or-less exclusive control of the six members of the Commission, still without much in the way of professional advice.

Ibbs had now given the House a body responsible for the funding of all its major services; but this did not solve all the problems of implementation and accountability. The new Finance & Services Committee, set up to advise the Commission on the financial implications of proposed new services, consisted largely of the chairmen of the old services sub-committees, now re-branded as "domestic" committees, to whom log-rolling was second nature. The new Director of Finance & Administration had direct access to the Commission, but remained merely one of the co-equal members of the re-vamped Board of Management. And the ancient dispute about whether or not the House service should have a chief executive, and lose its federal characteristics, remained unresolved. The Clerk of the House was formally recognised as *primus inter pares*, but was still not in a position to direct the affairs of the other departments. These problems were revisited time and again after Ibbs, one independent inquiry following another, decade after decade, and were still in dispute when Mr Speaker Bercow attempted, in 2014, to introduce an antipodean administrator as Clerk of the House, a post for which she appeared not naturally qualified, having minimal experience of parliamentary procedure. Technically, the reforming Speaker lost this battle, and the College of Clerks yet again held the field. My former colleagues battled on heroically but uncomfortably to sustain the dual roles of chief proceduralist and chief executive, and they at least succeeded in ring-fencing the nominal "primacy" of the man in the wig[*] at the Table. But in reality that primacy was already fading.

Meanwhile, by the time the Ibbs report was published its instigator had departed the scene, as had his nemesis. Geoffrey Howe resigned as Lord President, Deputy Prime Minister, and Leader of the House on Thursday 1 November, and was replaced as Lord President and Leader by John MacGregor, who did a workmanlike job in implementing Ibbs in the months thereafter. Geoffrey Howe delivered his rightly famous resignation statement to the House after Questions on Tuesday 13th November, and a challenge to the party leadership was already in train. On Tuesday 20th November Michael Heseltine came second in the ballot, on Thursday 22nd November Margaret resigned, and on Tuesday 27th November – the day we published the Ibbs Report – John Major became leader of the Conservative Party, and on the following day Prime Minister. Widely regarded as a stop-gap, John Major remained at No 10 for six and a half years (longer than famous and flamboyant predecessors such as Harold Macmillan), demonstrating the staying power and popularity of the nice guys.

Geoffrey Howe was certainly one of the latter, but he knew that in performing the duties of Brutus he would never be forgiven by the tsarina's remaining devotees in the party (particularly in the constituency associations), and therefore could never seek the purple for himself. In the days before he drove in the knife, I was one of those who had felt the intensity of his anger, knew at least some of his reasons for resignation, and was not surprised by his subsequent determination to bring down the woman who had spurned and betrayed his loyalty.

On the day before his resignation I was summoned to the Leader's office for a brief discussion of current Commission affairs – and over some substantial tumblers of scotch he retailed to me the main burden of what became the statement he eventually made to the House a fortnight later: loyalties had been strained to breaking point, and it was time other colleagues took the same step. As speculation bubbled over the next couple of weeks I could well have tipped off my media friends, but in true clerkly fashion I kept my own counsel.

From a personal point of view the most significant outcome of the Howe/Ibbs process was the regrading of my own post from Deputy Principal

---

[*] In a wig no more, following Mr Speaker Bercow's decision in February 2017 to present "a marginally less stuffy and forbidding image" of the chamber by meeting the wishes of what was claimed to be the "overwhelming majority of clerks" to dispense with what they regarded as "itchy" encumbrances, except on ceremonial occasions: if they were the same wigs of which I had custody thirty years previously it should have been no surprise that they had become a trifle uncomfortable.

Clerk (in civil service terms known as Assistant Secretary) to Principal Clerk, Grade 4 (which was half-way to a civil service Under Secretary). The immediate effect of this quite proper elevation of my office was something like a 15 per cent reduction in my take-home pay, since at that time the bottom band of Grade 4 was actually lower than the top band of DPC and – far more important – I was in honour bound to relinquish my regular post as Leader of the équipe anglaise in Strasbourg, a demanding job which had paid extremely well in hard (and untaxed) cash, but was in those days reserved by gentlemen's agreement to the merely aspirant bosses in the ranks of the Deputy Principal Clerks. When Sir Clifford Boulton personally delivered his oleaginous letter of promotion I received it through, as it were, gritted teeth.

30

Money Matters

The Treasury & Civil Service Committee: I predict the collapse of sterling; defending a creative writer; the dangers of underwriting; and other attempts to regulate the City; and back to the PBO, but no more dip pens

On Wednesday 16th September 1992 I took over responsibility from Douglas Millar for the Treasury & Civil Service Committee, which I had been shadowing since the General Election in April while running down my commitments to the House of Commons Commission. We held a kind of handing over ceremony during the day, attended by a selection of the eminent economists who had long served as advisers to the committee.

This was Black Wednesday. As interest rates rose, and as the Bank of England continued to sell the family silver, the experts around me expressed their collective confidence in both the Governor and the Chancellor: a further steep rise in rates would be bound to bring the run on the pound to an end, and Britain's membership of the European Exchange Rate Mechanism, of which they had collectively approved, would be secure. Knowing nothing whatever of the mysteries of the City, but having read and lived through a good deal of post-war history, I tentatively expressed the opposite conviction that by the end of the day we would have left the ERM: was this not a classic run on the pound, which could only end in devaluation? This unfriendly scepticism from a non-specialist tyro was universally poo-pooed. Around seven o'clock in the evening the unfortunate Chancellor, Norman Lamont, announced Britain's withdrawal from the ERM.

The Treasury later calculated that the day had cost something over £3 billion (which was a lot of money at the time), and the Conservatives' reputation for sound economic management seemed for the time being damaged beyond reasonable repair. In retrospect Black Wednesday proved the wisdom of Margaret Thatcher's long-running opposition to the ERM (and is therefore known in some circles as White Wednesday), and probably saved the UK from a much worse fate: memories of the horrors of the day undoubtedly helped to reinforce Gordon Brown's subsequent determination to resist joining the ERM's successor arrangements. So we stayed out of the Euro, to the relief of all save Tony Blair. From my own point of view it had the effect of launching my short career in the world of high finance with my ingrained suspicion of the experts apparently fully justified by events; although I soon came to recognise that mere instinct is not always the best route to sound decision-making.

There was a sort of inevitability about my translation to the powerful-sounding post of Clerk of Financial Committees,[*] since I had always made it clear to management that this was the one job in the House of Commons service that I did not want. I had always had a deep suspicion of the workings of the City and all other manifestations of the capitalist system. I might occasionally dress this up as political principle or as a moral aversion to usury but it was really just part of my genetic makeup: from my maternal grandfather, who was persuaded to accept almost all payment for his great engineering works in substantial quantities of shares, and was subsequently pauperised, along with his large entourage of well-bred daughters, when the South American governments took advantage of the Great War to nationalise their railroad companies without compensation; and from my innocent father, who inherited from an uncle a whole street of terraced houses on a prime site in Lincoln (the family's only prospect of riches), was so concerned for the welfare of his tenants that he regularly paid more in repairs than he received in rent, and was merely relieved when invited to sell the whole lot to a supermarket for peanuts.

I had therefore inherited a family tradition of financial insouciance. But by the time I was finally relieved of any responsibility for this major industry I had become more impressed by the individual and collective idiocy of the City than by its perfidy. To a great extent – subsequently confirmed by the appalling events of the 2008 crash – many of the practitioners were simply not much good at their jobs, although extremely well rewarded for their incompetence.

When I took over, the Treasury Committee was billeted in a newly-acquired building on Millbank, to which almost the whole Committee Office had recently been decanted from their former home on the Embankment. St Stephen's House was at last scheduled for demolition to make way for Portcullis House and the magnificent new station below. The interior of 7 Millbank, obtained initially on a short-term lease and refurbished accordingly, had something of the appearance of a multitude of eggboxes of various capacities, with styrofoam walls and suspended polystyrene ceiling tiles, all of which served as camouflage for the probably-listed 1920's walnut panelling and corniced ceilings of what had once been the headquarters of one of Britain's much-lamented industrial

---

[*] The Clerk of Financial Committees was really the Clerk of the Treasury & Civil Service, dressed up with a few managerial functions to justify a slightly higher grading.

conglomerates. Mercifully, however, staff had access for the first time to a decent self-service canteen for all ranks on the ground floor, open for most of the still lengthy parliamentary day, and at the top was a bistro-style restaurant with an outside terrace, with a limited but excellent menu. And there was no sign of a Pugin desk.

Following the General Election of April 1992 the Treasury Committee had acquired a new chairman in place of Sir Terence Higgins, who had planted his orthodox stamp on the committee for most of its existence. His replacement was a younger man of equal intensity – John Watts, the cost-cutting Thatcherite scourge of Hillingdon, who went on to implement the privatisation of British Rail as John Major's Minister of State for Transport. The committee's leadership was completed by several friends from Procedure Committee days - Giles Radice, who chaired the Civil Service Sub-Committee with similar high seriousness, and the Liberal interest represented, as so often in my life, by Alan Beith. My contemporaries and fellow-sufferers will understand that this was one period in my career when it became a trifle risky for the committee clerk to seek in traditional manner to break the occasional deadlock between the parties with any kind of light-hearted jest.

There were at least a few members who enlivened proceedings - even a few with a sense of humour – and all were notable rebels. On the Tory side, Nick Budgen, a Midlands barrister who served as successor to Enoch Powell, with a similar sharp intellect and disdain for the party hierarchy, and a wit not always appreciated by his more intellectually challenged colleagues and leaders; and Quentin Davies, a merchant banker and former diplomat whose military manner and occasional parade ground tones belied an entirely civilian, innocent and pacific life. In 2007 Quentin crossed the Floor, once the ruling New Labour party had proved itself indistinguishable from its nominally Conservative opponents, and spent a happy couple of years as a defence minister.

On the traditional Labour side was another sparring partner from 1978, John Garrett, a leading management consultant, another man of high seriousness, always out of sympathy with whoever was in charge of his Party; Diane Abbott, the first black woman elected to the House of Commons, who in her youth seemed destined for high office, and in a fair world would undoubtedly have reached it on merit; but her obvious lack of sympathy for the New Labour project didn't help; and Brian Sedgemore, a heavyweight left-wing rugby-player, former Parliamentary Private Secretary to Tony Benn, loathed by Jim Callaghan, and actively feared by the orthodox economists subjected to his forensic interrogation over many years in the Treasury Committee. He in turn did his best to do maximum damage to his party by crossing the floor to the Liberal Democrats in the run-up to the 2005 General Election; this came as no surprise to those of us who had experienced his entirely independent mind at work, and his loathing (which not a few of us shared) of the political correctness which was becoming the new orthodoxy in place of the various strands – syndicalism, Fabianism, chapel socialism, or even a smidgen of Leninism - which had created and successfully sustained Labour as a party of principle for the previous century or so. Although the Lib Dems were unlikely to have provided much of a refuge from the advancing tide of wokeness.

In this late twentieth-century Parliament - which was supposed to "represent" the ordinary people of Britain - only one member of the Treasury Committee, Barry Legg, hadn't had the privilege of an Oxbridge education (although I won't of course have a word said against his alma mater, the Victoria University of Manchester of beloved memory). He, like others in this laudably dysfunctional band, ended up out of favour with the party leadership of the time, and, variously maligned or praised in the media as an "unreconstructed Thatcherite", had no golden ticket back to the Commons after the Tory defeat of May 1997: instead he became chairman of the Bruges Group, and successfully harried the Tory leadership to concede a referendum on EU membership.

Although the "effectiveness" of the departmental select committees is an ongoing preoccupation of political scientists and journalists (and no doubt a recurring question in Finals papers) I am pretty certain that there was one area in which the Treasury Committee of that era did have a real and lasting influence over public policy-making.

During the first two years of my tenancy, the committee got to grips with the question of who in an ideal world should decide the basic rates of interest charged in the banking system and therefore to the public (still known at that time as the Bank Rate), and therefore who should be in effective charge of the country's monetary policy and, ultimately, of its international competitiveness. For many years politicians as well as economists had looked longingly at systems which seemed to have found some solution to the boom-and-bust cycle which had bedevilled the British economy since the mid-1950's. In those years the United Kingdom economy had suffered continuing turbulence, due at least in part to the upping and downing of Bank Rate, traditionally a matter for the Chancellor of the Exchequer: the rate had risen from 5 percent in 1970 to 10 percent in 1995, but with peaks of 17 per cent in 1980 and 15 percent in 1992 (the day we left the ERM and I joined the Treasury Committee), and with few notable troughs. How is it, we collectively mused, that the Germans and the Americans seemed to be able to avoid the wildest of these fluctuations and enable their economies to progress on a generally upward trajectory?

So the Treasury Committee embarked on an extended series of visits and consultations with overseas national banks and politicians. The committee's favourite port of call was the legendary Deutsche Bundesbank, which had engineered the post-War German economic miracle, and which the committee visited regularly in its comfortable headquarters building in

Frankfurt. As the threat of the Euro approached, the German bankers, led by their President Hans Tietmeyer, made no attempt to disguise their chagrin at the loss of the Deutschemark which they had so assiduously nurtured since the War, and at what they saw as the failure of the German political community to recognise the harm already done to the German economy, and its currency, by the earlier politically-driven one-to-one assimilation of the Ostmark at the time of reunification. Although it was expected that the new European Central Bank would, at least in theory, inherit the Bundesbank's independence in monetary policy, the appalling prospective blow of the submersion of their highly successful currency – and hence their economy - in a sea of floundering liras, pesetas, escudos, and drachmas was not much softened by the knowledge that the ECB would be based in Frankfurt, but under a foreign presidency. Despite (or perhaps because of) their current anguish, German bankers were unanimous in recommending the benefits of central bank "independence" – a view which appeared to be shared by the very political masters who by other means had in recent years been undermining its effectiveness.

The desirability of national bank independence was similarly endorsed by other central bankers in Europe and the Commonwealth – and there appeared to be an albeit grudging acceptance of the benefits even by the political elites. For the latter the loss of "control" over monetary policy was a serious challenge to their collective machismo, but it was difficult for them to deny the advantages of avoiding boom-and-bust: and there was also obvious political advantage in shifting the blame from their own shoulders to those of the bankers, who were already popular targets and expected to take it like men: that, after all, was why they were rather well remunerated.

This message was reinforced by meetings in Washington and New York. At the headquarters of the Federal Reserve Board in Washington DC the legendary Alan Greenspan, still in his relatively early years as chairman, was politely contemptuous of politicians who attempted to second-guess the monetary assessments of the experts. The need for politicians to be kept away from the direction of monetary policy was also strongly endorsed at the New York Fed, and urged on us by Michel Camdessus, the longest-serving occupant of the chair at the International Monetary Fund (by then an almost exclusively French fiefdom).[*]

Despite this endorsement by American and – horror of horrors – even French experts, the Treasury Committee overcame its chauvinism and was almost unanimously persuaded of the need to "give the Bank of England its freedom". Although the then Chancellor of the Exchequer Kenneth Clarke was reluctant to relinquish the power to set the "Bank rate", the committee's

---

[*] French politicians, bankers or administrators occupied the post for 41 out of 53 years to 2016, in which year Christine Lagarde, the former finance minister (and synchronised swimmer), was re-appointed for a further five-year term.

conclusions in 1994 went a long way to prepare opinion in all political parties for this change.[90] As a result, when his New Labour successor Gordon Brown handed control of interest rates to the Monetary Policy Committee of an "independent" Bank of England a few days after the General Election of June 1997, Ken Clarke was just about the only senior political figure to raise serious objections. And Gordon Brown generously acknowledged the debt he owed to the committee's work.[91]

During the mid-1990's the Treasury Committee was also involved in the slow and painstaking search for some better means of regulating the affairs of the City of London, a search which also preoccupied much of Whitehall and of academia. The abolition of exchange controls by the Conservative government after 1979 had triggered the opening of London to unlimited competition from overseas, to all the talents, and also to all the rogues. The Bank of England's rescue of Johnson Matthey Bankers in 1984 (which the Bank ended up buying for one pound sterling), and the failure of BCCI in 1991,[*] had by this time led to widespread calls for a serious review of the supervision and regulation of banking and other financial services. The Treasury Committee made its own contribution with five separate reports on different sectors of the industry, summarising its conclusions in a final offering[92] agreed only a few months after London's oldest merchant bank – Baring's – had collapsed as a result of the uncontrolled activities of a single derivatives trader in Singapore.

The indignities to which the temptations of Mammon could lead otherwise decent – if evidently simple-minded – middle-class folk were fully exposed during the last of our sectoral inquiries, into what was optimistically described as "self-regulation" at Lloyd's of London.

This inquiry came in response to a growing awareness that the Lloyd's collective had vastly overstretched itself, and was on the point of collapse. Lloyd's had started in 1688 in a London coffee shop where deals were arranged between merchants, ship-owners and ships' masters to cover individual ships and their cargoes on individual voyages to the unknown regions. The Society of Lloyd's eventually became the dominant marketplace for commercial insurance, its worldwide reputation secured by what was in retrospect a highly questionable reaction to the San Francisco earthquake in 1906, when leading Lloyd's "underwriters" agreed to meet all claims in full, irrespective of the terms of the policies invoked.[†]

Lloyd's was not an insurance company, with the limited liability protection for individual shareholders which that status would have

---

[*] The Bank of Credit and Commerce International, which was "locked down" and forced into liquidation in July 1991.

[†] Several of my maternal great-uncles were amongst the recipients of this irresponsible largesse, and their many descendants subsequently enjoyed the benefits: not least their long occupation of grand houses at the top of Nob Hill.

provided. Rather, it was a collection of rich people prepared to take large risks in the expectation of very large profits. Although some of the risk was spread by the establishment of "syndicates", the individual "Names" were ultimately liable to the full extent of their personal assets: they not only could take whatever profits accrued, but also had to meet all the losses. Suicides were therefore not unknown even in the early days.

In the latter half of the last century the inherent weaknesses of the system began to show, as the calculation of risk became increasingly difficult in a more complex commercial environment. To cover future claims against policies which might have been issued decades earlier, the syndicates persuaded themselves that they were happily protected by the practice of *reinsuring* their future liabilities, usually placing such reinsurance policies with other Lloyd's syndicates, often involving many of the same Names. Assisted by a UK tax regime which in effect allowed their profits to be treated as capital gains (which attracted a lower rate of tax than investment or "earned" income) the system worked well – or at least to the very great benefit of those already in it – so long as nobody actually had the temerity to claim on the ageing employers' liability and workers' compensation policies gathering dust in the cellars of the Royal Exchange.

Confidence therefore crumbled when courts in the United States began to admit actions from anyone thought to be suffering from asbestosis or similar as a result of their employment thirty, forty or even fifty years previously. Eventually the individual claims blossomed into "class" actions, which crippled several American insurance companies – and the buck was passed back to Lloyd's, whose underwriters and syndicates had accepted the long-stop role of reinsurers. Individual and class actions against the tobacco companies were soon to follow.

The underwriters and brokers who had effective charge of the Society of Lloyd's were not planning to go bankrupt in response to this transatlantic outrage. Instead, facing an obvious and growing gulf between incomings and outgoings, they appear to have opted for a natty way of increasing their collective income to cover their accumulating costs. They reduced the minimum capital requirements for membership, and were said to have sent salesmen into the shires to recruit a whole army of new Names from the châtelains and châtelaines of relatively modest country estates and other lowly folks, whose sometimes quite limited assets would collectively beef up the capitalisation of the syndicates; in subsequent (largely unsuccessful) court cases this was claimed to be a deliberate policy of "recruit to dilute". By whatever means, a substantial number of modestly wealthy individuals were enticed by tales of the remarkable profits made by their predecessors, and undoubtedly flattered to become known in local society as members of Lloyd's.

When our inquiry into the Society's affairs was announced we made it absolutely clear that, although anyone with an interest in the matter was welcome to submit their views, the Treasury Committee was not in the business of considering or adjudicating on individual cases, which would ultimately be a matter for the courts. Despite this injunction, uninvited files began to accumulate in the corridors of the second floor of 7 Millbank. On the last day for the submission of memoranda we were compelled to open up the Treasury Committee library as a depository: by the end of the day the room was stacked high with hundreds of thousands of photocopied pages, documenting the extreme foolishness of those who had succumbed to what these days we would probably describe as a scam. Hundreds of individuals had been brought close to bankruptcy as their unlimited liability was invoked for policies written decades previously, and of which, most alleged, they had not been warned.

We all felt a trifle sad for these previously well-heeled victims of capitalism. The committee's staff picked through most of the files, which certainly added flavour to our investigations. But as we had warned, the boxes were packed up again, and rapidly despatched to join the other millions of records of misadventure and disappointment in the Victoria Tower. The committee's report[93] added yet another contribution to the anguished discussions of how to save the wreck of the British insurance industry. Eventually a rescue operation to reimburse some of the Names' losses was launched, at enormous cost; corporate members with provable assets (ie real insurance companies) were admitted as underwriters; and the enrolment of individuals with unlimited liability was brought to an end. Lloyd's once again thrives, now a symbol of twenty-first century international corporate capitalism, rather than seventeenth century individualism, in its magnificent headquarters building in Leadenhall Street. By 2014 only about 2 per cent of Lloyd's capacity was provided by the last surviving individual Names.

The committee's running inquiries into financial services provided, as such inquiries so often do, a public forum for the scrutiny of issues being hotly contested in academic and professional institutions, in the corridors of power in Whitehall, or in the case of financial services and banking regulation also in international organisations like G7 (or 8 or 20, or whatever), the IMF, or the European Union. Some reports probably contributed little of real significance to the outcomes (although we were obviously keen to claim credit where our reputations for sagacity might benefit), and in any case the outcomes not infrequently created the next set of problems (for which those of us by then safely out of the way were only too happy to blame our successors). Different regulatory regimes for different sectors of the financial services industries came and went with some rapidity, while the less respectable practitioners (as well as some of the supposedly respectable) were equally rapid in discovering loopholes in each set of new rules – a practice at which they remain adept to this day.

In the final stages of these inquiries the Treasury Committee was led by a man of rather greater humour than his two predecessors.

The choice of chairman in those days was normally stitched up between the usual channels (who decided which party got which chair) and the individual whips' office (who decided which of their members would occupy it). Although each committee in theory chose its own chairman, in practice they usually endorsed the whips' agreed candidate, who was then simply "called to the chair". On some occasions, however, the system failed to deliver, or a committee rebelled, which provided the committee clerk with a rare moment of glory. Sitting in his normal place to the left of the (empty) Chair, the clerk "reminded" the committee that it was for some member to move that one of their number "do take the chair of the committee", that such a motion was debatable, and that members were free to nominate anyone including themselves. When John Watts was elevated to the ministerial ranks the whips seem to have failed to sew things up, and there was, thanks to bitter disagreements about Europe, no agreement amongst the Tory members themselves about who should succeed him. Several names were proposed in turn, but when I put the question to the vote, enough of the Tories abstained. The choice of chairman of the Treasury Committee was therefore left largely in the hands of opposition members, who duly waited for the most amenable name to be proposed, and then voted for it. As a consequence Sir Tom Arnold, scion of a theatrical dynasty, and staunch European,[94] was elected to the vacant chair, apparently more by accident than design. He did a good job as chairman – particularly from the point of view of the staff, since his appearances in 7 Millbank were only sporadic, and his textual emendations few.

Thankfully, I didn't have to write all the Treasury Committee's reports on my own – indeed I could not have done, given the technical complexity of many, and in particular those dealing with the annual Expenditure Reviews and Budgets, and esoteric subjects such as the introduction of "Resource Accounting". Although I still insisted on topping and tailing reports and looking carefully at the text of the formal recommendations, I was happy to leave it to the better qualified to draft the questions, assess the evidence and advance the arguments. This was in other words a committee which needed experts on tap all the time (but still not on top). As a relief from the great and good advisers from the City and academia, whose arguments might be *parti pris,* we always had a couple of outstandingly able young economists on the books as specialist assistants.[*] They all worked extremely hard, and didn't much complain, although Ken Clarke's decision to move the Budget to late November sorely tested our own and our

---

[*] By 2016 the two clerks were assisted by three in-House economists, together with five specialists seconded from the National Audit Office, the Treasury and the Bank of England, as well as the usual committee support staff, and the usual army of the great and the good as advisers.

families' patience, since the committee's report on the Budget was for a few years drafted over the Christmas recess: proof-reading on Boxing Day was very definitely not a phenomenon which we wished to pass on as a clerkly tradition.*

From the start of the new system in 1979 the Treasury Committee, like the Foreign Affairs Committee, was, despite acute staff shortages in the Department of the Clerk, provided with two clerks, since it had the power to appoint a sub-committee. The FAC used this facility (designed to compensate for the abolition of a separate committee on overseas aid) only sporadically, but the Treasury Committee had regularly appointed a sub-committee to cover the "& Civil Service" part of its brief, in my day chaired by Giles Radice, who after 1997 became chairman of the full committee. The committee's second clerk was mainly responsible for this side of the committee's work, while also rolling up his sleeves to assist when the main committee was in full flight, particularly at times of Budgets and Financial Statements.

For part of my time the second clerk's desk was occupied by an aspiring young novelist. Philip Hensher had joined the Clerk's Department as an Assistant Clerk in 1990 and had apparently so alarmed the boss men in his first procedural office that when he reached us in Millbank I was enjoined from above to keep a close eye on the burly young man from Sheffield, who seemed to me to do the job perfectly adequately, albeit with a slightly bemused air from time to time. I was eventually instructed to write something in his defence.

A paper of this kind was not to be allowed to pass over the desk of a mere typist – even though the Treasury's Committee's senior executive officer, Jane Fox, had served as PA to the Clerk of the House for many years and had handled more than a few "personnel" problems. Knowing that nobody else could in any case read my handwriting, I banged out an enormously lengthy script on the personal electric typewriter which travelled everywhere with me in those pre-laptop days. The whole job occupied several late nights, as I eloquently defended Philip from unsubstantiated suggestions of idleness, reminded my seniors that the tolerance of occasional departures from conventional behaviour (as also of, say, religious eccentricity) was one of the Department's most laudable traditions, and that we had historically been blessed by a succession of outstanding authors, including my first boss Kenneth Mackenzie as well as

---

* Fortunately my immediate successors didn't have to put up with this for too long, since Gordon Brown speedily reverted to a March Budget after 1997, a decision again briefly reversed twenty years on.

the rather more notorious author of *The Riddle of the Sands*,* and more than a few others who found the House a congenial adjunct to their more serious creative or academic endeavours.

My encomium had the intended effect, and Philip was duly confirmed in the college of clerks. Only a few months later, but after I had left my successor to cope with the realities of life with a by-now successful novelist, Philip was compelled to fall on his sword by a court of honour, hastily summoned in the office of the Clerk of the House in early 1996 to deal with some apparently indiscreet public references in the media to members of the House (which I never had the pleasure of reading). Philip was apparently not offered the bottle of malt and loaded revolver which might have appealed to his romantic temperament and his sense of history. But he departed for a glittering career. I have personally avoided certain of those novels in which I continue to fear that I might recognise myself, but have quite enjoyed some of his later works – risqué though they may occasionally seem – as well as his unquestionable excellence as a reviewer.[95]

Shortly after getting Philip temporarily off the hook, I was invited to return to the Public Bill Office, the hub of the operation where I had cut my parliamentary teeth thirty years earlier. I was offered – and foolishly accepted – the post of Clerk of Standing Committees, and imagined myself recreating the role of the avuncular David Scott in an atmosphere of dip pens, long lunches and relaxed bonhomie. I was resistant to the truth that the world which I desperately wanted to stand still had continued to turn. Of many bad decisions in my life, moving back to the PBO was without doubt one of the worst.

The long office over the Chamber to which I returned in 1995 looked almost the same, but was full of keyboards, with young men busily digitalising the legislative process. Their quest for a paperless world was a proper one, and they protected me as much as they could. I was still allowed to write up the proceedings of my committees, and record amendments to bills, in manuscript, all of which the bottom boy, Mike Hennessy, quietly transferred onto his computer. Even my ultimate boss, the Clerk of Legislation Roger Sands, had got up to speed, and I was quite fairly regarded (and played the role with some finesse) as a dinosaur slumbering away in the side office to which my post had now been relegated.

The desk in the main PBO to which I had thought I was moving had by then been colonised as the operational hub of the Scottish Grand Committee, which a few decades earlier had been simply a comfortable and occasional

---

* Robert Erskine Childers, born 1870, junior and then assistant clerk in the House of Commons 1894-1910, runner of German guns to the Irish Volunteers 1914, DSC in the British Army 1915, intelligence officer, secretary to the Irish delegation to the Anglo-Irish Treaty talks of 1921, executed by a Free State firing party in November 1922. A troubled life, but still a departmental legend of a heroic stamp.

opportunity to talk about the Gorbals in the Grand Committee Room (with its clerk located at the bottom end of the Office) but had now been elevated into a peripatetic apology for a Scottish assembly, in a rather sad attempt by the Tories in their dying days to appease nationalist aspirations - and the desk had therefore moved to the top end of the Office. The new Grand Committee's expensive travels around the northern kingdom were brilliantly masterminded by Frank Cranmer, who in any spare interludes from his travels mopped my fevered brow and substituted for me when the inevitable mid-life crisis finally grounded me at home and in the hands of the counsellors.

Two unexpected challenges confronted me in the PBO. First, I discovered that although the Clerk of Public Bills (subsequently known as the Clerk of Legislation) had overall responsibility for seeing the Finance Bill through the House, it was I who was supposed to do much of the day-to-day work, including clerking the interminable proceedings in standing committee, and also advising backbenchers and the Opposition on the drafting of amendments. I had no understanding of tax law, and no sympathy with the process, and I proved hopeless at the job. Eventually, at about two in the morning, when still trying to make sense of the amendment papers for the next day's sittings, I realised that I needed to take a break, or would break. Frank took over for a while, demonstrating that he was not only a Christian in theory, but also a true friend to a friend in need.

The second challenge came on the day I returned from my few weeks of unscheduled leave. That very afternoon I received a sympathetic visit from Donald Limon, by then Clerk of the House. After appropriate inquiries into my health Donald told me that his cricketing friend the Clerk of *Private* Bills, Roger Willoughby, was planning to take early retirement, and that he and his senior colleagues had concluded that the much reduced activity on the private bill front did not really justify the retention of a separate post: within a few weeks, therefore, I would be taking charge, as a side-line, of an office which had once been the powerhouse of the Department of the Clerk. Donald suggested that it might be sensible if I became acquainted with the esoteric mysteries of my new post as soon as possible, and if I would also work out the logistics, since Roger's office would now be needed for other purposes.

Although the "outer" Private Bill Office on the main Committee Corridor was for the time being retained (partly because it still housed an enormous library of Victorian parchment), and a young clerk would continue to do the donkey work, I suddenly found myself dealing with the parliamentary agents who promoted or opposed private bills, and I assumed at short notice the grand additional titles of Clerk of the Court of Referees, Examiner of Petitions for Private Bills, and Taxing Officer (which in theory empowered me to adjudicate and allocate costs to the warring parties). I quite enjoyed these new responsibilities, not least because private bill activity had reached such a low ebb that my expert services were called on only infrequently. But there were one or two occasions when wise counsel was called for, and I was relieved to find that my procedural antennae were still in reasonable working order.

I managed some of the jobs in my rebranded role as "Clerk of Bills" with reasonable success – I was expert at persuading reluctant members of the Chairmen's Panel to take on legislative committee responsibilities when their diaries (and their secretaries) clearly indicated that they were not available, and I even managed to non-plus the parliamentary agents from time to time. But my only contribution of any historical interest resulted in abject failure, from which Parliament and nation have suffered ever since.

As recounted earlier[*] the "reformist" members of the old Procedure Committee had with my help suffered a significant and I foolishly hoped conclusive defeat at the hands of Enoch Powell, when they were persuaded to drop all proposals for the routine timetabling of legislation in parliament, and even to recommend further restrictions on the ability of the Government to force "guillotines" through the House on occasions when a major bill was in extremis. Sadly, Enoch and I had won only a battle, and the war continued – a war of principle between those who believed in the primacy of the elected parliament, and those who were beguiled by the bright lights of ministerial Whitehall to believe in the primacy of party. In the early 1990's a clutch of procedural committees had sadly edged closer to the latter tendency. Although always carefully talking about "voluntary" timetabling, in the interests of "better-planned" legislative scrutiny, these committees were really giving in to the pressure from Whitehall to get their bills through the House with as little fuss as possible. John Major's government either had not the inclination, or the clout, to push the argument to its apparently logical conclusion: it was left to other more determined and less principled men. Mid-way through my second shift in the Public Bill Office, in April 1997, the administration changed hands, and the dazzlingly modern New Labour team moved rapidly to capitalise on their plurality at the polls, and (thanks to the glaring imperfections of the first-past-the-post system) their overwhelming majority in the Commons.

To achieve this, they invented a new select committee, which looked a bit like a traditional procedure committee but with the important difference that it was chaired by the Leader of the House, rather than a more or less independent backbencher, and was from the start intended as a vehicle to implement the new Cabinet's agenda. The Committee on the Modernisation of the House of Commons was ordered to consider "how" (not "whether") the procedures and practices of the House "should" (not "could" or "might") be "modernised", and to make appropriate recommendations. It made no pretence to be an objective all-party investigation into problems which

---

[*] see chapter 15 above.

might need solutions, but was a committee expected to endorse the Government's pre-ordained solutions to problems which they had already enumerated. Which it duly did, without any serious resistance from the new official Opposition. The Tories were in disarray, having immediately lost their leader,* and were deeply demoralised by the loss of more than 170 seats at the polls.

The Tories in Opposition were comprehensively wrong-footed. After all, when in government they had been steering procedure committees in similar directions, always aimed to benefit the party in power. They were no longer in power, but had not yet shaken off the attitudes of those in power. In the summer of 1997 I found myself invited to advise members of the new Shadow Cabinet on their best approach to the introduction of the more or less automatic timetabling of government legislation, which the Modernisation Committee was about to launch on a listless parliament. This was to replace the already formidable and loathed power of the Government to move for a guillotine when proceedings on a government bill got bogged down in committee – a procedure which at least required a separate three hour debate and vote, and could not respectably be moved until the Government could plausibly argue that the will of the majority was being unreasonably frustrated.

For a middle-ranking clerk to visit the dowdy Shadow Cabinet rooms at the back end of the corridor behind the Chair was unusual, and was understandably disapproved of by some senior colleagues. It also proved to be a profoundly depressing experience. I retailed the doctrine which I had helped to promote twenty years earlier – that delay was the only remaining weapon in the parliamentary armoury, and therefore must be retained at all cost. The surviving Tory grandees listened politely. But they nevertheless went off to sign up to New Labour's beguiling agenda. Disastrously, they accepted the proposition that motions for the programming of government bills from the start of their progress through parliament, normally to be agreed by a simple majority immediately after the vote on second reading, and without debate, would be ok so long as there had been prior inter-party discussions, and so long as the names of the Opposition party leaders were attached to them. The new procedure would not only obviate the need for the Government to argue the case for a guillotine later, but also dispensed with the need for them to move the "closure" (which requires at least a hundred government backbenchers to be around at all times of day and night) later in proceedings on the bill.

So new "temporary" standing orders were approved to this effect, and

---

* John Major, who is rightly held in almost universal respect, both as a not unsuccessful successor to his formidable predecessor and as a decent man who did his damnedest to hold his divided party together. He nonetheless set an unfortunate precedent by resigning immediately after the 1997 General Election.

the programming of legislation – long encouraged by the academic establishment – rapidly became the norm. It was of course no surprise that within a short while the Opposition found that they were not really happy with the system, did not want to sign up to the timetables, and wanted more time and freedom to discover and exploit what remaining procedural devices might be available to them. Instead, programming motions were soon the established practice, in 2004 were embodied in permanent standing orders, and were soon put to the House in the name of the Government alone, certain to be approved by the New Labour majority. And the Opposition discovered that there were actually few procedural weapons left to deploy. Centuries of latent parliamentary power thus finally drained away, never to be fully recovered, even under a coalition Government: or so, until 2019, it seemed.

31

Flying Solo

Around the world without Members; promoting the Westminster model in implausible places

Promotion did not mean that my travelling days were over. However, apart from the brief interlude in the mid-nineties as Clerk of the Treasury & Civil Service Committee, most of my travelling from now on was travelling *without* Members. I sometimes still came across them when I arrived at the latest odd destination; and these could be curious encounters. On some occasions – such as a delightful week at a Commonwealth conference on the Isle of Man in April 2000 – I spent many happy hours off the leash arguing deep political matters with old sparring partners. Diane Abbott, who had first enlivened my life as an effective and belligerent interrogator on the Treasury Committee, exchanged indiscreet views on the failures of the Labour Government's social policies on the steam-hauled line from Douglas to Castletown and back. And Michael Cocks (my Mother's long-suffering opposite neighbour) attempted valiantly and publicly to persuade me to support Frank Dobson, the official Labour candidate for Mayor of London. Voting for the Mayor was a new privilege which I was to exercise immediately on my return home, and like a majority of Londoners I was already committed to the cause of "Red" (and temporarily "independent") Ken Livingstone. Having something of a guilty conscience about my part (as clerk of the Transport Committee) in the process which had led to the termination of his earlier role as Leader of the Greater London Council, I felt that I at least owed him a vote.

On other occasions there was often little communication between wandering Members and a wandering clerk. In May 1995, for instance, I spent a relaxed ten days in a comfortable Novotel in Arusha, in northern Tanzania. Apart from giving my ritual talk on committee systems to African members of the Commonwealth Parliamentary Association, I was generally left to my own devices, enjoying glorious sunshine and the insistent attentions of the teenage girls of the night who roamed the hotel's estate at all hours. Fortunately my bank card wouldn't work, and I therefore remained penurious and undefiled. The only available cash had already been spent on a large and dangerous hunting knife, purchased from a young Maasai warrior named Albert, who I discovered rather incongruously teaching himself English from a tattered copy of the King James Bible at the side of a mountain road. The knife, illegally smuggled onto Lufthansa, was a present for my eleven-year-old son, who on my return immediately disappeared into the back garden and began cutting down trees.

In 1996 I spent a couple of weeks of the summer recess in Beijing, as part of a three-man team leading a seminar on comparative legislative systems for senior staff of the National People's Congress. I was in distinguished company: the head of plenary services in the Bundestag, Dr Wolfgang Zeh; and a big wheel at the Congressional Research Service in Washington, Dr Stanley Bach. It was quite hard work: during the five meeting days I delivered over eleven hours of formal lectures, listened to another twenty-two, and participated in "open forum" discussions for another eight hours or so, all over unlimited supplies of green tea. We also managed to visit the Forbidden City, Mao's dacha (with its cavernous but now largely empty railhead, the masses no longer required to make obeisance), and the world's largest MacDonald's, while grieving in politically correct posture in Tiananmen Square.

It was a heartening experience. We certainly put on a bravura performance: loads of documents from all three legislatures translated into mandarin, eloquent and sophisticated disquisitions on the finer nuances of procedure, and stirring and crowd-pulling encomiums on parliamentary privilege and the (sometimes theoretical) independence of parliaments from control by the executive or political parties. But we evangelists of pluralist democracy found a surprisingly sympathetic and remarkably well-prepared audience. Here we were, in one of the last bastions of the one-party state, locked in detailed arguments about Locke, Montesquieu, Rousseau and Walter Bagehot, with hardly a genuflection in the direction of Marx, Engels, Lenin or Mao Tse-Tung (and certainly not Stalin). We were engaged with officials of an assembly whose claims to "represent" the people of China were even publicly somewhat tentative and apologetic, and which was in practice controlled by and subservient to a ruling party with much blood on its hands: in western eyes flowing most outrageously and televisually in Tiananmen Square in 1989, but engraved on all Chinese hearts were the memories of the much greater collective humiliation, and the hundreds of thousands - or more likely millions - of deaths during Mao's Great Leap Forward and subsequent Cultural Revolution.

Twenty years on from the end of Mao's experiment it was clear that the new People's Republic was catching up fast. The smiling people we were dealing with were, first of all, reassuringly fluent in English English (thanks to the BBC) and often better drilled in western political philosophy and practice than the mass of graduates emerging from the politics departments of our own universities. Second, they were doing their damnedest to infiltrate some of the norms and practices of western parliaments into the work of the People's Congress, notwithstanding the peculiarities of the prevailing system of government. At this stage the main preoccupation of the NPC staff, who had grown in number from a few dozen at the end of the cultural revolution to almost two thousand twenty years later, was to work to establish what they (and the Party) billed as "constitutionalism and the rule of law", and in particular the establishment of a legal framework in which capitalism could flourish. This included close consultation with interest groups (albeit officially licensed interest groups), and public hearings – and therefore greater "transparency" - on legislative and budgetary issues. There was considerable pride in the extent to which they had already succeeded in asserting the constitutional primacy of the Congress (or at least its committees) and the principle of rule by law rather than by party diktat: they had even reached the point of sending back to party organisations draft laws which they considered defective under the rules of the NPC.

The experience in Beijing was typical of many encounters with legislatures in Europe at various stages in the process of emerging from people's republic to Strasbourg-certified democracy. I had already been quite impressed by the staff of the Supreme Soviet in Minsk, which I visited as part of a team sent out from Strasbourg in 1993 to assess the democratic credentials of Belarus as an applicant for membership of the Council of Europe.[*] The old CPSU had been technically wound up even in Belarus, but the staff we encountered admitted to being more than a little conscious of the continuing influence of its networks; the procedures of the new legislature were still the procedures of its communist predecessor; no new electoral law was anywhere near preparation, let alone promulgation; and fresh flowers continued to be laid each morning at the foot of the statue of Felix Dzerzhinsky across the road from the local Lubyanka.

Strenuous efforts were made to flatter and cajole the Council of Europe team, including a Beethoven/Rachmaninov concert specially staged for us in an otherwise empty and exceedingly draughty hall. But there was no chance at all of us recommending full membership of the Council of Europe. In January 1996 the Bureau of the Assembly in Strasbourg even suspended the "special guest status" which Belarus (like most former Soviet republics) had enjoyed for the previous four years; and the country has remained the sole pariah, so far as the Council of Europe is concerned, to the present day. And yet, and yet: the large staff of the Belarus legislature included many well-informed about the practices of more open societies further west, who showed a real hankering for change.

This was a golden age for clerkly travel. After the breach of the Berlin

---

[*] The team was by no means unsympathetic. It was led by Georges Charitons, a former long-serving head of the procedural services at the Council of Europe, who in his youth had fled to France from the Baltic states during the upheavals of the second World War, and was more attuned than the rest of us to the difficulties facing the politicians in the suddenly and unexpectedly independent capital of White Russia.

Wall in November 1989, and even more so after the assisted suicide of the Union of Soviet Socialist Republics two years later, just about every western government or parliament began to allocate generous funds in a competitive drive to support the development of "democratic" practices and attitudes in the capitals of the newly independent states of central and eastern Europe. Washington and Ottawa competed with Brussels, within Europe the British competed with the French, the British and the French competed with the Germans and the Swedes, and all competed with the European Union institutions in Brussels and their Council of Europe rivals in Strasbourg.

The Americans strove hard to export congressional practices – and where possible the whole US Constitution – to anyone who would take their money; the French and the Germans, as established "continental powers", advertised their own systems as infinitely more appropriate analogues for the "new" democracies; and even the British occasionally attempted to sell bits of the Westminster model (a non-party Speaker is, you know, a very good thing etc), however implausibly, to countries whose legal cultures were an uncomfortable amalgam of Napoleonic and Asiatic influences, and who had never heard of common law. Once the human rights credentials of central Europe (bar Belarus) had been signed off by the Council of Europe, a further race was on to prepare them for membership of the new western European empire, more or less immediately on offer from its separate civil and military headquarters in Brussels, however embryonic their political and legal systems or backward their economies, to replace the protective umbrella of the muscovite empire from which they had so recently been released.

For a decade or so, professional consultancies blossomed throughout the West to absorb all this new-found largesse, some emerging from respectable political studies or foreign affairs institutes, but not a few put together by fleet-footed civil servants who decided to go for do-it-yourself privatisation before they received a redundancy package in the post from their cost-conscious governments. They in turn quickly discovered that when dealing with parliaments little impact would be made by fielding academics alone – political science academics in particular being understandably suspect amongst professional parliamentary staff worldwide. They also quickly cottoned on to the fact that tradition required that serving parliamentary officers would require only their expenses, unlike the academics who would actually demand a fee: we therefore came very much cheaper.

The consultancies consequently competed to cultivate the Clerk of the House in Westminster or Ottawa, the *Secrétaire Général* in Paris, the *Greffier* in Brussels or the Parliamentarian on the Hill, in the hope that they would release reasonably senior staff to give credibility to their particular sales pitch in central Europe, and at minimal cost.

All this led to some duplication of effort and expense. When I first visited Kiev in 1997, for example, I discovered that a substantial American team was beavering away at codifying and digitising Ukrainian statute law in a building in the centre of town only a few shouts away from a substantial team from Brussels which was apparently also beavering away at codifying and digitising Ukrainian statute law. When asked, each team denied knowledge of the other, and there was nobody in the *Verkhovna Rada* who was going to officially enlighten them or the world: for, as all well-intentioned NGO's know to their (or rather our) cost, the more aid agencies in town the better, at least so far as the local elites are concerned. For the latter the prize was the prospect of a trip to the West, the tedium of endless seminars and interviews with the great and the good being easily compensated for by a week or so in a decent hotel (with or without your spouse, according to taste) in Paris or London or Berlin or Washington or Ottawa, and some spending money to be deployed in Bond Street. Who won these trips of course had almost nothing at all to do with the relevance of their jobs but almost everything to do with their position in the local hierarchy. As a result, after painstaking cultivation of mid-career officials who seemed to be on the right democratic wavelength in Budapest or Sofia or Bucharest, and after extending the usual invitations to training sessions back home, we would have the pleasure a few months later of welcoming to Westminster (or wherever) an assortment of occasionally unreformed Stalinists, with upholstered wives, who often slumbered through interviews with our well-intentioned colleagues, only rousing themselves to check that they were not going to be late for the Broadway musical lined up for them that evening, or the chance of impressing their own diplomats at the local embassy jollifications.

What was encouraging – despite these very human reactions to the sudden availability of hard cash – was the commitment of the middle-ranking parliamentary staff, in Kiev, or Bratislava, or Ljubljana, or Prague, to the objectives of representative democracy, alongside a fierce pride in the traditions of their own institutions. It was sometimes touching with what relish so many of them now welcomed the prospect of running parliaments for which they would no longer have to apologise, either to themselves or to fellow professionals from elsewhere. Imperfect though their revamped institutions (and their revamped electoral systems) might be, they were nonetheless proud and newly-confident activists in the international brotherhood of parliamentary officers, reinforced by their bosses' membership of the Association of Secretaries General of Parliaments, [*] and they believed moreover (and rightly) that they had experience and expertise of their own which others in the fraternity should take seriously.

---

[*] Founded in 1939, the ASGP was an offshoot of the Inter-Parliamentary Union, established in 1889 by a French republican and an English liberal, both of whom were early winners of the Nobel Peace Prize. The IPU makes some claim to be the forerunner of the League of Nations and, subsequently, of the United Nations.

Our central and eastern European interlocutors were therefore not to be easily fobbed off with assertions that "western" parliamentary systems had all the answers, and north American or other salesmen who hadn't done their homework were liable to be treated with a contempt which they generally deserved. In this respect Members and clerks from Westminster had something of a head start. Several decades of regular and frequent dialogue with our counterparts in the hundred-plus legislatures of the Commonwealth had prepared us to accept that we couldn't honestly claim to have all the answers, that other people might do things at least as well as or even better than ourselves, and that we might actually have much to learn.

32

Europe yet again

Saving the UK's honour at the Council of Europe; our man in Brussels; Giscard's Convention

The need for awareness of our own system's shortcomings was brought home to me very forcibly during my last appearance as *chef de l'équipe* at the Council of Europe Assembly in May 1992. I had been performing this illustrious role for a couple of years in succession to my contemporary Douglas Millar and as far as possible in the spirit of our eminent predecessors – Barney Cocks, who created the team in 1950, and more recently JPST (John Taylor) and JFS (John Sweetman), who had defined the British team's personality in the 1970's and 1980's.

I had said my formal farewells at the Assembly's part-session in February 1992, with a speech of great eloquence and interminable length in praise of Strasbourg and all it stood for, at my favourite restaurant, *au Pigeon*, before a final rendezvous at Julia's Bar. Thanks to the vagaries of office moves back home I nevertheless put in a final final appearance in Strasbourg in May (what better time?), foolishly hoping for a quiet handover thereafter to my successor, and several relaxed evenings *au Pigeon* or at the *Taverne des Tanneurs*. I had spent the usual frantic days getting the Assembly up and ready to run, and had celebrated my birthday, alone but happily, at the latter remarkable hostelry on the intervening Sunday.

But there was still work to be done on behalf of the fatherland. In the early afternoon of Monday 4 May the Parliamentary Assembly, with the *doyen d'âge* in the Chair, painstakingly following our carefully honed *dossier du president*, went through the required rituals, prior to the election of its President and umpteen Vice-Presidents, of formally approving the credentials of the national delegations at the start of the new Session. This was traditionally the moment for Turkish delegates to challenge the credentials of the wholly Greek delegation from Cyprus, for the Greek and Cypriot delegation leaders to respond in kind, and for friendly denunciations about who did what in 1974; and more recently for the Greeks to argue about the title of what eventually became known for the purposes of international organisations as "The former Yugoslav Republic of Macedonia -

291

FYROM"[*]. These traditions were duly observed, with the usual good humour, but on this occasion only following a démarche from the floor, when the credentials of the entire British delegation were challenged - not by some suspect foreigner in suspect French but in educated Yorkshire by the leader of the British Labour group.

Most arguments about credentials, whatever the organisation, arise from domestic squabbles, and this was no exception. In early April the Labour Party had yet again failed to overthrow the Tories in a General Election, despite or more likely as a result of the earlier departure of Margaret from No 10, despite the opinion polls, and despite Neil Kinnock's hubristic rallies. The Tory majority in the House had nonetheless been substantially reduced.

When the long-serving leader of the Labour side of the British delegation, Peter Hardy[96], came to see me on the morning of the first day of the new Strasbourg session I was already prepared. Much of the previous week in London had been spent to-ing and fro-ing between the Chief Whip, the Foreign & Commonwealth Office and our own Overseas Office, in trying to sort out the composition of the delegation following the General Election.

Like other international parliamentary bodies, the Council of Europe allowed delegations to continue for up to six months after an election to enable national selection procedures to follow their inevitably slow course. Earlier in the year the then Secretary of the British delegation, Richard Lambert, had sensibly advised the Chief Whip's office that if a general election were to be held at the wrong moment it might be wise to reappoint those members of the Council of Europe delegation who had survived the Election for its next annual session, making subsequent changes within the six-month period but after the new House had settled down and other more important appointments had been sorted out. The Whips failed to follow this advice after the surprise result of the Election, mainly because they had the complication that one senior Tory - Sir Geoffrey Finsberg[97] - had accidentally become President of the Council of Europe Assembly when the incumbent Anders Björck, a kind and level-headed man with whom I had greatly enjoyed working, had become a minister in the Swedish government. Sir Geoffrey's term could only last until the beginning of the April/May sitting of the Assembly, since the socialists were then due to take over; but the whips apparently thought it would be bad form if he were not to remain part of the formally nominated Westminster delegation up to that point.

This was one of those occasions when the Chief Whip's office – for which we all had tremulous respect – simply fell down on the job. Instead of going for our straightforward option, they decided to nominate a new delegation, for the most part picking only those Members who had retained

---

[*] The Greeks and Macedonians finally resolved the issue in June 2018, and since February 2019 the country has been known as the Republic of North Macedonia.

their seats, but exceptionally invoking the six-month dispensation for Geoffrey Finsberg – but for him alone, and not for three Labour members of the delegation who had lost their seats a few weeks earlier. As the party balance in the Commons had altered in Labour's favour at the General Election the result of this cag-handedness on the part of the Chief Whip's otherwise awe-inspiring private secretary Murdo Maclean[98] was that the Labour Party claimed to be seriously under-represented when the Parliamentary Assembly reconvened in Strasbourg: they should have had fifteen members in the delegation, but they only had ten. Protests of some kind were inevitable.

Under the Assembly's rules, Peter Hardy's credentials challenge was referred to the Committee on Rules of Procedure, who were required to report back within twenty-four hours. As soon as the Council of Europe's permanent staff looked at the problem they discovered that this was not merely an inter-party spat but that the United Kingdom, the founding member of the organisation, appeared to have been breaking the rules all the way back to 1950. Article 25 of the Council of Europe's Statute required that Assembly members should be either elected by the national parliament "from among the members thereof", or appointed from those members "in such manner as it shall decide". The House of Commons at that date had never elected anyone other than Mr Speaker, and it soon became apparent that for all those years the United Kingdom delegation to the Assembly had simply been promulgated by No 10, in the form of a written answer in the House of Commons, a procedure never authorised by any kind of vote in either House in Westminster.

The rules committee's secretary Mario Heinrich, a modest and self-effacing German-speaker from the Tyrol, hastily put together a brief text which, if adopted, risked the rejection of the credentials of the entire British delegation or – perhaps worse – of some but not all of them. This would have been extremely bad politics. So while Mario was doing his best to discover some route out of the rules, I abandoned the chair beside the President in favour of my elegant French counterpart Mme Danielle Freignaud, and as the only vaguely senior parliamentary official present rushed off to the UK delegation offices to make urgent calls, on what still seemed something like hand-cranked field telephones, to the Overseas Office in Westminster, and to the Whips. What I knew I needed was an undertaking from the Government that they would regularise the situation in the as-near-as-immediate future as possible, and no arguments.

I don't think I ever extracted quite the promise I was looking for, since it was taking a little while for the Whips to wake up to the small political and diplomatic storm which was threatening in the corridors of the usually somnolent Assembly. But I acted on the premise that something on those lines would eventually emerge, confidently assured the new President Martinez and the very agitated Secretary General, Heinrich Klebes, that this would be the case, and undertook to take Mario's draft away and try to recast it in politically acceptable terms.

Leaving the tradesmen's door at the back of the Palais de l'Europe at my customary time of about 9.30 pm, I as usual couldn't find a single taxi in the area since delegates and all other staff save the printers had long since departed, and heaved a bulging briefcase along Strasbourg's waterways back to the Place Gutenberg. Gratefully locating the only known off-licence in town en route I returned to my hotel, thankful that I had as usual booked the one room with something resembling a desk, and that I had remembered to bring my well-travelled portable kettle for its final engagements in Strasbourg. I then set up shop, interrupting my labours only for a short trip across the square for a large *omelette jambon* and a *pichet* or two before the last café put up its shutters for the night. Fuelled thereafter by generous quantities of scotch, chased down with a continuous supply of tea, I drafted four thousand words in indecipherable script, and by 6 am was back in the *avenue de l'europe*, queuing up at the tradesmen's entrance along with the cleaners, to go through security, and in search of a typewriter upstairs. By 8 am a beautifully typed draft report was on the Secretary General's desk, and I had gone in search of strong coffee and hardboiled eggs in the interpreters' bar behind the *hémicycle*.

Later that morning the Committee on Rules of Procedure met to consider the report of the rapporteur, the veteran Austrian social democrat Peter Schieder, which was identical in all but the typeface to my nocturnal text, and was endorsed unanimously and with some gratifying banging of desks.[99] The following morning the plenary Assembly also gave its approval, representatives of the political groups lining up to commend Herr Schieder's "excellent, swift and Solomon-like report", which "reflected the working of a mature democracy". It certainly made one of the "mature" democracies take note of the minimal standards to which the rest of democratic Europe now expected them to adhere, since the Assembly's resolution gave the Westminster government and parliament only a couple of months in which to set their house in order. And it was also testimony to the power of concentration (however short-lived) contained in a litre of Bell's and a couple of packets of Sainsbury's fig rolls.

I made occasional further forays to Strasbourg, first as a stand-in for others, and subsequently in a tentative and eventually aborted attempt to produce the next edition of the Assembly's procedural handbook, yet another "authority" first produced by Barney Cocks in 1951. I had ghosted much of the eighth edition in 1983, and co-edited the ninth (with John Sweetman) in 1990. I roughed out an outline of the book and some early parts of the text, but it was left to those closer to the Assembly to complete, which they did very well.[100] Yet another unfinished book to my credit.[*]

Around the turn of the century I had my last direct encounters with the European Union: in wet and muddy Brussels, rather than sunny or brilliantly icy Strasbourg. In 1999, after a below-par couple of years back in the Public Bill Office, I swapped jobs with Robert Rogers and inherited a new small empire which he had been busily creating across the road from the Palace in 7 Millbank. This was the short-lived post of Clerk of Delegated Legislation, designed to supervise and coordinate the work of the European Legislation Committee (which attempted to monitor all legislation in progress in the Commission, the Parliament and the Council), the Select Committee on Statutory Instruments (which assessed the *vires* of the vast deluge of subordinate UK legislation made by Ministers) and the Deregulation Committee, which passed judgement on the trickle of ministerial attempts to reduce the volume of regulations aimed at business, industry and the world at large.

In respect of the latter I merely succeeded, in a series of reports often ghosted on behalf of the nominal committee staff, in demonstrating the widespread indifference and incontestable ineptitude of government departments – the Home Office in particular – in implementing the Government's worthy aim of reducing the "regulatory burden" without recourse to primary legislation: the famous "bonfire of regulations", advertised by every incoming government from 1979 onwards, was never even to be ignited if officialdom had its way.

So far as concerned the scrutiny of statutory instruments, I very soon found myself looking not at what the scrutiny committees were doing but at the legal team who were acting on their behalf. On an opaque brief from the then Clerk of the House, Bill McKay, I prepared the relaunch of the ancient office of Speaker's Counsel, which had moved at truly Dickensian pace in addressing even the simplest legal conundrum referred to it. Taking advantage of the imminent retirement of the long-serving incumbent, and with the eventual blessing of the Speaker and the Commission, the operation involved moving the small legal team from their cramped but prestigious berths behind the House of Commons chamber to utilitarian accommodation alongside most of the rest of the workers across the road in Millbank. New posts were created, and new appointments made, and under their new boss, John Vaux, the Legal Services Office rapidly became a

---

[*] In the early 1980's I had similarly scuppered a rewrite of *The Parliament of France*, a somewhat pedestrian recitation of the French *reglement* which David Lidderdale had produced under the auspices of the Hansard Society in 1951. It should however have been obvious that a book about the parliament of the Fourth Republic could not simply be updated a few decades into the Fifth, and particularly not on the basis of a fortnight's sojourn on the Left Bank by Douglas Millar and myself (much though we enjoyed it).

highly professional and motivated service available to all branches of the House of Commons service, fully capable of taking on the government legal advisers across the road, and the courts.

And then there was even more of Europe. With his considerable organisational skills, RJR had created a new office, embedded in the European Parliament buildings, which was to become the eyes and ears of Westminster in Brussels. The National Parliament Office monitored what was going on in the Commission, the Council and the Parliament, and sent back a weekly summary and analysis of the main proceedings in the Brussels institutions. The Bulletin was initially designed for the Commons European Scrutiny Committee alone. But before long, select committees in both Houses found themselves at least one step ahead of the Ministers and officials from whom they were taking evidence, and for the next couple of decades the Bulletin remained an indispensable part of the parliamentary toolbox.

Our Brussels office was initially staffed by one mid-career Commons clerk who, uniquely, was a parliamentary officer granted diplomatic status, together with an assistant who might or might not be from the UK; in later years they were joined by a clerk from the Lords. They were housed in a couple of rooms in the Parliament building in Brussels, and in a single office in Strasbourg, and became passengers on the monthly wagon train between the two capitals of Europe. My only real contribution to the success of the venture was to approve just about every expenses claim which reached me (since there were no precedents for refusing them) and, in order to ameliorate the bleakness of the office accommodation in Brussels, to arrange the export of appropriate paintings from the Palace of Westminster art collection along with some of Pugin's excruciatingly uncomfortable furniture. There were prolonged tussles with the Parliamentary Works Office over the ultimate ownership of all this spare gear from the basement, and the logistics of their removal, and with the accountants over the exorbitant cost of shipping and insurance; and I am not sure whether Chris Stanton and his successor Nick Walker were overjoyed by having their limited space invaded by these lugubrious Victorian home comforts. But we were all agreed that planting the portcullis emblem (emblazoned on the backs of the chairs) firmly on European soil would make a small statement of our already qualified commitment to ever-closer union, and of our intention to fight our corner.

The UK office in Brussels was one of a growing band of similar national outposts in the new imperial capital, and my personal doubts about the Franco-German project were temporarily allayed by this evidence that the national parliaments were beginning to fight back. By now the chairmen of the various European scrutiny committees were meeting regularly together in COSAC*, and their staffs were increasingly co-ordinating their efforts to assert national parliamentary interests in decision-making in Brussels and in the European Parliament. There seemed at least a glimmer of hope that the project's onward progress might be challenged. In retrospect these signs of inter-parliamentary cooperation were probably indicative more of developing panic in the elected institutions of the nation states than of any real hope that the trend would be reversed.

Towards the end of 2001 an opportunity seemed at last to be on offer for a trial of strength between the federalist and nationalist tendencies in the European Community, with at least a possibility of some redistribution of functions and powers, and not necessarily in the direction of the federalists. At their meeting in Laeken, in Belgium, the heads of government collectively acknowledged what by then had come to be known as the "democratic deficit", declared the need for the European institutions to be brought "closer to the citizens", and established a "Convention on the Future of Europe" to define the powers of the Union and the member states and to create "democracy, transparency and efficiency". This initiative was greeted with some enthusiasm by the national parliaments as a last opportunity to preserve at least some protection against the onward march towards federalism.

Chaired by former French President Valéry Giscard d'Estaing, the Convention included representatives of the European institutions, and of the national parliaments and governments. It first met at the end of February 2002, and in June 2003 produced a draft European Constitution, to be submitted to an intergovernmental conference later in the year and then ratification by the member states. Drafting a constitution was not one of the tasks specified for the Convention, but once inspired by its presiding officer and encouraged by the media to compare itself with the Philadelphia Convention of 1787, a draft constitution was the more or less inevitable outcome.

It was not an exact clone of the United States Constitution. The latter comprised around four and a half thousand words and seventeen articles (including the first ten amendments), and very precisely established the respective powers, rights and responsibilities of the state and federal authorities. Giscard's draft ran to about four hundred clauses, covering something like three hundred pages of A4, and left the rights of the states undefined and therefore subject to the predations of the ambitious central power.

---

* Later known as the Conference of Parliamentary Committees for Union Affairs. COSAC was also attended by representatives of the European Parliament, presumably in the hope of legitimising them as members of the international parliamentary fraternity, but from what I saw of the proceedings their presence tended to underline their isolation from, and ignorance of, the political systems which actually mattered to the voters.

My role in all this was only as a facilitator. Indeed, I only discovered that I was to have any involvement at all when I had a phone call in late January 2002 from Gisela Stuart, the attractive contralto for Birmingham Edgbaston.[101] Gisela told me that she had just been selected by the Labour Party to represent them at the Convention, and that Bill McKay, the Clerk of the House, had told her (without any prior warning to me) that I would sort out any support services she might need. Shortly thereafter I had an almost identical call from David Heathcoat-Amory,[102] who had been chosen in a contested backbench election to represent the Tory interest at the Convention. After a few inquiries from each I ascertained that they needed (or seemed to have been promised) more or less unlimited travel expenses, a budget for additional staff, and office accommodation in Brussels. Much to my own surprise, and the frank amazement of some colleagues, I managed within a couple of days to rustle up around a quarter of a million pounds, while doubling the workload of our man in Brussels.

Together with Peter Hain[103] (who represented the government in the Convention) our man and girl worked enormously hard to find a formula which would make the European empire more palatable to the British electorate, who were widely expected to have a chance by one means or another to judge the results before the new constitution for Europe was promulgated (from the Reichstag roof, or so it was rumoured). Gisela, a German by birth, was expected to act as the epitome of the new European, and to reflect the famously harmonious relations which were then said to prevail in the ranks of New Labour, in stark contrast to the Tories, still torn apart by the divisions which had brought Margaret down and the bastards who had bedevilled John Major's otherwise tranquil occupancy of No 10.

David Heathcoat-Amory, elected by his peers, represented the civilised wing of the bastard tendency. He did the job very well, organising a small but the only effective "opposition" group in the Convention, tabling hundreds of amendments (but none was voted on, since there was an unwritten diktat that the Convention should move "by consensus"), and generally proving a thorn in the side of both Giscard and Sir John Kerr, the British diplomat landed with the unenviable task of drafting all the nonsense which the right-minded and politically-correct urged on their fellow delegates.[104] Gisela had the misfortune to be chosen to serve on the Convention's thirteen-man presidium, as the token representative of the national parliaments. She concluded from this experience that the draft constitution represented the work of "a self-selected group of the European political elite" who never once questioned "whether deeper integration is what the people of Europe want"[105]. She emerged a decade later as the chairman of *Vote Leave*. When I had told Gisela in early 2002 that my own periodic immersion had turned me into a convinced opponent of ever-closer union, she had offered up one of her benchmark peals of contralto laughter. But her own conversion also came as no surprise.

The draft Constitution so joyfully embraced in June 2003, and dressed up into a draft treaty in October 2004, seemed by the beginning of June 2005 to be a very dead letter, the French and Dutch electorates having voted it down by substantial margins. All subsequent referenda and parliamentary votes in other member states were thereafter cancelled, saving Tony Blair from the embarrassment of delivering on his belated and foolish promise to consult the British electorate also.

In accordance with time-honoured Brussels tradition, however, the Constitution for Europe was not dead, but only slept. In December 2007 all its essentials were resurrected, but in new apparel, as the Treaty of Lisbon, a deliberate makeover to avoid the need for further popular votes in the member states. This cynical disregard by the European elite for the democratic deficit which the whole constitution-building process was supposed to address, lit the fuse for the rise of nationalist oppositions throughout western Europe, and of UKIP and the *Front National* in particular, and for the cataclysm of 23rd June 2016. Populism, the patronising term applied by that same elite to any manifestation of democracy which challenged their own imperium, had triumphed. They had only themselves to blame. The people of England had spoken at last.[*]

---

[*] It may not have been entirely clear to his first readers to whom G K Chesterton was referring when in 1907 he described the "new unhappy lords, who dare not carry their swords", but "fight by shuffling papers", but it was evidently clear enough to the English electorate a century later.

33

A Farewell to Annie's

The cavaliers depart; Iraq; freedom from Freedom of Information; Tony Blair: his part in my downfall

Sometime in the spring of 2006, Annie's Bar finally closed. This latest Annie's bore little resemblance to the original taproom, located in brief staggering distance of the chamber across the Members' Lobby, from which a lady named Annie had once dispensed hospitality and bonhomie to Members, including party leaders such as Arthur Henderson and Winston Churchill - both said to be regulars - and to lobby journalists. She was bombed out in May 1941. When rebuilt, the premises, which didn't even have a cold water supply (glasses were said to be washed in a bucket refilled from the river), were absorbed into the Opposition whips' offices, apparently on the instructions of William Whiteley, Atlee's long-serving and strictly teetotal Chief Whip.

Nor was this Annie's that haunt of journalists in search of a story, of Ministers of the Crown eager to oblige them, of former front benchers denouncing their successors, of disaffected backbenchers, of whips in search of all the latter categories for disciplinary or voting purposes (or both), and of disaffected clerks and library clerks, to which I refer in earlier parts of this book. That second incarnation had come to life in 1967 in the north curtain corridor at the bottom of the Tea Room stairs during Cap'n Bob's brief but eventful stewardship of the Catering Committee. The original Annie had returned to pull the first pint and the notoriously unclubbable Opposition Leader Ted Heath had, astonishingly, cut the ribbon.

Annie's Mark II was just establishing itself as the hostelry of choice when I arrived in Westminster in 1968, and it went on to play a vital role during the more-or-less minority Labour Governments of the 1970's, when the whips of both sides needed to take the temperature of their own and the other parties on an hourly, or even a minute-by-minute, schedule.* Many of the great names of the time became habitués, and others – even Margaret herself – were occasionally prepared to compromise if there were votes to be secured. It was a place of discreet conviviality and occasional intrigue,

---

* James Graham's *This House*, which premiered at the National Theatre in 2012, gives an uncannily accurate flavour of the times, and of the main protagonists.

where the cavaliers of all parties or none could exchange political and other indiscretions with reasonable confidence that although much would appear in print it would be unattributable. Betty Boothroyd might reprise her role as a Tiller Girl (as she did), but it wouldn't be on the front pages of the tabloids in the morning.

This second Annie's was a small L shape, created from two even smaller rooms, once upon a time the offices in the 1880's of Charles Stewart Parnell, leader of the Irish Parliamentary Party: many of his compatriots were still to be found there in the 1980's. It had the advantage of an area around the corner where brief private conversations could be held. It might be Jack Weatherill and Walter Harrison, or Joe Harper and Fred Silvester, trading pairs in an emergency; it might be backbenchers (and occasionally clerks) putting together an Early Day Motion or an amendment designed to discomfort both front benches; it might even be a Principal Clerk conducting an unthreatening annual performance review with a subordinate friend; or it might be a brief liaison of a more promising nature, ahead of the long night ahead. Whatever the nature of the conversation there was a universally observed code of honour that if the dog-leg was occupied no-one else was to enter that end of the room, a breach of which convention could result in eviction from what was really one of the more discerning clubs in the parliamentary village.

Despite its historical importance, the patronage of Chief Whips and Cabinet Ministers, and its brisk trade at any time of day or night, the Mark II version was swept away in the summer of 1995 (along with the House of Commons barber's, another key rendezvous for the exchange of indiscretions, and the original Strangers' Bar across the corridor) to make way for the construction of new kitchens under the Tea Room and for the Terrace Cafeteria which came to occupy most of the river frontage west of Speaker's House.

In the autumn of 1995 stray souls might therefore have been found wandering disconsolately along the Terrace in search of their former hostelry, cursing the puritans who had razed the citadel. The Strangers' at least could still be located, having moved westward along the terrace, larger, lighter and less intimate, more comfortable and more crowded, but never quite the same again. For the real cavaliers a counterfeit Annie's was said to be located in the kitchen area somewhere below the Central Lobby. This had formerly served as the "Policeman's Bar", and the very fact that it was no longer needed for that purpose said much about the brave new and well-behaved world into which we were now moving. The journalists too, having deserted Fleet Street, had apparently also abandoned their traditional habits, and could be found in the unlikely occupation of drinking coffee. The few surviving members of the club eventually identified a rival establishment at the other end of the Terrace, and joined those who had gone before them, in the hitherto undiscovered Lords Bar, which thereafter enjoyed a few years of popularity and perhaps even profit.

When the Commons Administration Committee recommended its closure in April 2006, Annie's Mark III was said to have already been "disused" for several years. This is no surprise, since most of its former clientele were dead, de-selected, or simply couldn't find it. On my only visit I discovered the Iberian barman improving his command of English by reading Anthony Trollope, and the pool table – foolishly installed by those with little understanding of the essential dynamic of the place – gathering dust in lonely isolation. When questioned on the matter a decade or so later, nobody in what had by then become the Catering and Retail Service could remember quite exactly when the last pint was pulled.

Sometime after the closure of the real Annie's, and shortly before the expiration of its successor, I decided that it was time to move on. This was partly for personal reasons - not least my abomination of commuting through London's south-eastern suburbs, despite the vast improvement in the rail system, for which I of course claimed some credit. And my enthusiasm for the cause I had embraced three-and-a-half decades earlier was waning. The culture of Westminster had changed, and I had failed to change with it.

Parliamentary working hours were adjusting to those which it was claimed obtained in the world outside: the vanguard of what John Knox might have called the monstrous regiment of women were firing their first salvoes. To become more "family friendly", the Commons met earlier in the day, contested decisions in the evening were left over to the following afternoon, and, thanks to "programming", regular all-night sittings became a distant memory, as did any serious threat of government defeat. Opportunities for debates initiated by backbenchers were marginally increased, but were relegated to an artificially-created debating club in the Grand Committee Room off Westminster Hall. Much more of the operation was now centred on the scrutiny committees, which could certainly embarrass ministers (and did so with increasing adroitness) but could rarely de-rail the legislative juggernaut. I was proud to claim some responsibility for the remarkable success of the 1978 committee scheme, but I found it much harder to adjust to its consequences.

The small college of clerks which I had joined in 1968 was growing with alarming rapidity into something like a bureaucracy: much larger, inevitably much more rule-bound, and dispersed around the burgeoning parliamentary estate. So distant had the committee teams in 7 Millbank become by the turn of the century that a routine complaint of many recent recruits during annual reporting interviews was that they had never exchanged a word with the Clerk of the House, their nominal boss, or had even set eyes on him other than on the television stream which was fed to their rooms at all hours.

These annual staff interviews (which for a while became biannual) were symptomatic of the new era. The Clerks had actually been ahead of most of

Whitehall in introducing formal staff reports back in the early nineteen-seventies, but these were simple four-page documents, made out in long-hand by the reporting officer, with a box mark at the end – a box mark that might one day influence promotion prospects but had no effect on pay, which was determined almost entirely by position in the hierarchy[*] and length of service.

By the start of the new millennium, however, much of the time of anyone with "managerial" responsibilities was devoted to the painstaking completion of many interviews and of lengthy documents, which were required to be word-processed at each stage. The reports seemed designed to demonstrate that everyone (the reporter as well as the reported on) had either failed utterly, or had significantly advanced in every aspect of their performance every year, wage progression being now dependent on the outcome. Since the quality of most of the staff at every level could in normal parlance be described as good or more often outstanding, after a few years it became impossible to mark anyone higher, which threatened their future pay. However, the now even larger army of human resources experts in the Finance and Administration department justified their existence every few years by obligingly changing the criteria which had to be met, and the marking system on the forms, which enabled everyone to start again from scratch. Each change also forced everyone to go on yet more training courses to learn the new drills, to add to all the other training sessions – on fire precautions, first aid, desktop publishing, internet and intranet changes, and so on and so forth – which seemed to come round on an almost weekly basis: sessions on safeguarding, anti-discrimination, etc have no doubt been quite properly added to the regular round in recent years. Thus are empires built and sustained. At the same time we bowed further to political correctness, and became 'Investors in People', John Major's headline contribution to the onward march of the human resources industry.

During my years as a frontline clerk I had developed an irritating tendency to bang on to otherwise blameless members of either House, when cornered on a plane or a train, to follow my own practice of re-reading both *Brave New World* and *1984* around the turn of each year.[†] Although our new

---

[*] In those days both the *Civil Service List* and *Dod* set out the names of clerks at each grade in order of seniority, based on their date of arrival in the Department of the Clerk, and their original ranking at the Civil Service Selection Board, with salary scales published alongside. This published order was maintained, irrespective of assessed merit, until individuals were on the threshold of appointment to the handful of "principal" clerkships at the top of the tree (or were, alternatively, invited to leave). Despite "freedom of information" this particular information is curiously no longer easily obtained.

[†] To these great prophetic works I would in later years have added David Nobbs' original Reginald Perrin novel, which so graphically reveals the inner frustrations,

ruling class would no doubt find the idea laughably suburban, it was obvious to the surviving freethinkers amongst us that in many aspects of our lives we were already not that far away from both those dystopian worlds, and it was high time our representatives began to wake up to the danger and put up some kind of concerted resistance: if they wouldn't, who could? One assumes that both Huxley and Orwell would have been a trifle depressed to see how much further their nightmares had progressed than they intended – genetic engineering, cloning, the new lumpenproletariat, big brother, Newspeak, to name but a few[*] – but probably neither would have been particularly surprised. Within fifteen years of his original, Aldous Huxley had already advanced the establishment of the World State from six hundred years hence to a mere century.[106] And we are indeed more than half-way there: although most alphas have not yet acquired personal helicopters, they are already queuing up for the first generation of driverless cars; and only a late-afternoon vote in the Commons is needed to get the Central London Hatchery up and running.

In the end, two separate series of events persuaded me that my time would be more honourably spent at home. Both were largely, if indirectly, the responsibility of Anthony Charles Lynton Blair.

The first was the second Iraq War, launched on 20th March 2003. Like all right-minded people – encompassing the vast majority of the British (and indeed the world) population – I was saddened, if not surprised, by the blatant dishonesty of the Bush and Blair entourages as they created a spurious case for a military intervention which destabilised not only Iraq but the whole of the Middle East, and led to decades of bloodshed, some in Europe. But I was more appalled by the complicity of the majority of the House of Commons. Given the unusual opportunity of actually voting for or against a war – albeit only two days before the tanks were scheduled to roll across the desert and the oil wells began to burn – the House voted by comfortable majorities to authorise British participation.

The Liberals, a respectable minority of Labour backbenchers, and a handful of honourable Tories were principled and in some cases courageous enough to vote against or abstain, but the fact that the official Tory Opposition, as well as a majority of Labour members, encouraged each other to enter the lobbies to endorse the Government's obviously fraudulent prospectus was an abdication of political responsibility from which the political classes have not yet fully recovered, and deserve not to. It was from this point on difficult to understand how the House of Commons could claim

---

resentments, obsessions and daydreams of the middle manager: it should be compulsory reading for all boss men (*The Death of Reginald Perrin*, London (Gollancz), 1975).

[*] To which list we could of course add many others today: the Two Minutes Hate, for example, now organised hourly and with apparent spontaneity on Twitter, Facebook and other versions of the "social" media.

to "represent" the British people, when millions were demonstrating in the streets against what the man on the Hanley omnibus at any rate knew to be unjustified, unprincipled and unprovoked aggression. In my several decades in Westminster it was the only issue on which I found myself sorely tempted to break my oath of neutrality and to take to the streets along with my friends.

Disgust at the crimes Her Majesty's Government had perpetrated in my name was not assuaged during the following summer months. Friday 18th July 2003 was the first day of Parliament's summer adjournment, and it soon emerged that I was the only senior member of the Clerk's Department who had not sensibly departed for distant shores when news arrived of the apparent suicide of Dr David Kelly, the weapons inspector, near his Oxfordshire home. Apart from two nights on the Sussex coast, I spent every other day of that summer recess either in the office or working from home, dealing with the parliamentary implications of the Hutton Inquiry, set up in great haste by the Government to examine the "circumstances surrounding" Dr Kelly's death. This included trying to cope with the understandable distress of the staff and some of the members of the Foreign Affairs Committee, whose robust but honest public interrogation of Dr Kelly two days before his death was loosely and irresponsibly alleged in the media to have "caused" his apparent suicide. But the unprecedented demand by Lord Hutton for access to the committee's working papers, including the suggested lines of questioning prepared for the chairman and the clerks' other private papers, constituted a major challenge to the historic privileges of the House. By the time Parliament returned in the second week of September I was already mightily tired of anything to do with Iraq, and the "privilege" implications rumbled on almost up to the moment of the publication of the inquiry's report.[107]

It was parliamentary privilege which finally tipped the balance in favour of a slightly earlier retirement than originally planned. And in this case it was very definitely Tony Blair's fault. My last parliamentary job, to which I had moved at the beginning of 2003, was as Clerk of the Journals, an ancient post established in the mid-eighteenth century of which I was the twenty-eighth (or twenty-ninth) holder. So I was now on my third run in the Journal Office above the Chamber, this time in the large and disorderly lair at the end of the corridor in which many notables – such as the Rt Rev Dr Eric Taylor – had "read the Vote" and occasionally slumbered, their portraits, bewigged or be-whiskered, looking down on me like the Murgatroyds of Ruddigore.

Apart from being the custodian of the formal records of the House – the Votes & Proceedings, and the Journal itself – the Clerk of the Journals had in modern times come to be regarded as the in-House authority on all matters pertaining to the privileges of the House. This reputation was certainly deserved by some of my recent predecessors, notably Jim

Hastings, who had done the job for almost ten years and in the process had authored the most authoritative account of the subject to date. Amongst other things, Jim's report[108] sensibly recommended a new statute to codify the myriad common law, statute law, customs, Speaker's decisions and court rulings which continued to confuse the most agile legal and clerkly minds.

I managed, with the help of the new Speaker's Council, John Vaux, to get my head round the basic principles, certainly quite enough to provide routine advice to Members and government departments when required. But I made no claim to being an expert of the Bill McKay or Hastings variety.

The essential text on which the privileges of Lords and Commons are based in modern times is Article 9 of the Bill of Rights of 1689, by which the new monarchs from the Netherlands were bound, which stipulated that "the freedom of speech and debates or proceedings in Parliament ought not to be impeached or questioned in any court or place out of Parliament": this means that nothing said or done either by a Member, or by anyone giving evidence to either House or a committee, can be the subject of a prosecution or civil action, or examined by a court, except with the express permission of the House concerned.

This sounds straightforward enough until challenged. There is a mass of case law. Freedom of speech in debate is reasonably clear, but what constitutes "proceedings"? And what, apart from a court of law, is meant by a "place" outside Parliament? These were not merely academic questions, but questions which were and are frequently confronted. In a recent case, for instance, I as a mere select committee clerk had had the experience of ruling categorically against a Member who sought to attach "privilege" to reams of documents containing allegations against third parties which he encouraged a lobby group to present to a select committee, during a public meeting, as "evidence". The documents had not been sought by the committee but were marginally related to the terms of reference of the inquiry which the committee was then conducting. But there was no clear definition of what constituted "evidence" and might therefore be regarded as part of the committee's "proceedings". I, like many committee clerks before and no doubt since therefore had to guess and hope that higher authorities (like the then Clerk of the Journals) would back me up. And the Hutton Inquiry had resurrected questions both about the meaning of a "place out of Parliament", and what it meant in practice to "impeach or question", particularly when a parliamentary committee had voluntarily surrendered its internal working papers to outside scrutiny, as the Foreign Affairs Committee had now done.

During the course of 2003 it was agreed by those at the top of the service that in addition to being the man who knew all about privilege, the Clerk of the Journals would in future also adjudicate on requests for information submitted under the Freedom of Information Act 2000. As originally proposed by the Government, this new legislation did not extend to Parliament at all. It was, sadly, amended to include Parliament as a result of a recommendation by the Public Administration select committee during its scrutiny of the draft bill.[*] Although the resulting Act contained convoluted provisions to protect parliamentary privilege, in most cases any complaint that a request for information had been refused could now be examined and adjudicated on by the Information Commissioner, an ostensibly "independent" public servant appointed under the terms of the Act, and although it was possible for a "conclusive certificate" to be issued by the Speaker the very fact of doing so would thereafter be bound to open up to public debate the whole issue of what does and does not constitute "proceedings in Parliament", and in any case raise questions of motive of a wholly political character.

After months of juggling with the conflict between the ancient privileges of the House and the promises now given to the public and the media that requests for information would in general be met, I finally concluded that a solution was beyond my limited grasp. I was therefore relieved in late 2004 to be able to pass the baton on.

My successor as Clerk of the Journals was Robert Rogers (now Lord Lisvane) whose flexible mind might have been expected to find appropriate means of squaring the circle if such were possible. This was not to be entirely the case, however. In 2009 the "expenses scandal" broke, as a direct consequence of the Freedom of Information Act. The House authorities tried in vain to protect themselves – and Members – but were eventually compelled to release most of the information requested. There followed a swath of resignations, retirements, and de-selections. Many Members were required to repay relatively trifling sums, and a few faced criminal charges for false accounting. And for the first time in modern history, the Speaker was forced to resign.

All this of course delighted the media, who as always claimed to have been acting in the interests of the people. The reputation of Parliament, with the active help of the Fourth Estate, had fallen to a new low (although the depths were to be further plumbed in later years).

As a last pre-retirement visit I was invited to attend the annual "professional development seminar" of the Canadian Association of Clerks-at-the-Table, held in the youngest legislature in the Commonwealth, in Iqaluit, capital of the newly formed Canadian province of Nunavut. This was attended not only by clerks from the parliament in Ottawa and the

---

[*] The committee's chairman admitted to a seminar in Portcullis House a few years later that this recommendation had been a bad mistake (Dr Tony Wright, Labour MP for Cannock, and then Cannock Chase, 1992-2010; Chairman of the Committee on Reform of the House of Commons 2008-09; Professor of Government and Public Policy, University College London, from 2010).

provincial assemblies, but also by officers from several legislatures of the American states which still maintain some of the procedural traditions inherited from Westminster. The assembled colleagues expressed their collective horror at Westminster's "insanity" at allowing freedom of information legislation to impinge in any way on the privileges of parliament, a view previously expressed by incredulous clerks from all parts of the Commonwealth. It was only small consolation that a few years later Tony Blair – who had vociferously campaigned for Freedom of Information while in Opposition – conceded in his memoirs that he had been an "idiot", a "naïve, foolish, irresponsible nincompoop" in allowing his government to proceed with the Freedom of Information Act. He was certainly right about that, if about little else, and his successors have no doubt cursed him daily.

34

Forty Years On

an Afterword

In June 2019 I attended a conference in Westminster to celebrate the fortieth anniversary of the appointment of the first twelve "departmentally-related" select committees, just one of the seventy-six recommendations of the 1978 Procedure Committee.

The conference was held over two days in the Atlee Suite, the largest meeting space on the committee floor of Portcullis House. Like most others I had arrived via the Jubilee Line in the new Westminster Underground station which underpins the parliamentary building. Every time I make this journey I do so with a small frisson of pride, claiming at least a tiny proportion of proprietorial rights, and genuine exhilaration at this outstanding example of British design, taste and engineering.[*]

At the time of the conference the public standing of the British Parliament – and of the House of Commons in particular – was at yet another low point, and the United Kingdom's reputation around the world as the home and guardian of "democracy" was looking more than a little frayed. Out of a total of over 45 million registered electors in the UK, a mere 143,000 members of the Conservative Party, which had achieved less than 10 per cent of the popular vote in the most recent national poll (the European Parliament elections in May 2019) were at that moment in the process of choosing between two candidates to become the party leader and next Prime Minister of the country. In the preceding months the incumbent Prime Minister had survived only with the support of a small regional party, and the arrangements she had negotiated for the country's "orderly withdrawal" from the European Union, over which that small party had an effective veto, had been defeated at least three times in a distinctly disorderly House of Commons.

As a result of the 2016 referendum on membership of the EU, and the cavil decisions of too many Members to "respect" that result (thus forgetting their Burke, and their duties as representatives, not as delegates), the normal operational rules of the system of governance had gone into abeyance.

---

[*] see chapter 28 above. I of course made an irrefutable claim to a much larger proportion of such rights over the committee system which the conference was celebrating; irrefutable if for no other reason than none of the other original actors was around to stake any claims of their own.

According to the received model, the Government's job was to lead, and the job of their Commons majority to follow that lead. However, the Cabinet was in open warfare with itself, and although it might win an occasional confidence vote it was only because members of all parties were preoccupied by the fear of losing their seats, and so didn't want another General Election quite yet. On all the votes which mattered the Whips offices (themselves also divided) had simply lost control.

Particularly challenging to the traditional relationship between Executive and Parliament was that the Cabinet could no longer be certain of determining the agenda of the House, the historic instrument of control: the Cabinet no longer commanded a majority in the House, and its claim to the procedural priorities of the Executive could therefore no longer be easily enforced.

Instead they could be and with increasing frequency were claimed and exercised by whatever shifting alliance of Members could organise a majority on the day – early in 2019 the diehard Brexiteers, later in the year the diehard Remainers, with several misalliances in between. The House of Commons was at risk of reverting to an earlier, pre-modern, model which would have been familiar to Dean Swift and other satirists of the early eighteenth century; we appeared to be moving – at least temporarily – to something approaching the *gouvernement de l'assemblée* to which we idealists of the campuses of the sixties might in our youth have aspired. The parties were losing power, and the backbenches were for the time being taking control.

The gradual erosion of two-party hegemony of course had largely external causes. The rise of powerful regional parties in Scotland and Wales had reduced the solidity of the electoral base on which the Labour Party in particular had relied, and had led to the creation of power structures and centres of authority in Edinburgh and (to an increasing extent) in Cardiff which presented plausible alternatives and a serious challenge to those in Westminster and Whitehall. Economic and social changes had undermined the essentially economic base of the two-party system which had prevailed after the end of the Great War, and had forced the parties to try to appeal to electorates with less obviously identifiable common interests. And the decline of deference, triggered by post-war national service and outrageously celebrated by me and others on the sixties campuses, had been accelerated and then completed by the new technology, available to all. If you could advertise your own views to anyone who cared to read them – instantly - on Twitter, on Facebook, or through your own blog, if you could organise your own campaigns, what need was there to rely on the cumbersome machinery of a national political party indirectly to promote your interests, or misrepresent your prejudices? The traditional role of the big parties had been to "articulate" our interests and our grievances: but what purpose did they really serve when we could all do it ourselves, without their help?

Meanwhile in Westminster the control of the parties was being progressively and systematically undermined from within. And much of the impetus for this process can be traced back to the Procedure Committee established in 1976. Their appointment provided the first opportunity in a century or more for backbenchers to take the initiative. They picked up the ball and held onto it long enough to get it into play. The Committee's report in 1978, despite some far-reaching procedural proposals, had modest ambitions – at least in the sense that it set its sights on a shift in the balance of *advantage* between Executive and Parliament, and not the balance of *power*. It provided a framework, and the momentum, for sweeping changes in the internal mechanisms of parliament – but not intentionally in the fundamental relationships between the different elements of the unwritten Constitution.

From the appointment of the new select committees the following year the "balance of advantage" began slowly to shift. Pre-legislative scrutiny of draft bills, improved explanatory memoranda, evidence-taking public bill committees, research assistance for individual Members, the establishment of a formal Liaison Committee, the employment of fulltime committee specialists, the establishment of parliamentary control over the national audit service – even the payment of committee chairmen – all these and many other changes moved onto the reform agenda, and most were implemented. At the same time, thanks to the establishment of the House of Commons Commission, Members were for the first time provided with the staff and the facilities to enable them to act independently, in defiance of the parties.

There were certainly also some reverses along the way. Two decades on from 1978 the argument over the timetabling of legislation was lost in the euphoria of the Blair revolution. But by that time the departmental committees had become a permanent part of the machinery of the House. They had proved themselves over many years of weak opposition (Labour in disarray for the first decade of Thatcherism, the Conservatives in at least equal disarray for most of the Blair premiership) as far more effective tools for the sustained criticism and scrutiny of Government, and even for the formulation of alternative policy, than the Opposition front bench. Collectively, they had become a force to be reckoned with – a non-party alliance, with common interests of its own, which cut across and challenged the power, and to some extent the interests, of the mass parties. As they took imaginative advantage of technological changes – first broadcasting, then the internet, then the new social media – they were able to reach out to substantial sections of the public over the heads of the Government and the parties. The committees established their own sizeable constituencies, and were able to talk directly to them; and many committee chairmen became rather better known to the public than mere secretaries of state across the road in Whitehall.

The 1978 Committee had avoided any discussion of proportional representation – the elephant in the room - in order not to undermine their carefully constructed consensus. It remained the generally accepted view of practitioners and observers alike at the time that any change in the balance of *power* was dependent on electoral change, and that the first-past-the-post electoral system would meanwhile guarantee the two-party arrangement as the default.

Forty years on these assumptions no longer hold good. The many external factors – economic, social, ethnographic, cultural and technological – which had already eaten into the parties' authority in the country at large, were similarly at play within Parliament to further weaken their hold over the machinery. Even without electoral change the two-party system was transforming itself into an unstable multi-party and cross-party mix in which continuous single-party government appeared increasingly implausible. Even if a party did manage to win a majority at the polls its ability to sustain that majority in the House would be immediately challenged whenever the next critical policy issue arose.

Two centralised and disciplined parties had always provided the essential mortar in the received model of the Constitution, conceived by Walter Bagehot in the mid-Victorian era, refined by Richard Crossman a century later, and perpetuated in school and university course books. But if the mortar fails, how will the building hold together? Attacked from without by new electoral interests and alliances, eroded from within by acute and essentially irreconcilable policy differences, and together undermined by the growing independence of the subordinate institutions of Parliament, the Tory and Labour parties just about held on into the twenty-first century as custodians of the Constitution. But finally, unable to resolve their internal disputes, in 2016 the parties abdicated their control over policy to the electorate. Whether they (or any other parties) would be able to fully repossess the building was an open question after the events of 2019. The outcome of the General Election in December of that year suggested that the two-party model retained some resilience. The previous three years, on the other hand, demonstrated that the model was now extremely vulnerable. There can be little confidence that when the next major policy crisis arises the forces of populism – now so easily unleashed by the new media, and accessible in the pockets and handbags of all – will not undermine the structure once again.

The unprecedented spectacle of a minority Government roundly and repeatedly defeated on what at any other time would have been regarded as matters of confidence was peddled in the media as a failure of the House of Commons as an institution, rather than the failure of the two parties which had up to that year successfully collaborated in keeping Parliament in its proper place. To some of us, however, the first nine months of 2019 was a reminder of where power ought to reside – in the elected representatives of the people. With a non-conformist Speaker, the Commons performed one of its historic roles: as I argued earlier in this book, we elect parliaments not only to legislate on our behalf but also on our behalf not to legislate. In not embracing the Executive's proffered solutions to the impasse created by the referendum in 2016, the House of Commons was merely reflecting the deep-seated divisions in the country as a whole. It was, in other words, doing its job, albeit in rather clumsy fashion. Meanwhile – upstairs and in Portcullis House – committees of members of all parties were collaborating in the other part of the job – to investigate, criticise, and constrain the aspirations of those who wish to legislate in order to further control our lives and further limit our freedoms. And doing it better than it had ever been done before. If the parties were not fit for purpose, the House of Commons as an institution was not wholly unprepared for the uncertainties of the future.

Index

Endnotes

Chapters 1-2

[1] The Civil Service Selection Board
[2] Sir Barnett Cocks, *Mid-Victorian Masterpiece: The story of an institution unable to put its own house in order* (Hutchinson, London, 1977)
[3] S E Finer, *Comparative Government* (London, Allen Lane, 1970)
[4] 'G E Edwards', "The Scottish Grand Committee, 1958 to 1970", *Parliamentary Affairs*, Autumn 1972, pp 303-325

Chapters 3-9

[5] *Erskine May's Treatise on The Law, Privileges, Proceedings and Usage of Parliament* (first published 1844), 25th edition 2019.
[6] Sir Barnett Cocks, *The European Parliament: Structure, Procedure & Practice* (London, HMSO, 1973)
[7] *Motion for a Resolution on the establishment of a temporary committee of the European Parliament to examine the procedure and practices of the Parliament, together with an explanatory memorandum* (European Parliament document PE 32.103 (BUR) (1973).

Chapters 10-13

[8] This particular Park Hotel now seems to have decayed completely (and not surprisingly). There is a whole string of small hotels bearing the same name in today's Istanbul, but not, apparently, the original.
[9] The Fourth Baron Strathcona and Mount Royal, who went on to various middling ministerial positions in Margaret Thatcher's first Government, and was eventually Deputy Leader in the Lords.
[10] *Washington Post*, 23 May 1976.

Chapters 14-16

[11] Science and engineering graduates as a proportion of the England & Wales total actually fell from 55% in 1963 to 46% in 1974 (and of postgraduates from 67% to 51%), despite the white heat of the technological revolution.
[12] MP for Nottingham West (1964-83), Michael English had apparently read the whole of Erskine May when confined to his sickbed as a child.
[13] Even more than Michael English, Nigel Spearing (MP for Acton, 1970-74, and Newham South until 1997) was a staunch (some might have said obsessive) anti-marketeer whose unlimited eloquence was sufficient to exhaust all but the most robust of opponents. He was an early pioneer of cycling to work at Westminster, and rather more regularly and genuinely committed to that environmentally friendly practice than later and more famous politicians of the same public persuasion.
[14] David Renton, bland though he seemed to many, became one of my greatest allies in the battle against the forces of reaction in the Whips' offices on the one hand and, on the other hand, against the happy band of lunatics who endangered the production of any sensible committee report. It was an absolute delight to learn that in July 2003, when he was approaching his 95th birthday, the then Lord Renton comfortably passed his driving test for the first time (having driven contentedly since the pre-testing days of 1934), becoming the oldest person in the UK ever to do so.

[15] A child of the Welsh valleys, Tom Williams served successively as MP for Hammersmith South, Baron's Court, and Warrington (and probably would have done so for anywhere else that wasn't Wales). He was for a time President of the Inter-parliamentary Union. He appeared to have one of the most obtuse minds of all the many parliamentarians with whom I had to deal over the years, and was therefore undoubtedly well-qualified when appointed a High Court judge in 1981.

[16] Enoch Powell was obviously the complete antithesis of the aforementioned. He was the youngest ever Professor in the English-speaking universities (Professor of Greek at the University of Sydney at the age of 25) and was subsequently the youngest brigadier in the British Army (like Fitzroy Maclean, and nobody else, having risen from the rank of private to brigadier). His was one of the most invigorating minds I was privileged to work with during my parliamentary career.

[17] First Report from the Select Committee on Procedure, Session 1977-78 (HC 588-I).

[18] HC Debs, 19th & 20th February 1979, cols 44-213, 276-386 *passim.*

[19] The final tally, on 11th June, showed 265 signed-up supporters for EDM 13 (Procedural Reform).

[20] Unlike his predecessor the new Leader of the House was merely Chancellor of the Duchy of Lancaster, rather than Lord President of the Council, the latter role and title having passed to Christopher Soames, former Ambassador to France and European Trade & External Relations Commissioner, nephew of Baden-Powell, and son-in-law of Winston Churchill. Lord Soames, armed with the title of Lord President, served as Leader of the House of Lords for the first two years of Margaret Thatcher's Government, and simultaneously (until April 1980) as the last Governor of Southern Rhodesia.

[21] Appendix B to the 1978 Report.

Chapters 17-19

[22] Tom Bradley was what was then a typical Labour backbencher (but would be something of an anachronism today). Educated at the Central School in Kettering, employed in the mines during the War, Tom had by this time become President and acting General Secretary of the Transport Salaried Staffs Association - real heights in those pre-Tebbit days when the unions still constituted the Fourth Estate in the land. Tom's particular strength as well as his particular weakness was his loyalty to colleagues, staff and friends - the latter in particular. He had long served as PPS to Roy Jenkins, in his various roles of Chancellor, Shadow Chancellor and Home Secretary. Tom regarded Roy as his true political friend and mentor; Roy treated Tom largely as a tame gofer. Tom's loyalty in the end cost him the remains of his career in national politics.

[23] Both were subsequently knighted. Sir Peter later became the Chairman of the Federation of European Bingo Associations. Sir David, an Etonian and former intelligence officer with the Scots Guards, became an assiduous campaigner for the disabled, and for residential care for the mentally ill. He had achieved some notoriety in the Tory Party as an abstainer over Suez, but like others was forgiven by Macmillan. He achieved applause for his coinage of the phrase "the Winter of Discontent" to describe the difficulties of both the Tory and Labour Governments in the early months of 1974 (a coinage stolen by *The Sun* five years later to describe the Callaghan Government's similar problems in January 1979).

[24] First Report from the Transport Committee (*The European Commission's Green Paper on Transport Infrastructure*), Session 1979-80 (HC 466-v).

[25] Second Report from the Transport Committee (*The Channel Link*), Session 1980-81 (HC 155-I).

[26] Obituary in *The Independent*, 4 November 1996.

[27] Fifth Report from the Transport Committee (*Transport in London*), Session 1981-82 (HC 117).

Chapters 20-27

[28] Labour/Co-operative MP for South Ayrshire 1979-83, and for Carrick, Cumnock and Doon Valley 1983-2005, and subsequently Baron Foulkes of Cumnock.

[29] Son of a police sergeant, ex-RAF, double first in history from Emmanuel College Cambridge, MA Yale, former Foreign Editor of *Newsweek*; Tory MP for Bury St Edmunds 1964-97; Minister for Sport under Ted Heath; progressively disappointed thereafter. His relatively lowly origins no doubt enabled both Grocer Heath and Daughter-of-Grocer Thatcher to look down on him from their lofty social positions, and his vocal pro-Europeanism didn't exactly endear him to the latter.

[30] Minutes of the Proceedings of the Foreign Affairs Committee, Session 1982-83, HC 380.

[31] Fifth Report from the Foreign Affairs Committee, Session 1983-84, HC 268 (*Falkland Islands*).

[32] Tory MP for Hertford & Stevenage from 1979, and from 1983 to 2001 for Hertford & Stortford. From 1997 to 2001 he chaired the Select Committee on International Development.

[33] Fifth Report from the Foreign Affairs Committee, Session 1981-82 (HC 47).

[34] Tory MP for Conway 1951-66, and for Hendon South 1970-87; thereafter Baron Thomas of Gwydir. He appeared for many years at the Eisteddfodau as Pedr Conwy.

[35] Sir Paul Scoon, *Survival for Service* (MacMillan Caribbean, 2003) pp 134-5, 145

[36] Richard Hart, *The Grenada Revolution: Setting the record straight* (Caribbean Labour Solidarity/Socialist History Society, SHS Occasional Paper No 20, 2005) pp 44-5

[37] NUM-sponsored Labour MP for Don Valley from 1979, and Doncaster North 1983-1992.

[38] West Indies Records (Barbados), W186 (1983). One side of the sleeve is emblazoned with revolutionary slogans, the other with advertisements for local businesses, including the St George's University School of Medicine.

[39] Second Report from the Foreign Affairs Committee (*Grenada*), Session 1983-84 (HC 226), para 113.

[40] *Trinidad Express*, 5 February 2011

[41] George L Proctor, *The Greenland Adventure* (London: Harrap, 1950); George and Anne Proctor, *Provincial Poison* (written 1934-38, privately printed 2010).

[42] Third Report from the Foreign Affairs Committee (*The Forthcoming Fontainebleau Summit*), Session 1983-84 (HC 480).

[43] First Report from the Foreign Affairs Committee (*The Abuse of Diplomatic Privileges and Immunities*), Session 1984-85 (HC 127).

[44] 1932-2017. Labour MP for West Lothian, and then Linlithgow (1962-2005). Like many left-wing contemporaries (and many since) Tam Dalyell was educated not in the shipyards but at the Edinburgh Academy, Eton and King's. But at least he did his National Service as a mere trooper in the Greys, which no doubt provided a certain cachet in his dealings with constituency Labour parties. As my innumerable Scottish relatives might have said, every laddie loves a laird.

[45] officially the Overseas & Defence Committee (South Atlantic) (OD(SA)).

[46] House of Commons Debates, 21 December 1982, col. 902

[47] London (Secker & Warburg), 1984

[48] Dennis Canavan, *Let the People Decide*, pp 154-55

[49] Fifth Report from the Foreign Affairs Committee (*United Kingdom membership of UNESCO*), Session 1984-85 (HC 461).

[50] Third Report from the Foreign Affairs Committee (*Events surrounding the weekend of 1-2 May 1982*), Session 1984-85 (HC 11); the Labour members' alternative draft is set out on pages lxvi-cxxiii.

[51] Interview with Leonid Zamyatin, *Kommersant*, 04/05/2005.

[52] Mikhail Gorbachev, *Memoirs* (Bantam, 1997), pp 205, 207

[53] (Sir) Ivan Lawrence QC, (b 1936), Conservative MP for Burton 1974-1997, Chairman, Conservative Friends of Israel, Home Affairs Select Committee (1992-97), UK branch of the Commonwealth Parliamentary Association (1995-97).

[54] After the collapse of the Soviet Union the National Hotel became the usual kind of serially sold and resold property – a Forte Hotel in 1995, a Méridien Hotel in 1996, and part of the Starwood Luxury Collection in 2009. To complete the inevitable circle, it was eventually bought by a local dollar billionaire in 2011, and is now managed by Marriott.

[55] Sir Ivan Lawrence, *My Life of Crime: Cases and Causes* (London 2010), pp 228-232; Ivan records one of Sasha's better jokes, with which we all regaled the rest of the world on our return from Moscow.

[56] Ivan recalls that he subsequently wrote to the Procurator-General to accept his invitation, but not surprisingly never had a response. Ivan was nonetheless not infrequently on duty in Moscow over the next few years, and assisted in drafting the legislation (the so-called Exit Law) which eventually allowed several hundred thousand Jews and others to leave the USSR legally. Ivan Lawrence, *loc.cit.*

[57] Ben Macintyre, *The Spy and the Traitor* (Penguin, 2019), chapters 13-14.

[58] Second Report from the Foreign Affairs Committee (*UK-Soviet Relations*), Session 1985-86, (HC 28-I).

[59] Foreign Affairs Committee, Minutes of Evidence, 7 July 1986, QQ 241-243

[60] *loc cit*, p 260.

[61] Daphne Park (who was also a successful British spy), in her Valedictory on leaving Hanoi in 1970. Reprinted in Matthew Parris & Andrew Bryson, *The Spanish Ambassador's Suitcase*, London 2012, pp 367-74.

[62] Ivan Lawrence, *op cit*, p 261.

[63] First Report from the Foreign Affairs Committee, (*South East Asia and Indochina*) Session 1986-87 (HC 114), para 101.

[64] Later Sir Nicholas Fenn, subsequently Ambassador in Dublin (1986-91) and finally High Commissioner in Delhi until 1996. After retirement he served as Chief Executive (and later Chairman) of Marie Curie Cancer Care, and a trustee of Sightsavers International.

[65] A genuine miner, MP for Don Valley 1979-83, and for Doncaster North 1983-92.

[66] Fifth Report from the Foreign Affairs Committee (*The United Kingdom and South East Asia: The Philippines*), Session 1985-86 (HC 368).

[67] Speech by the Chancellor of the Exchequer, George Osborne, to the Federation of German Industries (BDI), 3rd November 2015.

[68] Third Report from the Foreign Affairs Committee (*The Single European Act*), Session 1985-86, HC 442.

[69] Sixth Report from the Foreign Affairs Committee (*South Africa*), Session 1985-86, HC 61-I

[70] "For the United Kingdom government or Parliament to listen officially to the provinces or (worse) to enter upon an inquiry into the extent and sufficiency of provincial consents must in my opinion be condemned as 'an objectionable foreign interference in Canadian domestic affairs'." (P W Hogg, in *Canadian Bar Review*, vol 60 (1983), p 333).

[71] Geoffrey Howe, *Conflict of Interest* (1994), p 323.

[72] Sir Brian Urquhart KCMG MBE (1919-2021), one of the founders of the United Nations, and its Under-Secretary General 1971-1985.

[73] Andreas Papandreou (1919-1996), Prime Minister 1981-89, 1993-96; son of Geórgios Papandreou, Prime Minister 1944-45, 1963, 1964-65; father of Giórgios Papandreou, Prime Minister 2009-2011: a surprising democratic tradition.

[74] see K C Wheare, *Federal Government*, OUP, 4th edition (1963), pp 50-51 and *passim*.

[75] Third Report from the Foreign Affairs Committee, Session 1986-87 (House of Commons Paper 23), Q 179 (the Rt Hon Julian Amery MP).

[76] W Hepworth Dixon, *British Cyprus*, Chapman & Pincher, London, 1879, p 181. This is a beautifully crafted and remarkably detailed description of Cyprus in the first years of British administration on behalf of the Sultan.

[77] Rauf Raif Denktaş (1924-2012): Barrister of Lincoln's Inn, served in the colonial Crown Prosecution Service 1949-58; founder and leader of the Turkish Resistance Organisation (TMT) set up to counter EOKA in 1957; nominal Vice-President of the Republic of Cyprus 1973-74; elected President of the Turkish Federated State of Cyprus from 1974; President of the Turkish Republic of Northern Cyprus 1983-2005: a friend of Glafcos Clerides (1919-2013), graduate of King's College London, an RAF prisoner of war in Germany from 1942, a leading member and defending lawyer of EOKA, and President of Cyprus 1993-2003.

[78] Third Report from the Foreign Affairs Committee (*Cyprus*), Session 1986-87 (HC 23).

Chapters 28-34

[79] Second Report from the Select Committee on House of Commons (Services) (*Access to the Precincts of the House*), Session 1987-88 (HC 580).

[80] Sir Alan Muir Wood FRS (1921-2009), senior partner in Sir William Halcrow & Partners.

[81] House of Commons Debates, 24 May 1960, cols. 213-4.

[82] Liberal/Liberal Democrat MP for Berwick-on-Tweed 1973-2015, later Sir Alan, subsequently Lord Beith. An active member of the 1976-79 Procedure Committee. Member of the House of Commons Commission 1979-1997. He was responsible, amongst other things, for answering written and oral parliamentary questions on our behalf, and until the establishment of the coalition government in 2010 was therefore probably the only Liberal MP to have done so since the end of World War II.

[83] My first boss eloquently described the process of the "squalid infilling of courtyards and more building of huts on the roofs" in his entertaining account of the *Mid-Victorian Masterpiece: The story of an institution unable to put its own house in order* (Sir Barnett Cocks, Hutchinson, London 1977).

[84] Sir Michael Hopkins CBE RA (born 1935).

[85] Rt hon Bernard Weatherill (universally known as Jack), later Baron Weatherill (1920-2007). A tailor by birth, with a thimble to prove it. Conservative MP for Croydon North-East 1964-92. Conservative deputy Chief Whip 1971-79, and hero of James Graham's *This House*; Chairman of Ways & Means 1979-83; elected Speaker unopposed 1983, with the support of the Labour Party but in defiance of Mrs Thatcher. The last Speaker to wear the full-bottomed wig, which he described as "a wonderful device that allows the Speaker to pretend not to hear some things".

[86] Charles Irving (1924-1995), Conservative MP for his home town of Cheltenham from 1974 to 1992. In 1990 he was knighted by Margaret Thatcher, of whom he was a grovelling admirer (he regularly sent her flowers). He was an adviser to the Conservative Campaign for Homosexual Equality, and, to his credit, was one of the founders of NACRO (the National Campaign for the Care and Resettlement of Offenders).

[87] Sir Robin Ibbs (1926-2016) went on to become chairman of Lloyds Bank.

[88] *Report to the House of Commons Commission: House of Commons Services*, House of Commons Paper 38 (Session 1990-91), 27 November 1990.

[89] Geoffrey Howe, *Conflict of Loyalty*, London 1994, p 621.

[90] First Report from the Treasury & Civil Service Committee, Session 1993-94 (*The Role of the Bank of England*) (House of Commons Paper 98).
[91] see First Report from the Treasury Committee, Session 1997-98 (*Accountability of the Bank of England*) (House of Commons Paper 282).
[92] Sixth Report from the Treasury & Civil Service Committee, Session 1994-95 (*The Regulation of Financial Services*) (House of Commons Paper 332).
[93] Fifth Report from the Treasury & Civil Service Committee, Session 1994-95 (*Financial Services Regulation: Self-Regulation at Lloyd's of London)* (HC 187-I).
[94] Thomas Richard Arnold (born 1947), theatre producer and publisher. Knighted 1990 (at a remarkably young age). Conservative MP for Hazel Grove 1974-97. Vice-Chairman, Conservative Party 1983-92.
[95] Dr Philip Hensher FRSL (born 1965), Professor of Creative Writing, Bath Spa University.
[96] Peter Hardy (1931-2003), later Lord Hardy of Wath, teacher of English, sponsor of the 1973 Badgers Bill and other wildlife legislation, renowned song-bird mimic. Labour MP for Rother Valley from 1970, and for Wentworth 1983-1997.
[97] Sir Geoffrey Finsberg (1926-1996), later Lord Finsberg of Hampstead. A former Bevin Boy. Conservative MP for Hampstead from 1970, and for Hampstead & Highgate 1983-92.
[98] Murdo Mclean, private secretary to the Chief Whip 1979-2000. Knighted 2000.
[99] Council of Europe, *Report on the Credentials of the United Kingdom delegation*, Assembly Document 6610 (1992).
[100] *The Parliamentary Assembly: Practice and Procedure* (Tenth edition, edited by Paul Evans and Paul Silk), Council of Europe Publishing 2008.
[101] Gisela Gschaider Stuart, born in Bavaria 1955, Labour MP for Birmingham Edgbaston 1997-2017, Parliamentary Under-Secretary for Health 1999-2001, Foreign Affairs Committee 2001-2010, chairman of Vote Leave in the 2016 referendum, subsequently chairman of Change Britain. Now Baroness Stuart of Edgbaston, Chairman of Wilton Park from 2018, and non-executive board member of the Cabinet Office from 2020.
[102] David Heathcoat-Amory, born 1949. Educated Eton and Christ Church, Oxford. Conservative MP for Wells 1983-2010. Minister of State, Foreign & Commonwealth Office 1993, Paymaster General 1994-96. A longstanding Eurosceptic.
[103] Rt hon Peter Hain (Lord Hain), born Nairobi 1950, childhood in South Africa, leading ant-apartheid activist, Labour MP for Neath 1991-2015, various ministerial offices 1999-2010 (Leader of the House of Commons, 2003-2005).
[104] David Heathcoat-Amory, *Confessions of a Eurosceptic* (London, 2012), pp 109-126.
[105] Gisela Stuart, *The Making of Europe's Constitution* (Fabian Society, London, 2003), p 3.
[106] Aldous Huxley, in his Foreword to the 1950 edition of *Brave New World.*
[107] *Report of the Inquiry into the Circumstances Surrounding the Death of Dr David Kelly CMG*, House of Commons Paper HC 247 (Session 2003-04), 28th January 2004.
[108] *Report* of the Joint Committee on Parliamentary Privilege, Session 1988-89 (HL 43-I/HC 214-I).